DATE DUE

ILL STH 940384		
10·20·01		
JUN 08 06		
158 583420 14/19/15		
ILL NNE 158 586193 12 9-15		

COLLISION at HOME PLATE

––––––––––– · The Lives of · –––––––––––
Pete Rose and Bart Giamatti

James Reston, Jr.

University of Nebraska Press
Lincoln

Photographs in the insert are credited to the following: Page 1: Courtesy of Rosemary Sweeney. Page 2: Jack Klumpe. Page 3: New York Times Photo Library. Page 4, *top:* Archives and Rare Books Department, University of Cincinnati Libraries; *center left:* Jack Klumpe; *center right and bottom:* New York Times Photo Library. Page 5, *top:* Jack Klumpe; *center and bottom:* New York Times Photo Library. Page 6, *top:* Jack Klumpe; *center:* Bill Serne; *bottom: Inside Sports.* Page 7, *top and center:* New York Times Photo Library; *bottom:* Paul H. Roedig, Philadelphia Phillies. Page 8: New York Times Photo Library. Page 9, *top and bottom left:* Courtesy of Mary Giamatti; *bottom right:* Mount Holyoke College Library/Archives. Page 10, *top left:* Carol Reis; *top right:* Michael Marsland/Yale University Office of Public Information; *bottom: Yale Daily News.* Page 11, *top left:* New York Times Photo Library; *top right and bottom:* J. D. Levine/Yale University Office of Public Information. Page 12, *top:* Frinzi Studio, Hamden, Conn.; *center and bottom left:* J. D. Levine/Yale University Office of Public Information; *bottom right:* Peter Tobia/*New Haven Register.* Page 13: Bruce L. Schwartzman. Page 14, *top left and right:* New York Times Photo Library; *center left:* Chuck Solomon; *center right:* New York Times Photo Library; *bottom left:* Jack Klumpe. Page 15, *top:* Chuck Solomon; *center:* Courtesy of Dick Wright; *bottom:* Mark Lovewell, copyright © 1989 Vineyard Gazatte Inc., reprinted by permission. Page 16, *top:* Chuck Solomon; *bottom:* Michael Marsland/Yale University Office of Public Information.

♾ The paper in this book meets the minimum requirements of American National Standard for Information Sciences—Permanence of Paper for Printed Library Materials, ANSI Z39.48-1984.

First Bison Books printing: 1997
Most recent printing indicated by the last digit below:
10   9   8   7   6   5   4   3   2   1

Library of Congress Cataloging-in-Publication Data
Reston, James, 1941–
Collision at home plate: the lives of Pete Rose and Bart Giamatti / James Reston, Jr.
p.   cm.
Originally published: New York: E. Burlingame Books, c1991.
Includes bibliographical references and index.
ISBN 0-8032-8964-2 (pbk.)
1. Rose, Pete, 1941–   .   2. Baseball players—United States—Biography.   3. Giamatti, A. Bartlett.   4. Baseball commissioners—United States—Biography.   I. Title.
GV865.R65R47   1997
796.357′092—dc21
96-46316   CIP

D.B.L.

for all the cheers and boos

made of yron mould
Immoveable, resistlesse, without end
Who in his hand an yron flale did hould
With which he thresht out falsehood,
and did truth unfould.

—Edmund Spenser, *The Faerie Queene*

Why'd you come the first time?
Because I hate to see a hero fail. There are
so few of them. Without heroes, we're all plain people
and don't know how far we can go. . . . There are so many
young boys you influence.

—Bernard Malamud, *The Natural*

A guy must pay his bookmaker, no matter what.

—Harry the Horse

Contents

Illustrations follow page 182

Prologue

LOOKING FIVE BLOCKS down Vine Street, through the low-slung stone buildings, you can see the stadium settling low upon land reclaimed from the river. Though settled low, it dominates this city of modest resources and hard work, of railroads and machine tools and soap, of the proverbial beer and a shot. The ballpark is accessible to the downtown, giving it life, even giving it a daytime ball game—the "businessman's lunch." A vision of geometric, white perfection, the amphitheater is beautiful, especially at night, when it twinkles like the lights of the floating bars and restaurants along the big river, and throws a soft light across John Roebling's suspension bridge, newly dubbed the Pete Rose Suspension Bridge.

But the stadium is not admired by the commissioner. He often complained about the conventional architecture of modern ballparks and compared their style to the social realism of Mussolini. Why couldn't architects build "idiosyncratic" ballparks, with odd angles and uneven walls and irregular distances to the fence? That would elevate the strategy of the game, force its players to use their heads as well as their brawn. A stadium should be a box rather than a saucer like this one in Cincinnati, he had argued, a place of strange angles and beautiful ricochets.

Old Redland Field might have been his ideal. It had been the first great stadium of the Cincinnati Redlegs, and it was known as the "Palace of the Fans," largely because of its ornate Roman colonnade and because of its box seats, the first in baseball, which were known as Rooter's Row. Toward the end of the nineteenth century, when the Palace was in its heyday and such future Hall-of-Famers as Charles "Chief" Bender, Charles "Kandy Kid" Nichols, and James "Pud" Galvin had played there, you could purchase twelve mugs of beer for a dollar. The commissioner was not so sentimental about that, for drunks and violence and crowd control had become a constant preoccupation, marring family enjoyment of the national pastime. He feared events such as the one that occurred in 1988, when the Reds manager, Pete Rose, had provoked an ugly and dangerous and nearly uncontrollable situation by shoving an umpire after a questionable call. Such behavior was cause for concern to the commissioner, whose whole life had tended to cultivate a respect for civilized manners and good conversation.

The Palace of the Fans burned in 1911, and the Reds moved to what eventually would be Crosley Field. With its seats so close to the baselines that you could hear the infielders' chatter, its right-field bleachers called the Sun Deck, and with a laundry and a brewery across the street, Crosley Field had the spirit of Boston's Fenway Park. The commissioner would have approved, even if its amenities were few, for Crosley Field flourished in the days when sports writers could still write poetry in their columns, odes to ball players and bleachers.

> Goodbye, dear pal, farewell for aye,
> Your life was long and sweet;
> And now you're dead as barleycorn,
> Old two-bit bleacher seat!

But Crosley Field was no Campus Martius on the banks of the Tiber. It was a bandbox near Mill Creek. In the great flood of 1937, a couple of Cincinnati pitchers named Lee Grissom and Gene Schott climbed into a dinghy at home plate and rowed over the centerfield fence. The waters of the mighty Ohio had backed into its estuary and spilled into the ballpark, but, as the commissioner would say, baseball is a resilient institution, able to transcend even floods and pestilences. The glory of the game would survive in Cincinnati.

Cincinnati was the smallest city in America to have a professional baseball team, and yet attendance at Riverfront Stadium equaled that of all the other American cities combined. It even exceeded them during the dynasty years of the Big Red Machine. The crowds came from the hills of Kentucky and the factories of Mill Creek Valley and the bottomland tenements of the neighborhood known as Over the Rhine, a name that was a remnant of the age when canals crisscrossed the downtown. But they thought of themselves as a close and stable family, a family on a healthy outing just for the sheer pleasure of their hard-won leisure. When they sang "Take Me Out to the Ballgame" during the seventh-inning stretch, it might well have been "Nearer, My God, to Thee," for it was sung with respect and even reverence. The commissioner himself had once remarked on the near-religious quality of American baseball, on how a trip to the ballpark was really a search for paradise, a quest for a place only slightly east of Eden.

Walking the few blocks to the stadium from the downtown, crossing over the freeway, you are prepared for an historical experience at the very least. The plaques along the catwalk memorialize the home team's great events: the Cincinnati Redlegs were baseball's first professional club, established in 1869; the Victorian owner of the Reds, the much-maligned Gerry Herrmann, is honored as the father of the World Series; William Howard Taft began his training for the U.S. presidency as a Cincinnati ball player; Johnny Vander Meer became, in 1938, the only pitcher in major league history to pitch consecutive no-hitters; the Reds sweep of the Yankees in the 1976 World Series made the Big Red Machine one of the greatest teams of all time; and, finally, in 1985, "on a warm September evening, Cincinnati native, Pete Rose, smacked a single to left center field to become baseball's all-time hit leader."

The late afternoon of August 25, 1989, was also warm, and the Reds languidly took their turns at batting practice several hours before their night game with the fifth-place Pittsburgh Pirates. The near-empty stadium was unadorned. For seven months, the ballpark had been transformed, its magic destroyed. The world of sharpies, hangers-on, drug-dealers, and gamblers had invaded it. The fans could not look over at the Reds dugout and see the team's manager in his customary place, leaning on the second railing, eye level to the field, without wondering if he was a crook, perhaps even a cocaine dealer.* They had supported him in the beginning, but now they were embarrassed. How could they, to use the commissioner's words, "aspire to paradise" in their ballpark, when their sports pages were filled with reports of low-lifes, cocaine dealers, and tax evaders? Moreover, the Reds were losing, mired now in fourth place, having lost thirty-three games out of forty-six at one stretch. To some, that was the real dishonor.

As the small crowd began to arrive, only two banners appointed

---

* Despite his associations with cocaine dealers, Rose was never implicated in a cocaine deal.

the railings of the upper deck. They were neutral. Far out in right field, the number 14 was simply painted on a sheet in red. Along the third-base mezzanine, less carefully painted, as if it had been scrawled in haste, was a sheet that read: THANKS, PETE, FOR 4256. The number marked Rose's total career hits.

By the batting cage, the players talked in undertones, out of the hearing of the national press. Somewhere in the catacombs of the stadium, engineers and technicians tested the electronics of the huge scoreboard. From the colossal television screen over the centerfield bleachers, the rich voice of Mel Allen suddenly boomed across the near-empty stadium like a tremor: PETE ROSE BANNED FROM BASEBALL.

The commissioner had handed down the verdict the day before, on an off day for the Reds. This was the first game back at Riverfront without Rose.

As Allen's powerful staccato voice, lilting a bit now with age, continued with the report, the face of the commissioner flashed up on the screen. It was huge and big-brotherly, but to those who might wish to hate him, Mephistophelian. He did not look like a man of baseball—he was manifestly no former athlete. He did not even look like one of those buttoned-up, icy executives who hover around the management of the game, men who hail from the cautious precincts of the law. There were deep pouches under Bart Giamatti's eyes. His teeth glistened under the television lights, contrasting with his olive skin. His goatee was speckled, and his hair was gray at the temples. Orotund sentences rolled from his mouth with practiced, scholastic precision. "To pretend that serious charges of any kind can be responsibly examined by a commissioner alone fails to recognize the necessity to bring professionalism and fairness to any examination." That was the language Giamatti had once called "high-institutional."

The sentences were exotic. He spoke of integrity: the integrity of baseball and the integrity of his investigation. He spoke of honesty and high principles and ideals. And baseball men had listened, listened intently, and they had been moved. The commissioner was talking about baseball, but his message applied to all American institutions; therein lay the power of the moment.

At Riverfront, batting practice stopped, and the Reds players stood watching the big screen, as Giamatti's words filled their stadium.

Allen's report cut to Rose's press conference of the previous day, which had followed Giamatti's. Perhaps for the last time, Pete's image was up there on the screen. "This could have went on for another year," he said. "I was tired of it." He firmly believed he could have won a trial because the evidence against him, he proclaimed, was soft, but there could never be a fair and impartial trial.

"Pete, do you think you have a gambling problem?" a reporter asked. "If so, will you seek any sort of rehabilitation?"

"I don't think I have a gambling problem. . . . Consequently, I will not seek any help of any kind."

Suddenly, the Riverfront television screen went dark in mid-sentence, as if the engineers had decided to stop Rose from answering further questions. The hitters completed their turns at bat hurriedly and returned to the clubhouse to change into their white uniforms. The game must go on. Their new manager was Tommy Helms, who had played with Rose on the Reds in the sixties, until the Reds traded up at second base, sending Helms to Houston for Joe Morgan and thus revving up the engine of the Big Red Machine. Helms had had a busy day, an endless round of media interviews. "It's an ugly way to get a big league job," he quipped. Then he took his seat on the left end of the bench, by the bats, and began to litter the boards in front of him with the shells of sunflower seeds while his players took the field.

The workhorse of the Reds, Rick Mahler, climbed the mound and promptly got bombed for eight runs in four innings, dropping his summertime record to 1 and 8. When the night was over, the score was 12–3. During the game, Helms had noticed that the crowd was sedate, unengaged, inattentive. "It's the kind of game when you just turn the page," he said afterward. "We'll go out and get them tomorrow."

As the Reds played through their doldrums, the commissioner retreated to his cottage in Edgartown on Martha's Vineyard, as he had done every summer for years. He was tired and eager for a time of relaxation, when he could read history, the crime novels of Robert Parker, "junk and self-help junk and whatever obsession I have at the moment." The clutter of his living room reflected his summertime leisure and his generic obsessions: tomes on the Renaissance mixed easily and naturally with *The Armchair Book of Baseball*. (In the latter, a few pages were devoted to "quotations from Chairman Pete," including Rose on his love for the game: "I'd walk through hell in a gasoline suit to keep playing baseball.") Under the light from the skylight, Giamatti's own book, *Earthly Paradise and the Renaissance Epic*, served as a coaster for his coffee cup.

He was always greeted with curiosity and amusement on his arrival on the Vineyard. It was no different this time. To the literary, urbane vacationers on the off-shore island, the former Yale University president's romance with baseball was appealing. "I admire the speed, the grace, the beauty of the sport," he had told the *Vineyard*

Gazette three years before. "At the moment where an athlete makes something happen, everyone watching is elevated. That's what we say about great works of art. It's done with the body, but it's done with the mind and the spirit too. Whether you're a great ballet dancer or a great singer, athletes and artists have a lot in common."

The first days of his 1989 vacation would be interrupted by more than the friendly curiosity of the summer residents. Far west on the mainland, Rose had given his first interview after his banishment. He howled betrayal. His lawyers had worked for weeks on a compromise that would not officially find that he had bet on baseball, but then the commissioner had proceeded to double-cross them. After all the legal negotiations, Giamatti had announced at his New York press conference, "Yes, [Rose] did bet on baseball." On Martha's Vineyard, the commissioner's phone rang off the hook. He finally had to call a halt. Until he could log in a few walks on South Beach, the Rose case was closed.

Even so, on Friday afternoon, September 1, Yankees owner George Steinbrenner reached Giamatti in Edgartown for the second time that day. The two maintained a jolly, bantering relationship. Steinbrenner, proud of having majored in English literature at Williams College, occasionally quoted Keats and Shelley to the commissioner to show that he knew more than cleats and ships and solvent, race horses and Billy Martin. Giamatti would scoff at such posturing as outpourings from the "potted Ivy League." Steinbrenner, in turn, would take delight in citing a recent poll that ranked Yale as merely the fourth best university in the nation.

Still, the Yankees owner appreciated the commissioner, especially the way Giamatti never lorded his erudition over the baseball owners. On that day, however, they pursued serious matters: a subject of high confidentiality in the baseball world, and one close to Steinbrenner's heart and pocketbook. They needed to be in touch over the weekend. Steinbrenner gave Giamatti the phone number at his horse farm in Ocala and said if he was not at the main house, the commissioner was to have the help fetch him. But Steinbrenner was skeptical about Giamatti's commitment to follow through on his request, and he said so. There was a pause on the line.

"Do you doubt the Chair?" Giamatti chided in a significant, Elizabethan tone.

"Only since you have been sitting in it," Steinbrenner responded. Giamatti roared with laughter and cried, "Sir, you are a lout!"

Steinbrenner hung up in satisfaction and went off to the stables. An hour later, Giamatti was dead.

River Rat and Water Boy

DOWNSTREAM, west of the city, the great river makes a wide bend to the north, leaving behind the bowl of Cincinnati. Then it straightens for three miles before it slouches gradually toward Louisville. Low hills braid the muddy banks, affording long vistas up and down the river of tugs and barges inching their way toward Pittsburgh and St. Louis.

A veteran of the Continental Army, Colonel Cornelius Sedam had settled here in the late eighteenth century, purchasing a large tract of land around the mouth of Bold Face Creek. He set himself and his sons up as river traders. Upon his death in 1823, his sons took over the flatboats, his eldest son inheriting the property east of Bold Face Creek and founding a village called Sedamsville, his other son, David, getting the western parcel. High on the hill above the river, David Sedam built a stone mansion called Riverside. In the 1840s, when Cincinnati was known as the Paris of the West, when Charles Dickens and Frances Trollope came to observe the crude manners of genuine Americans, the neighborhoods of Riverside and Sedamsville were popular, fashionable places for beer barons and prominent meat packers and soap manufacturers to drive their families for a Sunday carriage ride in the summer or a sleigh ride in winter.

With time, the area became the site of a steel mill and a cooperage, of oil storage tanks and river depots. A rail line was laid along it, and the villages were annexed into the city and ceased to be fashionable. The West Side of Cincinnati became working class and Cath-

olic and stable. Its residents worked in the fine machine tool plants of
Mill Creek Valley or at Procter and Gamble, or, as in the case of Harry
Rose, in the banks and businesses downtown.

At the mouth of Bold Face Creek, a community park had been
carved out of the hillside, with a ball diamond sunk below street
level, so that the outfield fences were sharp, sloping banks. Across the
street, the spire of Our Lady of Perpetual Help church began to lean
in a slight genuflection toward the river.

Bold Face Park became the hub of these three-river communi-
ties. It was the dominion of a legendary baseball coach named Joe
Hawk, who distinguished a league called Knothole. To join a Knothole Club, a youngster had to sign a solemn pledge:

> I will not at any time skip school.
> I will attend no game against the wishes of my parents.
> I will practice clean speech, clean sport, and clean habits.
> I will try by attendance, deportment, and effort at school or
>   work to prove my worthiness to membership in the club.

In the summers of the 1940s and 1950s, there was little for boys
to do but to show up at the park at eight in the morning and stay until
dinner. Ball games went on continuously through the day under the
orderly instruction of Coach Hawk. In those days, the boys of the
river gloried in the label "river rat." Some, like the Zimmer brothers,
Don and Junior, came from across town to become honorary river
rats, because they wanted to play for Joe Hawk. In 1945, Don Zimmer
would walk nearly a mile to catch a bus, then transfer to a trolley in
order to get to practice. He became a shortstop, rifling his pegs to a
kid called Jim Frey on first base. Zimmer and Frey became the heart
of successive championship teams, before they graduated to American Legion ball and made a team called Bentley Post famous by
winning the national championship in 1947. They won it in Hollywood and got their pictures taken with Lana Turner and Clark Gable.

Sports were everything down by the river. In addition to the
youth leagues, young Don Zimmer played evening softball on the
same team as his father. But his father insisted on playing shortstop,
so Don got moved to second base. On the same team, a stocky bank
accountant, Harry Francis Rose, played in the outfield. He was a
well-built, well-liked, handsome, and intense man who poured his
passion into sport largely as an antidote to his dreary accountant's
life. Softball was pure fun to Harry Rose, but the ledger sheet had
dulled his eyes, and he couldn't hit. He tried boxing, too, but football
was his real forte. In Riverside in the 1930s, Harry was famous as

"Old Swivelhips" in the Feldhaus Sunday League. Competing against such powerhouse teams as Captain Al's Trolley Tavern, Harry played halfback on offense and linebacker on defense. In their flimsy cotton-stuffed leather helmets and thin pads, the players hit one another with fierce abandon. Harry Rose, so straitlaced and exact during the week, let the leather fly. He was known as the fiercest competitor in semi-pro football that Cincinnati had seen for some time.

At the end of the season, when professional football coaches came to recruit for the National Football League, Harry was turned away. He could not be signed, he was told, because he did not have a college education. At the professional level, football remained elitist. Its fans consisted of college graduates who came to see their old college stars compete on a higher plane. It was just business, nothing personal, the scouts said, though it was probably Harry's small stature as much as his limited education that disqualified him.

Harry Rose played on, because he was a sporting man in a sporting culture and because playing released his professional frustrations. Several thousand fans turned out to watch him on Sundays, including his young sons, Pete and Dave. Harry was to play semi-pro football until he was forty-two years old, when the average league player was half his age. In him, the virtues of ruggedness and durability were transcendent. He never complained, even when he was hurt. He was always aggressive, in defeat and in pain, as well as in glory, and from this grew a story that Pete would tell over and over later. The year was 1952, when Harry was forty years old and Pete was eleven. The old man kicked off, ran downfield, and was hammered by a tremendous block. He went down with a fractured hip. But, Pete would say, Harry crawled after the ball carrier and made the tackle. "That's the kind of guy my father was."

The Roses lived down at Anderson Ferry, a river crossing, where a sidewheeling tug called Boone Number 7 powered a barge, ferrying people and cars back and forth to the Kentucky shore. Ever since the Civil War, the Kottmyers had operated the ferry, and young Pete Rose earned spare change by working for them on the weekends, taking tickets. His family lived in a two-story, clapboard house on Braddock Street, above River Road, where the drivers of heavy trucks and hot rods bore down on their accelerators to make up for time lost on the curves near town. To the families of Riverside, the road became known as Slaughter Avenue. Between the noise, the grim, bloody River Road, the railroad tracks parallel to it, and the dangerous river beyond, the perils were enough to make any mother anxious.

The Rose family bought a rudimentary television set, a seven-inch circular screen enclosed in a wooden box. Through its electrical blizzard, they watched Otto Graham, Marion Motley, and Dante Lavelli of the great Cleveland Browns sweep aside the competition. There was little else to keep an active stiff-haired kid around Anderson Ferry. Harry's wife, LaVerne—also known as Rosie—was consoled by the thought of her boys playing ball at Bold Face Park, from sunup to sundown, especially when she worked at a tavern called Twin Trolleys to supplement the family income.

Among the German, Polish, and Irish of the river bank, Pete Rose grew up slowly, little noticed. With his flat, plain, pug-nosed face and his wide-set eyes, his gapped teeth and freckles, his dime-store clothes, cuffs rolled up on his jeans, there was little to distinguish him from the other children. He was just another river mouse destined to carry on the working man's tradition. He was small, often smaller than the girls in his grade school and junior high school classes, and had a small boy's cockiness: intent to show he could not be pushed around and ready to fight to prove it. Besides endlessly bouncing a ball off the brick wall of the local tavern, he had almost nothing else in his life, except perhaps collecting pop bottles and camping out on the ridge above the river, stealing the occasional watermelon and riding the ferry.

As he grew older, Pete might ride the bus to the end of the line in Saylor Park, which was considered a swanky step up from Riverside, because the houses had big lawns and the boys actually went on to college. There were the inevitable tests of manhood. Against the edict of every Riverside mother, the boys would occasionally swim in the Ohio River, whose current was swift and whose eddies were unpredictable. Occasionally, they even swam all the way across, a true brace of river rats, ending up a half-mile downstream on the wicked Kentucky side. Hopping the occasional freight train was another forbidden pleasure, but hopping off when the train began to pick up speed was important, lest you end up in Greenburg, Indiana, which was no fun.

As a natural extension of his sporting life, Harry Rose liked to take his boys to the racetrack, to the venerable River Downs, east of Cincinnati. He also took them to the taverns that sponsored his teams. There, men engaged in passionate debates that usually began with the line "How about them Reds!" Harry was no drinking man, but he didn't pass up the flutter on the game. His joy in gambling went back to his own childhood along the river, when Mexican laborers were brought in to build a railroad roundhouse in Riverside and were housed in abandoned passenger cars on a siding. There, little Harry

Rose could be found shooting dice, and when he told his son Pete about it, he made it sound very romantic. If gambling added a bit of spice to Harry's life, there was nothing especially evil about it. He would never have considered anything truly wicked like a secret trip across the river to wide-open Newport, where there was serious gambling in real casinos with naked ladies and the like.

Mainly, Harry poured his hopes and his frustrations into his eldest son. On the playing field, he used every physical and psychological strategy to stoke Pete's hunger and desire for sports. As Pete began to play baseball at the hallowed Bold Face Park, where his father and grandfather had played before him, Harry, resorting to a little poetic license, told of the time his own father had stepped to the plate and poled one of the old dead balls so hard that it cleared the bank of the ballfield, went past the railroad yards, and landed in the middle of the Ohio River, where it struck a sternwheeler that promptly sank.

By 1953, Don Zimmer had broken in with the Brooklyn Dodgers organization, after being paid the enormous bonus of $3,900. His teammate, Jim Frey, was then playing Class AAA for the Boston Braves organization, and the solid Junior Zimmer was catching for a minor league team in Hazard, Kentucky, where he was taking the pitches of the promising Johnny "The Point" Podres. These were the heroes and the models at Bold Face Park. Others besides Pete Rose caught the eye of Coach Hawk. A kid called Bernie Wrublewski had considerable natural talent as a pitcher, but he horsed around a little too much and would end up as the village priest. A string bean named Eddie Brinkman had everyone talking. He could hit the long ball and was a graceful fielder with a bullet peg to first. His brother, Charlie, was a gem of a catcher, with an equally strong arm.

Against this stiff competition, Pete had to fight for attention. He compensated for his unremarkable skills with aggressiveness and hustle and cunning. His father hounded him from the sidelines and worked with him one on one, shouting at Pete to keep his eye on the ball. Sensitive about his size, the boy took to hanging for great blocks of time from the parallel bars at the playground next to the ballfield. He fantasized that he could stretch himself into a bigger boy and a better player. To work on his fielding, he would bounce a ball endlessly off the side wall of Schulte's Beer Garden until the metronomal pounding of leather against brick annoyed the rough clientele inside, and the drinkers, with their schooners of beer, ran the boy off. To work on his weaker left arm, Harry forced him to shoot baskets endlessly with his left hand.

Besides Harry, Pete had another adviser in these early days. His mother's brother, Buddy Bloebaum, was also a consummate baseball man whose dream of becoming a big league ball player had gone aglimmering. He had achieved a measure of success as a shortstop on a Cedar Rapids minor league team by becoming a switch-hitter but had seen the value too late, at the ripe age of thirty. Uncle Buddy, who had a steady job managing a pool hall, umpired in the summer leagues, but, more impressively, he was an unpaid scout for the Reds. Bloebaum persuaded Pete to take up catching as a youngster because there were fewer good catchers in professional baseball than any other position.

Uncle Buddy is also sometimes given credit for starting his nephew out as a switch-hitter. As Pete remembers it, Harry and Uncle Buddy made a devil's bargain with Coach Hawk: "Let Pete switch hit, and I'll guarantee his presence in every game," Harry said to Hawk. At home, before bedtime, Harry stood over Pete and forced him to swing the bat a hundred times from the right side and then a hundred times from the left side. So long as his son succeeded in baseball, Harry Rose was quite content to leave the rest of child rearing to someone else. If Pete did not excel in sports by some extra effort, a life of drudgery surely lay ahead of him. Harry's was a working man's intuition: sweat on the playing field was far preferable to sweat in a factory.

Pete understood his father's message. Then and for the rest of his sporting life, he would do anything to win.

In his early teens, Pete graduated to American Legion ball, playing sixty games in a summer for a team sponsored by S&H Green Stamps. Pete would come home, stand in front of a mirror, and swing a weighted bat his Uncle Buddy had given him to strengthen his arms. But the dream of becoming a big league ball player seemed misplaced. He went off to Western Hills High School and promptly got cut from the varsity football team. For the son of the local football hero, this was a devastating blow. Pete drifted into the streets, making only an occasional appearance at school and flunking all his subjects.

He also got in trouble. It was not serious criminal trouble, by modern standards, but a punk's trouble. Combative and argumentative, he was ready to pick a fight whenever there was any provocation. He hung out with other neighborhood toughs, shooting marbles and dice behind buildings with the other apparent losers. In another day and place, he would have been a prime candidate for drugs or reform school. It was all too familiar a pattern in Riverside—yet another kid with a chip on his shoulder—and his teachers and coaches began to lose interest in him.

A defining moment for both father and son came when the teachers announced that, after all the absences and the poor performance, Pete Rose would have to go to summer school if he wanted to move on to tenth grade. Harry Rose considered the proposition and vetoed it. Pete could not go to summer school because he had to play summer baseball. Harry knew his priorities. Baseball was the alpha and omega. Pete Rose later came to idealize this decision. It showed how wise his father was. Perhaps Pete's whole future in baseball might have been destroyed if he had gone to summer school. Harry knew best.

Subconsciously, Pete had to prove that his father had been right, for Harry had set up an all-or-nothing situation for him. As it turned out, this decision implanted such a deep and fundamental ambivalence in Rose's subconscious that during his efforts at rehabilitation after his banishment from baseball thirty-five years later, his relationship to his father was considered an explosive and almost untouchable subject.

The immediate consequence of Harry's decision was that Pete had to repeat ninth grade. He never quite got over the embarrassment. Many years later, when they got around to naming a street after Pete in Cincinnati, he said, "They should have named an alley after me, the way I acted in high school."

In his second sophomore year, however, he made the football team, at a compact 130 pounds. This saved Pete Rose for better things. It restored hope. He turned out to be a decent halfback, quick and tough and determined. He made a few memorable runs, when it counted, against the dirty-playing Panthers of Elder High. By his senior year, it seemed possible that he might land an athletic scholarship at a small college, where a 150-pound halfback might be able to compete successfully. In baseball, scouts doted on his classmate, Eddie Brinkman.

At Western Hills High School, the baseball coach, Pappy Nohr, was comfortable as a pair of old slippers, and he was a legend in Cincinnati equal to Joe Hawk as a developer of talent. By the mid-1960s, Coach Hawk and Coach Nohr could claim to have developed more major league players in a radius of three miles than any other place in the United States. Besides the Zimmer and Brinkman brothers and Pete Rose, there was Dick "the Hummer" Drott of the Cubs, Art Mahaffey of the Phillies, Clyde Vollmer of the Reds, Russ Nixon of the Red Sox and Twins, Herman Wehmeier of the Reds . . . and, by the mid-1980s, four products of Bold Face Park were major league managers: Rose, Nixon, Don Zimmer, and Jim Frey. Coach Nohr was a gentle motivator who understood the vulnerabilities of adolescents. Never angry with a player when he screwed up, Nohr had a policy of waiting overnight to discuss the mistakes of the playing field. During the school year, practices were held at 7 A.M. in the gym, where the coach laid out mover's mats on the basketball floor so the team could practice sliding techniques. On Sundays, his teams practiced in the afternoons, on the untested assumption that his boys had to attend Sunday school and church.

To Coach Nohr, the river rats were not bad boys, certainly not thugs. They were only a bit raw. He understood their dreams and appreciated how important sports were to them. Once, one of his boys, a pretty good ball player, was late for practice for good reason. A neighbor's house had burned down behind them.

"Did you go over and help them fight the fire?" Pappy asked.

"Heck no," the youth replied. "They were stealing our vegetables."

In Eddie Brinkman, the coach knew what he had. Brinkman could do everything except hit "outshoots," as sliders were called in those days. In one of their seven-inning games, with a platoon of scouts in the stands, Pappy Nohr (who was himself a scout for the Chicago Cubs), played Brinkman at every position on the field just to display the full range of the boy's talent. Brinkman was a bona fide high school superstar of national importance, and he signed with the Washington Senators in 1959 for an enormous bonus of $75,000.

In contrast to his appreciation of Brinkman, Coach Nohr had a wry, bemused attitude toward Pete Rose. There was something poignant about young Pete, the determined boy who tried harder than anyone else but simply didn't have the talent. The way Pete idolized his father particularly touched Nohr, as Pete would often mention to his coach that he wanted to achieve in baseball what his father had achieved in football.

It was just not in the cards. Pete was "a good ball player, not a Brinkman," Nohr would say, as if comparing a Ford to a Cadillac. "I don't mean to be disrespectful," Pappy would say, "but I don't think I would have recommended him for the big leagues when he was in high school. . . . Pete Rose could not have made the minors on his own, but his Uncle was a scout."

Six hundred miles northeast of Cincinnati, in the low foothills of the Holyoke mountains of western Massachusetts, there is another river community, very different from Riverside and yet in a few respects the same. South Hadley is a quiet town on the Connecticut River, with a deep sense of history and a strong set of Yankee values. Its founder was "the worshipful Major" John Pynchon of the colonial Massachusetts militia, who came from Springfield in 1662 and paid 150 fathoms of wampum to a Norwottuck Indian for 500 acres, south of the notch leading to Amherst. Upon this sloping land, a town of classic New England features slowly developed. It had a village common and a succession of meeting houses, two paper mills, a tannery, and a rousing tavern. The nation took note of it in 1837, however, when a teacher named Mary Lyon from nearby Buckland established the first seminary in America dedicated exclusively to the higher education of young women. Mount Holyoke became a model to educators, and the eldest of the "seven sisters" colleges. In this idyllic setting, lines of poetry and strains of the lute mixed with somber scholarship.

In 1936, to the consternation of many alumnae who regarded the event as a rejection of feminist values, Mount Holyoke College appointed the first male president in its history, an associate professor of English literature from Yale University named Roswell Ham. He brought with him a number of male professors and their families to South Hadley. Among them was a large, genial professor of Italian literature named Valentine Giamatti.

Val, as he was known to his friends, had grown up in the Italian tenements of New Haven. His father, Angelo, an immigrant laborer, and his mother, Lavorgna, came from Telese, a town forty miles northeast of Naples. Neither spoke English when they came to America. (Lavorgna, in fact, would never learn the language.) Angelo was, however, a great spinner of tales. Along Lilac Street, the immigrants often gathered at his feet to listen to him tell stories in his fluid Neapolitan accent. It was never clear whether they came from true life or from his imagination.

While Angelo went off to work as a laborer at the New Haven Clock Company, Valentine had shown promise early. Even though he had entered the first grade speaking no English, he eventually attended Hill House High, which in the 1930s was contiguous to the Yale campus. Then, in a highly unusual step for a local Italian boy, Val entered Yale on a four-year scholarship. He rode to the campus every day on the trolley, as his patrician classmates strolled from the pleasant digs in their Gothic colleges. This difference remained vivid in his mind throughout his life. He was deeply grateful to Yale for all the university had done for him, but he never forgot the indignities that he had suffered at the hands of the upper class boys. Nor did he forget his upbringing in the tenements of New Haven. His eyebrows bore the scars of ethnic beatings he had received as a child, when he was pummeled and called a wop.

Val excelled, distinguishing himself first with a Phi Beta Kappa undergraduate degree and then with a Ph.D. from Harvard. Thus, in one astonishing leap, the Giamatti family went from immigrant labor to academic respectability in a single generation. While he was studying in Florence, Italy, Val met his future wife, Mary Claybaugh Walton, who was taking her junior year abroad from Smith College. Her forebears had been colonial sea captains and shoe manufacturers in the tired industrial towns of northern New England. When their first son was born in 1938, his christening as Angelo Bartlett Giamatti reflected this union of immigrant Italian and Congregational Massachusetts. His mother had liked the name, Bartlett, for the way that the two *tt*s in Bartlett Giamatti came together. Val preferred Bart as a nickname because he knew that Angelo would inevitably be shortened in the school yard to Angel.

The Giamattis arrived at South Hadley in 1940 and settled into a comfortable but modest academic's existence. They lived on Silver Street, a quiet lane north of the campus, in a spacious colonial on a corner lot with an expansive lawn and a view across the Holyoke playing fields. Val's commodious library reflected his special interests. He was a scholar of Dante. His modest academic credits included, apart from a primer on elementary Italian, a reinterpretation of *The Divine Comedy* in the light of "modern dynamic psychology" and a schematic outline of the Inferno, Purgatory, and Paradise.

What he did not write was as significant as what he did write, especially to his own son. He never wrote "the Book," the definitive study of Dante that would demonstrate his superior knowledge and establish him as the foremost Dante scholar in America. When he wrote in English, he lacked confidence, and therefore did little of it. For this insecurity, Val compensated in the education of his children. He emphasized the many and wondrous uses of their native tongue.

Val's hobby was collecting different editions of *The Divine Comedy*. In his library, there were shelf upon shelf of carefully arranged leather editions. In time, it became perhaps the best collection in America and included a 1481 edition illustrated by Botticelli, a six-volume edition illustrated and autographed by Salvador Dali, and an ornate, leather-tooled edition from the 1920s, three feet by three feet, that covered the top of a card table. These Giamatti treasures were kept on special shelves in humidified, illuminated cases in the library and were shown grandly to visitors.

Smoking was another of Val's pleasures. He usually smoked four packs of cigarettes a day. At the age of fifty-one, he would suffer a massive heart attack, a significant warning that made him change his ways. But there was a darker secret in the Italian side of the family: a congenital ailment of the muscles called Charcot Marie Tooth disease, a rare variant of multiple sclerosis that hung like a shadow over Val and succeeding Giamatti generations. After his heart attack, Val would walk laboriously, first with one cane and later with two.

At Mount Holyoke College, Val Giamatti was a popular teacher who was known affectionately as Mr. G to his students. His Dante course was a rite of passage. Even as he protested that he was shy and naive, Mr. G was approachable and well mannered, worldly and friendly. In his hands, *The Divine Comedy* was made to seem contemporary and relevant, particularly in a world that had been ravaged by global war. Consequently, young Bart was asked to learn the epic poem, canto by canto, over the breakfast table. Dante's classic, he was told, made life better, and more interesting and worthwhile.

In 1951, Val went so far as to establish a Dante Fair as a pretext to promote the cause of the Italian orphans of World War II. Mount Holyoke students seldom ventured outside their ideal world. To Giamatti's new idea for festivity, however, the college responded enthusiastically. Students and faculty gathered at the steepled Mary Lyon Hall and marched north, behind the Mount Holyoke fire engine, to the arch of elms on Silver Street and the Giamatti house. There, they munched popcorn and peanuts, took pony rides, and clustered around a table where they could make donations to Italian orphans. The Dante Fair became an annual event.

In this cozy, cloistered setting, Bart Giamatti had a quiet and graceful upbringing. He was instilled with the decorum and public-spiritedness of a Yankee village, surrounded by the artifacts of ancient Italy, taught the value of ceremony, and schooled in the poetic meter of Dante and his concerns for damnation, purgatory, and salvation. Dante's dominance of the household impressed on Bart the importance of allegory and symbolism, as well as Valentine's belief that these poetic concepts had relevance to real life. Youthful Bart was also cultivated with an Italian sense of nobility and with the Latin sense of the expansive gesture. If his skill at communication was always ahead of his peers, it was because of the great emphasis on the uses of language in the home.

All told, Bart's emulation of his father was every bit as powerful as Pete Rose's. In both cases, there was a strong drive to realize what the fathers had been so close to achieving but never had.

In 1947, when Bart was nine years old, the Giamatti family went off to Rome for a sabbatical year. They found themselves in a ravaged land where there was still no hot water and where transportation remained uncertain. They lived in a spacious three-room apartment in the Hotel Eliseo in the Via di Porta Pinciana, next to the Villa Borghese, the largest public park in Rome. Bart went to the Overseas School, which was then situated in an old Mussolini villa in the Via Nomentana. His Italian quickly became fluent. This childhood residence in the old country gave him a "bifocal sense, a doubleness of view," he was to say, making him an "amalgam" of both Italian and American cultures. This year, along with a second year in Italy seven years later, when he was in his mid-teens, imparted to him, he said, an Italian fatalism—a sense of history and a concern for the fragility of institutions—together with an American sense of possibility.

In Italy, he also acquired his first real baseball glove, a relic left behind by an American soldier.

Toward the end of the Giamattis' first year in Rome, the visiting professor, along with other members of the American community, was granted an audience with Pope Pius XII. A photograph of this audience was printed back home in the *Holyoke Transcript*. It showed the classic Roman profile of the diminutive, bespectacled pontiff, raising his crooked ringed finger to young Bart, whose eyes appear respectfully downcast. Actually, to the mortification of his parents, Bart had refused to kneel for the Pope, nor would the boy kiss the pontiff's ring.

In physical stature, young Bart lagged behind his peers. He was, however, quick of mind and of foot, and he gravitated to the sports world with passion and yearning. From the beginning, he was a Red Sox fan, for that was in the air and water of his town, the lingua franca of the place. "The Red Sox in South Hadley, the Red Sox in small New England towns, that was the big league in every sense of the word," Bart would say many years later. "That was the universe, that was the firmament, what the Lord had put out there to give one stability, coherence, and purpose in life." On any given day in the summer, Bart could be found under the canopy of Gene's gas station off the town common, in a clutch of twenty men and boys, listening to Curt Gowdy call the Sox game.

As the kids listened to the Sox games on the radio, they could play pinball for a nickel. This gaming device was thoroughly illegal, for it paid real money to the winner: on a good day a kid with a nickel might walk away with a quarter. But no one seemed to mind, not even the estimable Professor Giamatti.

Just as Pete Rose doted on Johnny Temple, the second baseman of the Reds, Bart's favorite player on the Sox was Bobby Doerr, who by 1946 was considered the best second baseman in baseball. His reliable fielding was exceeded only by his surprising power at the plate. Bart, however, admired Doerr's off-the-field demeanor nearly as much as his skill on the field. The second baseman had been a steady, stabilizing force on the great teams of the late forties. He neither drank nor smoked nor cursed nor womanized. He had a fondness for goldfish and in the winter raised mink on his farm in Illahe, Oregon. In the 1946 Series, when the great Ted Williams had choked so embarrassingly, Doerr hit .409.

In the fall of 1946, after the major league season was over, Dom DiMaggio, then the center fielder of the championship Red Sox, came to South Hadley to be interviewed at the local radio station that broadcast the Sox games. Suddenly, there on Main Street, sitting in a booth of a downtown luncheonette, was a star of the first magnitude in Bart's firmament. Val brought Bart down the hill to join the crowd of kids who swarmed around "The Little Professor," as DiMaggio was known. Like any good American father, Val wanted to partake of his son's dreams and fantasies. Moreover, Val had a baseball memory of his own. He remembered when the Yankees came to New Haven to play an exhibition game when he was a rising student, and he had seen Babe Ruth and Lou Gehrig play catch on the Yale Green.

The kids peppered the center fielder with endless, burning questions about the World Series the month before against the St. Louis Cardinals of Stan Musial, Red Schoendienst, and Enos Slaughter. Why had Ted Williams collapsed so totally in the Series? Why couldn't the Sox hit Harry "The Cat" Brecheen, who won three out of the four Cards victories? How did The Cat learn to pitch like that in Broken Bow, Oklahoma, anyway? How had it felt when DiMaggio scored the deciding run of the fifth game on a hit by Pinky Higgins? And how did it feel when he hit a double off the right-field wall to tie the seventh game in the eighth inning? Most of all, why, for God's sake, had Johnny Pesky hesitated in throwing home on the relay, allowing Country Slaughter to make it all the way home from first on Harry "The Hat" Walker's single?

As the kids grilled DiMaggio, Valentine stood off on the side, chatting with the proprietor of Conti and Veto's luncheonette. Val and Mr. Conti spoke not so much about baseball, because Conti was a Yankee fan, but about the old country. Both their fathers had been immigrants, so they understood these dreams. Baseball brought them together. It gave them a sense of belonging, of participation in the American experience. It imparted a commonality to three Italian families called Giamatti, DiMaggio, and Conti.

As it happened, young Lou Conti, a year above Bart in school, was the best athlete in town. By the time he was a sophomore at South Hadley High, Conti was excelling in three sports, most notably in baseball, where he was the center fielder and star pitcher. In the summer, he played for the Highland Volts in the Holyoke League and, one summer, took them to the national championships in Johnstown, Pennsylvania, where he blanked a team with a hot prospect named Al Kaline.

Bart, by contrast, remained a scrawny little kid who tried hard on the baseball diamond, but he couldn't hit, he couldn't throw, he couldn't catch. Far from dampening Bart's enthusiasm, this hard truth stimulated it. If he couldn't make the team, he nevertheless wanted to be around people who played the game well. He doted upon the talented Lou Conti, tagging around after him in school, plying him with endless questions about future games, most especially against arch-rival Palmer High, and making endless offers to help. This same offer of help was put to the South Hadley High School coach, Tom Landers, a fair and gentle teacher of sport, who was every bit the legend to western Massachusetts that Coach Hawk and Pappy Nohr were to Western Hills in Cincinnati. Bart promptly landed the job of manager of the baseball team. By all accounts, the bats were always in the right place, the oranges were ready to be eaten when they were wanted, and the official scorecard could always be relied upon.

Young Lou Conti was to Coach Landers what Eddie Brinkman was to Pappy Nohr. The highpoint came in Conti's junior year, when South Hadley High, a school with only 405 students, faced the much larger Holyoke High for the first time. With Conti on the mound and Giamatti at the end of the bench, South Hadley won, 15–0, as Conti pitched a shutout and hit a homer and a triple besides. This performance brought the scouts to South Hadley in earnest. For Coach Landers, that was competition in itself, for he was a secret scout for the Chicago Cubs.

Among the eight teams who offered contracts to the spry Lou Conti was the Boston Red Sox, and Bart was in awe. The Red Sox in 1952 was a team undergoing a face lift as it sent Johnny Pesky and "Moose" Dropo to the Tigers in exchange for Dizzy Trout, Hoot Evers, and George Kell. That year was also when Bobby Doerr retired. No wonder Bart could remember all the names of the rebuilt Red Sox of 1952 thirty years later (including the right fielder, "Zeke" Zarilla). He hoped that his schoolboy idol, Lou Conti, would find a place on the team. He was living the best dream of his youth through young Lou.

Bart began to follow Lou Conti around all the more, hounding him with questions tinged with advocacy: Was Lou going to sign with the Red Sox or not? Lou replied with grand professional hauteur: he was going to listen to all the offers before deciding. No sentimentalist he. Bart seemed disappointed, but only briefly, for Lou did sign with the Sox for the same standard figure that Pete Rose would sign with the Cincinnati Reds several years later: seven thousand dollars.

There was a difference. Young Lou Conti lasted a month in Boston before he was shipped to the minors in Nova Scotia. He eventually drifted into the navy, and then back to South Hadley, to end up running a small, popular dinette in town just like his father.

"Lou Conti had tremendous ability as a high school athlete," Coach Landers would say. "If he had had someone pushing him, he could have gone much farther in professional baseball. But he had grown up pretty comfortable in South Hadley. His father owned a good restaurant, and things came easy for Lou. When he got into the minors and found himself up against people with equal ability, he had a tendency to back off and not be aggressive enough."

As for Bart, he was full of desire, full of love for the game, full of vicarious joy and eventually pain for Lou Conti, and totally lacking in talent. "I've always found baseball the most satisfying and nourishing game outside of literature," he would say later.

With Lou Conti gone, and the Red Sox sinking into sixth place, Bart turned to literature. As a ball player, he was a brilliant student . . . and still a pretty good dreamer.

· 2 ·

The Bush Leaguer and the Valedictorian

IN THE ACADEMIC YEAR of 1954–55, Val Giamatti took another sabbatical to Italy, and Bart again went to the Overseas School, which had moved from Mussolini's villa to more modest quarters on the Via Cassia. In those days, the Overseas School still had a spotty reputation, especially as a finishing school, and Valentine and Mary Giamatti worried about this for their son. In the fall of 1955, upon the family's return from abroad, the sixteen-year-old youth was sent to Phillips Academy in Andover, Massachusetts, where Mary's father had gone.

Andover was steeped in Yankee tradition. It had been founded to promote "the virtuous and pious education of youth of requisite qualifications." Ever since, the academy groomed the brightest of patrician New England for the Ivy League. Bart was neither Cabot nor Lodge, but his father's Yale and Mount Holyoke connections sufficed. Moreover, Andover had a policy of aiding families of modest means. For diversity's sake, Andover's founder, Samuel Phillips, had invited the presence of "youth from every quarter" at his academy. While Bart Giamatti entered the school from the lower social regions, Val did not ask for financial aid.

In short order, Bart (or Matts, as his classmates called him) became known around the Commons for his spunk, his wit, and his differentness. Amid the white bucks, khaki trousers, and blue blazers of Andover, Bart was a genuine original, at a time and place where there were not many originals. It seemed to serve his purpose to flaunt an image of the threadbare immigrant, newly off the boat, and he had picked up a bit of swaggering from the teenage street life of Rome. Just as the severe side of his mother's Yankee roots bored him, his Italian side excited him, and he adopted a pose of "them versus us," which he exaggerated for effect with a leather jacket and studs. When he worked in the kitchen as part of his common duties and found a rich boy in his midst, he tended to harness the victim to slop jobs "to do him some good."

In general, sports—and little else—made one famous at Andover. The academy celebrated the Greek ideal of the scholar-athlete. Its athletes were its natural elite and real power group, for they represented the goal of well-roundedness that Andover was keen to project in its graduates. Actually, the academy was celebrating two lofty ideals of sport at once. (Later, Giamatti himself was to separate them and find them to be antithetical.) On the one hand, the Greek ideal of the scholar-athlete was a joyless cultivation of inner strength and spiritual toughness: triumph in games was a measure of superior manhood and deserved to be rewarded and celebrated as a symbol of superior skill in the combat that lay ahead in life and war. This, of course, was embraced by the boys who were becoming men.

But there was another ideal that concerned the Andover educators, and it was Celtic rather than Greek in origin. (In the nineteenth-century English public schools, from which Andover derived its traditions, it had a Christian element as well.) In this ideal, games promoted brotherhood and fellowship and moral fiber, sportsmanship and fair play and respect for the rules, team spirit and strength of character for later life. In the Greek tradition, winning was everything; in the Celtic, the struggle alongside one's comrades was paramount and revealed how one would behave later in more important, competitive pursuits.

If there was to be a piece of either ideal for young Bart Giamatti, it lay in equating athletic prowess with artistic prowess. In Ancient Greece, the great athlete was on the same plain with the great artist. For Aeschylus or Sophocles or Euripedes to win a three-day dramatic contest in Athens, they had to be great athletes as well as great playwrights.

Bart was as clumsy as he was skinny. He had entered a school where cliques and friendships had had four years to establish themselves. Yet, he penetrated those imposing walls with ease and speed. Conversation was his sport. He gravitated naturally to activities in which his skill at communication could be handsomely displayed: to debating and foreign languages and drama. On Wednesday evenings at the Philomathean Society, students turned out to see this newcomer perform, especially when the issue dealt with such a self-congratulatory theme as whether genius was the product of heredity or environment. In January 1956, before a packed crowd and broadcast on a Lawrence, Massachusetts, radio station, Bart took up the banner of heredity. "For the most part casting aside his peerless wit," wrote the school newspaper, Bart argued that genius was in-born, and that the quality could be noticed in the first or second day of life. Environment, he said dismissively, could only nurture essential genius, not create it.

To his classmates, Bart's charisma arose more from his originality than his humor or his brilliance. He seemed to view the world through different glasses. "It was as if there were a poet in our midst," his classmate, John McBride, would say, where even the most mundane event was seen with a wry and sometimes absurd perspective, but one totally devoid of cynicism. Cynicism was the exclusive dominion of the Andover old-timers, and "Bart would have been murdered at Andover, if as a one year post graduate, he had tried to make fun of people," another classmate, Dan Catlin, has said. "Bart was funny by virtue of his perceptions." Students sought him out and competed with one another to sit next to him at dinner because he was so entertaining. This included the athletes who enjoyed Bart's wry observations about their exploits. After dinner, on the steps of the Commons, where seniors were allowed the privilege to smoke, a slouchy, unhealthy-looking, and chain-smoking Bart held court for a group of world-beating preppies.

His Roman years made Bart seem older and more worldly to his classmates, and he knew how to play that for all it was worth. At this furtive age, their dreams were not of the baseball diamond, and the homeruns they imagined were not achieved on the base paths. In January 1956, after Christmas vacation, Bart published a little piece in the *Phillipian* entitled "Dreams of Glory."

> As I sat in my acrid little room with my nose pressed against the cracked, dirty pane, I watched them return. Looking at the long files of returning boys, with their lean, debauched faces still sleepy with dissipation, I felt moved. In fact, it moved very hard and very deeply; and as I picked myself up off the floor on the other side of the room, I thought just how good it was to be back.
>
> Soon all the dirt and dust that had been allowed to settle during the last nineteen days would be up and flying again as roommate met roommate. And the "Can You Top This" phase of the winter term would begin. Orgies would be relived; boys would be men again; New Year's . . . Christmas . . . the first night home . . . all this would be retold until the truth was out. Then the fun would begin.
>
> Neatsy!

To his teachers as well, there was something special about this boy. For history teacher Fritz Allis, Bart's outrage at the inhumanities and frauds of American history particularly set him apart. When they were discussing the Pullman Strike of 1894 and how Eugene Debs took 50,000 rail workers out on strike, only to have President Cleveland send in the troops to bludgeon the strikers back to work, Bart was horrified.

"They couldn't have done that!" he exclaimed in disbelief.

"I'm sorry to say that they did, Mr. Giamatti," the teacher responded, touched by his student's disillusion.

The English teacher at Andover exercised a particularly strong influence on Bart. Ted Harrison had returned to his alma mater to teach several years earlier. Besides Andover, his roots were decidedly Yale, where he had been the quintessential Bulldog jock, winning eight or nine letters, depending on who was telling the tale. As a defenseman and the captain of Yale's hockey team, he was the mainstay of the offense. In baseball, the day he struck out fourteen Dartmouths on a team that had a first baseman named George Bush was remembered twenty-five years later. Most important to the lore was the story that Harrison had given up a contract to pitch for the New York Yankees to join the U.S. Army and fight the Nazis. These rumors quivered thrillingly in the air at the Commons.

In addition to teaching English at Andover, Harrison was the hockey, baseball, and assistant football coach. He had a tolerance for literature but an absolute passion for baseball. If he expected his students to master their Wordsworth, he demanded that they excel on the baseball diamond. And he demanded that his teams win. This was something new at Andover. Up until the Harrison era, sports had a certain gentlemanly aspect. Except perhaps in a close game against Exeter, every man on the bench could expect to play. Not with Harrison. He won, and he played favorites, and as a result, his stars were his fervid loyalists and his bench warmers were bitter detractors.

Bart stood on the side of these rivalries and jealousies as an ardent observer. He adored Harrison as a scholar-jock who appreciated equally the playing fields of poetry and the poetry of the playing field. Harrison responded with high praise. In Bart's school record, Harrison wrote that Bart was "the finest student I ever taught" and found him overall to be "an unusually fine boy." Much later, Bart would say that the coach never praised anyone if the boy was merely fulfilling his potential. "Talent is sacred," Bart said of Harrison's philosophy. "If you have it, you have an obligation to use it. If you use it well, that is how it should be. No one ought to be specially praised for doing a job well, if he has the ability, any more than a man should be praised for telling the truth."

Bart had an eight o'clock class with the coach in a cramped room with a wistful sideview of the gym. At that beastly hour, when the boys were often not operating to their fullest potential, indeed, when quite a few of them were still half asleep, Harrison plied his unorthodox pedagogy. To deal with flagging attention, Harrison had a propensity to throw chalk—with both arms. By Bart's own testimony, the old Bulldog still had excellent control, and he never beaned anyone: "He only moved them back a little, the puffs of white dust from the explosion on the wall a reminder to them of the need to concentrate. They were brush-back pitches, designed to encourage the batter to dig in . . . to plant his feet . . . to take a real cut at the ball at that ungodly hour."

Sometimes, Harrison went overboard. In the class was a student named Tom Bagnoli, who was Harrison's second baseman. At 8:00 in the morning, Bagnoli could not be aroused, or even intimidated, by Harrison's bullets. One fine spring day, Harrison got fed up when, as Bart later related it, "the gifted Bagnoli was not covering the bag and the great Wordsworth, no swift baserunner, but strong and purposeful, stole second on him." With a move of "speed and coherence" which Bart never forgot, Harrison picked up not chalk but a massive, dog-eared *Webster's Unabridged Dictionary* and arched it gracefully at Bagnoli, who was wedged in daydreams in the corner. "Bagnoli, now alert, caught the accumulated efforts of seven hundred years of English-speaking people without great effort," Bart recalled. "Perhaps Harrison did not throw the dictionary at Bagnoli; perhaps he threw it to him. But Bagnoli's face registered the shock of his teacher's and coach's skill and attention."

Harrison had "connected" with his student, and thereby with all his students.

"The language was his fundamental medium and his final care," Bart said . . . not to mention, his ultimate weapon.

In his fifth and final year at Western Hills High School, Pete Rose was ineligible to play sports because he had flunked his sophomore year and had to repeat it. Unable to play in the scholastic leagues, he joined an amateur league in Dayton and played three times a week after school, sometimes at the position of catcher. This was Double A amateur ball, not bad in quality, and ideal to attract the attention of scouts. On the days he trundled up to his team in Lebanon, Ohio, in his 1937 Plymouth, Pete roomed overnight with two blacks, one of whom was a close friend of the great Frank Robinson.

Pete felt close to greatness that spring. At first, he was tight and did poorly, but his uncle Buddy Bloebaum relaxed him, and before long he was batting .500 against such teams as Wright Patterson Air Force Base. A scout for the Baltimore Orioles took notice, especially after watching a game when Pete went 5 for 5. Harry Rose kept from his son the fact that there was initial interest in him from the big leagues.

On graduation day in 1960 at Western Hills High, the Cincinnati Reds were holding a baseball clinic in Piqua, north of Dayton, so Harry Rose was surprised when Uncle Buddy, instead of spending the day scouting for the Reds, showed up at his door. By this time, young Pete was out celebrating. It was just as well, for Buddy had an announcement of some significance: the Reds were ready to offer Pete a contract for $7,000.

"Is that good?" Harry asked.

"It's better than what the others are offering him now," Buddy replied drolly.

"What about the Orioles?" Harry asked.

"A bird in the hand is worth two Orioles in the bush," said Buddy. Actually, the Reds were unenthusiastic. The kid was too small, a scant 155 pounds. But Uncle Buddy, willing to stake his reputation for his nephew, convinced them that the Roses were late bloomers.

The following morning, Harry and Pete went off to Crosley Field. They had been there many times before, but Harry's procedure had been different in the earlier years. Harry would buy a ticket and have Pete cadge his from the gathering crowd. This time, though, Pete didn't need an Annie Oakley to get into the ballpark. Father and son spoke little as they reverently walked onto the field.

The Reds needed extra work that day. Even though they had knocked out starter Moe Drabowsky in the second inning the night before, they had been shellacked by the seventh-place Cubs. The loss to Chicago was Cincinnati's sixth straight.

Meanwhile, gamblers were getting "bolder by the day," noted Lou Smith of the *Cincinnati Enquirer*. They had begun calling the press box to find out the next day's pitchers. "I don't blame them for calling," cracked a press box wag. "I'd like to know when Moe Drabowsky is pitching too."

The series had one special feature: Danny Murphy, a seventeen-year-old "bonus beauty," had just reported to the Cubs after signing for $125,000.

"What's the kid weigh?" Reds pilot Fred Hutchinson inquired of the Cubs manager, Lou Boudreau.

"About 180 pounds," replied Boudreau.

"I'd want more weight for that kind of money," Hutch quipped.

As Harry and his featherweight son walked the field, Uncle Buddy sat in the stands with Phil Seghi, an executive for the Reds. In a few minutes, they commenced the real negotiation. The offer came as Uncle Buddy had predicted: $7,000 to sign, another $5,000 if Pete made it all the way to the majors and stayed thirty days. As Pete later described it in his autobiographies, Harry mentioned his promise to the Orioles scout that he would do nothing before talking with him. Uncle Buddy stepped in. This happened all the time, he assured Harry. He would talk to the Orioles man.

"The fact that this kind of thing happens all the time doesn't make it right," Harry objected. "I owe him the courtesy to talk with him."

Pete began to sink in his chair, worrying that his father was about to queer the deal.

"Listen, I shouldn't be making this decision at all," Harry said finally, turning to his son. "Pete, what do you think?"

"I'd like to sign," the kid stammered. "I'd like to sign and go right now."

"If you're sure [the scout of the Orioles] will accept this thing all right, let's say yes," Harry said to Buddy. And so it was a done deal.

"You can do one of two things," Seghi said, turning to his new prospect. "You can go up to Geneva, New York, and play right away or you can wait till next spring to sign, go down to Tampa, and start off even with everybody else.

"I'll be honest with you, Pete," Seghi continued. "I know you've been playing ball a couple times a week, but you're going to have to face facts. You're really not in shape to play. Three times a week isn't enough. But if you want to go to Geneva, fine." The management did not mind if Pete only hit .100 at Geneva, Seghi said unconvincingly. "They'll be tearing you apart ... but Pete, if that thought doesn't bother you, and you still want to go ..."

"I want to go right now," Pete blurted out.

"At least wait till Monday, kid," Seghi said. "That's when the plane leaves."

The next day, Lou Smith, the sportswriter for the *Enquirer*, announced that a local boy had signed with a Reds farm team, "the son of Harry Rose, one of the finest all-around athletes ever developed in this area." It seemed to be a good day generally for the Reds. They turned the tables on the Cubs, pounding them for a load of hits, including two homers off another Cincinnati boy and product of Bold

Face Park, Dick "Hummer" Drott. The Cubs ivory, Danny Murphy, played his first game in center field and went 0 for 4.

In Geneva, a boxcar town of 18,000 on the north tip of Seneca Lake, the team called the Redlegs was struggling. They were managed by a journeyman named Reno DeBenedetti, who would be fired six weeks after Pete's arrival, as the Redlegs would finish in the cellar, nineteen games behind the champions of the New York–Penn League. Young Pete arrived somewhat dazed after his very first ride on an airplane. His teammates greeted him frostily, viewing him as the sentimental, hometown choice of the Reds organization and a player who was not likely to last.

At first, Pete's play confirmed the suspicion. He hit a little higher than .100—a decent .277 in fact—but he made an unacceptable 36 errors in 85 games. Balls shot straight at him on the ground were a particular problem. No matter how much the coach told him not "to let the ball play you," Pete seemed afraid. Moreover, his double-play motion was no thing of beauty. His pivot was slow and jerky. At the plate, still insisting as always on switch hitting, he got few hits left-handed.

Even though the Redlegs were mired in last place, the team had a few bright prospects who, unlike Pete, seemed to have a real future in baseball. A complement of Cubans was led by a graceful and powerful, if somewhat skinny, player named Tony Perez, who was having a fine year (27 homers, 132 RBIs, and an average of .348). Perez was livid when he was moved from second to third base to make a place for this newcomer from Cincinnati.

With his drive and desire, Pete did his best to compensate for his apparent lack of natural talent. He was hungry and was perhaps the most willing student the coaches had ever seen. He seemed to carry the desperation of his situation on his sleeve, as if the ghost of his father was always looking over his shoulder. He knew that if he didn't make it in baseball, he was not going to make it anywhere. That might have been true of a number of young players there in the horse-and-buggy league—it was certainly true of Tony Perez, who faced a future in the sugar factories of Camagüey, Cuba, just like his father and brother, if he didn't make it. Yet, Pete seemed more aware of playing out his last chance.

A month into Pete's "professional" career, Harry Rose came to inspect the progress. At a game in Erie, Pennsylvania, Harry was pleased at his son's evident improvement but frightened by the stiff competition. Then Harry had a private talk with Manager DeBenedetti, who was looking for any excuse to explain the poor standing of the Redlegs. To Harry, the skipper spewed out a string of complaints about Pete, wondering if this bad habit or that was something Pete had always done back in Cincinnati. Once again, Harry kept this bad report from Pete, because, as he said later, it could have broken his son's heart, although Harry was just as worried about his own heart. Instead, Harry returned to his fixation of hustle and criticized the lazy kid in left field, Art Shamsky, for giving up on a long ball.

In deportment, Pete was loud and vulgar. His cockiness earned him a reputation as a hotdog and even the inapt nickname of "Hollywood Rose." From the beginning, his working man's ethic made him popular with the fans, partly because he was seen as playing above his abilities. Devoid of racism, he quickly became friends with the more talented Cubans, even those who spoke no English and with whom he communicated with gestures and grunts. Because he was younger than most of his teammates, the poignancy of the lonely kid away from home for the first time invited charity. His mother, LaVerne, came to Geneva and stayed in a tourist home for a few weeks to cut the loneliness. After some clubhouse thief stole a portion of his meager $400-a-month salary, Uncle Buddy helped the banker's son open a checking account.

Back in Cincinnati, Harry had another jolt. He had the misfortune to encounter an executive in the Reds front office, who handed Harry the scouting reports without comment. "Pete Rose can't make a double-play, can't throw, can't hit left-handed and can't run." To Harry, this was "the grimmest day" of his life.

"Does it say that Pete does anything right?" Harry asked.

"Well, it does say that Pete seems to have a lot of aggressiveness," the front man replied. "Does that help?"

"Not much," Harry replied.

Nevertheless, after the season, the Reds met their side of the bargain. Pete would get a shot the next spring in Tampa under Johnny Vander Meer. As the nineteen-year-old Rose left Geneva, he received his first gift as a player, a token of appreciation for his effort: two Samsonite suitcases. He traded in his jalopy and bought a spiffy 1957 Plymouth with running boards and window shades.

By the end of that first short professional season, he knew all too well the value of heft. Back in Cincinnati, work and his mother took over. He took a job in the railyards, unloading boxcars for the Railway Express Agency to build himself up. Every noontime, LaVerne turned up with a hearty lunch and a cup of warm cocoa. Over that winter, Pete grew two inches and reported to Tampa in the spring twenty pounds heavier.

Johnny Vander Meer, the manager of the Tampa Tarpons, was a quiet, unassuming, unexcitable sort of fellow who could teach Pete Rose a great deal more baseball wisdom than merely how to be a disciplined hitter . . . if Pete would listen. For Vander Meer possessed one of the great records of baseball history. As an unheralded rookie portsider for the Reds in 1938, he had pitched back-to-back no-hitters, a record that was considered every bit as unassailable as Ty Cobb's 4,191 hits. The son of a Dutch stonecutter, Vandy entered the majors with a terrific fastball and a sharp-breaking curve, but a reputation for wildness that was well deserved for every year he pitched in the major leagues except the first year. His battery mate was Ernesto Lombardi, unquestionably the most popular player in the history of the Cincinnati Reds up to that time, who was the son of an immigrant, an Italian grocer from Piedmont. With his gigantic size and Roman nose, Lombardi was tagged with a number of nicknames, including Big Ernie and Bocci, and the one he loathed: Schnozz. Big Ernie was idolized by the fans, especially the women, and his popularity embarrassed him, so much so that he refused to sign autographs. He refused, that is, until once several kids approached him, baseballs in hand. When Schnozz waved them away, one kid turned to the other and said, "See, I told you he couldn't write." Thereafter, Big Ernie always signed autographs.

On June 11, 1938, before 10,000 fans on Knothole Day at Crosley Field, the fireballing Dutchman pitched his first no-hitter against Boston, blanking the Bees, 3–0. Four days later, Vandy's turn to pitch came again, and this time, the scene was more imposing. The Reds were in Brooklyn for the first game of night baseball ever played at Ebbets Field. Larry MacPhail, who was known as the Barnum of Baseball, was in charge of the spectacle. He had recruited Jesse Owens, fresh from his Olympic victories in Berlin two years before, to race two baseball players 100 yards in an exhibition before the game, spotting the ball players a 10-yard head start. MacPhail had also invited Babe Ruth to the game, and the Bambino made a royal entrance.

Vander Meer was even sharper that night than he had been four days earlier in Cincinnati. His fastball had more movement, and his curve was breaking even sharper. By the fifth inning, he felt he had a shot for his second no-hitter, and he kept "fogging them in." By the bottom of the ninth, his no-hitter holding, the stadium was on its feet in excitement. He got the first batter. And then, abruptly, unexplainably, he seemed to lose everything, walking the next three batters to load the bases. The Reds pilot, Bill McKechnie, trotted out to the mound to calm Vandy down, telling him, as he stood there on the brink of an epic achievement, just to relax, not to get too excited, not to worry. The batter was Ernie Koy, a dangerous hitter with terrific speed (he had been chosen to race Jesse Owens earlier in the evening). With the count at 1 and 1, Koy hit a bounder to third, and the Reds third baseman, Lew Riggs, fielded it cleanly, but took such deliberate care in his throw to the plate that Big Ernie Lombardi had no chance to turn a double play to first. With two outs, Leo Durocher stepped up. He hit a looping fly ball to center. When the Reds center fielder, Harry Craft, gathered it in, bedlam broke loose. Later, on the rubbing table in the clubhouse, Vandy admitted that "I felt a little tired in the final two heats and it was certainly a relief to me when I turned around and saw Harry circling under Durocher's fly."

So Johnny Vander Meer had a few things to teach his young players about fame and its vagaries, about records and their transience, about the struggle for the top and its sometimes bitter afterglow. Before he settled into his job as a minor league manager, Vander Meer pitched another thirteen years, wildly. He had only one other noteworthy achievement: in 1946, he pitched fifteen scoreless innings in the longest double shutout in baseball history, a game that was called for darkness after nineteen innings without a score. Vandy knew a lot about the relation, as Bart Giamatti put it in a different context many years later, between life and art.

Pete Rose arrived in Tampa physically transformed but fretful. His negative advance billing from Geneva clouded his future, and he was placed on the second team, from which only the real surprises survived. At the beginning of the season, Harry Rose went to Tampa to cheer his son and perhaps to live out the last vestige of his own vicarious dream. On the grass of Al Lopez Field, Harry hit grounders to Pete and assumed that this would be the closest he and his son would get to the majors. After their extra practices, Harry took Pete to the dog track or to the jai alai fronton, further nurturing Pete's fondness for the bet and encouraging the vice with paternal sanction.

Into May, Pete began to play as if he were possessed. The Old Dutchman quickly tore up the reports from Geneva which no longer bore relation to this dynamo. Rose sprayed his liners into the gaps and seams to the point that he was batting .376 one month into the season. Moreover, he was sustaining the pace equally from both sides of the plate and hitting with power. By the first week in June, with two and a half months left in the season, he had seventeen triples, which was near the League record. His final total was thirty, which stood as a record in the Florida State League for years.

Many of those triples were the result of stretching a stand-up double into a headfirst-slide triple. The art of stretching a hit by a base is essentially the craft of the gambler. It is a question of odds: the outfielder might have time to catch you, but only with a perfect throw, and what are the odds of that happening? Rose began to analyze the skills of the opposing outfielders and worked out his calculations intuitively. His aggressiveness began to be tempered with discipline. His father had hammered into him early that when he got a hit, he should think third base rather than settle for second or first. Now he was realizing there was a science as well as an art to the triple. This constant, relentless, nerve-racking pressing rattled the opposition and forced it into mistakes.

To Vander Meer, Rose ran like a "scalded dog." The manager passed the word to Cincinnati that he wanted to keep the kid, who had now acquired the nickname of "Scooter Rose." The Tarpons swam far ahead of the competition, leading the League by ten games in mid-season. On the day he hit two inside-the-park homers in a double bill against the St. Petersburg Saints, Rose was named the League's player of the month. Vander Meer told the *Tampa Tribune* that his team was in first place because his young players were going so hard they even ran out a walk to first base.

"Speed is the thing in this league," Vandy said. "The parks are so big, it's foolish to go for a home run."

To the joy of the Tampa owners, worried as they were that the Cincinnati Reds would sever their association with the franchise, attendance at the games rose to about six hundred fans a game. They were not fans before whom Pete especially enjoyed performing, however. Many were leather-skinned retirees from Cincinnati. "Seeing us was about the only real touch they would ever have again with home," Rose would write later. Beautiful old people they might be, but "in some way they always made me sad. It seems like everybody had stopped loving them. That's the sad part about being down there in Florida. At times, it's like being surrounded by thousands of ancient people who are sitting on park benches in the sun, waiting for their Social Security check or death. I hadn't come there to die. I had come there to begin."

If Pete Rose did not understand why the old people of Tampa turned out to watch these bush leaguers, Bart Giamatti did: "I'm always interested when I watch the older people in the stands in Florida or Arizona," Giamatti would say. "Watching them watch a baseball game. Watching them watch young men. . . . What do they see? They don't just see youngsters in relief. They see Vic Raschi and Lefty Gomez and Walter Johnson. You see history out there in every one of those young players because they all remind you of a past you can't see anymore."

Hot as he was at the plate, Rose still showed fundamental flaws on the field. He was limited in his range, particularly to his right, and his double-play pivot was so rough that "he wouldn't ever get a good major league runner," Vander Meer believed. So marked was this flaw, that the manager wanted to move the kid to the outfield, but the Reds front office blocked the move. Pete Rose was too small for a major league outfield, management believed. The executives continued to distrust Uncle Buddy's insistence that Pete still had some growing to do.

Vandy would not tamper with Rose's hitting, however, not when he was hitting over .350. As a matter of principle, Vander Meer knew the problem of overcoaching. He did concentrate on Rose's discipline to wait for the good pitch. The manager did not want his aggressive leadoff hitter swinging at the first pitch, partly because a quick out made it easy on the opposing pitcher and harder on the hitters in the heart of the order. You had to make the pitcher work and give him a chance to screw up. Pete should not be afraid to take a first strike, Vander Meer counseled. If the first pitch was a ball, the second pitch was likely to be a fastball over the plate. A pitcher certainly didn't want to go 2 and 0 on the batter, because then he had to throw a fastball.

"Pete Rose looked to me like one wonderful hitter," Vandy announced with the pride of prophecy. The statistics bore him out. While Rose's average slacked off to .331 at the end of the season, the Tarpons won the pennant in the final game of the play-offs, as Rose smacked two doubles, while his hulking first baseman, a product of the Birmingham Negro League, Lee May, contributed a home run.

Not surprisingly, Rose was named the player of the year in the Florida State League after the season, but this settled nothing about his future. Two other bush-league second basemen in the Reds farm system were also named players of the year in leagues that were tougher than the Florida State: Tommy Harper in the Three I League in Topeka and Cesar Tovar in the PIN League. Moreover, in Don Blasingame, the Reds had a solid performer on their championship team in 1961.

To the outside world, Rose's year in the Cigar City was a resounding success. He went home with the reputation as the "hard hitting, sharp-fielding second baseman" of the Florida League. Abruptly, the front office began to concentrate on him as a hot prospect. But Pete still felt his vulnerability. In his own mind, his skills remained inferior. "I'd stay around after the regular practice and work out with anybody who would work out with me. I had to. I was running real fast just to stand still in those days," he said ten years later. "Let the other guys go out and give 100 percent if they want. They're good. Me? I got to give 110 percent to keep up with them. The minute I slack off, I've had it. Baseball is a hard game. Love it hard and it will love you back hard. Try to play it easy and ease off and the first thing you know, there you are, on the outside, looking in, wondering what went wrong."

Over that winter, the Reds had Rose play in the Instructional League, largely to work on his fielding. The following spring, he reported to Macon, Georgia, leaping from Class D to Class A ball. If he could make it in Macon, he would make a major jump and save himself several years in the minors.

Now, Pete's manager was Dave Bristol, a native of Macon, who himself was something of a phenomenon—for his wiles rather than his hits. Bristol had been a journeyman in the minors for ten years as a player. His cunning was recognized early, however, and at the age of twenty-three he became a player-manager in the Reds organization. He was now twenty-nine and no longer playing, but he had been promoted to the top rank of the Reds farm system and was headed for still bigger things. Besides his canniness, Bristol was also known as a fierce, main-event fighter who always lost his fights. That he always lost did not seem to deter him. Once, when he was coaching third at Macon, he got into a rhubarb with Elmo Plaskett, the catcher from the other team. Plaskett hauled off and hit Bristol in the face with his catcher's mask. Bristol went down, bleeding from his nose and mouth, but at the count of four, he hopped up, slipped into his best fighter's stance and said, "Had enough, Elmo, or do you want more?"

The first time Bristol saw Rose—running as hard as he could to every assignment he got on the field—the manager wondered to himself whether the guy was real or whether "he was putting me on." Was Rose going to be like that all the time? Bristol was not sure he could handle all that kinetic energy.

For his part, Rose picked up where he left off in Tampa, hitting .330, leading the league in triples (seventeen) and runs batted in, and getting thirty-five doubles. Some thought Rose should be moved to San Diego, the top Reds farm team, in mid-season, but Dave Bristol expressed his opinion about that by spewing a stream of tobacco juice contemptuously on the dugout steps. Rose's love of the game matched his own, and Bristol wanted Rose around for personal as well as professional reasons. The Scooter's enthusiasm rubbed off on the other players, and it also made the long bus rides more fun.

"Pete was the greediest player I ever had . . . and that's no knock," Bristol said years later. "A lot of players, when they get a couple of hits up front, they cruise. Particularly if the game is one-sided. They don't bear down on their last at bats. Not Pete." Bristol remembered well a game in Greenville, North Carolina, where in a big first inning, his team went way ahead, but Pete went 0 for 2. His poor start and his team's lead did not discourage him. He ended up 6 for 8.

In Macon, other future big leaguers were acquiring their final polish. Among them were Tommy Helms and Art Shamsky. One who would not make it was a catcher named Larry Himes, whose peg to second on steal attempts had a tendency to sail into center field. A helpless Himes eventually began shouting to his second baseman, "Pick me up! You gotta pick me up!" One day, arriving late for batting practice, Bristol found Himes behind the plate and Rose atop a stepladder at second base (with Helms midway down). Pete was shouting, "Pick me up! You gotta pick me up!" Bristol liked that.

For some in the minors, like Bart Giamatti's childhood friend Lou Conti, the sight of hotshot competition made them wilt. Rose understood instinctively that this could work to his advantage. He cultivated his hotdog image studiously, matching his hustle on the field with a jock's cockiness in the locker room. And he carried it over in the precincts of that sleepy southern town where ball players hung out (although he lived in the spartan YMCA). He acquired a green Corvette, which began his love affair with fast cars. Whenever he could, he drove it to games in nearby Atlanta and Augusta.

Most of the road trips were made in the club's station wagon, six oversized, loud ball players shoehorned into a cramped space. Pete was always on the lookout for anything to break the monotony. Once, on a seventeen-hour drive to Lynchburg, Virginia, as the others slept and Shamsky drove, Rose slipped to the back, quietly opened the rear window, and climbed on the luggage rack as the station wagon zipped along at 60 mph. Eventually, he clawed his way forward. Suddenly, there in the dull haze of a long drive, in the middle of the night on a rural road, Shamsky saw two ghostly palms slap across his vision on the windshield. Bristol was not so amused when he heard this story.

In Macon, when it rained during the sultry summer months, frogs emerged by the hundreds to hop around the grass. This pestilence could work on the mind, especially a Latin mind that knew of poisonous frogs. This could give a fellow a notion. In the summer of '62, the Macon team had a player from Venezuela who seemed particularly spooked by the amphibians underfoot. So a locker-room wiseguy with the improbable stage-name Mel Queen taped a frog to a baseball and then hurled a fastball to the unsuspecting Latino. It is said that the terrified Venezuelan was last seen galloping for the piney woods.

"When in Macon, look out for the frogs," Rose would say later, "or at least, when it rains, watch out for Mel Queen."

The Yale that Bart Giamatti entered in the fall of 1956 had the quality of an elegant and self-contained Renaissance city-state. With its moats and ornate gates, its enclosed quadrangles and crenellated battlements, it looked the part. Its puritan charter in 1701 defined the school's mission to be a place where, under Almighty God, youth were to be trained for service to church and civil state. In its dedication to humane and charitable citizenship, Yale liked to distinguish itself from its competitors. Later in life, Giamatti would write that Yale preferred to define most problems as ethical and then search for political solutions, whereas Harvard defined most problems as political and then sought to solve them with money, while Princeton did not acknowledge that there were any problems.

Yale is a place of congregations, where joiners rather than loners flourish and where a sense of community is valued above individual freedom. The University was, and is, divided into residential colleges of about two hundred students each, designed to break down the impersonality of the larger whole with the intimacy of smaller parts. In 1956, Yale College did not admit women, and it turned its back or, more aptly, raised its nose, toward the city of New Haven, whose original Italians, then blacks and southerners, then Puerto Ricans and Southeast Asians, bore no relation to the high-minded pursuit of excellence and knowledge that the effulgent name of Yale had come to mean.

It was the late 1950s—Godless, apathetic, Bohemian—where the rebel without a cause was the model, where James Dean, Sal Mineo, and Natalie Wood represented the standard for deportment and romance and social irresponsibility. In Sal Mineo, Bart might have felt a connection. Those sad-eyed, troubled juveniles of the Italian street gangs whom Mineo, a Puerto Rican, played so well appealed to Bart. He wore a black leather jacket, dangled a cigarette constantly from his lip, struck a studied slouch, and even adopted a starchy, anti-intellectual style of speaking. He lapsed easily into a mock Italian accent. In his best guttural, he insisted on being called "Angie," while somewhere, no doubt, his father winced. It was a transparent pose to mask his superior intellect and grasp of the language.

That, at least, was the first impression of his Yale compatriot,

Dick Cavett. To Cavett, there was nothing phony in Bart's pose. Rather, it was a genuinely amusing act put on by this emaciated product of the cloisters of Mount Holyoke, ancient Rome, and patrician Andover. At the time, there was nothing unusual about the young men of Yale, particularly freshmen, playing any manner of roles.

Naturally enough, Bart's relationships with his Andover mates—he was one of about sixty Andover grads at Yale—survived through his first year in New Haven. Still, he broadened his circle rapidly. For one thing, he knew New Haven. In the first few weeks of college, he could show the newcomers where the movie theaters and the Bohemian joints and other assorted wickednesses were located. He became Virgil in the local inferno, divinely funny along the way. He and his Andover friend Dan Catlin set off religiously once a week for the Mediterranean precincts of South New Haven for a pizza at Pepe's.

For Bart, it was a sentimental journey, for the owner of Pepe's had known Val Giamatti as a boy. This was the neighborhood where Bart's grandfather, Angelo, had lived and labored for the New Haven Clock Company. In 1956, for a Yale lad to venture into these mean streets was downright risky, for the gown of Yale was like a red cape to the toughs of Worchester Street. Young Bart proposed an ingenious solution to this unpleasantness, and he worked it out carefully with Catlin: whenever they were confronted by a few hostile *contadini*, Bart immediately switched into his best and most fluent Italian, and Catlin, the heir to the Havemeyer sugar trust and a Yankee blueblood, was to say "Sí" emphatically whenever Bart paused. Inevitably, they were passed by as brothers.

After his freshman year, Bart entered Saybrook College, "pinned" to a clutch of Andover mates who went to the residential college as a group. With its five floors of cramped rooms and its pinched, narrow dining hall, Saybrook was known as the "anthill," a place for the gregarious. Its men were "seals" who swam happily in schools, sometimes gossiping about the "oysters" of Branford College, to which Saybrook is joined architecturally in the famous Memorial Quadrangle. (Branford men liked their nickname as well, for it suggested a reflective, if private, sensibility that often harbored pearls of wisdom.) Saybrook's portals and seals and figurines celebrated the heroes of the place: Samuel Morse (Class of 1810, inventor of the electric telegraph), Eli Whitney (1792, inventor of the cotton gin), Samuel Tilden (1837, Democratic candidate for President), and William Howard Taft. Also memorialized is one William Graham Sumner, class of 1863, an estimable sociologist and economist, who was regarded as the greatest teacher at Yale in the late 1800s. Sumner's insistence upon strict rules was legendary, and students like Bart were meant to pay attention to the legend. At the beginning of the semester, Sumner laid down the law to his crowded lecture hall: "This rule applies to everybody. It applies to graduate students. It applies to undergraduates. Applies to you. Applies to me. It's a good rule. I made it."

The drama school beckoned powerfully to Bart. As his Yale education progressed, he spent more and more time around theatrical types like Cavett and a fine if slightly stout actress with a powerful voice and presence named Toni Smith, whose father happened to be the football coach for a Plainfield, New Jersey, high school. Bart dreamed of a career in the theatre and showed some promise in Constance Welch's stage speaking class, although the acting teacher, Nikos Psacharopoulos, had a mild antipathy toward this ersatz immigrant and tried to discourage the growing romance between him and Toni Smith. "Get rid of Giamatti, Dick," Psacharopoulos once said to Cavett. "He's a loser."

Giamatti got a minor role in a musical version of *Cyrano*, which featured Cavett as Ragueneau and Toni Smith as Roxanne. Bart was one of four Spaniards, and his most memorable line came after the overture, when he belted out, "Let the Play Begin!" In one performance, he made the mistake of rolling the wheel of a flower cart onto the foot of Cavett's future wife, Kerry Ney, as she was in the midst of a stage speech: the actress bravely but wanly pressed on.

That he was perceived as a lesser theatrical talent—and began to perceive himself that way—instilled in him an enduring awe for those who made good on the stage. Throughout his life, Bart followed the entertainment business avidly and kept up with Cavett's career with special fascination, admiring his collegemate as much for his chutzpah as his talent. The delight in Cavett's chutzpah derived from a time at Saybrook College when the two stood in the dinner line, and Cavett, on impulse, turned to Bart and proposed that they take a train to New York at that very moment and try to persuade Peter Ustinov, who was then performing on stage, to come to Yale for a talk. Hours later, they stood outside Ustinov's dressing room, knees shaking, before the actor invited them in and heartily agreed to the proposal. Giamatti and Cavett threw themselves into promotion of the event. At the appointed time, on a pleasant spring afternoon, a huge crowd gathered, but Ustinov did not show up! Cavett was pushed forward to try to explain, asserting boldly that Ustinov was coming "any hour now," whereupon a drama professor stood up and shouted, "Fiasco, Cavett!" and stomped out. As the disgusted professor disappeared around one corner, Ustinov's blue Alfa Romeo appeared around another. The actor's triumphant appearance reprieved Bart and Cavett from permanent disgrace.

For Bart, the urge to act found its eventual home in the medieval pageants and ceremonies of Yale and in the classroom. The robes, cowls, medallions, processions, and grand titles of high academe were in touch with the thirteenth and fourteenth centuries, which he loved, and presented him with the opportunity to act without being too severely reviewed for his performance. More important was the act of teaching itself, which Bart undertook with theatrical ebullience, as if for each class the curtain was rising and the audience had the right to expect something wonderful.

All in all, Bart's Yale undergraduate years were rich and varied. Besides the Dramat, he was active in the Elizabethan Club, affectionately known as the Lizzy, where faculty and students of a literary bent met for tea and tomato sandwiches in the late afternoon. He pledged Delta Kappa Epsilon, the fraternity of jocks. This was one more indication that if he couldn't be one himself, at least Bart wanted to sit among the stars, whether they were athletic, theatrical, or literary.

Toward the end of his undergraduate years, Giamatti began to gather in the honors. In the glow of remembrance, a classmate, Lewis E. Lehrman, the drugstore mogul who later ran for mayor of New York, said of Bart upon Giamatti's inauguration as president of Yale: "He was endowed with the spirit of the Great Bard, the felicitous rhetoric of Cicero, and the compelling force of a Sforza. Behold my friend, the Prince!" Overblown though that may have been, the special combination of humanity and humor in Giamatti seemed to be widely appreciated. He was swept into the most prestigious senior honor societies. He was made a Pundit, one of ten undergraduates who were theoretically Yale's greatest wits and whose past members included Stephen Vincent Benét, Cole Porter, and Peter Arno. The Pundits had lunch together regularly at Mory's, engaging in dazzling and self-conscious repartee around its carved and worn tables. Once a year, in May, the Pundits threw a lavish dinner on the steps of Sterling Library. In 1960, champagne and lobster were served (under the watchful eye of the campus cops), and the entertainment consisted of the members in ballerina costume, posing as a contingent from the Bolshoi and performing pas-de-deux and pirouettes from *Swan Lake*. Another of Bart's honorary societies was the Aurelian Society, named for Roman emperor Marcus Aurelius, who embodied scholarship, leadership, and sportsmanship. Bart was one of only thirteen senior-class members to be inducted.

Most significantly, however, he was tapped into the mysterious and prestigious senior society known as Scroll and Key. About these secret societies at Yale, little is known officially—or is supposed to be known: whether it is really true that the society called Wolfshead has a secret swimming pool, because it has the largest water bill at Yale; or whether in Skull and Bones, young men, including George Bush, really wrestle naked in mud or bond by masturbating together over a coffin filled with bones . . . who can say for sure? The honorees are sworn to secrecy. But Keys met twice a week for dinner at the Tomb— that much is known—and the club usually broke up around 1:00 A.M., for its members could be heard belting out their Troubadour's Song at that hour from the Tomb's steps.

Keys had signaled to Bart that they wished to tap him late in his junior year, and he had signaled back that he would accept. When word of this spread, Keys got every other candidate it wanted in the rising senior class, including the titans of Yale sport that year: the captains of football, baseball, crew, wrestling, lacrosse, and the tennis captain, Donald Dell. This was company truly to Bart's liking. Joe Mathewson, the editor of the humor magazine (and future playwright), took the role of the elegant sophisticate, and Giamatti became the ribald vaudevillian; together, these two supplied the hilarity during the society's meetings. Bart's most memorable performance within the windowless Tomb, it is rumored, was reciting Kipling's *Gunga Din* in a cockney accent.

A variation of Bart's role at Keys was to needle the heroes of Yale sport and to make sure that their heads did not swell unduly. After Donald Dell received a couple of notes from Gardnar Mulloy, the great doubles champion, Dell began to wonder whether Mulloy, who had teamed with Vic Seixas and Billy Talbert in past triumphs at Wimbledon, was looking for a new partner. It was not until Bart stood up in Keys some time after, with a third message from Gardnar Mulloy, that Dell finally understood what was going on.

Bart's role as the stand-up comic at Keys only made quasiofficial the role he was ascribing to himself for life in general. To his friends, he always seemed to be "on stage." Unlike most actors, who subsumed their own personality in the persona of their roles, Bart was forever acting out Bart Giamatti, and the role was demanding. As his friends looked forward to the next performance being better than the last, Bart did his best to meet their rising expectations. It took a lot of energy to keep this perpetual one-man theatre rolling.

In the grand tradition of Yale civic-mindedness, Bart also found time for good works by chairing the Charities Drive. Seniors at Yale were intensely aware of the need to build their resumes for the future. For this, the Charities Drive sufficed nicely. This work landed him the

Fellows Prize at Saybrook College and the distinction of having his name carved into the oak panel of the dining hall. For his senior thesis, upon which his magna cum laude came to rest, he chose to write about mystical poetry, where rapture comes from being taken out of oneself.

Bart's crowning achievement came on graduation day, when he was accorded the high distinction of delivering the class oration. This was a signal honor, akin to being valedictorian, but the oration was a measure of being well liked beyond top grades. At last, he was a star in his own right. It was a remarkable speech for a twenty-two-year-old: literate, worldly, and heartfelt. His theme was the apathy of their Anxious Age. Their indifference, he told his classmates, was only the symptom of a deeper disease. Afraid to look inward, they feared that if they did, they would find nothing of substance. Their generation was self-centered and spiritually barren. "I have met too many people here at Yale who not only do not know what they are going to do, but who do not even know what they would like to do." He quoted Yeats to chill them: "The best lack all conviction, while the worst / Are full of passionate intensity."

The central problem—the degenerative disease—Giamatti said, was their lack of myth. "There is a void, for what we lack is a myth, a unified body of belief," he told his classmates. "Here is the disease of which apathy [and self-centeredness] are merely symptoms." To overcome the void within, they needed the courage to look at themselves first, before they looked at their role in society. "There is a difference between the man who shouts aloud that he is going to shoulder all the responsibility of the race, and the man who has faced himself, has found himself to be strong, and who will then proceed to act," Giamatti proclaimed. "This is the difference between the man who cultivates his own garden because he doesn't have anything else to do, and the man who first cultivates his own garden, because that is the only way he can ultimately produce anything for anyone else. . . . Let us not seek a sedative for what ails us, but let us seek the cure."

In one form or another, for the rest of his life, this image of the garden—one's own garden, the garden within the larger society that is the university, or the paradise that is the baseball park—would be Giamatti's central preoccupation.

· 3 ·

The Rookie and the Renaissance Fan

IN 1962, the Cincinnati Reds finished a close third in the National League pennant race, winning ninety-eight games and losing sixty-four, a mark only three games behind Willie Mays's Giants. Frank Robinson was the Reds leader and superstar extraordinaire, finishing with an average of .342, while the sleek center fielder, Vada Pinson, led the National League with 204 hits. The pitching staff boasted two twenty-game winners in Bob Purkey, the change-up artist, and Joey Jay. Its dean was Hamilton Joe Nuxhall, who, at age thirty-four, had added a new slip pitch and had things totally under control. He had issued fewer walks per nine innings than anyone else in the majors. If Nuxhall was beginning to feel old, he could scarcely complain. He had the distinction of having entered the National League at the age of fifteen, the youngest pitcher in major league history. In the two-thirds of an inning he pitched as an adolescent in 1944, however, he walked five batters, gave up two hits, and yielded five runs. As a consequence, his ERA in his first year in the majors was statistically 45.00. It got better.

The team was managed by the Great Stone Face himself, Fred Hutchinson, a burly, hulking, bull-necked perfectionist, who, with a former pitcher's sense of exactitude, was intolerant of mental mistakes. He sent his big leaguers to night classes to bone up on the basics of their positions and was not above breaking up a few chairs in the privacy of his clubhouse office after a tough defeat. Perhaps as a hedge against his own anger, Hutchinson had ordered the corridors

43

from the dugout to the clubhouse at Crosley Field made of steel without accessible lights because the players kept punching out the bulbs and violating the flimsy walls with their bats when they were rattled.

In February 1963, Pete Rose reported to the Reds spring training camp as a top minor league prospect, but he was not on the Reds big league roster. He joined platoons of other minor leaguers who had high hopes and dreams but no realistic chance of making this pennant-contending club. His expectation was to do well and to impress Hutchinson before he was optioned to the Reds top farm club in San Diego for yet another year of seasoning. Second base on the Reds was anchored by the nimble though unspectacular Don Blasingame, who had come off a solid year, hitting .281. Publicly, Hutchinson spoke of the Blazer in complimentary terms. "He knits the entire infield together," said the skipper, and Blasingame came to camp relatively unconcerned, with his wife, the former Miss Missouri, in tow. At third base, the Reds had Gene Freese. He came to Tampa fully recovered from the ankle fracture that had kept him out for most of the 1962 season. Because Freese had hit twenty-six homers in 1961, the conventional wisdom around the Reds organization was that if Freese had been healthy in 1962, he would have accounted for at least another four victories for the Reds . . . and the pennant. Now, the team seemed to be back in world championship form. The only position up for grabs was center field, and it was indeed captured by a rookie, Tommy Harper, who elbowed Vada Pinson to left field.

Before the competition began in earnest, Hutchinson made the familiar noises about the fine chances for the Reds in 1963. He was pleased about the return of Freese and remained in awe of Frank Robinson, and he was upbeat about the great looking youngsters who were coming to camp. As Hutch was putting out this line to a reporter in early March, Freese popped his head in and said, "Pete Rose is another Nellie Fox with power. He can not miss making it big in the majors . . . in another few years." That seemed to be the feeling. Rose had a great future and was the probable successor to Blasingame, eventually. As long as the kid was no instant threat, the veterans were generous.

In the first game of the Grapefruit League, Blasingame went meekly 0 for 3. The second game was against the White Sox, and Hutchinson gave the minor leaguers the day off. As Rose prepared to leave the park, Mike Ryba, a former big league catcher and the manager of the Reds farm club in Cedar Rapids, turned to him.

"Why don't you stick around, kid," Ryba said. "You might get a chance to play. . . . You never know."

Rose's break came when the game went into extra innings. The Blazer pulled a groin muscle, and Hutch needed a pinch runner. Pete raced to first in his usual split-second time, and then, in the process Bart Giamatti later mythologized as Nostos, the poignant quest to return home in baseball, he raced around the bases to tie the game. The score remained knotted, until Rose got his turn at bat. He doubled, but died on second (the poignancy, to Giamatti) and the game went on . . . and on, until Rose had a second chance to hit again in the fourteenth inning. He doubled again, came home, and the Reds won the game. Rose was Ulysses for a day. Hutchinson liked what he saw: the enthusiasm and the willingness to hang around, as much as the hits themselves. With the Blazer out, Rose was inserted.

This was getting uncomfortable for the veterans. Cliques are normal on any professional team, and the Reds were no different. Blasingame was popular, an eight-year veteran who deserved his position back if anyone did. If this flash could threaten the Blazer, who was safe? More uncomfortable still, the press was swooning over Rose. To the *Enquirer*'s sports columnist the local boy was husky and fleet-footed, refreshingly brash, reeking with color, and loaded with ability. With each week, Smith strengthened his advocacy. First, the kid was Blazer's eventual successor in a couple of years. Next, he was making a determined bid for Blazer's job; then Hutch was dogged with the decision of whether to platoon Blasingame and Rose. Finally, the writer saw shades of Enos Slaughter in the guy.

Predictably, the veterans began to turn on Pete. They made fun of his grandstanding, made cracks about his alpaca sweaters and his language and the gap in his teeth, and snubbed him overtly. Gene Freese, Bob Purkey, and utility infielder Eddie Kasko led the freeze out by the white players. So Rose turned to Frank Robinson and Vada Pinson, the two best players on the team, who themselves formed a daunting and troublesome clique. The black superstars welcomed him, for they knew all about snubs. This was 1963, and in Florida and elsewhere in the South, Robinson, despite his .342 average and Most Valuable Player Award in 1961, and Pinson, with his .343 average in 1961, often had to eat in the bus or in their rooms. (Indeed, Frank Robinson was jailed for a night in 1961 after an ugly racial incident in a restaurant, where in his fury over a racial remark, he had pulled out a concealed revolver.)

One night, Rose's roommate bolted the door at midnight. (In the player's defense, he seemed to have a late-night visitor.) Rose wandered down to Pinson's room, where he was greeted warmly and given a bed. In the morning, Pinson ordered his customary room-service breakfast—an extravagance to Rose but a necessity to Pinson—and a lasting friendship was forged. From Robinson and Pinson, Rose learned other social amenities, such as how to tip and how to dress. "Nobody had to show Pete how to hit," Robinson was to say years later, "but they wouldn't even show him how to be a major leaguer. So we did."

These kindnesses made a deep impression on Pete. It expunged any trace of racism he might have had. In the years to come, he was to return manyfold this generosity to a rookie who came to camp raw and cocky and ostracized, as he had been.

The competition for second base was the most interesting story of the 1963 spring training. Back in Cincinnati, sports fans rooted for their hometown boy, as Hutchinson fomented a wartime atmosphere. He split the team into the Wolves and the Lambs in the early intrasquad games and said, "These games are going to be for blood. I want everybody playing to win. I want the base runners sliding hard and trying to break up the double play." For the carnivorous Lamb, Pete Rose, that was a license to kill. By March 21, when Pete stretched a single into a double in what was to become his trademark, Hutch was saying that "as of now" he's on the roster. "There isn't anything he hasn't done well so far." But the skipper wanted to see Pete face more big league pitching. The Cincinnati writer Lou Smith kept boosting Pete, but he was still betting that the kid would end up in San Diego. Twelve players still had to be cut from the roster, and the Blazer had returned from his groin pull to have some good games. Goaded by the writers, even the players were betting on whether Rose would make the squad, and they were betting against the possibility—all except one, Don Blasingame.

Ironically, a brief slump in late March revealed just how deep the rookie's inroad had become. The team was split in half, with a touring contingent sent off to Mexico City for a three-day stand. A number of veterans groused about having to make the trip, but not Pete. He went buoyantly south, partied excessively in low-life strip joints, and promptly fell flat on his face, hitting a sickly 2 for 25. This performance provided a valid excuse to bench the kid and save face. But Hutchinson put him right back into the starting lineup when he returned, and the writing was on the dugout wall.

On March 29, when the Yankees honored the Reds camp by turning up for a game at Tampa, all the talk was of Mickey Mantle's gimpy legs—and the fact that Mantle had just joined Willie Mays as the only other player in baseball with a $100,000 contract. That day in Tampa, Whitey Ford was in good form. The Cincinnati writers gathered around the slick southpaw and asked yet again whether breaking Babe Ruth's World Series pitching streak of twenty-nine and two-thirds scoreless innings (the Babe had done it in the 1916 and 1918 Series for the Red Sox) had been Whitey's great thrill in baseball. Ford had accomplished the feat at the expense of the Reds in the 1961 Series.

"I don't know," Ford replied, apparently thinking hard and deeply about this tough question. "I remember once pitching the Maspeth Ramblers to a 17–14 win over the Astoria Indians, and that was a good one too."

When the game with the Yankees began, Ford and Mantle sat on the dugout steps, taking the sun together. Rose came to bat, drew a walk, and made it to first in 4.1 seconds, considerably faster than Mantle could cover the distance with a single.

"Look at that. There goes Charlie Hustle," Mantle said, affixing a permanent label.

For Pete, the last week of spring training was akin to a stretch drive. On the day he reached base four times—twice on doubles, and was robbed of another hit—in a game against the Dodgers, Lou Smith was writing that Pete's chances of making the club were fifty-fifty. The Reds owner, Bill deWitt, promised a decision in five days, saying Hutch wanted to see the rookie face a few more big league pitchers. On April 2, Rose went 3 for 4 against the White Sox. On April 3, he was 2 for 3 against the Mets and scored three runs. The Reds broke camp and went north for a game in Macon with the White Sox: 2 for 5. On the Saturday before Monday's Opening Day, before a crowd of 5,000 in Charleston, West Virginia, Rose managed only 1 for 4, a double. After the game, Hutchinson took him aside.

"Pete, I've had them book you into a hotel room. I don't want you going home."

"Why not?"

"I'm promoting you to the Reds," he said, spreading a contract before him. "You're our starting second baseman. The word is going out and I don't want the neighbors bothering you all night."

When the word went out, Hutchinson said Rose had a helluva spring. "I'm sure he's ready," the skipper said. "He's been improving in all departments of play." When Harry and LaVerne Rose heard that Pete had been signed by the Reds, they wept for joy.

On the train ride to Cincinnati from Charleston, Blasingame wandered by Rose's seat. "Well, rook, you got big league pants now. Let's see if you can wear them."

Just a few days shy of his twenty-second birthday, Pete Rose was now 5 feet, 11 inches and weighed 192 pounds. "You're a little guy to be talking to me that way," he replied.

April 6 in Cincinnati broke warm and partly sunny, temperature in the mid-sixties, with a breeze from the south. Gregory Peck won an Oscar that day for his role in *To Kill a Mockingbird*. In Washington, D.C., a movement to draft Senator Barry Goldwater for the 1964 presidential election was unveiled. In Paris, Secretary of State Dean Rusk proclaimed that the United States would resist Communism anywhere in the world, wherever it arose. But at Crosley Field, 29,000 fans gathered for the really important event in their world.

Crosley Field belonged to Pete on Opening Day in 1963. Hometown sentiment went only so far, however. The last native Cincinnatian to start for the Reds, old Herm Wehmeier, another product of Bold Face Park, had pitched on Opening Day in 1952, only to be shelled for eight hits and five runs in four innings. He went on to become the most vilified player in Reds history. The local fans might have forgiven him for the trick knee that kept him out of the military service in 1944, even if it wasn't so bad that he could make his major league debut the following year. They might even have forgiven his terrible temper. But not wildness. Not the gift of home runs. The cruelty of the Cincinnati fans toward Wehmeier was so vicious that another product of Bold Face Park, the Hummer, Dick Drott, refused to sign with his hometown club and went to Pittsburgh instead.

The fans rose in tribute as Pete went to bat for the first time. Their son had come home. He walked on four pitches and sprinted to first. He stayed there, in danger of being stranded, until, with two out, Frank Robinson came up. Robie ran the count to 2 and 2, and then blasted a homer into the left-field seats.

When it was over, the Reds had won, 5–2, and the youth was mobbed in the clubhouse. To be sure, he had gone 0 for 3, but for a few days the fans were willing to be tolerant. They gave him credit for sporting a classy mitt in the field. He had started two double plays, pivoted on another, and made two sparkling grabs. Instead, he dwelt upon his error in the eighth.

"When I booted the ground ball, my mind was somewhere else at the time," he said sheepishly. "Just the inning before, I struck out. I was still thinking about that, I guess."

Who could resist that?

To his fellow graduates at Yale in 1960, Bart Giamatti had seen the lack of a myth as the source of his generation's apathy. Now, as he prepared to go to graduate school, he turned his thoughts to the place where a myth might be pondered. The image of the garden in literature, the garden where a spiritual, almost mystical experience might be had, began to preoccupy him. The perfect garden especially fascinated him, the earthly paradise, where mankind might find perfect harmony and inner peace and where an ideal of human existence might be simulated.

During the summer of 1960, other concerns were also on his mind. He and Toni Smith were married only a few days after graduation. Their first son, Marcus, would follow in a year. Housed in a small apartment in Branford, Connecticut, they settled into the staid life of a married graduate school couple: long hours in class and the library; small, inexpensive dinners with spirited debate. Giamatti initiated his friends in the art of preparing spaghetti: you cook it, you drain it, and then you throw it against the wall. If it sticks, it is . . . *Ecco! . . . al dente!* At one such gorge in 1960, Giamatti and friends watched Kennedy and Nixon debate. He was an enthusiastic Nixon supporter, with a visceral distaste for Kennedy and all things Kennedyesque. His contempt for the Kennedys originated in the sense of his own Italianness, which made him disdain the ill-gotten wealth of these Irish upstarts and their ill-deserved place among *i grandi* of Boston high society.

In his course work at Yale, Giamatti studied with the legends of the place: Henri Peyre on Baudelaire and the Symbolist poets, Marie Borroff in Old English and Elizabethan poetry, R. W. B. Lewis on Faulkner and modern American Literature, and Cleanth Brooks in poetic criticism. His mentor was Maynard Mack, the respected biographer of Alexander Pope, whose lecture course in Shakespeare was considered imperative for every Yale undergraduate. Mack had been a classmate of Val Giamatti's at Yale College and then a fellow member of the Yale faculty, and he had watched over Bart as a surrogate father through his undergraduate years. They even shared the mysteries of Scroll and Key: Mack had written the standard primer for the new initiates, and later, Bart was to update it for modern novitiates. Indeed, Mack took special pride in persuading Bart to take his graduate work at Yale rather than to desert New Haven for Harvard. Mack knew that Cambridge exerted a strong pull on Bart, partly because Val had received his Ph.D. there, but more compellingly because Fenway Park was only one subway stop from Harvard Yard. But Mack knew that money for the graduate student was a problem, especially with a new wife and a child on the way. With Mack's help, Bart was able to secure a Woodrow Wilson fellowship, which he supplemented with an instructorship in Italian.

From the beginning of his relationship with Bart, Mack had been impressed with the young man's way with language. Graceful and startlingly original metaphors seem to roll off the young man's tongue effortlessly. "Sometimes I thought of him as a glassblower," Mack was to say. "He could blow iridescent creatures out of his mouth, turn them over and consider them . . . then, he would put them on the table and pull the cloth out from under them, and gaily, watch them go tinkling on the floor." Not everyone was taken so completely by the creations that Giamatti blew out of his mouth. To some, their "orotundity" was overwrought and ponderous, like a garish piece of Murano glass.

For all his skill at declamation, Giamatti bridled under the constraints of graduate life. Secretly, he deplored the smugness and pomposity of the senior professors. While he could talk their high Elizabethan on demand, he preferred to deride the literature he disliked with crisp four-letter words and to praise what he liked with simple statements about tone and feel. For his pleasure, he continued to be drawn to the artistic community, to the theatrical types and aspiring poets who read their work in smokey basements—the scriveners, he called them affectionately. Indeed, at these furtive sessions, he provided most of the smoke. One cigarette followed another without interruption. It was said that when you were around Giamatti, you became addicted to tobacco, whether you smoked or not. If Giamatti loved the struggling artists and yearned to be one himself, they thought he was headed for a career as an actor. They besought him to read at their sessions or in their classes, for he infused the reading of the classics or their own work with such thespian energy and flair.

In 1961, an old friend of Giamatti's from undergraduate days and a brother from Scroll and Key, Steve Umin, returned to New Haven for law school after having been away for two years at Oxford on a Rhodes Scholarship. Heading down College Street one day, Umin recognized a familiar figure walking toward him: threadbare tweed coat, collar turned up, dark glasses, hands in pockets, hunched-over shoulders. Umin knew instantly who it was. When they came face to face, Giamatti issued no standard greeting of long-lost friends. Instead, in a confidential tone, he leaned toward Umin and said, "Blake's in. Donne's out."

His course work complete in 1964, Bart turned to his dissertation. He fell under the direction of Lowry Nelson, Jr., a medievalist who had managed Giamatti's undergraduate senior thesis on mystical poetry. For his topic, Bart chose to study the role of the garden in literature, particularly in the epics of the Renaissance. In these epics, the heroes wander the world in search of tranquility or truth or glory. The tales usually involve leaving home, traveling great distances over land and water to faraway places, and encountering great dangers and misfortunes, as the hero seeks something final and fixed.

The search for a quiet place of bliss and delight and repose is a profound instinct of man, Giamatti wrote. "In the garden, meadow or field, poets have always felt Nature most nearly approximates the ideals of harmony, beauty and peace." Remote and beautiful, this *locus amoenus* is a haven where the ideal of perfection is simulated and where man comes to realize the impossibility of attaining that ideal. But the enchanted garden of the Renaissance poets, Giamatti wrote, is a false paradise. The dreamer is torn between what he wants and what he can have. Man, however, never ceases to search or yearn, for in the yearning he finds pleasure.

Of particular interest to Giamatti was the rose garden, for the rose itself was a symbol to the Renaissance poets both of the good things of life and of the passage of time from youth to old age. "Gather ye rosebuds while ye may," the English poet Robert Herrick had written of youthful pleasures. "This same flower that smiles today /Tomorrow will be dying." To Pierre de Ronsard, in his "Ode a Cassandre," written in 1553, the life of the rose was even shorter, and thus, it was all the more important for the lover of beauty to gaze upon it while he could:

> Darling, we'll go together, see if this morning's
> New-opened rose—it opened crimson to the sun—
> Has lost its crimson pleatings now that it is evening.

Paradise, real paradise, was reserved for Dante. The divine poet had portrayed the City of God, or heaven, first as an amphitheater with tiers—some might say with grandstands—and then as "the eternal rose, which doth expand, rank upon rank, and reeketh perfume of praise unto the Sun that maketh spring for ever."

The 1963 baseball season saw several important changes in the rules. The strike zone was lengthened from the letters to the shoulders. On a big hitter with a straight-up stance, that gave the pitcher another six inches in which to position a strike (although with Pete Rose's tight crouch, the difference was measured in millimeters). During spring training, that old expert on tight corners, Johnny Vander Meer, now the national ambassador for a Tampa brewery, wished he were still pitching under these new conditions. There would be a lot fewer .300 hitters in 1963, Vandy predicted.

What advantage was given to the pitchers with one hand was taken away with the other, for the balk rule was tightened simultaneously, requiring that the pitcher pause in his stretch one full second before delivering the pitch to the plate. The Reds twenty-game winner in 1962, Joey Jay, was to blame for that change. When the Reds had played the Dodgers the summer before and the premiere base stealer, Maury Wills, was on first, Jay had adopted a trick motion, sometimes pausing not at all, sometimes pausing some seconds before delivering. Jay's cunning had infuriated the Dodger manager, Walter Alston, and the fakery precipitated a few rhubarbs.

On April 13, in a game against the Pirates, these factors came together. Bob Friend took the mound for Pittsburgh and proceeded to tie a National League anti-record with four balks. Meanwhile, Pete went into his fourth game of the season 0 for 12 and could hear the loud grumbles already. "He'd better play good ball, because he's got a fine ball player sitting on the bench ready to come in," mumbled one veteran. Hutchinson was prepared to be patient a while longer. To the Reds pilot, being "long on patience" was the key to being a good manager.

In his first time at the plate against Friend, Rose lashed a pitch into the gap. It was a clear stand-up double, but Pete refused to stand up. He raced on toward third and slid headfirst under the tag. His trademark slide began with his first major league hit. Vada Pinson drove him in. But then Bill Mazeroski and Roberto Clemente took over for the Pirates, and the afternoon turned into another drubbing, 12–4, for the slow-starting Reds. Days later, when Rose's weak hitting ran to 4 for 23, Hutch benched him and put in the Blazer, an old story apparently in the making. The pressure on the local kid was too great, explained the skipper.

The benching did not last long. Ten days later, Pete was back in the lineup. Hutch quickly congratulated himself on his managerial wisdom. His rookie looked more relaxed in the box, and he began to hit. On May 3, Nux hurled a shutout against the Cards, as Rose smacked his first major league homer over the center field fence and sweetened the glory with a triple. The next day, he was on base five times against the princely Bob Gibson: two singles and three walks. In his *Enquirer* column, Lou Smith wrote that the kid had a terrific eye . . . for a rookie. By May 24, his average had doubled to .261.

In Chicago, on a steal attempt, Pete was hit on the head by the catcher's peg. Rose shook it off. His wild, harried, headlong style of play reminded a UPI writer of the Gashouse Gang of the 1930s, especially of Pepper Martin, the "wild horse of Osage." Martin too had a bent for sliding hands first. The grimy, stained, wrinkled, and spiked quality of his uniform after a ball game had given the Gashouse Gang its name—this was a working-man's outfit. To refer to Rose as a "throwback" to the Gashouse Gang, to compare him to the wild horse himself—well, that was high praise indeed.

In late May, people began to talk about Rose as a candidate for Rookie of the Year. At that point early in the season, Rusty Staub of the Houston Colt .45s and Ed Kranepool of the Mets were the competition, but they faded as the summer progressed. The Blazer was traded to the Washington Senators in July to team up with Eddie Brinkman and go on to obscurity. Rose finished the season hitting a respectable .271 in 157 games. To six homers, he added nine triples and twenty-five doubles. His fielding average was .971, an impressive mark that was near the top of the league for infielders.

At season's end, Rose trundled off to Fort Knox to squeeze in six months' active duty in the army before spring training began. Across the road in another barracks was Brinkman. On November 26, the nation was deep in mourning over the assassination of President Kennedy four days earlier, and little attention was paid to the triviality of sport. Private Rose was waxing a kitchen floor when the duty officer brought the news that he had been voted the National League Rookie of the Year, garnering all but three votes. The last Cincinnati Red to get the honor was Frank Robinson in 1956. Pete reacted characteristically.

"I didn't think I'd win," he said, "by such a big margin."

He spoke of being only a raw rookie in 1963 and of all the polish he still needed: moving to his right, drag bunting, hitting behind the runner, that sort of thing. "Making the club" even remained a question mark for him.

"I know I'll have to hustle to hold my position," he said, ever the overachiever in fear of being found out. "There are some real good infielders in the Reds organization."

During the 1964 season, Rose ran smack into the sophomore jinx, but neither the Reds organization nor the fans seemed to pay much attention. They were preoccupied with the slow dying of Fred Hutchinson. Over the winter, Hutch's own brother, a surgeon in Seattle, diagnosed lumps in Hutch's throat and chest as cancerous. It was a death sentence. By stages, the condition presented itself. At spring training, the skipper needed the use of an electric cart to get around. In May, he had difficulty getting his jacket onto his locker hook and needed a hefty painkiller. However, he was not too sick in June to bench Rose when the sophomore was hitting .214, and Pete felt he was in real jeopardy of being sent down to the Triple-A farm club in San Diego. By mid-July, with Rose scared for himself and scared for Hutchinson, the batting coach, Dick Sisler, was running the team. Hutch ceased to make the road trips. Still, the skipper kept up a brave stoneface, insisting, whenever asked, that he was feeling better.

Would he quit as manager? "I'll never quit until the Man Upstairs tells me I have to," he replied.

On August 12, his forty-fifth birthday, Fred Hutchinson appeared in a Reds uniform for the last time. The Reds and the local boosters made a huge occasion of it, producing a maudlin melodrama in which the teams lined up on either baseline while a five-hundred-pound birthday cake was wheeled to home plate. The icing read: "To a Nice Guy Who Finishes First." Reds owner Bill deWitt blubbered openly as Hutchinson declared he was the luckiest fellow in the world. The man who had given Rose his break in big league ball had shrunk from his bearish 220 pounds to a skeletal 140.

With the first pitch against the Dodgers, the sentimentality ceased. The product of the University of Cincinnati named Sandy Koufax was merciless, hurling a cruel five hitter. Rose went 0 for 4 and made an error.

Still, the Reds were in the race for the pennant until the last day of the season, when the Phillies drubbed them 10–0, while the Cards beat the Mets to take the championship. In the clubhouse afterward, Dick Sisler conducted the dirge. With a drawn Hutchinson parked on a nearby couch in street clothes, Sisler said, "I'm sorry that the team couldn't have won for that gentleman over there."

"I'm sorry that they couldn't have won for themselves," Hutchinson replied, ever the sportsman.

Knowing his future was in doubt and eager to improve his play, Rose requested that he be allowed to play winter ball in the Caribbean on a team managed by Reds coach Reggie Otero. With Hutchinson's consent, he got the okay and took off for Caracas soon after the last game of the season. Otero was a taskmaster who, from humble roots in Havana, had clawed his way into the big leagues for fourteen games in 1945. His philosophy stressed that the game of baseball consisted of departments, and Rose was weak in the double play department. To Otero, good play came from good habits. Pete had bad habits in the field that were deeply rooted, and Otero meant to break them. Pete's problem remained his slow release from second to first; he cocked his arm too far back, and that slowed his throw. So, on the dusty practice field, Otero positioned someone at shortstop; his coach, Alex Carrasquel, was around home plate with a bat. (A one-time pitcher for the Washington Senators, Carrasquel had been suspended from the major leagues between 1946 and 1949 for playing winter ball in the Mexican League. He represented one of the few players ever to be suspended and then reinstated by the Commissioner of Baseball.) Perhaps 150 times a day under the tropical sun, as Carrasquel hit grounders and Rose took the throw from short and threw to first, Otero would stand over Rose and yell for him to shorten his release. All of this effort would have been unnecessary if the Reds had moved Rose to third, to which he was more naturally suited.

Despite the hard work, Rose enjoyed Caracas. By his lights, he was maturing as a player and as a man. He hit well. For the pool table after work, his buddy, Tommy Helms, was around. When he made four errors in an inning once, he was proud of himself for not getting on the next plane to Cincinnati. And he was appreciated. "I get a kick out of the way fans are in Caracas," he would say. "They gamble. They gamble on every pitch. But they're really enthusiastic. If I make an error, I get booed. When they see me diving for balls, they cheer. There's nothing halfway about them. Besides, I had my work cut out for me. I knew if I didn't improve, I might not stay with the majors."

On November 13, the Caracas Lions were on a bus, heading toward the downtown of Santo Domingo in the Dominican Republic. Rose sat next to Otero, who was listening to a Spanish station on a portable radio when suddenly he gasped.

"Hutch?" Rose stammered.

"He die."

And they both broke into sobs.

With efficient dispatch, Giamatti completed his graduate work in 1964 and looked ahead. No doubt, he would have loved an invitation to move directly onto the Yale faculty as a junior professor, but life is not so easy, and no such offer was made. Regretfully, he went instead to Princeton. He went, moreover, in a situation not altogether to his liking, not as a professor of Comparative Literature or English but as an instructor in the Italian language. Still, this was the mid-1960s, when academic jobs were plentiful and grant money prodigious, when tenure came easily and junior faculty members were more relaxed about their future. Shortly after his arrival at Princeton, he learned that his dissertation, *Earthly Paradise and the Renaissance Epic*, had been accepted for publication by Princeton University Press. Upon receiving the news, he called a friend to come over for champagne and said that he and Toni were "bumping into walls like happy, drunken elephants."

The Giamattis had an apartment in a low-rise for junior faculty overlooking Lake Carnegie, where the Princeton crew trained, and life was good. Bart's greatest sport was to repair to a classic diner on Nassau Street called Petrinferno's (its regulars were disappointed when its proprietor anglicized the name to Firestone's). He went with his friend, the Dantista, Bob Hollander, for provolone on a hard roll and endless passionate discussions of *The Divine Comedy*. Joyfully and intensely, they argued for hours over such questions as whether Dante had love or contempt for Virgil, his guide through heaven and hell.

Now that the Giamattis' second child, Elena, had arrived, "Toni and the trolls" frolicked with hordes of other faculty children. While Bart was, in the opinion of most, one of the least athletic human beings ever to exist, he sometimes joined the gay evening volleyball game by the lake. But the first symptoms of a menacing degenerative disease were beginning to show. Giamatti dismissed the condition as gout, and his friends did not pry further, even as his limp became more pronounced. He also was having circulatory problems, was plagued with a chronic kidney disorder, and suffered from terrible migraine headaches, which forced him to recede into the darkness and "pull the curtain down." He bore these afflictions with silence or a quip. His friends were seldom aware of the pain he was enduring. When the subject of his reported gout arose, he remarked that, in the Renaissance, the condition was considered a mark of intelligence and the symptom of too much red wine and red meat at medieval feasts. He usually got a laugh.

If the Renaissance man was his ideal, the one thing Giamatti lacked was the fine body. In the prototype of the Renaissance man, Leon Battista Alberti, athletic powers accompanied superior intelligence, social grace, noble bearing, artistic sensibility, civic responsibility, and creativity. Alberti had been a playwright and a mathematician, a musician and architect, a poet and philosopher, but he had also been a skillful runner and wrestler and mountain climber in his youth. It disappointed Bart that he could be only half a Renaissance man.

With familiarity, he became disenchanted with Princeton. The intellectually placid, self-contented, irenic quality of the place annoyed him, and he felt constrained as a language instructor. Moreover, his infant son, Marcus, contracted meningitis and nearly died from sloppy medical care, a negligence that furthered Giamatti's disenchantment with Princeton. "We are all fleas on the belly of Mother Yale," he said in explanation to his friend Bob Hollander. Hollander saw in the remark a yearning to return to New Haven. Nevertheless,

Giamatti was, as always, immensely popular with his peers. He was noticed by the elders, but not always favorably. At faculty teas, he could amuse his colleagues with such high jinks as improvising "Giamatti's list of academic afflictions," starting with "dissertation dysfunction" and "tenure tremens." A few supercilious members of senior faculty were not amused by this ribbing about academic life and interpreted Giamatti's attitude as a lack of seriousness. Bart, they thought, was too much of a regular guy to be a real scholar.

Luckily for him, these disapproving full professors did not accompany him on his trips to Yankee Stadium. When the Red Sox came to the Bronx, Giamatti was there to see them. He occasionally went with Hollander, who was equally passionate about baseball and liked to think of himself as the Duke Carmel of the Romance Language Department. (Carmel was the utility first baseman of the lowly, pre-miracle Mets who hit .235 in his one year in the majors and posted a fielding percentage toward the bottom of major league infielders.)

One trip to Yankee Stadium was particularly memorable to Hollander. In July 1966, he and Bart went to an afternoon doubleheader, when the Red Sox had a firm grip on last place, twenty-five games out, and the Yankees were playing mediocre ball. Only pure fans like them showed up, for the sheer spectacle of it. They drove to the Bronx while engaged in a heated discussion about the Vietnam War, but once the field stretched before them, Bart lost all interest in faraway wars. Perhaps in some remote niche of his soul, the aesthetics of the white ball against the green field, the parabola of the sphere, the perfection of the enclosed space moved him. Perhaps he knew he was about to have the "quasi-religious" experience about which he wrote later, or perhaps a mystical experience in which he would be taken out of himself, in the same way that mystical poetry transported him. You would never know it. He was a screamer, a boorish bleacher bum from Revere. Hollander enjoyed watching the transformation of his friend, up to a point.

The professors found themselves seated next to two thick-armed teamsters who did not share Giamatti's enthusiasm for the Red Sox and who, with every succeeding beer, became menacingly intolerant of Giamatti's shrill boosting of the visitors. His epithets regarding the manhood of various Yanks were especially unwelcome, particularly when the Sox beat the Yanks and Whitey Ford in the first game, despite a homer by Joe Pepitone and because of an inside-the-park homer by Carl "Yaz" Yastrzemski. Giamatti seemed oblivious to the fact that his burly neighbors were becoming increasingly sore. He insisted on competing for elbow room on the thin metal armrest between them until, during the tight second game, nasty remarks began to be exchanged. Hollander suggested a hot dog. Giamatti refused. More hostile exchanges. Hollander insisted on a hot dog. Bart declined. Joe Pepitone was on deck in the sixth inning, and Bart despised the Yankee first baseman as only one Italian can despise another. In the nick of time, Hollander grabbed his friend by the collar, pulled him out of his seat, and dragged him out to the concession stand.

"Look, Bart, that guy is about to throw a punch at you," the Dantista said. "When he does, his even bigger friend is going to hit *me!*"

Hot dogs in hand, they started back for the seats—different seats on the opposite baseline—when the roar of the crowd swelled the stadium. They raced up the ramp, just in time to watch Pepitone trot triumphantly around third and head for home for his second homer of the day. Bart waited in disgust for the deafening noise to subside to silence. Then, full-throated and joyful, his scream reverberated around the horseshoe, like an acoustic wave from Death Valley to Mantle's upper deck: "Pepitone! You shiiiiit!"

The day ended satisfactorily, with a second Red Sox victory, as Boston beat that black-hearted scoundrel, Jim Bouton, 5–4, and without class violence in the stands.

Ever since Giamatti had slipped away to "the lotus eating life of Princeton," his mentor at Yale, Maynard Mack, had been scheming to bring this flea back to the belly of Mother Yale. In Bart's first year away, Mack had written to him about returning home. Bart replied that it would be unseemly to leave after only one year, but he would consider it after two years. Into the second year, Mack sprang his plan with the deft skill of a corporate raider. He offered Giamatti an assistant professorship on a Friday and gave him only until the following Monday to accept or decline. Hollander, furious, galvanized Princeton into making an attractive counteroffer—an astonishing feat for an academic institution to achieve in a weekend.

But the call of Yale was primordial. Much later, Mack took immense pride in luring Bart back to the "rocky Ithaca that Yale has always been, where only snow foxes and mountain goats and caribou survive."

· 4 ·

Wild Horse, Stern Rider

REGGIE OTERO'S sweaty tutorials in the fleshpots of Caracas took hold, and Rose came to camp in 1965 smoother and quicker at second base—70 percent better, by the estimate of his shortstop, Leo Cardenas. Rose made the All-Star team for the first time that year, polling more votes than any other Cincinnati Red. By the end of the season, he had made seventeen errors—a mark slightly above average. He wanted to do better. Bill Mazeroski of the Pirates was his idol now, and Maz made only eight errors that season. It was said that if Mazeroski had played only on AstroTurf, he would never have made an error. In any event, in this year when he earned a courtly $13,500, Rose batted .312, fifth in the league, and led the league in hits.

The following year, however, the inevitable switch to third base took place. It disheartened Rose, probably because Otero had planted the idea that such a move represented a player's demise. Even so, he had become enough of a professional to coast a little, and confessed later that 1966 was the year that Charlie Hustle hustled less. The year after that, 1967, Tommy Helms took over second base for the Reds. Dave Bristol, the Reds manager, switched Rose to left field.

Along the way for this clubhouse wise guy, there were the memorable moments that he would later recount with gusto and poetic license in assorted autobiographies. His sometime left fielder in those years, Alex Johnson, was the straightman in some of Rose's best stories. There was the one about A. J. and the press. A. J., you see, didn't like the scribblers and rarely responded with more than a grunt. At

59

Connie Mack Stadium, in Philadelphia, Johnson, a line-drive hitter, blasted his ninth home run. Afterwards in the clubhouse, a reporter sidled up and said, "A. J., last year you only hit four homers, and this year you've got nine already. What's the difference?"

"Five," A. J. replied.

"I'm surprised he didn't say four," Tommy Helms added at this telling.

Then there was the one about A. J. in the field. A sterling fielder he was not. One day in Atlanta, Rose was in center and Johnson in left when Henry Aaron hit a long drive that pushed Johnson back, back to the wall, where he leaped tremendously. Sensing that he could not catch the ball, he slapped at it with his web. The ball blooped up, falling to the playing field and landing in the glove of Pete Rose, who had hustled over to back up A. J. A routine 7–8 putout. Several innings later, a hot line drive was hit right at Johnson, waist high, and the "ole clank" dropped the ball, then looked up to watch the winning run cross the plate.

"Where the hell were you?" he yelled over to Rose.

Rose, the raconteur, knew how to reverse a good joke. At Connie Mack Stadium in 1966, he was the impossible out for the Phillies, until one day, he came to the plate and the Phillies catcher, Mike Ryan, on orders from his manager, Gene Mauch, said, "Gene told me to tell you what pitch is coming." Rose twittered, dug in, and for the next three times at bat, Ryan told the truth, and each time Rose was out. Unable to contain his frustration, he began shouting at the umpire to make Ryan shut up. "I don't want to know what's coming." Then into the ninth inning, with two out, one man on, and the score tied, Rose came up again.

"Curve," Ryan mumbled.

It dawned on Rose that this late in the game, with a strategy that had worked three times, they were not going to change. He primed himself for a curve, lined it squarely off the scoreboard, and the Reds won the game. When Rose came to the plate for the first time the next day, Ryan said, "Gene told me to tell you to go to hell."

It was not always fun and games in the ballpark. On July 1, 1967, the Reds were at Wrigley Field for a four-game series with the Cubs, when Rose laid down a bunt and powered to first. The play was close. Rose stretched during his last, furious stride to beat the throw, and the Cubs much-beloved first baseman, Ernie Banks, also stretched to grab the throw. Unwittingly, Banks planted his foot in the middle of the bag, and it was too late for Rose to avoid it. He came down squarely on Banks's ankle, tearing open a wound that would require ten stitches. As Banks writhed on the base path, Wrigley Field erupted in fury, accusing Rose of deliberately spiking their Southside prince. Catcalls, boos, beer cans, and even a crutch rained down on Rose when he returned to right field. After the game, as Rose was leaving the stadium, someone snuck up behind him with a small souvenir bat and was about to club him in the back of the head. Bob Lee, a lunk of a pitcher, clobbered the fan with a solid right to the nose. Then an old lady brought her umbrella down on Rose's head, but, as Rose would later put it, a cop "decked her."

This episode began a lusty relationship between Rose and the Bleacher Bums of Wrigley Field. They greeted him routinely with chants and imprecations. "Rose is a fairy! Rose is a fairy!" was their favorite . . . and Rose's as well. These were his kind of people, and he jabbered with them in a running dialogue. Meanwhile, in the four-game series when he became a villain in Chicagoland, he went 12 for 18.

In 1968, Rose sustained his first major injury. He broke his thumb and missed three weeks. The injury came at Dodger Stadium, a place that had become something of a jinx to Rose. In fact, he would be injured more than once in L.A. Perhaps more important to him, he couldn't seem to buy a hit there.

In 1968, the collective average of major league hitters was the lowest since 1903. Rose, however, had no problem at all. With three days left in the season, he was tied for the league lead with the Pirates' Matty Alou with a .331 average. On that day, Rose had a bad game, going 1 for 7 in a twelve-inning affair, but Alou also did poorly: 0 for 4. On the next-to-last day, Alou got hot and went 4 for 4. Rose calculated what he had to do to win. With constant updates from the bleachers and opposing players on Alou's performance, Rose, facing the spitball king, Gaylord Perry, was even better. He posted an impossible 5 for 5, with two doubles. The final day was a denouement: Alou went hitless, while Rose went 1 for 3 and had his first batting title.

When the writers got together to vote the honors after the season, they chose Bob Gibson of the Cards as the National League MVP. In the American League, they gave the prize to Denny McLain for his thirty-one victories that year. This caused some grumbling in baseball circles over the question of whether starting pitchers, who played only every fourth or fifth game, deserved to be the most valuable player over the everyday guys. Rose, who was Gibson's runnerup, could only silently agree. In any event, he had joined the elite. Behind him in the balloting was Willie McCovey of the Giants, while Rookie of the Year honors went to Pete's teammate, catcher Johnny Bench.

In 1969, déja vu. On September 22, Cleon Jones of the Mets was on top of the league at .346, Rose was at .340, and Roberto Clemente stood at .335. Two days later, the Mets clinched their Eastern Division, but Jones went 0 for 4 and began to fade, while Rose went 4 for 5, raising his average to .347. Clemente, however, went on a torrid streak, closing the gap as he hit an incredible 16 for 30 in his last seven games. Entering the final game, Rose was ahead of the Pirates' right fielder by two percentage points. As the final game proceeded, the bleacher bums kept giving Rose an update on Clemente's flawless performance. Rose whiffed and Clemente hit, and by the time of his last at bat, Rose was 0 for 3, and Clemente was 3 for 3.

"What do I do?" he wondered aloud to Tommy Helms.

"Lay one down," Helms said.

He did and beat it—and Clemente—out.

The Reds weren't as fortunate. They finished behind Atlanta in the Western Division, and after the season, Dave Bristol was fired. In his place, Cincinnati hired a flinty, old-fashioned straight arrow from California, Sparky Anderson, as the manager. Anderson's first act, on October 23, was to appoint Rose the team captain.

Until the 1970 All-Star Game, the public perception of Pete Rose was uniformly positive. He was the irrepressible and refreshing pepper pot, the hard-nosed tough-out, the cocky, indomitable, reckless overachiever. He was the archetype of how the game, at its best, should be played. He was the personification of success through sweat and sheer passion—the competitor's competitor and the central example to young dreamers about the possibilities for a player of limited natural skill. He wasn't supposed to achieve half as much, and what he did achieve was hard won. A fan could live vicariously through him— live, as Bart Giamatti would put it, the best hopes of his youth. His success was accessible, not esoteric like Roberto Clemente's, whose gifts seemed superhuman and therefore beyond reach. Rose was great because he seemed to try harder than anyone else. If he tried only as hard as everyone else, the fan felt, he would have departed the major leagues for a minor job at something like the Cincinnati Sanitation Department.

The opposition booed Rose because he was so maddening to them. It was more fun to see him strike out than make a hit, partly because it was more rare, but largely because he was so aggressive. When he was beaten, he seemed to take it so personally. He dared you to get him out. When you did, which was not often, there was a special satisfaction. To the pitchers with junk rather than blinding speed, the pleasure was unmatched, for there would be Pete, on the steps of the dugout, pounding his bat on the ground and shouting at you, "How can you get me out with that shit!"

His image changed in July 1970 and then changed forever in October 1973. Rose simply carried his style of play to its logical extreme. Suddenly, to many, his competitiveness went too far. The stallion had become destructive rather than exciting and needed to be reined in.

The two episodes involved slides and were malicious attacks of such virulence that they seemed more a part of football than baseball. They were akin to the cheap shot of the cornerback who hits the receiver in the back ribs just as his arms are fully extended for the football. In each case, Rose's victim was defenseless and dangerously vulnerable.

Rose's actions were borderline. They may have violated the spirit of the game, especially as a Bart Giamatti would see it, but his actions were not overtly outside the letter of the rules. This heightened their controversial nature. No professional baseball players, even his victims, ever criticized Rose openly for his actions. Their managers usually said Rose's violence was within his rights.

But the episodes left a deep, unspoken disquiet among a large sector of baseball fans. Decades later, they are vividly remembered and hotly debated. They put Rose in the category of Ty Cobb long before there was a race for the all-time hit record—the category of players whose mean-spiritedness was outside the accepted norms of the game. Gentility and civility attracted intellectuals such as Bart Giamatti to the game: the sheer pleasure of competition without violence. Rose's violent actions destroyed that illusion.

Riverfront Stadium in Cincinnati was so newly minted for the All-Star Game of 1970 that for some weeks before the game, it was not clear that the stadium would be structurally ready. Commissioner Bowie Kuhn threatened until the last to shift the game to Atlanta. The 1970 All-Star Game was also the first to be played on AstroTurf. Whereas Rose loved the surface because it was faster and made his liners more difficult to stab, the sages of the game, including his own manager, Sparky Anderson, wondered whether baseball on a carpet was baseball at all or some new game altogether. Casey Stengel was one of the doubters. Several years before, when Stengel came to manage the All-Star Game on the new turf at Busch Stadium in St. Louis, on a day when the temperature was near 100 degrees, an eager reporter full of civic pride approached him.

"Well, Mr. Stengel, what do you think of Busch Stadium?" he asked.

The Old Professor thought for a moment, as he tried to recede deeper into the shade. "It holds the heat very well," he said.

Rose entered the game with an average of .323. He had won the National League batting title for the past two years, yet he was on the roster as a reserve rather than a starter. The fad-crazy fans had voted Rico Carty of the Braves, a write-in candidate, as their favorite left fielder. (Carty had been batting over .400 for most of the balloting period.) Roberto Clemente had no trouble making the first team in right field. But the fans were down on him. A few days before the game, he complained about a little "pain in the neck" that might prevent him from playing. The problem of star players feigning injury to avoid the exhibition game was so severe that the American League manager, Earl Weaver, suggested a screening process to ensure a player's injury was real.

All this had nothing to with Rose. As always, he was in an "I'll show you" frame of mind. Among the 50,000 fans in Riverfront was the president of the United States, Richard M. Nixon, who was billed on the huge video screen as Baseball's Number 1 Fan. He threw out the first pitch, more of a soft hook layup from basketball than a pitch. Playing before the president, his hometown, and the nation, Rose once again had to prove himself.

The game had the mark of perfection. Earl Weaver's nest was crowded with Orioles: Brooks and Frank Robinson, Boog Powell, Davey Johnson, and Jim Palmer on the mound. They were fortified by the bats of the massive Frank Howard, the princely Carl Yastrzemski, and the powerful Harmon Killebrew. On the National League squad were Willie Mays and Hank Aaron, as well as the nucleus of the future Big Red Machine: Tony Perez, Joe Morgan, Johnny Bench, and Pete Rose. At first, it seemed as if it would be a pitcher's game. Jim Palmer dueled the Mets' Tom Seaver in three scoreless innings. Sam McDowell of the Indians relieved Palmer and pitched brilliantly.

By the top of the sixth, the American League had only two hits. Then Ray Fosse, the brilliant young catcher from Cleveland who was in his first full-fledged season, singled, went to second on a sacrifice bunt by McDowell, and scored the first run for the American League on a single by Yaz. An inning later, Fosse again came to bat with Brooks Robinson on third and brought him home with a sacrifice fly. Going into the top of the ninth, the American League seemed to have the game wrapped up. They were leading 4–1 by that time, their pitchers had held the Nationals to only three hits, and they smelled their first victory since 1962.

But Dick Dietz of San Francisco opened the bottom of the ninth with a homer off Catfish Hunter: 4–2. Bud Harrelson of the Mets, Joe Morgan of Houston, and Willie McCovey of San Francisco followed with singles: 4–3. Next, Roberto Clemente, sore neck and all, reached down to his ankles for a low fastball and drove it into deep center for a sacrifice fly that scored Morgan and tied the game.

That brought Rose to the plate with two on and two out. Here was his chance to show his hometown fans what a true champion he was. Batting left-handed against the Yankees' right-hander Mel Stottlemyre, Rose took the first pitch for a strike. Then he took a vicious, classic cut . . . and whiffed. Then, he whiffed again to strike out. He was embarrassed. So much for the storybook ending, or so it seemed.

The game remained knotted until the twelfth inning. Joe Torre and Roberto Clemente went down meekly, but Rose, batting this time against the Angels southpaw Clyde Wright, singled up the middle. He moved to second on a grounder through the hole by the Dodgers third baseman, Bill Grabarkewitz.

Jim Hickman of the Cubs came to the plate. With the count at 1–0, he lined a fastball to center that dropped on two bounces in front of Amos Otis of the Royals. Otis fielded the ball cleanly, as Rose barreled around third. The Cubs manager, Leo Durocher, waved him on and even ran down the line with Rose, screaming and motioning to his player to slide, slide. Otis's peg was true, but it faded slightly, slicing a few feet up the line toward third. Fosse moved up to receive it as Rose came toward him. The catcher positioned himself in a crouch, straddling the line, never taking his eye off the ball.

Technically, Fosse was not allowed to straddle the base path. He was supposed to leave a passage to the plate for the runner. But Fosse knew that blocking the plate was rarely, if ever, called by the umpire—certainly not in the twelfth inning of a tight All-Star Game. He prepared to catch the ball and swing his mitt around in one fluid, circular motion to tag a hook-sliding Rose. He expected a hook slide, but his rationale was doubtless more instinctive than conscious.

Twenty feet from the plate, Rose's body leaned forward in a massive, concentrated spasm of effort to leap headfirst and slide around Fosse's legs. His chest stretched forward, nearly horizontal to the ground, as an airplane does when it readies itself for its final approach to touchdown. All his competitive spirit was distilled into this one moment.

Rose knew this was the most dangerous situation possible for the headfirst slide: his hands and fingers stretched forward and exposed, trying to reach the plate amid the spiked, unpredictable, stamping hooves of a powerful catcher. Then, in a nanosecond—the same nanosecond in which a pilot tries to abort a landing and avert disaster when terrible danger suddenly reveals itself on the runway— Rose changed his mind. He shoved his throttle forward in a desperate attempt to stay airborne. His upper body, low at the waist, began to rise, as a plane rises. In this case, the plane had become a missile.

Just as Fosse, his arms fully extended, reached for the speeding ball, Rose's left shoulder crashed into him with calamitous force. The catcher never touched the ball. He was removed from its path, tumbling backward, writhing in pain, as Rose scored. For a moment, Rose hovered over the stricken catcher, either in triumph or in concern or both—but only for a moment, before he limped toward the dugout. His jubilant teammates rushed to congratulate him. At the dugout steps, he turned again to see if Fosse would get to his feet, and then he was swept away in celebration.

The fallout from this violent collision took some months, even years, to poison the ground for Rose. The immediate reaction was one of satisfaction and praise. To Bowie Kuhn and the doges of baseball, it was a splendid finish for a game that had everything. Richard Nixon and his statistician, son-in-law David Eisenhower, went away feeling that they had been presidentially entertained. A few American Leaguers questioned whether Rose's vicious body-block had been necessary, given the fact that the ball had not arrived in Fosse's mitt at the moment of collision, but they couched their mild complaints in the diplomatic language of the locker room.

Was Rose's attack a cheap shot? Did he know full well, even in that split second, that his action could injure, even maim, Fosse? Only Rose could say what his real intention was. Only he knew what had gone through his mind in that instant when he changed his slide.

Immediately after the game, Earl Weaver came to Rose's defense. To Weaver, Rose's play was proper. "I thought Rose got there a little ahead of the ball, and Fosse was trying to block the plate," Earl said. "They did what they had to do."

For several days, Rose nursed a badly bruised thigh before he returned to the lineup. Fosse was not as lucky. In terrible pain, he had been rushed to a hospital where he was X-rayed and told that his collarbone was severely bruised, but not broken or fractured. In the Cleveland press, where he was being cast as "Fearless Fosse," he was gracious about the collision: "I thought Rose would go around me. He said he started to dive but had no place to go. If he had, it would have saved me a lot of pain. Amos Otis threw the ball real well, and I knew if I got it, he was out."

Fosse was back in uniform several days later, slated by his manager, Alvin Dark, to catch the Cleveland ace, Sam McDowell. When he took batting practice, however, he found that he could scarcely swing the bat. He had no power in his swing, and he could not lift his left arm higher than his shoulder. When he told Dark about the problem, the manager sloughed it off.

"Don't worry about offense," Dark said. "Just handle the pitchers."

The spirit of those times, before the age of huge contracts, was different than it is today. If a player said he was hurt but couldn't prove it, he was expected to play. If he complained, he risked acquiring the label "Jake," for faking an injury. He was paid to play. Dutifully, Fosse took his cortisone shots and obeyed Dark's order.

In the next two months, before he fractured his right index finger—an injury revealed by X-rays—Fosse did the best he could. He altered his swing to compensate for the pain. Even though he did not have the same fluid stroke he possessed before the All-Star Game, and nothing approximating his old power, it was a source of satisfaction to him that he hit two more home runs that year.

Fosse was twenty-three years old, the most promising young catcher in the majors. He had entered the All-Star Game with sixteen homers and batting .313. He was the best hitter on the lowly Indians and was coming off a streak in which he had hit safely in twenty-nine out of thirty games. From this point, however, his career went into a decline.

The following April when Fosse's shoulder was X-rayed again, the radiology showed an old fracture and separation from the year before. He had played two months with the separation caused by his collision with Rose. The doctors defended their earlier prognosis by telling him dryly that an inflammation can sometimes mask a bone fracture. With his altered swing, he never regained his stroke, never hit more than twelve home runs in a season, never hit close to .300 for the next three years he played as a regular. In 1973, he was traded to Oakland, where he played creditably, including in the World Series against the Mets. But he was never the same again.

Fosse went on to become the much-beloved, down-home voice of the Oakland A's in the broadcast booth. In his frequent speeches to fan clubs around the Bay Area, his collision with Rose was always the best-remembered moment of his playing career. The question lingered about whether the crash was a cheap shot. For a few years, he harbored no bitterness toward Rose. The event had just happened. It was just part of the game. Only Rose knew what was really in his mind as he barreled toward home that day, Fosse would say. If he harbored any bitterness at first, it was toward the Cleveland organization for forcing him to play when he was hurt. Had he been allowed to rest and recuperate, his subsequent career might have been different. That was just the way it used to be in baseball.

Rose, too, was asked frequently about the collision. He was given to telling the story in a way that boosted his own reputation as a fierce competitor. He boasted about how he and Fosse had socialized the night before, as if this demonstrated the athlete's code: even the closest friendship had no bearing on how a great competitor plays the game. It was nothing personal. He was just trying to win a tight game.

In fact, Fosse and Rose were not friends at all. They had never met before the All-Star event. In Rose's rendition, he and Fosse became closer with every retelling. The socializing the night before the game became, first, dinner at the Roses' house; then they became good friends. Before the retelling was over, Rose was claiming that they were bosom buddies who were out carousing the night before until 4 A.M. This hurt and angered Ray Fosse. The truth is that after a press conference, Rose and Fosse, along with Sam McDowell and their wives, all named Carol, had gone out for dinner. They had ended up at Rose's house briefly to talk baseball before the Cleveland players left at a decent hour with their wives. There was no prior existing friendship, and no carousing.

If the Rose braggadocio was annoying to Fosse, an item in a sporting magazine in 1974 was something more. There, once again, Rose was asked about the collision, and he responded, "I could never have looked my father in the eye again, if I hadn't hit Fosse that day." To Fosse, that amounted to an admission of criminal intent.

And so the collision went into baseball folklore. In the world of sports, Fosse's fate began a much-ballyhooed superstition called the "Cleveland jinx." This is not to be confused with the "Chicago jinx" which held, until the 1989 season, that any team with the fewest number of former Chicago Cubs is sure to win the pennant. In the Cleveland jinx, the town is supposed to curse promising athletes with career-threatening injury. Injuries which befell such greats as Michael Jordan and John Elway in Cleveland advanced the theory. But the Cleveland jinx began with Ray Fosse.

Then came the third game of the 1973 National League play-off between the Reds and the Mets. At Flushing Meadows that year, the Mets were on the way to staging their second miracle in five years.

Since 1969, they had been also-rans, finishing no higher than third place. Only a few months before October 1973, they were mired in last place. Now, the championship series was knotted at one game apiece, as the series moved from Cincinnati to Shea Stadium for the first postseason game since the histrionic, confetti-filled day of October 16, 1969. The New York players and fans were high, and they became higher after Rusty Staub blasted two homers to give the Mets a 9–2 advantage.

When Rose came to bat in the top of the fifth with one out, he was already feeling frustrated. His anger increased as Jerry Koosman, the Mets pitcher who had had superb control all day, threw a high inside pitch to brush Rose back. Rose dug back in, pawed the dirt, and singled up the middle for his second hit of the day. That brought Joe Morgan to the plate.

With no hits in the first two games, Mighty Joe was also frustrated. He bounced a sharp grounder right at the Mets first baseman, John Milner, who snared it and fired to second, where Bud Harrelson was sweeping across the bag for a close but seemingly routine double play. Rose went in hands high, body high, taking out Harrelson in a bone-crunching mismatch—well after the ball was on the way to first for the double play. As Pete rose from the base, his elbow caught Harrelson's nose in a final insult.

"You cocksucker!" Harrelson snarled fiercely as he got up from the dirt. Twice before during the season, on plays like this, he had broken bones in his hand and ribs from similar, late hits. "You tried to elbow me!"

"What're you talkin' about?" Rose snapped, turning to leave.

Harrelson shoved him. Rose shoved the scrawny shortstop back . . . and back . . . and back toward first base. Suddenly, they were on the ground, Harrelson trying to punch, while Rose had him pinned firmly to the ground. The benches emptied instantly. The Mets third baseman, Wayne "Red" Garrett, arrived first and caught Rose with punches to the back and the ribs before Rose could pull Harrelson on top of him to shield himself from the blows and wait for help.

Near second base, the riot was total; it remains one of the most spectacular melees in baseball history. The pitchers raced from their bullpens to throw themselves into the fight. The best sideshow was between two relievers, Buzz Capra of the Mets and the Reds Pedro Borbon. Borbon blindsided Capra with a spectacular roundhouse punch to the right cheek, only to have Duffy Dyer strike back for the Mets. When Borbon and Dyer were finally separated by some of their teammates, Borbon grabbed his hat hotly and stomped away, only to find that it was not his hat at all but a Mets cap—not only a Mets cap but Buzz Capra's. He swept the despicable thing off, put it in his mouth, and took a huge bite out of it before he tossed it contemptuously to the grass.

The action was not over. After order was restored, Rose trotted out to left field, only to have garbage rain down on him: beer cans and hot dogs, programs and epithets. He picked up a can and threw it back at the fans. This brought a second deluge. At length, play was resumed. Two outs were made. Then, with Felix Millan at bat, a whiskey bottle whizzed by Rose's ear. Throwing his hands up in surrender, he called time and started to walk off the field. Sparky Anderson was out to meet him in a second.

"Spark, they just threw a whiskey bottle at me."

"That's enough for us today," the skipper replied. "Let's go."

"We'll get this straightened out," the ump said.

"Let me know when you do," Anderson replied, waving his troops off the field.

That brought the president of the National League, Chub Feeney, onto the field. If the fans in left field could not be quelled, the Mets would have to forfeit the game, 9–0. A blue ribbon peace delegation was suggested. Yogi Berra, the Mets manager, empaneled it: Tom Seaver, their best pitcher; Cleon Jones, their best hitter; Staub, the hero of the day; and the Met emeritus, Willie Mays, who was in his last days as a player. The panel strode purposefully to the left-field bleachers. Berra laid down the opening position, his hands extended in supplication before the mob.

"Keep quiet," he yelled. "Why let them beat us? We're ahead, 9–2."

"Look at the scoreboard," said Willie. "We're ahead. Let 'em play the game."

A cease-fire was finally achieved, and the contest resumed dispiritedly, without further scoring.

After the game, Rose and Harrelson hid from the press for forty-five minutes in their respective trainers' rooms, as if the bruises to their bodies and their pride needed urgent attention. Other analysts filled in for the hungry press. Sparky Anderson suggested that Red Garrett had been the real culprit by rushing in to clobber Rose with his rabbit punches. Without that, it would have remained a one-on-one scrimmage. This comment was greeted with guffaws.

The press rushed over to the Mets locker room for a reaction. "Bullspit," said Garrett (as the *Daily News* reported it). "If I tangled with a midget, I could do anything too," he said of the bully Rose.

Harrelson emerged at that moment to thank Garrett for sticking up for him but not for insulting him while he did so. Harrelson had calmed down enough to adopt a jocular tone. "Hell, I'm not a fighter. I'm a lover!" he said sweetly. Indeed, with a cut above his eye, he did look the worse for wear. The scrape came from his field sunglasses rather than Rose's elbow, he said graciously.

Of his cocksucker remark, Harrelson issued a clarification: "I just wanted to tell him, I'm not a punching bag."

Rose remained totally unrepentant. "I play hard, but I don't play dirty," he said. "If I was a dirty player, I could've leveled him. It's like the 1970 All-Star Game. I played that game to win. I've been criticized ever since for that. But that's the way I play. I don't feel it's my obligation to apologize to anyone over this, because I think I did the right thing."

Over and over, he stated his position, and he would do so for years to come. Indeed, the position stiffened in the telling, until he confessed he was trying to loft Harrelson into the left-field bleachers. As for the game the next day: "I might even slide harder, if it's possible. If I have to do it in the first inning, I will. I don't have any feeling about it."

After the game, Rose and Joe Morgan had dinner in their hotel, because Rose had been advised to stay out of sight. Room service brought him a deliberately burned steak, a discourtesy he was often to cite in the future. Morgan tried to cool him down and to get him to tone down his provocative remarks. For once, Rose worried about his image, but not greatly. He was certain that he was headed for a very bad press in the morning. As they watched a football game, Morgan told him to forget it and just play his game.

Rose was right about the press. The next day, in the *Daily News*, where the collision knocked the Mideast war off the front page, Dick Young wrote the hometown defense: "Bud Harrelson needs the protection of the rules, particularly from hyperactive outfielders who run the bases savagely, secure in the knowledge that when the teams change sides, the outfielders are standing a safe distance from the other guy's spikes." If the league was sincere in deploring "rowdyism," Young wrote, it should require the umpires to enforce the rule on "wayward slides." For the infielders had the tools for reprisal: spikes accidentally planted in the slider's chest or "low-bridging" a down-under sidearm peg aimed at the slider's forehead.

The next day, Shea Stadium was replete with messages for Rose: about roses that stink or wither, were pansies or weeds, roses that die where buds bloom, and so on. As the angry fans came through the turnstiles, they were ready to take up the straightforward chant of the day before: "Rose Eats Shit!"

In the Mets locker room, Bud Harrelson had grown even sweeter overnight. He donned his customary Superman undershirt that always went beneath his uniform, and in his pregame interviews he sported it openly with an *X* taped across the *S*. The press found this "classy." He even recalled his rookie year in 1966, when the Mets were playing in Cincinnati, and Bud was having trouble in the field. After the game, Rose had been standing with Tommy Helms when he called out to Harrelson: "Hey, kid, come over here!"

To Bud, Rose was already an idol. He stood in awe before Rose. "Listen, why don't you use a smaller glove," Rose suggested. Bud took the advice, and he never forgot it. The smaller glove would soon enough become golden.

The league officials worried about a second day of riot. Donald Grant, the owner of the Mets, called Harrelson to his box with the bright idea of Bud and Pete going to the plate when the managers exchanged their cards, and shaking hands.

"He won't do it," Harrelson said flatly.

"If he will, will you?" Grant asked. What was a player to say to his boss?

So Grant rushed to Bob Howsam, the Reds general manager, with his brainstorm, and Howsam put the idea to Rose. "That's not the way I compete," Rose said, but then softened. "If I get to second base during the game, I'll shake hands with him."

He did get to second base, twice, amid the chorus of boos that had a strange undertone of admiration. But he did not shake hands. "I decided I didn't want to make a spectacle of myself," he explained later.

The game went into extra innings. In the twelfth, Rose came to bat again and ran the count to 2 and 2. The next pitch came over and Rose barely foul-tipped it as the ball went into the catcher's mitt, but Jerry Grote couldn't hold it. Keep the ball lower, Grote motioned to his reliever. The next pitch was another fastball, sailing up in the strike zone, and Rose plastered it with a Mickey Mantle swing. The ball rose and sailed over Rusty Staub's head and landed in the right-field bleachers. As Rose rounded second, he raised his fist in a defiant salute of Red Power.

Harrelson was to have noble and sweet revenge the season after the slide. At the first Mets game at Riverfront Stadium, Harrelson came to bat, and the crowd erupted in boos and catcalls. It was their turn for reverse flattery. A switch-hitter like Rose, he dug in against the right-hander, Fred Norman. Norman wound up and threw him an inside fastball, and Bud tagged it, gently lofting it high, over Pete Rose's head in right field until it just barely cleared the fence. Rose, in disbelief, watched it go. As Bud trotted around the bases—he would hit only seven home runs in his entire major league career—Rose turned to his worshipers in the right-field bleachers and mugged a Rodney Dangerfield gesture of disbelief.

"What the hell was that all about?" he muttered.

In late September 1969, while Rose was locked in a tense struggle for the batting title of the National League with Roberto Clemente, a horse named Arts and Letters won the Woodward Stakes at Belmont Park to soar ahead as the leading money winner of the racing season. The thoroughbred, which went on to become Horse of the Year, was owned by the millionaire philanthropist Paul Mellon, a member of Yale's class of '29. He had named his horse in honor of a popular course of study in the humanities division at Yale College. History, arts, and letters were at the core of Yale College's mission: to provide a broad liberal arts education, steeped in the classics, in preparation for a well-rounded life outside the work place.

It was within this mission that Bart Giamatti began to flourish as a star of the Yale undergraduate faculty in the late 1960s and early 1970s. After his brief detour to lotus-eating Princeton, Giamatti quickly became a wildly popular teacher. Meanwhile, he pursued his scholarship apace. His essays and criticism in Renaissance poetry showed promise, so much so that he was made a full professor at the early age of thirty-three.

This eminence gave him the confidence and the security to branch out, to pursue his hobbies as well as his central academic concerns. Indeed, he tried to combine the two. To Peter Brooks, his friend and colleague in the humanities division, he proposed that they teach a summer course called "Games and Literature" on Martha's Vineyard. They might start with the funeral games of Hector in the first book of the *Iliad*. To Giamatti, games were space for the imagination. Their absolute rules were imaginative rather than restrictive constraints and were akin to the strict rules that governed a Spenserian poem. Baseball was the best example. To Giamatti, the game was "cultural perfection."

In an essay called "The Forms of Epic," he drew a parallel that he longed for his fellow academics to take seriously. "Aeneas is asked: How can I get home? What must I do? What will it cost me in terms of myself? What is it going to take to establish stability?" All epics ask these questions, he wrote. They were about a quest, the quest to destroy Troy or establish Rome, to defeat the infidel, to find the Grail, to worship at the court of the Faerie Queene. Why not to enter the Hall of Fame?

Giamatti's appeal to his students lay in this ability to make his courses on Dante and Edmund Spenser fun and amusing as well as profound and relevant. His particular gift was to make connections between the seemingly esoteric concerns of the Renaissance poets and the concerns of modern America. Somehow, these connections never seemed overstretched or facile. From the classical to the modern, he could take his students' breath away with his analogies. Then he would dismiss them jauntily with the catch-all phrase, "It's like anything else."

He was deeply romantic about the teaching experience. To Giamatti, a class was a canvas on which the painter was supposed to impart shape and contour, as well as beauty and drama, with the colors he applied to the surface. Or, he could change the image: the teacher was a weaver whose tapestry should have logic and a sense of completion. His manner in class was formal. He addressed his students as Mister or Miss So and So. There was often an exception to this rule, especially in his freshman class of English 25. He might pick out a tall, gawky newcomer, say, one Rick Godley, and knight him as Noble Godley. Giamatti had the habit of undercutting this old-fashioned approach with rough and occasionally vulgar interjections. Spicing his lectures with slang and street talk, in the midst of otherwise erudite discourse, was intended to shock, and Giamatti was good at shocking. This technique endeared him to the students of the Vietnam War era, in whom rebellion against authority, including academic authority, was strong and growing stronger.

Teaching freshmen was a particular joy for Giamatti. He loved their fear and their spirit and their curiosity. English 25 was an introduction to Great Poets: Chaucer, Spenser, Donne, and Milton. His students' first assignment was always to memorize the opening seventeen lines of *The Canterbury Tales* and to listen to a tape with the proper diction, so that, in class, they might recite "Whan that Aprille with his shoures sote" with the proper inflection. One of his students in the early seventies, Leslie Anderson, took to this task with special enthusiasm, but when the time came to write her first paper, she found the topic intimidating, and she froze. Giamatti, ever the taskmaster, had threatened that no late papers would be accepted. When he discovered there was no paper from Anderson, he boomed her name out to meet him after class. Terrified, she presented him with all the normal freshman excuses. In patient dismay, he said, "You know the other evening, I was walking by Sterling Library, and I heard a student reciting the Prologue to Chaucer's *Canterbury Tales.* You were saying it with such excitement. And you had it down perfectly. . . . Leslie, I know you can write this paper." She did, and she got an *A*, and Giamatti wrote on its face: "I have learned a good deal from it." She would never forget him.

Giamatti had begun to adapt his teaching methods to the turbulence of the times. His fear as a teacher was that he might lose touch with his students. The interchange, the back and forth, was the heart of the educational process to him, and he was intent to keep that interchange civilized, regardless of the incivility that might lie beyond the parapets of Yale College. On any given day, it was common to find Giamatti standing on a corner of Wall Street near the Bienecke Library, dressed in a beat-up sports jacket or parka, engaged in spirited debate with students or faculty or maintenance men on the issues of the day, especially the issues that affected Yale.

But he did not adapt comfortably. By nature and by upbringing, he was conservative, both in his educational philosophy and in his politics. Both were, for him, rooted in the verities of the classics. When the question had arisen at Princeton several years earlier whether the Latin requirement for graduate study should be abolished—Princeton being one of the last institutions of higher learning to have it—Giamatti was the only member of the Princeton faculty who voted to retain. Order and disorder preoccupied him. Standards and rules were the instruments of order. And he seemed inordinately interested in punishing those who violated traditional standards.

During his teaching days at Yale, Giamatti liked to spend time in his backyard in Westville, in batting practice with his son Marcus. The senior Giamatti would be dressed in faded red chino pants, a Coop button-down shirt, and a rumpled Red Sox cap. They would use a plastic dish for home plate. As the boy picked up the bat, Giamatti would say, "Marcus! Concentrate Your Forces! Keep your eye on the ball. It's like anything else." Or: "Marcus! Never argue with the umpire. Try to understand him. Remember that he has an important job to do: he keeps and protects the laws of the game. It's just like anything else."

Giamatti's love of order was especially evident in his attitude toward language. He believed deeply in the poetry and the awesome power of language and hated the thought that the bullhorn, the slogan, the placard, and the bumper sticker had begun to replace the declarative sentence. If someone could not express an idea, then the idea did not exist for Giamatti. Moreover, he viewed with alarm the growing sentiment among the young that language was somehow sullied and dishonest, a tool for the manipulation of the masses by the intellectual elite. The fault was not entirely the students', for they were, to Giamatti, the products of the "anti-structures" of the 1960s: the new math, open classrooms, Legos, and, worst of all, the Filthy Speech Movement of Berkeley, where the by-product of uttering obscenities was "to free us from the shackles of syntax, the racism of grammar, the elitism of style."

Never did the "assault on literacy" become more worrisome than in the fall of 1969, when Yale finally experienced the kind of crisis that had already disrupted Columbia, Cornell, and Harvard. Kingman Brewster, Jr., the president of Yale, had been expecting a student rebellion for a year and had drafted a policy or "scenario" to meet a disruption with stiff measures. The policy called for the immediate suspension of any Yale student who engaged in force or intimidation or coercion. The Yale faculty had approved Brewster's plan in the abstract. Then, on November 6, 1969, under the banner of student mobilization, radical students occupied Wright Hall and held a university official hostage overnight. If Giamatti feared the bullhorn as a symbol of uncivilized discourse, it was now the Yale provost who stood with the instrument on a police car for much of the night and warned the students inside of the fate that awaited them. When the Students for a Democratic Society (SDS) emerged the next morning and gave up their occupation, the provost suspended them all, as he had promised and as Brewster's scenario of swift and summary justice provided.

Then the inevitable academic committee convened. It recommended that the students' suspension be lifted and replaced with warnings about future misconduct—a recommendation that clearly undercut President Brewster. This bugle call to retreat was put to the entire Yale faculty for a vote.

At the meeting in Sprague Hall, Giamatti found himself seated next to Robert Brustein, the dean of the Yale Drama School, who had been active in the protest against the Vietnam War and yet was outraged at the weakness of the committee. Giamatti had a strong but secret antipathy toward Brustein. Giamatti loved traditional theatre and classical theatre performed in a classical manner. (Two years earlier, on a faculty questionnaire, Bart had written in the box for avocations that he loved the theatre and the Boston Red Sox "in reverse order.") He and his wife, Toni, were devoted to the Yale

Repertory Theatre and the undergraduate Dramat that predated Brustein's controversial tenure as dean. Brustein, however, had revolutionized theatre in New Haven, as he had downgraded the role of amateurs. He brought modern translations to classical pieces—"Shakespeare on rollerskates" as it became known by his detractors—as well as a heavy accent on the avant garde.

As an actress of the previous regime, Toni Giamatti was especially critical of what Brustein was doing to her beloved institution. At Brustein's early productions, the Giamattis (according to Brustein) enjoyed going to the Yale Rep to laugh derisively from the audience at what was happening on stage. Toni Giamatti later confronted Brustein on the street and laced into him for his innovations.

At the faculty meeting concerning punishment for the students (as Brustein later told the story), Giamatti was witty and charming. He was also scornful about the timidity of his colleagues. Muffling his voice behind his hand, Giamatti urged the dean to deliver a stinging soliloquy in defense of President Brewster.

When the vote finally came, Brustein voted boisterously against the recommendation. He, for one, would be loyal to his president. Then, to his surprise and disgust, after all that charm and conspiratorial whispering, Giamatti voted with the majority to lift the suspension. To Brustein, this discrepancy between private and public behavior on Giamatti's part showed a weakness of character. He would say so six years later, when he was consulted about the list of candidates who were being considered to succeed Brewster. Brustein would say pointedly to the head of the search committee, William Bundy, that A. Bartlett Giamatti did not have the strength of character to be president of Yale.

Armageddon came a few months later. On May 2 and 3, 1970, the bullhorn and the slogan took over the Yale campus completely. The situation came about as a result of the imminent trial in New Haven of the Black Panther party chairman, Bobby Seale, on murder, conspiracy, and kidnapping charges in connection with the death of an alleged police informant. The famous line "Off the Pig" was taken up as a rallying cry in the streets of New Haven, and demonstrations took place. The invasion of Cambodia by American troops several days before made the anger and the danger of the moment seem that much greater.

President Nixon ordered federal troops to New Haven to keep the peace, for the May demonstrations brought to that city the sloganeers of the Left, Yippie leaders Jerry Rubin and Abbie Hoffman. Another fifteen thousand demonstrators joined them. Yale University had no official connection with the rallies, but the events were centered on the New Haven Green, whose northern edge was demarcated by the Yale campus.

What would Yale's response be? Would it close itself off or would it become involved? The university wanted to be open, but it wanted no part in violence or bloodshed. How were these contradictions to be reconciled? It was one of those rare events in which an academic institution had to reexamine its essential mission as the nation looked on. The crisis was front-page news all over the country.

The faculty watched the events unfold in high anxiety, for the situation was palpably dangerous. Just how dangerous campus confrontations with the National Guard could be was shown only two days later in Ohio at Kent State University. Kingman Brewster, Jr., decided that Yale could not turn its back. He sanctioned the students to invite the visiting demonstrators into the residence halls to sleep and authorized the Yale cafeterias to nourish the hordes. Classes were suspended, and that freed students to participate.

Most controversial was Brewster's statement during a faculty meeting that Yale shared the social concerns of the demonstrators. He told the faculty that he personally doubted that Bobby Seale or any other black revolutionary could get a fair trial anywhere in the United States. When his statement was leaked, it brought a call from Vice-President Spiro Agnew for him to resign. Agnew's statement had the happy but unintended effect of rallying students to Brewster's side. If Agnew was against you, you couldn't be all that bad. "Spiro Agnew? What class was he?" read one telegram to Brewster.

The banners of rebellion were everywhere. One helmeted youth, identifying himself only as Jung, explained to the *New York Times* what the symbolism of the new Yippie flag was: "The black is for anarchy. The red star is for our five-point program. And the leaf is for marijuana, which is for getting ecologically stoned without polluting the environment." The New Haven police made a point of greasing the sixty-foot flagpole above the World War I monument on New Haven Green, so that Old Glory would not be replaced by this lurid Yippie standard.

At the rallies on the Green and on the campus, the throngs hung on the words of Rubin and Hoffman. "To free Bobby Seale, we have to go to the only court left, the court of the street," exclaimed Rubin, and then he got everyone's attention by shouting, "Fuck Kingman Brewer [*sic*]." Abbie Hoffman pointed at the Greek Revival courthouse where Seale would be tried and shouted, "There's the house of death right there. If they find Bobby guilty, we're going to pick up that building and send it to the moon."

This was rhetorical flourish, and Giamatti acknowledged grudgingly that it could be effective in moving crowds toward a political goal. What Hoffman said on the Green did not concern Giamatti so much. But when the Yippie leader entered the sanctuary of Yale itself to preach his atavism, Giamatti was incensed.

On a warm evening before a big rally, Hoffman came into the very courtyard of Ezra Stiles College, where, a year later, Giamatti would become the master.

"Don't listen to people who say we got to be serious and responsible," Hoffman told Giamatti's students. "Everybody's responsible and serious but us. We gotta redefine the fucking language. Work—w-o-r-k—is a dirty four letter word. . . . We need a society in which work and play are not separate. We gotta destroy the Protestant ethic as well as capitalism, racism, imperialism—that's gotta go too. We want a society in which dancin' in the streets isn't separate from cuttin' sugar cane. . . . We have picked the Yale lock." To Giamatti, such rhetoric was downright traitorous to the educational process and "corrosive as acid."

Yale survived May 1970, but the events left a deep impression on Bart Giamatti. In three days, he would write later, there had been more rhetoric for more causes than in the forty-five-year reign of Elizabeth I. That "the pageant," as he later called it, had been sponsored by Yale gave him scant comfort. Order and rules, civilized discourse and manners, grace and eloquence were his paramount values, and they had been trampled. The university was a sanctuary for the refinement of these values. The Philistines had invaded and defiled Giamatti's garden. Hoffman had even tried to redefine his garden as a place where work and play were inseparable, where togetherness came from redefining language in a way that made all simply feel good. To this academic, nothing could be more repellent.

After the troubles of 1970, Giamatti became a visible and vocal foil for Brewster in faculty meetings. He always adopted the conservative point of view, as he harped on order and regularity. Brewster took this young Disraeli seriously, encouraging his opinions· even though the president disagreed with them. He appointed Giamatti to increasingly important academic committees. On "the troubles" themselves, Giamatti never criticized his predecessor. There was a certain resignation in Giamatti's voice when he spoke of them. Nothing noble or Machiavellian or weak or passive had marked the university's stance. Yale had simply done what it had to do to survive.

Meanwhile, in his literary life, Giamatti focused on the image of the wild horse in several of his academic essays. The unchecked, riderless horse is in Renaissance poetry a metaphor for "appetite run

wild, a people completely leaderless." The rider, by contrast, represents the rationality of man. The combined image of the horse and
the rider were the halves of man himself: man's beastial power and
energy needed to be tamed and controlled and guided by his higher
intellect. "The horse is a symbol for the part of man we must govern
most wisely," Giamatti wrote in an essay called "Headlong Horses,
Headless Horseman." "Even more, it represents the energy in life
most dangerous to the established conventions and norms." In the
work of the poet, Ludovico Ariosto, the horse out of control is a symbol for human despair. "How one rides is an index of one's spiritual
state," Giamatti wrote. And he concentrated upon the act of taming
itself in the poem *Morgante*, by the fifteenth-century Italian poet Luigi
Pulci,

> Rinaldo sat awhile to watch;
> but then, seeing the game had gone far enough,
> and that with bites and hooves
> that big horse was smashing up his Baiardo,
> he resolved to strike a blow in his favor.
> And while Baiardo was reeling,
> he gave that other a fist between the ears
> with his glove—such as few would want;
>
> and it fell as if it had fainted.
> Baiardo ran to one side, he was afraid.
> For the good while the horse lay stunned
> then he recovered and checked himself over.
> Rinaldo quickly went to him,
> took his mouth by the hard jaw,
> put in a bit he had brought,
> and that horse became docile.

Giamatti went on to describe the process of curbing, after
the hero applied the mailed fist to the forehead of the wild beast. The
curbing is done by hand, he wrote, "by the shaping power of the human, the higher part fashioning out of the energy of the lower something that transforms them both. The wild horse becomes a lamb."

The homecomings of exiled and defeated heroes in epic literature also fascinated Giamatti. When the homecoming took place, it
was a time of celebration. It was a restoration, the "restoration of
lacerated heroes," a making whole again of one who had been muti-
lated. "The humanist enterprise," Giamatti wrote of the mangled

Virgilian heroes, "is a celebration of the way limbs, or a people dispersed like the Trojans, may be brought home—home to Italy where they live out their lives whole, healthy, and secure."

In his years as a popular teacher at Yale, Giamatti never imagined that he could be a judge, much less an executioner of anybody. He was a detached and disengaged professor who had long since accepted his fate as a man of words, not a man of action. But he had downright awe for judges and a profound respect for the courts, which he viewed transcendently as an institution of language. In the summers of 1975 and 1976, he lectured on Dante and Spenser in the pastoral setting of the Breadloaf School of English in the mountains of Vermont. As usual, his course was among the most popular. In the words of his student DeWolfe Fulton, he taught the Renaissance virtues and verities from the epic poems "with an articulate often theatric Mediterranean passion, his voice at once booming and forceful, then mellifluous and soothing. He read Dante's original Italian as a maestro reads music—with love." With considerable force, he pressed his point that these medieval works could be used as a guide for living in modern times.

To his Breadloaf students, Giamatti was intimidating, largely because he was so smart, partly because of his gift to bring this material alive and make it relevant, but also because he adopted a tough-guy style that brooked no laziness or silliness. *The Faerie Queene* was serious stuff. In evident contrast to his esoteric material, he dressed like a hoodlum. He came to class draped in a denim jacket with upturned collar and sporting sunglasses. Together with his speckled, cropped goatee, his dark skin and baggy eyes and that cigarette constantly dangling from his lips, he reinforced more than one stereotype.

When he came to focus on Book V of *The Faerie Queene*, which is an allegory on the virtue of justice, there was no missing his sympathies. Through the righteous decrees of Artegal, the knight who personifies justice, and the power to back up the decrees, represented by Artegal's groom, Talus, the oppressed are freed, the right is distributed, and the injuries to the kingdom are redressed. He gave the enforcer, Talus . . . and Talus's flail . . . special emphasis. Talus was:

> made of yron mould
> Immoveable, resistlesse, without end
> Who in his hand an yron flale did hould
> With which he thresht out falsehood,
> and did truth unfould.

After a class on Book V, in which Giamatti had discoursed upon Spenser's concept that justice was connected to God (for it was God's way of meting out good on earth), his student DeWolfe Fulton, caught up to him afterwards on the dirt road leading to the lunch hall, and they fell into conversation about the justices of the U.S. Supreme Court. The personal agony of a judge interested Giamatti: how any mortal could bear the immense responsibility of deciding weighty questions like abortion and capital punishment or simply judging another human being. His admiration was evident. Taking up the Spenserian lesson of the day, Fulton asked,

"How can one mortal know rightly to impose God's will on another?"

"The answer to that," Giamatti replied, "God only knows."

When DeWolfe Fulton would think back on that interchange fifteen years later, he would say, "In the Rose case, Bart must have doubted his right to judge and doubted his own humanity a thousand times over."

At the end of the course at Breadloaf, Fulton got together with another student who said she could sew. They bought a Wrangler denim jacket and some sequins and sewed on the back the name of Talus, a freehand design of the iron groom's spiked club of righteousness, and the words "Justice with a Flail." The words and the symbols might have been a fitting garment for a motorcycle gang . . . or for a subsequent meeting in the baseball commissioner's office.

When the students presented the jacket to Giamatti at the last class, it was the only time they ever saw him at a loss for words.

· 5 ·

Big Red Machine and Mother Yale

IN 1966, the Reds approached the general manager of the St. Louis Cards, Robert Howsam, about taking over in Cincinnati. Howsam was a quiet, unassuming, old-fashioned Coloradan who had engineered a few key trades such as bringing the Baby Bull, Orlando Cepeda, and the base thief, Lou Brock, and even the aging and declining home-run king, Roger Maris, to St. Louis. (At the same time, he gave away Mike Cuellar to Baltimore, where Cuellar put together a few twenty-game-winning championship seasons.) Howsam had fashioned the teams that brought two world championships and three pennants to the River City between 1964 and 1968. But he felt constrained under the ownership of Augustus "Gussie" Busch and was having trouble making the trades that he wanted. To him, trades were the apogee of excitement—the offers, the calls, the dreams of perfectly synchronized teams, the surprise acceptances, the·hopes and uncertainties for the future.

In his early career, Howsam had been with the Yankees of Mantle and Ford. He had admired the way the dour and conservative George Weiss had built his dynasties and made them even more powerful at World Series time with extra acquisitions. (Johnny Mize in 1949 was the prime example.) To beat the Yankees of Weiss, you had to beat not Mantle and Maris, DiMaggio and Ford, but twenty-five players, perfectly shaped and molded and matched, so that there were no weak joints or imperfect fixtures. Even more than the way of Weiss, Howsam admired the manner in which Branch Rickey and his son, Branch, Jr. (Branch and Twig), had built the Cardinals, the Dodgers, and finally, the Pirates. Howsam considered the senior Rickey to be the greatest judge of ball players ever.

Balance was paramount to winning ball clubs, and Howsam longed for the freedom to follow his instincts without interference from the ownership. In Cincinnati, he got his chance. Given total control of the club, he began with values. His conservative tastes squared nicely with those of his adopted city: clean-cut, traditional, midwestern. He set out to meld the image of his ball club to the image of the city and its surroundings. His metropolitan area was the smallest of any in America with a major league team. Only about 20 percent of the crowds came from the inner city. The Reds drew heavily from all the places within a fifty-mile radius of Cincinnati, from cities as far away as Columbus, Louisville, and Indianapolis, and from small towns in four different states. The mores of those far-flung places were even more traditional than Cincinnati's.

Howsam engaged in a shrewd marketing strategy. He began with the stadium. In meetings with the city fathers, he pressed for a new stadium to be located downtown, on the river, for he had seen what the downtown location of Busch Stadium had done for the spirit of St. Louis. It should have quick access to the interstate system, so his far-flung fans could get in and out of the city quickly. The new stadium should be state of the art but should not have any new-fangled innovations that separated the fans from the action. He wanted the bullpens on the field, in full view, rather than hidden behind the outfield fences, because to him second guessing the manager about his choice of relief pitchers was as important to baseball as Cracker Jack.

In a good German town such as Cincinnati, the pipe organ should be sprightly, the beer robust, the restrooms clean, and even the hot dogs should be nutritious. In this last idea, he went overboard. The all-beef hot dog he introduced might have been the best made, but this dog was a dud. The beef made it too chewy. Howsam knew this by personal inspection. After games, he saw too many half-eaten half-smokes. So he had to retreat to the filler hot dogs. He even experimented with a powder, developed in association with scientists at the University of Denver, that could be sprayed all over the stadium to simulate the odor of fresh baked bread.

To this Michelangelo of Baseball, as Howsam was once called, the field was a canvas. His players were his paints. And the composition should be extravagant. He considered AstroTurf to be superior to grass and dirt. As a matter of principle, no ball game should ever be lost or won on a bad bounce. Nor should one ever be lost or won because a wicked owner let the grass grow too long to decelerate the hop of the ball or wet down his basepaths to slow down a quick opponent. On Howsam's rug, the bounce was quick but true. The carpet did not wear out or have bald or brown spots in August.

Most of all, the appearance of the players concerned him. They should be neat and well groomed. On the road, they were to wear coats and ties. No beards or long hair or Afros were permitted. Their uniforms should be pristine white against the green of the playing field. Their Red stockings should be uncluttered with stripes. Their shoes should be stately black. Indeed, the 1972 World Series between the Reds and the A's, the latter with their white shoes and garish, pastel colors and muttonchops and mustaches, was so fascinating precisely because it reflected the reality of baseball as the national game of a diverse nation. (That was the Series where Rose hit Catfish Hunter's first pitch in the fifth game over the fence, but in the end, the Catfish and Rollie Fingers and Blue Moon Odom were too much for the traditionalists.)

Cincinnati was not so innocent, nor so detached from the realities of American life in the sixties, to escape the strife over matters such as race hatred and Vietnam, which were changing old-fashioned standards of civility and decency and public spiritedness. The city exploded in racial violence in 1967, Howsam's first year in town, when a black man named Posteal Lasky was tried for the rape and murder of several elderly white women. The following year, there was more violence and riot over the assassination of Martin Luther King, Jr. Tensions remained high, and feelings were bitter between the blacks and the white Appalachians who lived in uneasy proximity in Over the Rhine, the bottomland that was a short walk from the riverfront. Through this social unrest, the city remained in the hands of a paternal oligarchy. Old and quiet money dominated. These old-line Cincinnatians appreciated the importance of the Reds to the happiness and tranquility of the city. They quietly exercised an influence over the team and particularly over Howsam. They gave him the stadium he wanted, and he gave them the team they wanted.

Baseball did not escape the strife of the wider society either. Racial tension in the clubhouse was a constant worry for baseball owners. And there were other nefarious temptations. Denny McLain won thirty-one games for the Tigers in 1968, only to be suspended during the first half of the 1970 season for involvement in a bookmaking scheme, then suspended again later in the same season for carrying a gun. McLain's second suspension was a harbinger of what was to happen to Rose nineteen years later, for it happened because McLain, upon advice of his legal counsel, refused to give a full account of the episode to the then baseball commissioner, Bowie Kuhn.

Closer to home, Frank Robinson had been arrested in the early sixties on weapons and disorderly conduct charges, and over the next few years he and Vada Pinson formed a knot of black power on the club that was ultimately disruptive. Howsam felt that one or the other had to be traded, and among the new general manager's first acts was to deal Robinson to the Orioles, even though Robie was at the top of his game. The Reds meant to be faithful to the upstanding traditions of the past, an island of immutability in a troubled sea. That at least was the goal and the hope.

After the 1969 season, Howsam brought in Sparky Anderson, a manager who was comfortable with strict rules of conduct and who was prepared to enforce them. Anderson admired Howsam's inflexibility on the dress code—he would later call it Howsam's greatest legacy—for it led to good discipline and good baseball. Its flip side was that, so long as there was no smudge on the uniform or chip on the helmet, Howsam did not interfere with the strategies of the playing field or intrude upon the private camaraderie of the clubhouse. Among Anderson's first decisions was to appoint Pete Rose the team captain, a first in the history of the franchise.

"Pete, I think you deserve to be captain," Sparky said on the phone beforehand. "With the career you've had here, the way you've dedicated yourself to the Cincinnati Reds, I have to make you captain."

Rose was skeptical. It was not an unmixed blessing, nor the purest of honors. The new manager might be trying to turn him into a tool of the management. That could drive a wedge between him and the other players.

"If you think this will help the club, I'll do it," Rose nevertheless replied.

Sparky did have Rose in mind as a tool, something like a needle or a jackhammer, to prod the players on to better effort. Two months later, in January 1970, Howsam supported his manager by signing Rose to a contract worth $105,000. This met a long-standing and much expressed goal of Rose's: to become the first singles hitter in the majors to make more than $100,000. Two months after that, in spring training, Rose lived up to this charge by working so hard that Anderson dubbed him "the animal." This was high praise. Other Reds were amazed that Rose could stand in the batting cage and take batting practice for forty full minutes, whereas their muscles tightened after ten minutes. Moreover, Rose hated a day off. With Rose as his exhibit A, Anderson established himself in spring training as a stern commandant, so much so that there were grumbles about a "slave camp." Half-joking, Johnny Bench called Anderson's Florida "Stalag 17."

Anderson had another reason for admiring Rose. As his captain became a legitimate superstar in the majors, he seemed to have an absolute genius for public relations. Pete knew how to be a star. He understood when to speak, when to be quiet, when to step forward, and when to recede into a corner and let the crowd follow. In public, Rose was jocular with the fans. He took the time to be courteous, in his special jock's way, and to jolly the kids. He merrily signed autographs, cracking those stale jokes kids like so much, such as the one about where a gorilla can go to the bathroom.

Rose's ability to be a star endeared him to Howsam as well. Being pleasant to the fans was a quality Howsam particularly liked to see in his players. Courtesy took so little effort, and it meant so much. Howsam remembered well a time when he was with the Yankees: he had watched Mantle and Ford snub some fans, shoving them aside on the way to the clubhouse. Howsam had followed them into the locker room and scolded them, "You might hit a hundred homers in a year, Mickey, and you can win thirty games in a season, Whitey, but if there's nobody in the stands, you won't get paid one lead nickel."

The gentle pace of Cincinnati made it easy for Rose and the other players to be pleasant. Their heroic status did not separate and exalt them but included them in the civic affairs of the small city, as if they were honorary burgomasters. They were treated as real people rather than as untouchable, unapproachable icons or steamy prima donnas from whom the fans expected bizarre and eccentric behavior. As a result, players liked to play there. In the Queen City, they were mortals, albeit with special talents, who had families and problems like anyone else. Indeed, Howsam looked for family values in building his dynasty. It was a hedge against the growing drug problem, racial tensions, and swollen heads. So long as he had a strong farm system, and therefore, a large supply of homegrown players to draw upon, he promoted the notion that no one was indispensable.

On November 29, 1971, Howsam made the trade of his career. When it happened, it shocked the baseball world, but jolted Cincinnati even more. In an eight-player deal, one of the largest in the history of the franchise, Howsam sent Lee May and Tommy Helms (and a utility infielder) to Houston in exchange for Joe Morgan, Jack

Billingham, and Cesar Geronimo (and a minor leaguer and aging third baseman). The reaction in Cincinnati was dismay and anger. Lee May, otherwise known as the Big Bopper from Birmingham, had just had his best year in the major leagues, with thirty-nine homers, a .278 average, and ninety-eight runs batted in. The well-liked Carolinian, Helms, was a Golden Glove fielder.

What were the Reds getting in return? To be sure, Morgan was fast, with forty stolen bases, and the Reds needed speed and left-handed hitting in their new park. But Morgan had hit only .256 that year, and his throwing arm was barely adequate. Moreover, he had a reputation as a clubhouse troublemaker and an annoying motor-mouth. Geronimo and Billingham? Geronimo, the Indian Chief from the Dominican Republic, might be fast in center field, but he had played sparingly in Houston that year and was considered by the Astros to be lazy. Moreover, he had arguably the worst slapping, uppercut swing in baseball. Billingham was a solid workman, nothing spectacular.

The hometown howled. The sages of the press resoundingly agreed with one another that Houston got a sweetheart deal. An *Enquirer* headline expressed the fans' reaction: TRADE HOWSAM FOR A TRAINED SEAL. "If the United States had traded Dwight Eisenhower to the Germans in World War II," wrote *Enquirer* columnist Bob Hertzel, "it wouldn't have been much different than sending May and Helms to Houston." Not only did the Reds get the short end on talent, Hertzel proclaimed, but in May and Helms the team lost leadership, an "intangible that is irreplaceable."

As the press howled, the management chortled and congratulated itself. In his more detached moments, Howsam wanted the fans to second guess him just as much as they second guessed his manager. Sparky Anderson admired Howsam's "gambler's instinct" and contemplated deliciously what this burst of speed could do for his club. After the deal was announced, the skipper turned to Howsam and whispered, "I just want to tell you, boss, you just won us a pennant with that deal."

In the following spring training, Anderson followed a hunch by putting Morgan's locker in the clubhouse next to Rose's. He felt that "a little of what made Rose tick as the game's most exciting player might rub off on Joe. It would set up an honest kind of competition between them for attention." Rose created challenges for the other players. "He's like a speed horse at the racetrack," Sparky observed. "If you just let him get out there in the lead and go, you're in trouble. You're not going to catch him. The way he plays, he creates embarrassment for other players."

Early in spring training in 1972, Anderson laid down the challenge for Morgan: "Joe, when you can come to the park and play like Pete every day, then you're going to be some player. And remember, he never gets disgusted with himself. You'll never find him pouting." When the regular season got under way, Anderson returned to the theme: "You're getting down on yourself a bit, Joe. But you can't pout and still be like Pete. You're getting close to being another Pete Rose in attitude, but you've got about twenty-five percent to go."

The rest of the story is well documented. Chief Geronimo was delivered into the meaty clutches of the hitting coach, Ted Kluszewski, who went to work on Geronimo's swing and had the center fielder hitting above .300 by 1976. The Chief established himself as the best fielding, strongest throwing center fielder in the major leagues, as he won five consecutive Golden Glove Awards. The workhorse, Billingham, delivered two nineteen-victory seasons for the Reds and a World Series record that was among the best. And Joe Morgan became simply the most powerful offensive weapon in the game.

But not for several years. In 1973, Rose, the speed horse, gave Morgan a mark to shoot for. That year, Pete was voted the league's Most Valuable Player, as he won his third batting title with a .338 average and collected 230 hits. That made six seasons out of nine with more than two hundred hits, and his eighth of nine seasons over .300. If he had quit there, he would already have been regarded as one of the most consistent hitters in major league history. In July 1973, he passed the two thousand hit mark, and it made him feel old, as if the mere thought of three thousand hits meant his career was coming to an end.

For the second time in two years, Willie Stargell of the Pirates was second in the balloting, and he was disgruntled. With forty-four homers, an average of .299, and 119 RBIs in 1973, Stargell raised an ugly specter. "Politics" had been involved in Rose's selection, he suggested. He meant racial politics. "Awards are fine, but if it's done on a political basis, I don't want any part of it. . . . I don't know what goes into [the selection process] . . . I don't know if it's politics . . . if there's certain guys that people like. I know Pete's the kind of guy that people like . . . the way he plays."

Everybody knew what he was saying, including Pete Rose. Going back to his rookie days, Rose had shown himself to be totally devoid of racial prejudice. When he was being protected and nurtured by the Reds' black superstars, Frank Robinson and Vada Pinson, management had cautioned him to stay away from "the niggers" for his own good. Rose had told them to go fly a kite. Now, he knew what to say and what to leave alone. "I'd have been disappointed if I didn't win," he said. "I had a good year, and so did Stargell. I'm just trying to prove that there's a place in baseball for the guy who doesn't hit home runs."

The relationship between Rose and Morgan deepened during this period, and their closeness was a visible demonstration of the absence of racial division on the ball club. Anderson himself contributed to the colorblind atmosphere. He had grown up on the fringe of Watts in Los Angeles. Indeed, after the Watts riots of 1967, his mother found thirteen bullet holes in her porch. His parents had stressed the lesson of a single humanity as he had grown up, and as a child, Anderson had flourished in mixed company. As an adult, Anderson believed that misguided religion was responsible for promoting the difference between the races. The only difference he could see in the clubhouse was that his black players loved their music and tended to recede with it into the corners, while his white players liked to hang out in bars.

The skipper's attitude made more poignant a situation concerning Bobby Tolan in 1973. After an Achilles tendon injury in 1971, Tolan returned in 1972 to have a solid year and a fine Series. He was voted Comeback Player of the Year. But he came to spring training in 1973 out of shape. More disturbing, there was an angry belligerence in his attitude. In years past, he fit in comfortably with the bantering that was the trademark of the Reds clubhouse. To Anderson, this needling and ripping was part of the Reds' charm. "You give it, you take it or you die," he said. Anderson had loved the time when he had scratched Joe Morgan from the lineup because his second baseman had a 103-degree temperature on a day when the Reds were to face the Mets and their ace Jerry Koosman. Tony Perez left a sleeping bag, a pillow, three aspirins, and a note in Morgan's locker that read: "Take these and you'll be over Koosmanitis tomorrow." Amid the cackles outside in the locker room, Morgan came storming into Anderson's office and demanded to play. "There's no way that damn Cuban is gonna get me with Koosmanitis!" he exclaimed.

Suddenly, Tolan was neither giving nor taking, especially when he went into a slump in the early season. Anderson realized too late that Tolan was "dying inside." For a time, the skipper coddled his black player, hoping for a turnaround, despite the protests of his coaches. Then Tolan did the unthinkable: he started growing a mustache. Not once but twice in the mid-season Anderson knew this testing for what it was. At first, he was able to defuse the situation quietly because Tolan shaved. But before the play-off series with the Mets, a player came to Anderson and said, "What are you gonna do about the beard Tolan's starting to grow?"

This was no skirmish but a declaration of all-out war. Anderson called Tolan in and told him not to suit up if he did not shave. "I'm putting on the uniform . . . and I'm not shaving," Tolan sneered. He turned on his heel, put on his uniform, and trotted onto the field.

Anderson asked Kluszewski and Rose to retrieve Tolan from the field for one last try. At last, Rose had become the tool of management.

"I told you not to put on the uniform, Bobby, and you've done it," Anderson scowled. "I told you not to go out on the field, and you've done that."

"Yeah, and I'm going back," Tolan snapped, and did.

Minutes later, on the field, Anderson confronted his player for the last time. "You won the war today, Bobby, but don't return tomorrow because your uniform will be packed away." Suspended, Tolan missed the play-offs and was traded after the season. Sparky Anderson would always regret the incident as his biggest mistake as a major league manager. Perhaps if he had only talked to Tolan more. Perhaps if he had protected him during his depression. Perhaps. Perhaps.

Three years later, when the Phillies faced the Reds in the National League play-offs, Tolan, then a Phillie, frosted the Reds by proclaiming that Rose was only an average third baseman, certainly not in the league of Mike Schmidt, and Johnny Bench did not deserve his superstar status. The Reds swept the Phillies in three games.

The year 1973 was a vintage one for Rose, but the following year, the grapes went a bit sour, as he hit only .284, his first under-.300 average since his rookie year. No one on the Reds hit over .300 that year. Still, the team muddled through with ninety-eight wins, finishing behind the Dodgers, who won 102 games. This downslide by Rose provided Morgan with his opening. The following two years, the great championship years for the Big Red Machine, Mighty Joe was the National League's Most Valuable Player. In 1975, he hit .327, stole 67 bases, and scored 107 runs while driving in 94. In 1976, he hit .320, stole 60 bases, and drove in 111 runs. The year after that, 1977, Rose and Morgan were outdone for the MVP Award by yet another Redleg, the awesome and strange George Foster.

Foster had been another of Howsam's "gambles." Like Geronimo, he had played very little with his previous club and needed work on his technique. When Howsam acquired Foster from the Giants in 1971, he knew that the outfielder could not hit a curve; indeed, "he could not hit me if I was on the outside of the plate," Howsam was to say. Foster's early play for the Reds was inconsistent, so much so that in 1973, he was sent down to Indianapolis. There, he performed poorly until he fell under the care of a hypnotist, who must have known the mysteries of the curve. By 1975, Foster came into his own. As a result, in May of that year, Rose was moved from right field to third base so that Foster could play regularly. (At his new position, Rose was a "jackhammer third baseman," knocking down everything in sight. This proletarian label, which Sparky Anderson applied, further deepened the affection of the hard hats for Rose.) In his MVP year, Foster hit fifty-two home runs, one of which, so the flight engineers said, would have traveled 720 feet from home plate, if it had not hit the top of the upper deck.

Thus, between 1972 and 1977, the Cincinnati Reds took the National League's Most Valuable Player Award every year (1972 had been Johnny Bench's turn). Between 1970 and 1975, the team won more games and championships than any other: six Western Division championships, four National League Championships, and two World Championships. Every man on the field ranked number one at his position in the league. To Sparky Anderson and many others, they were the best baseball team of all time. "I used to get mad at them," Anderson recalled. "I'd say, 'You guys think you're so good that you can turn it on and turn it off when you want to.' The truth is: they could."

In 1971, the year before he became a full professor at the age of thirty-three, Giamatti took his first administrative post at Yale. To be a master of a residential college was, to many professors, a romantic job. The scientists and the teachers in the professional schools particularly sought the post, for it involved them with the raw passions of underclassmen. It was also a job that required a good deal of care and feeding *in loco parentis*, and not every professor had the shepherd's patience. But the job did entail a free house in the college for the master, which was a considerable financial inducement for many modestly paid junior professors. Given the choice, Giamatti would have preferred to be master of Saybrook College, where he had been an honor student, but Ezra Stiles College was a worthy second choice. The college married the traditional with the contemporary. It is named for a president of Yale in colonial times, who had been a force for tolerance and progressivism in an era of religious and ethnic prejudice, and this, no doubt, appealed to Giamatti's sentimental side. Designed by Eero Saarinen with a sloping inner green and a sweeping vista to the tower of Graduate Studies, it was built in 1966. Open, breezy spaces with polished flagstone floors grace the elegant master's house.

For the first time, Giamatti became a public man. Though he had always been gregarious on campus and on the street, he had been exceedingly private about his family and his home. The home was for the family, and his friends, even close friends, had rarely been there. They consigned this keen sense of privacy to Italianness and dismissed it as a cultural peculiarity of Giamatti's upbringing. Thus, when the new master of Ezra Stiles gave his first cocktail party, it was a major event. Many were seeing the Giamattis as hosts for the first time.

To the students, he was open and engaging. He was far from a remote otherworldly Renaissance scholar. Not only did he know his baseball, but he knew his movies and popular television shows and singers such as Ray Charles and Aretha Franklin. He made a point to engage the "radical" SDS students in public discourse, where he publicly disagreed with their harsh tonic for America, disagreeing in clear and succinct and often withering repartee, a style that gained him the reputation in certain quarters as a hard-nosed conservative. This will to engagement got mixed reviews among the students, for he seemed all too clearly to be of the school that radical students were acting like children and should be treated as such.

Soon enough, the reality of living in proximity with boisterous and messy students who played loud music and lofted beer cans into the quadrangle at their late-night parties got on the Giamattis' nerves. Not only did they treasure their privacy and want a healthy, serene environment for their young children, but Professor Giamatti needed peace and quiet at night to read and write. Such hours now came only after midnight. The family was ready to move out after the first night. It would have to wait two years. The master put the best face on his grim situation that he could muster. Once, in a session with the parents of some students, a mother stood up indignantly and said, "I've just been to see my son's room, and it's a mess, and his roommates' rooms are a mess. The entryways are all terribly messy. Can you explain that to me?"

Giamatti puffed himself up, with the eighteenth-century formality of a Samuel Johnson, and announced, "Madame, your children are slobs." For a moment, there was stunned silence, then the parents broke into laughter and applause.

Giamatti's mastership was to be short and turbulent—and in the end, roundly unsuccessful. This would be considered a negative factor seven years later, when he became a candidate for the presidency of Yale.

Among the special offerings that Giamatti inaugurated during his two years at Ezra Stiles was a seminar in Sports and American Society. To gain the authority to make such a seemingly trivial pursuit into a substantive course, worthy of the Yale imprimatur, Giamatti had to make a case to the university that this was something more than basket weaving. The seminar proposed to study "the relationship between games and a society in which sports had become an obsession." Students were required to bring the knowledge and methods of other fields to this "study of man as a playing animal." To elevate and dignify the offering, Giamatti invited the distinguished sports columnist of the *New York Times*, Red Smith, to Ezra Stiles to be the pilgrim of the quest. Smith agreed to come, even though he had a visceral distaste for academics who overintellectualized sport and tried to glean profound lessons about American life from American games. Giamatti assuaged Smith's concern by arguing that the seminar would be, as much as anything, a writing course. For he had a genuine admiration for certain sportswriters, such as Smith, and for the political columnist of the *Times*, James Reston, who began his newspaper career as a publicist for the Cincinnati Reds and then wrote sports before he took on world wars and presidents.

"Sports is where one really learns to write," Giamatti proclaimed.

To this, Red Smith replied tartly. "There's nothing hard about writing. All you do is sit down at a typewriter, open a vein, and bleed."

Giamatti's passion for baseball was becoming known outside the parapets of Yale. In the winter of 1971, Erich Segal, the garrulous Classics professor at Yale who was basking in the astonishing commercial success of his novella, *Love Story*, invited Giamatti to an evening in New York with Tom Seaver and sportswriter Dick Schaap. During this period, Segal was drawn to sports figures, especially after quarterback Fran Tarkenton had told him a few weeks earlier about entering the Vikings locker room to find several 300-pound offensive linemen sitting on a bench, reading *Love Story* with tears rolling down their mountainous cheeks. (Tarkenton had made up the story.)

By his own account, the normally talkative Giamatti spent the evening in star-struck silence, partly, he would say, because he was the only person in the room whose name was a household word only in his own household. The professor observed the great pitcher of the Mets as if he were in the presence of a doge. Above all, Seaver's dignity impressed Giamatti. It was as if he had never observed such a special aura before.

Much of Giamatti's admiration lay in symbolic thinking. To

Giamatti, Seaver was an icon who stood for much more than 200 strikeouts a year or the miracle of 1969 or an ERA of 1.76, which Giamatti compared to having an IQ of 175. "Tom Terrific" did not merely excel in his sport—he embodied it; he was gentry. This romantic notion of the sport existed in Giamatti's imagination and his class consciousness.

Moreover, Seaver was, to Giamatti, a hero in a time of anti-heroes. The pitcher's heroism lay in his contrast to the political activists of Seaver's own generation. Seaver's Fresno contrasted favorably to Mario Savio's Berkeley. His clean-cut performance at Shea Stadium was an antidote to the ragged, chaotic grandstanding of the student rioters such as Mark Rudd across town at Columbia University. Giamatti adored Seaver because he seemed cerebral in his work and excelled within civilized rules, both on and off the field. The pitcher represented the tradition of baseball, as Giamatti wanted to see it, but also the conservative tradition of America that appealed to Giamatti. Of Seaver, he wrote: "His was the respect for the rules that embodied baseball's craving for law; his was the personality, intensely competitive, basically decent, with the artisan's dignity that amidst the brave but feckless Mets, in a boom time of leisure soured by divisions and drugs, seemed to recall a cluster of virtues seemingly no longer valued."

It was an elitist sentiment. Had Pete Rose been the guest that evening instead of Tom Seaver, Giamatti's emotions would have been much different. Rose had played no less hard than Seaver during the previous summer, and he had played every day. How would Giamatti have viewed the way Rose held his fleshy hands? or arranged his polyester suit? or combed, if that's the word, his bristled hair? or fashioned his crude and ungrammatical sentences? What symbolism would Giamatti have found in Rose? What connection did Rose have to the rebellion of youth? Rose had experienced an off-season, batting only .304. Would Giamatti have connected that only to a slightly above-average intelligence, with an IQ of, say, 120? No, the elegant style and the traditionalism and even the mock-preppiness of Seaver moved Giamatti because he could connect these values to his own. With Rose, he would undoubtedly have retreated to the wry bemusement of the superior.

Upon Giamatti's departure from Ezra Stiles College, he broke with tradition. The practice of the college was for a departing master to have a portrait painted and hung in an honored place in the dining hall. Giamatti declined the honor. Instead, he donated a stuffed moosehead for his place on the wall. The trophy became more revered than a portrait ever could have been: the A. Bartlett Giamatti Memorial Moosehead.

Eight years later, when Giamatti was president of Yale, the attention of the nation was distracted by the World Series between the Phillies and the Kansas City Royals, and Yale students were tortured by midterm exams. The day after Pete Rose caught a deflected ball off Bob Boone's catcher's mitt, the A. Bartlett Giamatti moosehead was stolen from Ezra Stiles College.

A day later, President Giamatti received the ransom note, made up of letters cut from magazines and pasted together. It read:

> Dear Bart:
>   We have your moose. Cancel midterms or we'll EAT him.
>   The Moose Liberation Army

Giamatti's successor as master at Ezra Stiles College, the Classics professor, Heinrich von Staden, was not amused. He proclaimed that Stiles students were devastated. "What muses were to Theseus and Homer, the moose is to the Ezra Stiles College community. On humanitarian grounds, return it to its natural habitat. Do not mistake its stoic silence for a lack of suffering or a lack of indignation." Giamatti was even more indignant. He would not give in to "terrorist" demands, he proclaimed, nor to threats about eating the poor moose.

"Let them eat mousse," he said disdainfully.

As the master of Ezra Stiles, Giamatti had gained his first real visibility on the Yale scene. In 1974, he moved up a notch by taking over a program for visiting faculty, and in 1976, he became the director of the humanities division, which was a major post. In 1977, championed by Kingman Brewster, Giamatti became the first John Hay Whitney Professor of the Humanities.

The chair was endowed by the fabulous Jock Whitney, the millionaire philanthropist, former ambassador to London, and the publisher of the *New York Herald Tribune*, to whom sports were the natural accoutrement to the elegant style of the privileged class. His father, Payne Whitney, had been the stroke on the Yale crew in 1898 and a superior polo player. Jock Whitney followed both on the Yale crew and in becoming a member of national champion polo teams. At Greentree, his six-hundred-acre estate on Long Island—one of eight residences Whitney owned—there were three grass tennis courts, a nine-hole golf course, and the famous Greentree Stables, which had produced Twenty Grand, the Kentucky Derby winner in 1931.

Whitney's sister, Joan Payson, also had sporting interests: she brought the New York Mets into existence in 1962, aggrieved as she was by the loss to the West Coast of the Dodgers and the Giants four years earlier. When Jock and Joan inherited the Greentree Stables in 1944, they often gave their racehorses baseball names, including Shutout, Third League, and Hall of Fame.

It was undoubtedly in Kingman Brewster's mind that Giamatti was the perfect choice to be the first John Hay Whitney professor. Believing it was important that the benefactor personally like his first chaired professor, Brewster arranged a meeting between them. To Brewster, Giamatti represented the new spirit of youth and ethnic diversity that Brewster had tried so hard to foster at Yale, as well as the reverence for Yale traditions. Because of their mutual love of sport, Giamatti and Whitney were sure to hit it off, and they did. They also shared a love of the theatre. Whitney had backed about forty Broadway productions and had been the principal backer of the movie *Gone With the Wind*.

These various academic posts in the mid-1970s embroiled Giamatti ever more deeply in campus politics. He found that he loved the jealousies and conspiracies of the campus, when faculty members argued so vehemently and schemed so wickedly over matters esoteric and devoid of real weight. To Giamatti, campus politics was the only world he knew that brought into practice an aspect that interested him in medieval poetry: the uses of artifice and artificiality. His former student and later a reporter for the *New York Times*, Steven Weisman, would write later that Giamatti could ask in class about Milton or Spenser: "Why in these poems are the evil seducers always the best speakers and rhetoricians? Doesn't that mean that those with artistic skills know their skills can be used for both evil and good ends?"

To Hanna Gray, who had become provost of Yale during this period, Giamatti was an eager practitioner of what she wryly called "the academic way," namely, "a professional commitment to see complications, and if complications do not immediately appear, to create them." Gray taught a course on Machiavelli and the Renaissance with Giamatti and admired his imaginative technique of playing roles in the classroom and trying to understand ancient texts through this role playing. She also noticed that Giamatti had a "slightly conspiratorial view of the world," a view in which the players never said exactly what they meant and often expressed motives for their actions that were not the real motives. To Gray, Giamatti saw the world in gamelike terms.

In 1974, Giamatti had given a lecture on Machiavelli on a local television station in which he spoke of Machiavelli's view of politics as art. "Machiavelli," he said, "saw the political process in the same way as a poet sees the process of artistic creation." Machiavelli was "the poet of power," who drew "lessons about political life from the ancient historians he so loved." Giamatti was intent on dissuading his audience from the notion that Machiavelli was devious and treacherous. He portrayed his poet of power as "shrewd, warm, full of sly humor, with an extraordinary capacity for friendship, loyal to his patron and his employers, a fond father; scrupulously honest in his personal dealings and financial affairs—he never profited at all from his official positions." Was Giamatti describing Machiavelli or himself?

To his discomfort, this lecture would be remembered later. When he was asked about it, Giamatti was always sensitive about the way people imputed cunning to him on the basis of his love for Machiavelli. Did he resemble Machiavelli at all, he was often asked later.

"If I'm lucky," he replied unrepentantly.

Winning by whatever means were at hand, winning regardless of the cost, winning as the only end preoccupied Pete Rose every bit as much as Machiavelli. As he entered the 1975 season, Rose was piling up the individual honors, but the big victory, total team victory, still eluded him. The muscular Reds of 1970 and 1972 had lost in the World Series. With the acquisition of Joe Morgan, the team was less muscular—less lumbering, some would say—and was learning how to win without crunching the ball. Still, they lost to the Mets in the play-offs of 1973 and finished a disappointing second to the Dodgers in 1974.

With his subpar .284 average, 1974 was the off-season for Rose. Moreover, he had been put through the humiliation of being asked to take a 20 percent cut in his $160,000 salary. (He acquiesced to 5 percent.) A case could be made that his 1974 season had not been as bad as the Reds management was posturing. He led the league in doubles and on-base percentage, for example. The difference was that, for the first time, he had to make the case vocally and defensively, because the case was not compelling from its numbers. He talked openly about the law of averages catching up to him. "I'm thirty-two and I feel good," he said. "I've had some good years, and I think I have some good ones left." Not everyone was convinced.

Then came 1975, when the Machine meshed with the power of Roman conquest. The tribunes of Morgan, Rose, Bench, and Perez overshadowed the centurions of Foster, Geronimo, Dave Concepcion, and Ken Griffey. They worked so fluidly together that opposing teams watched them take batting practice in worshipful astonishment. The opposition could only fall back on the charge of arrogance, but Johnny Bench turned the phrase around. It was not arrogance but "inner conceit" that the Reds possessed. It was a confidence that in any given baseball situation the Reds could outperform any opponent. Forty-seven times that season they came from behind to win. They had won forty-four out of fifty games after Sparky Anderson switched Rose to third base to make room for George Foster in left field. At season's end, they had won the National League West by twenty games, and they sent Pittsburgh away in a three-game play-off as though they were not pirates but petty thieves.

The Cincinnati Reds were going for their second "honest" world championship. In 1940, they had beaten the Tigers fair and square in seven games. Before that, they "won" the Series of 1919, in which the infamous Chicago Black Sox threw the games in a fix.

The Reds entered the 1975 World Series against Giamatti's heart throb: the Boston Red Sox of Carl Yastrzemski and Carlton Fisk, Luis Tiant and Bill "Space Man" Lee. Lee was the entertainment: a blooper pitcher who was cast, in contrast to Tom Seaver, as a symbol of the Woodstock generation, and who did not share Giamatti's low opinion of Kurt Vonnegut, Jr. Indeed, the southpaw was given to quoting Vonnegut's line "In nonsense there is strength," to the utter befuddlement of nearly everyone who listened. That was when he was not talking about biting off someone's ear, or "Van-Goghing," him. The Red Sox also had Fred Lynn, the only rookie in baseball history ever to win the MVP Award, and an Italian kid from Detroit named Bernardo Carbo, whom, along with his constant companion, a stuffed gorilla, the Reds had cast away after the 1970 season, even though Carbo had been the National League Rookie of the Year. Giamatti once described Carbo as "erratic, quick, a shade too handsome, so laid back he is always, in his soul, stretched out in the tall grass, one arm under his head, watching the clouds and laughing." Despite the notable presence of Jim Rice and Cecil Cooper, some would later say that the Red Sox of 1975 was the last great "white" team of modern baseball.

"We're Sending the Big Red Machine Home in a Little Red Wagon" read a hopeful banner of the long-suffering Red Sox fans, who had not seen a World Series victory since Babe Ruth pitched them to one in 1918.

As the Series began, Rose defined his own special inner conceit:

he wanted to be remembered as the best switch-hitter who ever played the game.

"If someone came down from heaven and offered you the choice between winning the World Series or making the Hall of Fame, which would you choose?" he was asked.

"I'd plead with him, 'Can't I do both?' " Rose replied. "If he came from up there, he'd understand: I just love to play baseball. Play and win. We've won 114 games so far this year, so if you have fun winning, this is the funnest year of my life."

The 1975 Series remains the greatest Series of modern baseball. Perhaps in the twenty-first century, it will be rivaled in the imagination by the 1924 Series, which the Washington Senators won over the New York Giants in the twelfth inning of the seventh game, after the Giants catcher Hank Gowdy got his foot caught in his mask going after an easy fly ball and when the winning run scored on a bad bounce over the third baseman's head. The Big Train, Walter Johnson, the fourth Senator to pitch, got credit for the win. President Calvin Coolidge attended three out of the four games in Washington.

In 1975, Boston led in all seven games, only to lose the lead in five of them. Two games went into extra innings, and two others were decided in the ninth inning. Five were decided by one run. Moreover, a nor'easter caused three rainouts and extended the agony and the tension and the drama and the conflict and the beauty of the Classic.

For Rose, the best of times had terrible moments. Vividly, he remembered the days of pounding rain where at one point, the Reds, primed and in uniform, were trapped in their rain-drenched bus, after their driver got lost while searching for some place called Tufts University, where they were supposed to practice. It was difficult to concentrate under those conditions.

More vividly, Rose remembered the unlikely hero, Bernie Carbo, trotting past him at third base, having just hit a pinch-hit three-run homer in the eighth to tie the sixth game. Carbo shouted out to him, "Don't you wish you were that strong!" Pete replied, "Hell, this is the way baseball is supposed to be played!"

Later, Rose would claim that the Boston fans had just willed Carbo's homer into the seats, as if he were a disciple of that other "Dutchman," Immanuel Kant.

Rose's joy in the sheer beauty of the contest was evident when he came to bat in the tenth, turned to the Boston catcher, Carlton Fisk, and uttered perhaps his best-known line, "Some kind of game, ain't it?" Pudge grumbled back, "Yeah, some kind of game." Two innings later, Fisk won it with a homer off the screen inches from the foul pole in left field.

For every wistful Red Sox fan, the memory of Carbo and Fisk in the sixth game is frozen in glory. The vividness is akin to Pearl Harbor or the Kennedy assassination: they all remember just where they were at that crucial, fleeting zenith of Red Sox history. Bart Giamatti was no different. "Toni and I were home in bed on Central Avenue in New Haven, with the set on," he would recall. "It was after midnight, and our three kids were supposed to be asleep, but of course, they were outside, prowling around. Then they heard us yelling, and they came rushing in pretending they didn't know what was happening. We all ended up jumping up and down on the bed together."

For Rose, there was an even more glorious memory, because his individual effort came together with his team's triumph. His personal accomplishments peaked in the final game, when they were needed the most. In the sixth inning, with the Reds down by three runs, he singled, frustrated a double play with a take-out slide at second, and scored on Perez's subsequent two-run homer. At that moment on Central Avenue, no doubt, the Giamattis groaned. The following inning, Rose's single scored Griffey to tie the game; he would later consider it one of the most important hits of his career. In the eighth, he began the double play that erased the Red Sox's last baserunner. And in the ninth, he walked, before Joe Morgan got a blooper to drop into center to score Griffey for the winning run. Rose reached base on eleven of his last fifteen appearances at the plate. His Series average was .370 (10 for 27), and he was selected as the Series MVP.

"I can't describe the feeling of being world champion for the first time," he would say years later. "What people don't realize, with all these records I've had, is that my biggest ups and downs came in play-offs and World Series. And that was the Series where I was lucky enough to be MVP, for my home city. It's quite a feeling and stays with you a long time."

In that memorable Series, there had even been a touch of cleansing for the curse of 1973. In the sixth inning of the final game, Rose was "stomping around the dugout like a whiffling Che Guevara," as *Boston Globe* reporter Pete Gammons put it, screaming and exhorting his teammates, before he stepped to the plate and singled. An out later, Johnny Bench sent Bill Lee's sinker on the ground toward second in what appeared to be a routine double play to end the inning. This time, the shortstop sweeping across the bag was not Bud Harrelson but Denny Doyle, and Rose bore down on him, untroubled by past vilifications. He leapt at second base, making sure that the Boston shortstop saw his airborne hulk flying high from ten feet away. Doyle threw the ball high over his first baseman's head. Bench took second on the error. The table was set for the carnivorous Tony Perez.

"Somebody's gotta win and somebody's gotta lose," Rose said once. "I believe in letting the other guy lose."

If Machiavelli and Pete Rose were obsessed with winning, Bart Giamatti, especially after the 1975 World Series, was more and more preoccupied with losing. What was it about the Boston Red Sox that broke one's heart so? They had had every chance to win that classic series, despite that Hun from Cincinnati. In the great sixth game, which was to Giamatti the best game in fifty years, his team could have won it in the ninth, when they loaded the bases. But they threw away the opportunity. Then, in the eleventh inning, as if to toy with their fans' frazzled emotions, they barely averted disaster when Dwight Evans leapt over the wall in right field and plucked Morgan's long drive out of the seats and turned it into a double play. In the final game, they let their last three-run lead slip away when Rose got hot.

Giamatti turned to his Elizabethan poet for comfort and found him wanting. Edmund Spenser, Giamatti said, was a melancholy man who thought he knew it all. "He did not. He had never loved the Red Sox. While he knew of Eden and its loss, he knew nothing of the fall in Fenway. It is not enough to think, as he did, that only once were we to go east, out into the land of Nod. Such a passage occurs without end. It happens every summer, with a poignancy that knows no bounds, in that angular, intimate, ageless green space in Boston. There, whenever autumn comes, comes the fall again."

During this period of near wins and inevitable losses for his Red Sox, Giamatti confessed that the pace of his summers was more and more bound up with baseball. He was counting on the game's "deep patterns" to set the order of his day. He tried to write about the Renaissance, but the work was fitful and "camouflage."

"The real activity was done with the radio," he said. With the broadcast on, he played the game "in the only place it would last: the enclosed, green field of the mind." Never mind that in the end the Red Sox, sometimes called the Team of Destiny, was destined to lose. Giamatti learned to cope, with "acquiescence and avoidance, and a sense that an old law had asserted again its iron hand."

These sentiments would carry forward to the last day of the 1976 season, when the Red Sox had to win and the Yankees had to lose for the Sox to make the play-offs. Of course, the Sox lost. "One pitch, a fly to center and it stopped," Giamatti wrote at the time. "Summer died in New England and like rain sliding off a roof, the crowd slipped out of Fenway, quickly, with only a steady murmur of concern for the drive ahead remaining in the roar. Mutability turned the seasons and translated hope to memory."

In his unique way, Giamatti had latched onto Edmund Spenser's Dame Mutability and had transported her into the ball park. She was the goddess who represented the power of change and held sway over all things below the moon, including night games. She knew that "nothing is sure that grows on earthly ground," even the inevitability of defeat. Dame Mutability never lost. She was there in the stands every autumn in Fenway Park. She ended the season, but perhaps she would be more whimsical next year, kinder to Boston while she frowned on New York and Cincinnati. In the meantime, Giamatti took to heart the first lines of Spenser's *Mutability Cantos:*

> What man that sees the ever-whirling wheele
> Of Change, the which all mortall things doth sway,
> But that therby doth find, and plainly feele,
> Mutability in them doth play
> Her cruell sports, to many mens decay?

The tragic quality of the Red Sox suited Giamatti's sensibility, both the operatic Italian side of it and the austere, puritan side. He was more interested in illusion than in reality. If he had grown up in Sardinia, Ohio, instead of South Hadley, it's doubtful that the constant winning of the Cincinnati Reds in 1975–76 would have engaged his imagination as much as the near winning of the Red Sox. Hope and bittersweet memory and illusion and denial are more interesting than outright triumph to the poet, just as change is more interesting than sameness. His mood reflected what the novelist John Cheever would say about the Sox two years later: "All literary men are Boston Red Sox fans. To be a Yankee fan in literary society is to endanger your life."

As the tragic Red Sox fled for their homes in 1976, the perennial powerhouses, the Reds and the Yankees, gathered once again for the fall classic. This would be the first Series to employ the designated hitter, an innovation Giamatti detested because he felt it impoverished the mental side of the game. For the rest of the nation, it would be the most forgettable of World Series. The Reds, now the Big *Mean* Red Machine, had won 102 games during the regular season, had the highest team batting average in the majors, with five hitters over .300, had hit 141 homers as a team, had averaged more than five runs a game, and had committed the fewest errors in the major leagues. They also had Joe Morgan, the National League MVP for the second consecutive year. To top it all off, in a three-game play-off they had swept the Phillies. In their Series lineup, Rose would lead off with his season average of .323, and Geronimo would bat ninth with his season average of .307.

Before the first game, a provincial New York reporter sidled up to Rose, confident in his knowledge that the last time the Reds and Yankees had faced each other, in the World Series of 1939, the Yankees swept the Reds in four games.

"Does the Yankee legend bother you?" the reporter asked.

Rose might have replied with history. This Yankee team was the first to play in a World Series since 1964 and was but a mere shadow of the great Yankee teams of the 1950s. "No," Rose replied instead, "because we have a legend here in Cincinnati. Does it worry them?"

Casey Stengel had handled the question differently in 1958, when he testified before a Senate anti-trust subcommittee.

"I want to know whether you intend to keep on monopolizing the world's championship in New York City?" he was asked by a midwestern Senator.

"Well, I will tell you. I got a little concerned yesterday in the first three innings when I saw the three players I had gotten rid of, and I said when I lost nine what am I going to do and when I had a couple of my players. I thought so great of that it did not do so good up the sixth inning I was more confused, but I finally had to go and call on a young man in Baltimore that we don't own and the Yankees don't own him, and he is doing pretty good, and I would actually have to tell you that I think we are more the Greta Garbo type now from success. . . .

"We are being hated, I mean, from the ownership and all, we are being hated. Every sport that gets too great or one individual—but if we made 27 cents and it pays to have a winner at home, why wouldn't you have a good winner in your own park if you were an owner? That is the result of baseball. An owner gets most of the money at home, and it is up to him and his staff to do better or they ought to be discharged."

Mickey Mantle had then been brought forward and asked for his opinion. "My views are just about the same as Casey's," he replied.

Rose was at the zenith of his career. He had just tied Ty Cobb's record for the most two-hundred-hit seasons (nine) and had done it in fourteen seasons, compared to Cobb's twenty-three. In May, he had received the Roberto Clemente Award, given annually to the player who best exemplified the game of baseball on and off the field. In presenting the award in Cincinnati, Baseball Commissioner Bowie Kuhn had said, "Fans in Cincinnati and throughout the country have been captivated by the way Pete Rose plays baseball. This enthusiasm is obvious off the field as well, as evidenced by his willingness to participate in any number of activities which benefit his community."

The Yankees and Bowie Kuhn and Pete Rose went on to have a rotten Series in 1976. The Reds swept in four games, becoming the first team in baseball history to have seven straight victories in post-season play and the first team since the 1922 New York Giants to win back-to-back World Series. Forgettable as the play on the field was for the rest of the country, the image of Bowie Kuhn was memorable. He had acquiesced to the network television demand for night games in prime time. Twice the temperature dipped below freezing, and there sat the commissioner, pretending it was summer, coatless and hatless, his long johns (which baseball writers later said should go into the Hall of Fame) hidden from view, while the fans suffered.

For his part, Rose hit only .188 in the Series. Dame Mutability had something grander in mind, however, than the mere decay of Pete Rose. Free agency went into effect that winter.

In mid-1976, the search for a new president of Yale University began. It had been clear for some time that if Jimmy Carter were elected, he would choose the consummate Yale man, Cyrus Vance, to be his secretary of state, and Vance, in turn, would tap another accomplished Yale man, Kingman Brewster, Jr., to become the United States ambassador to Great Britain. With his intelligence and savoir faire, Brewster was, of course, perfect for the Court of St. James's, as was his graceful wife, Mary Louise. This scenario played itself out as expected, and in May 1977, Brewster resigned. (In his sendoff, his friends gave him a silver pillbox to house his aspirins.)

Hanna Holborn Gray, the provost of Yale and daughter of a Yale faculty member, was appointed to be acting president while the official search got under way for the permanent president. The small search committee was headed by former Assistant Secretary of State William Bundy, and it went into action almost immediately. Composed exclusively of Yale trustees and Yale Corporation members, the committee was untainted by any of the "populist" elements, such as a token student or faculty member, that had complicated a recent search at Brown University.

Bundy saw the selection process as a combination of Wimbledon and primary politics. In the first "challenge round," some two hundred members of the Yale faculty were interviewed, as well as a number of promising outsiders. Hanna Gray remained the leading candidate after the "early spring returns."

By then, Bart Giamatti's name had emerged on the list of serious candidates. The thought that he was presidential timber had already entered his mind. Bowdoin College in Maine, which his son Marcus attended, had put his name into consideration that year for its presidency. But after a look, Giamatti withdrew. Bowdoin's location was too remote, its library too meager for serious scholarship, and its name did not have the magic of Yale.

For the Yale presidency, however, Giamatti's name was by no means near the top of the list. He was seen as brilliant, charismatic, wonderfully dedicated to Yale, but at thirty-eight, he was probably too young. With another five years of "seasoning," he might be a serious contender. Moreover, he was seen as a gadfly. His mastership at Ezra Stiles had been a disappointment; he had no grounding in economics; and his credits as a college administrator were minimal.

These last two points were extremely important because Yale was in deep financial trouble. Kingman Brewster had made it into a great, modern university. With ambitious building and a radical improvement in the graduate school, with coeducation and a sensitivity to ethnic concerns, not to mention the political adeptness it had shown during the "troubles" of 1969–70, Brewster's administration had been an historic one. The price was fiscal unsoundness. Far too high a percentage of the endowment was being spent on improvements, and the endowment was dwindling. During the past decade of Brewster's stewardship, Yale had developed a $16 million deficit in operating costs. In 1976 alone it had a deficit of $6.6 million.

As Bundy saw it, Yale was simply not running a tight ship. It needed a strong, proven administrator, preferably an economist who knew his spread sheets and could balance his budgets. The university faced a difficult period of consolidation, and even contraction. For the new president, it would be an office full of frustration and resentment. The times called for a manager, not a visionary. A Renaissance scholar did not seem to fit either category.

The search committee dreamed a little at first. A promising prospect was a Canadian who headed the University of Toronto, and he checked out wonderfully on all the criteria. The search committee started to get excited with the delusion that this was not going to be so difficult after all. As feelers went out, however, it was learned that the candidate had ambitions not for Yale, but to be prime minister of Canada. He was preparing to run in a by-election in a French-speaking district. After his name disappeared from the search, this academic-cum-candidate did run in the by-election and was defeated. As far as Yale was concerned, he was never heard from again.

Horace Taft, the fourth son of the Ohio senator and a descendant of William Howard Taft, was another strong candidate. A physics professor who had been a successful master and dean, he was a live wire whose only liability was an eccentric wife. (Whether wives could be considered as part of the selection process became a point of debate among the trustees, with a female member of the search committee protesting at this apparent sexism. The subject immediately became a silent, unspoken factor.)

The most entertaining dream of the search was to have the thirty-eighth president of the United States become the eighteenth president of Yale. (William Howard Taft provided the precedent for a post-presidential return to Yale. Indeed, in the historic, oak-paneled Yale Corporation room, where the search committee held its deliberations, there was even a William Howard Taft chair, enormous enough to accommodate the prodigious contours of President Taft's posterior.) Gerald Ford had gone to Yale Law School, where he was remembered with respect and affection. He had taken time to make his mark: his law school career lasted five years rather than three. The extra two years were necessary because Ford moonlighted as the boxing and assistant football coach.

During the summer of 1977, while other faculty members drifted away to libraries and summer retreats, Giamatti helped his cause. He served on a Priorities Committee that took a hard look at the precarious condition of Yale's finances and sought to identify areas of waste and expendable fat. The committee came back with the austere recommendation that spending on the endowment should be slashed from 7 percent to 4½ percent. Giamatti comported himself effectively and impressively on the committee as a tough-minded voice for draconian measures. Because the committee existed for the benefit of the next Yale president, his stock for the post rose.

Throughout the summer, Giamatti played the role of the reluctant candidate. People often asked him about the fact that he was under consideration for the Yale presidency. He replied in August with a famous remark, "The only job I've ever wanted was to be president of the American League."

That was not the only thought he had about baseball during this heady summer of 1977. In June, the priorities of the New York Mets shoved aside the priorities of Yale University. On June 15, the Mets stunned the baseball world by trading Giamatti's prince, Tom Seaver, to Cincinnati. There was a tearful scene at Shea Stadium, as Tom and Nancy bade farewell to the franchise he had, in a real sense, created. In an article he wrote in the days that followed, Giamatti compared this melodramatic scene in the "graceless precincts" of Shea Stadium to a fresco in the Brancacci Chapel in Florence, *The Expulsion of Adam and Eve*. Painted by a young innovator called Masaccio and filled with passion, the fresco depicts two nude figures departing the Garden of Eden, Adam seized with shame and remorse, Eve with howling grief. When *Harper's* magazine published the article, its display contained only the pictures of the tearful Seavers and not the Masaccio nudes, so it is doubtful that most of the magazine's readers got the connection. But they could not miss Giamatti's feeling about the symbolism of Tom Seaver in the age of rebellion. Here was a case where a baseball owner had put high salary demands above the importance of an irreplaceable emblem of New York and of baseball. Giamatti referred to a banner on a railing at Shea the day after the Seavers left: I WAS A BELIEVER, BUT NOW WE'VE LOST SEAVER.

"I construe that text to mean, not that the author has lost faith in Seaver," Giamatti wrote, "but that the author has lost faith in the Mets' ability to understand a simple crucial fact: that among all the men who play baseball, there is, only occasionally, a man of such qualities of heart and mind and body that he transcends even the great and glorious game, and that such a man is to be cherished, not sold." Some in Cincinnati would feel the same way two years later, when Pete Rose was sold away from the franchise he embodied, but Bart Giamatti did not write about that.

With the good reviews about Giamatti's performance on the Priorities Committee during the summer of 1977, the search committee removed his relative youth as a disqualification. Ironically, while he became a top contender, he turned again to the world of sports. On September 29, he attended a championship fight between Muhammad Ali and Ernie Shavers. If Tom Seaver appealed to the intellectual and the poet and the political conservative in Giamatti, Ali appealed to the intellectual and poet and actor in him. To the extent that Giamatti himself was engaged in a kind of title fight of his own, his tension led to the best piece of sports writing he ever produced.

In this *Harper's* article, Giamatti returned to his refrain of the importance of excellence within the rules. In Ali's theatricality and his psychological baiting of his opponent, Giamatti saw a lesson he might apply to his own fight. "For Muhammad Ali, sport is work conceived as theatre," he wrote. "Ali has known from the beginning what every good athlete learns: make him play your game, fight your fight, and you will beat him every time. But Ali has also learned a lesson kept from most athletes precisely by the pleasure of their work . . . a pleasure in work [which is] exhilarating to one who has the art born in him, the art of filling a scene. And the subtler lesson is that while you can only beat him if he fights your fight, you can destroy him if he acts in your play."

Giamatti was adapting these lessons about the tactics of the fight to his own situation. "[Ali's] fear of being marginal accounts for the savagery of his desire to get in, to land the first blow, and for the outlandish intensity of his acting center stage, before the bell has ever rung or the lights have dimmed." He saw Ali's fury as a black man as an advantage. Implied was his own fight for recognition as an Italian American. "Ali cannot stop until he has fought down the need, compounded of fear and fury, to act out completely what, in his view, it is to be black in America," he wrote. "To be always living at the margin, on the edge, in a position where, despite the pain of your work and the beauty of your play, a man may announce with superb casualness at any given moment that you have been counted out."

In the early fall, it seemed likely that Giamatti would be counted out for the Yale presidency with that same superb casualness. He seemed to know it, even as he wrote about Ali, as if Ali was code for himself. When the search narrowed its list, Giamatti made Bundy's semifinals of ten, but he was eliminated for the finals. In December, the committee invited five finalists to Washington for the final interview. Bart Giamatti did not get an invitation.

Even before the Washington interviews, the leading contender was Henry Rosovsky, the Dean of Arts and Sciences, not of Yale but of Harvard. A Jew born in Gdansk, Rosovsky was a man of power and of wit. An economist by training, his administrative experience was substantial and replete with achievement. He was his most comfortable in the back rooms of academic politics, and he was quite satisfied to be known around Harvard Yard by fifty significant professors as the real power at Harvard. Already, he had turned down the presidency of MIT and of the University of Chicago.

In his four years as dean, Rosovsky had concentrated on budgetary problems. He had started with a sizable deficit and had brought the figures into balance. Just as important, he had faced the legacy of the 1960s, of which the Harvard faculty was bitterly and passionately split along political lines between conservative and liberal caucuses.

Rosovsky was, however, best known outside Harvard Square as the force behind the definition of a "core curriculum" for Harvard. This was an attempt to redress the drift of the 1960s toward freewheeling choice for students and to bring undergraduate education back to a structured examination of critical thinking, rooted in Western thought. Harvard's core curriculum was to be a major educational initiative, and it was much anticipated by the entire world of American higher education.

Besides Rosovsky, Hanna Holborn Gray remained in contention, but her stock had fallen a bit since the spring. Her Yale roots were as deep as Giamatti's. Her father, Hajo Holborn, had been one of the great refugee scholars to flee Nazi Germany, and he had been installed in the Berlin chair at Yale, which was endowed by the Carnegie Foundation. She had followed with solid academic distinction of her own as a Renaissance historian. But upon examination, it seemed that she had some difficulties with budgets as the Yale provost, and a few trustees began to question how effective she would be as an advocate for Yale, for she was not an especially charismatic speaker. Unspoken but important in the background lay the question of whether Yale was ready for a woman president.

The university was clearly ready for a Jew, however. Henry Rosovsky was not an orthodox "observant" Jew—in the sense, as he would say himself, that he believed no shibboleth prevented him from giving a speech on Saturday—but his religion and his heritage were an important part of his life. Married to an Israeli, he had been active in Jewish organizations and causes all his life, including serving as chairman of the board for the American Jewish Congress. That Yale—long considered the bastion of the American WASP—might choose a Jew as president had been unthinkable only a few years before. Moreover, if Rosovsky were chosen, he would become the first Jew in history to head an Ivy League college.

Within the search committee, this powerful notion, far from something to shy away from, attracted. The mere consideration of Rosovsky showed how far Yale had come. Ironically, Kingman Brewster, the very epitome of the Episcopalian WASP, was given considerable credit for creating the environment in which this break with tradition was possible.

But Rosovsky had his doubts. His tie was to Yale's archrival, and he knew full well that moving from Harvard to Yale was nothing like moving from General Motors to Ford. The culture of an Ivy League college was important because each institution tried to distinguish its product from the others. Moreover, he was not a man who needed the limelight. With these hesitations, he was on the verge of declining to go for his interview, until his wife protested that it would be the height of discourtesy not to respond to such a distinguished invitation. With strong reservations, he went.

The trustees worried about the secrecy of their process, so the Metropolitan Club in Washington was suggested as a secure safe house for their final interviews. But women had not yet penetrated this fortress of the exclusive Washington establishment, and Maxine Singer, the distinguished biochemist who was on the Search Committee, objected to this lair of male chauvinists. So the committee chose a different den: her husband's law firm in the Watergate complex. There, Henry Rosovsky was immediately noticed in the waiting room by a female *Washington Post* reporter who was covering the search and whom William Bundy had mistaken for a secretary.

When the news of Rosovsky's consideration broke, Bart Giamatti was devastated. The nearer he had gotten to power, the more attractive it had become to him. At this stage, he desperately wanted the job. When he heard the news, Giamatti was with his friend Peter Brooks, who also had been interviewed for the presidency. Giamatti sat glumly in Brooks's car outside their children's prep school and tried to absorb the news. He was as disconsolate as Brooks had ever seen him. Giamatti knew now that he had finished twelfth on the list.

Moreover, he railed bitterly against Rosovsky. How could Yale tap a Harvard man as its president, especially this Rosovsky, whose core curriculum would be so alien to the spirit of Yale College? To Giamatti, the Yale curriculum might be somewhat "formless," but choice was its essence. It was part of the Yale ethic that students should not only make the choices themselves but learn to live with the consequences of those choices. (Ironically, when Harvard's core curriculum was finally promulgated, it was criticized vociferously for having too much choice.)

In the week of December 7, the trustees flew to Boston and formally offered the job to Rosovsky. He asked for a few days to ponder the offer. They asked, in turn, that he maintain the strictest secrecy. The latter was an idle hope, for the Ivy League was following the process with avid interest. U.S. Secretary of State Cyrus Vance had asked that he be kept abreast of developments as he pursued shuttle diplomacy in the Middle East. To arrange these communications, the news had to pass through the State Department, which was riddled with fascinated Yale and Harvard men. Moreover, President Derek Bok and a few other top Harvard officials were consulted about the offer. They did not want to lose Rosovsky, especially not at this critical stage of the curriculum reform. Their tongues flapped more freely than Yale might have liked, but then they did not have Yale's interest foremost in their minds.

The most touching deliberations came between Rosovsky and his wife. She wanted him to take the job and become the first Jew to head an Ivy League college. "I thought we were beyond that," he replied tartly. "I don't have to do something any more just because I am a Jew."

He had no tie to Yale, and he did not want to desert his colleagues who had worked with him so tirelessly on the core curriculum. Moreover, he was fifty years of age. If he took the job, he would have to do it until he retired. In the end, he refused the post.

After his official refusal, he disappeared for a few days and left his disappointed wife to field the phone calls. Among those who called was William Beinecke, the millionaire businessman and heir to the S & H Green Stamps Fortune, who had been a prodigious benefactor for Yale, and who was on the search committee.

"I'm going to talk him out of it, because I'm not used to being told no," Beinecke said to Mrs. Rosovsky in a courteous but firm way. "He owes it to his humble roots to do this." When Rosovsky was told of the comment, he was reminded of a remark of Disraeli's: When your ancestors were painted blue, mine were the princes of the earth.

To the profound embarrassment of the Yale community, and to the search committee in particular, Rosovsky's refusal was leaked to the press. Instantly, the Harvard dean was villainized far and wide, and he would stay a villain to some Yalies for many years to come. It was widely believed that Rosovsky had led the search committee down the garden path. That a Harvard man had done such a thing to Yale made the refusal especially bitter.

If Yale was embarrassed, Rosovsky himself was no less so. It had been a difficult time for him too. He knew what the search committee had gone through to choose him. Moreover, he hated the reverse pride that Harvard took in his decision, boasting that a mere deanship at Harvard was more important than the presidency of Yale.

While the search committee regrouped, the Yale community exerted considerable pressure on the committee to turn back to the Yale family. Bart Giamatti was the instant beneficiary. Ever since the previous spring, his name had been kept alive by two younger trustees, Strobe Talbott (Yale '68) who was a *Time* magazine reporter and had been a student of Giamatti's, and Lance Liebman, a Harvard Law professor, who had been two years behind Giamatti at Saybrook College. In the wake of the Rosovsky disaster, they pressed their advantage.

Several days after Rosovsky's refusal, Giamatti was formally scheduled for an interview in the vacant Yale president's mansion on Hillhouse Street. Talbott and Liebman paid a call on him the night before and helped to prepare him for the interview. Giamatti was intense and sardonic and wonderfully theatrical, all the while managing to suppress his eagerness for the job. To Talbott the next morning, he spoke of the job as if it were at least handled, if not damaged, goods. He even referred to himself, with evident displeasure, as the "rebound candidate."

When Giamatti came before the full search committee, however, he was magnificent. Seated in a high-backed nineteenth-century chair, he projected his total identification with Yale. They asked simple questions, and he gave them rolling, elegant paragraphs. His brilliance as a potential spokesman for the university was wonderfully on display. Here was a candidate who could charm the crustiest (and most tight-fisted) of Yale alumni around the country. His wit and his irreverence and his passion stood out. One unique trustee, the Right Reverend Paul Moore, the Episcopal Bishop of New York, assumed, no doubt from the surname, that Giamatti was a Catholic and would feel uncomfortable in the low-church chapel of Yale. The Bartlett in Giamatti discarded the problem with a wave of the hand. He made light of his Congregational roots in South Hadley.

And he shocked them. They were not to think, if he were offered the job and if he accepted, that he would be a long-term president. His love for scholarship was great, he professed, but he was unwilling to devote the rest of his life to university administration. They should not assume that he would stay as long as Kingman Brewster (fourteen years), he announced boldly. Indeed, they would be lucky if he stayed eight years. This reluctance and brassiness made him all the more attractive.

Moreover, Giamatti asserted, with all due respect, that he was not the type of person they wanted at all. "I have no interest in being a butcher," he said. Giamatti was talking about slashing budgets, but his remark meant more, and it was disarming. Still in the mind of the search committee was the advice of Kingman Brewster: find a scholar who understands education and whom the faculty respects and let him hire the "moneychangers" who understand balance sheets and can slash budgets.

The committee chose him overwhelmingly. When he was informed of the decision, Giamatti asked for twenty-four hours to think over the offer. Inevitably, the likelihood of his acceptance leaked to the *New York Times*.

The following morning, naked in the steam room at the Army-Navy Club in Washington, his old Scroll and Key buddy Steve Umin read the item and rushed excitedly to the phone. He had thought the idea of a Giamatti presidency was dead. Toni Giamatti answered. The offer was genuine, she told Umin, but "You better talk to him, because I don't know if he'll accept it." When Giamatti came on, Umin was effusive, recalling that he had once suggested the idea of Bart being president of Yale when they were undergraduates.

"You must do it," Umin exclaimed excitedly.

"But I want to be a Renaissance scholar," Giamatti replied curtly. His ambivalence was evident. "If I take this, I know I'll never go back to scholarship."

By afternoon, all doubt was swept away, and he had a few demands. One was nonnegotiable: he would not consider the job unless cable television were installed in the president's house, so he could receive his full complement of baseball games.

The announcement was major news around the country. Giamatti became a national celebrity overnight. He gave Edward Fiske, the education writer for the *New York Times*, a light-hearted interview. Giamatti's love for the Red Sox came up early.

"The origin of my fascination with sports is the whole sense of play which is in both sports and literature—the sense of fiction, the sense of the game, of the projection of the mind as well as the body," he said.

What about his remark about wanting only to be the president of the American League, Fiske wanted to know. Was the presidency of Yale still his second choice?

"I wouldn't say second choice," Giamatti replied. "I said that about the American League about four months ago and figured I would sit back and see if there was any movement. The baseball meetings came and went, and the big trades took place and nothing happened. There were no phone calls from the commissioner. Then I got this extraordinarily gracious call from the Yale Corporation. So I thought: Well, you do what you have to do."

Wasn't it true that he admired Machiavelli?

"I admire Machiavelli because he told the truth, at least the truth as he saw it," Giamatti replied. "But I certainly don't see him as a role model."

"Your preparation for the Yale presidency will not include rereading *The Prince*?" Fiske needled.

"I don't know that I would make that promise," Giamatti responded.

"Some time ago, you suggested that Yale was waiting for someone to come in on a white horse and solve its financial and other problems," Fiske said. "Do you have a white horse?"

"No." Giamatti smiled. "I have a yellow Volkswagen."

A busy few days stretched before him. He was in rehearsal for the role as Drosselmeyer in the Connecticut Ballet's production of *The Nutcracker*.

· 6 ·

Superstars

IN HIS ROOKIE YEAR, Pete Rose had lived the enviable existence of a high-spirited, unmarried, twenty-two-year-old baseball star, before whom the treats of celebrity were spread like some medieval banquet. He had no responsibility, and some money upon which he could indulge his taste for fast cars and fast women. His attitude toward the opposite sex was vintage Cro-Magnon. There were no qualms about displaying his appetites with breathtaking vulgarity. For a time after he was out of high school and in the minor leagues, his steady girlfriend was a fourteen-year-old with a sensational body, a fact that occasioned considerable gossip and not a small amount of envy at Western Hills High School. In his first year in the majors, he counted among his exploits an incident in Newport, the seedy sin city across the river from straitlaced Cincinnati, in which he displayed his bare crupper out the back window of a friend's car. The Reds' front office frowned upon this moonlight spectacle and hushed it up, but took no harsh action. In Pete Rose, all significant things were elemental.

Besides this unsurprising stunt, Rose had continued to pursue his favorite pastime of following the horses, which he considered to be superior athletes. He went frequently to the racetrack with his father or with his mates. One such occasion proved to be particularly lucky. Peering through binoculars at River Downs, his eyes came upon a fetching brunette in a short blue skirt with a revealing V neck and with her foot on the rail.

"Who's got the lead?" one of his friends nudged.

"I ain't got time for that," replied the rookie. "I got something better in the binoculars."

She was Karolyn Ann Engelhardt, a bookkeeper and ebullient Catholic girl, and an avid sports fan. Her father was a German carpenter, and her mother was a vaudeville singer. Karolyn herself had been "Miss Popularity" in her high school class. Every bit as earthy and hot-tempered as Rose, she was, nevertheless, principled about marriage and determined to stay within the rules of her upbringing. By Karolyn's account, his marriage proposal came in anger after she had resisted his advances yet another time. "That's it," he said in a huff. "Either we get married right now, or we forget it."

The blessed event took place on January 24, 1964. Immediately afterward, before the wedding reception, the newlyweds rushed to a dinner of Cincinnati baseball writers, where Rose was prevailed upon to speak. "I'm going for more doubles next year," he told them, now that he was no longer single. Then it was on to the reception, with 1,200 people in a fieldhouse. The cost of the party broke them, and they sold their gifts so the bride could accompany him to spring training.

Of Pete's marriage to Karolyn, his own mother-in-law, with the handy stage name of Pearl, was to say, "If there's such a thing as a match made in heaven, this is it. No one else could stand either one of them." Pistol that she was, Karolyn endeared herself instantly to the Reds organization and became part of the Riverfront entertainment. As Rose's fame grew, she was put forward as the perfect baseball player's wife: loyal, subservient, voluptuous. Behind home plate during home games, she was a booster with an ear-splitting whistle that she produced by putting her fingers between her teeth. She did not need to whistle to get attention, however. Just as her husband ascribed his durability to the fact that he took good care of his body, so did Karolyn, in the early years, take care of hers. A diminutive but compact 5 feet, 2 inches, she had tremendous breasts that were frequently described as heaving. These she displayed in tight-fitting sweaters or T-shirts with off-color slogans, and complemented the effect with equally tight fitting miniskirts, massive beehive hairdos (and wigs), huge dangling earrings, and a raspy-voiced barmaid's charm. This presentation inspired a good-natured Houston fan once to call out to Rose in left field:

"Hey, Rose, your wife's sure got some big tits!"

Soon enough, her celebrity grew with his in Cincinnati. So alluring was she to ballpark cameramen that in due course they had to be instructed not to focus on her so much since it disheartened the wives who were less well endowed. She was recruited by WNOP, a small radio station in Newport, Kentucky, to do a thrice-weekly radio spot, and she began to fancy herself as a straight-talking female version of Howard Cosell. With her inside track, she could sweeten up the toughest of interviewees, such as Johnny Bench, who taught her the fine art of spitting tobacco juice and how to chew bubble gum and tobacco at the same time.

Karolyn stories became legion: how she had been transported by the maracas music at the beginning of a ball game in Venezuela in 1964 and began dancing, only to find out it was the Venezuelan national anthem; how she dressed at their famous Halloween parties, once as a roller derby queen, another time as a werewolf, Frankenstein and a duck, all in one outfit; how Joe Garagiola had asked her once on a TV show if she had any good luck charms and she began to strip off her blouse slowly, down to a T-shirt that said "Pete Rose 14," while Garagiola nearly fainted; how on long nights during spring training, she loved to do jigsaw puzzles that slowly revealed the image either of her husband or of some other X-rated hulk. Karolyn became immortal in Cincinnati after she informed her listeners about an upcoming hockey game by saying, "Puck-off time is eight P.M." Less well known is the time she agreed to referee a wrestling match between the Sheik and Bobo Brazil and came home with her sweat suit splattered with blood. It was their blood, not hers, but only because she had ducked just in time as Bobo threw a chair at the Sheik. Karolyn had had a wonderful time.

In 1965, the Roses' firstborn, a daughter named Fawn, arrived; five years later, a son, Pete II, followed. Amid the wild and bizarre notoriety that came from dirt and blood and grit, Karolyn Rose presided over the domestic life of the family and strove for a kind of tranquility. To all appearances, she adored the celebrity and the riches, especially the riches. "I do like diamonds," she said once. "I wear them with blue jeans. I say, what's the difference? If you've got them, you might as well wear them."

They lived in a spacious brick house in the upscale neighborhood on the bluff above the river. With her two children and their half-poodle dog, King Tut, Karolyn tooled around town in a yellow and burgundy Cadillac—license plate: 14–PR—whose use was provided free by a local car leasing company. Meanwhile, the real King Tut of the house went to work in a brown Stingray, which was provided free by another company. Later, Porsches and a Rolls-Royce became the preferred mode of transportation, and there was a nasty spat when Pete vetoed Karolyn's request to put a CB radio in the Rolls.

When Rose left on a road trip, he bade his wife farewell with a hearty "Hooray!" instead of saying good-bye, and she didn't seem to mind these absences because when he returned it was like a honeymoon, or so she said. When he was home, he was distinctly out of sorts. He applied a white glove standard to his wife's housekeeping, yet he himself lolled around the house, spending countless hours in front of their outsized television set, watching every conceivable sports event, sometimes three at once, as Karolyn dutifully brought the soda and chips. There was no pretense about this pleasure. "I'd even watch the Rhode Island Reds of the Chicken Shit League, if they were on TV," he readily confessed. When it was suggested that he mow the lawn or something equally domestic, he demurred, saying he might injure himself. Fear of injury, however, did not prevent him from washing his newest car every day and carefully painting the Firestone letters on its tires.

One day, when he was having trouble on the playing field, Karolyn provided sympathy: "I think you're crouching too much," she offered consolingly.

"How many home runs have you hit lately?" he snapped.

In 1974, Rose's eleventh year in the majors, Judy Klemesrud, a writer with a wry and salty view of the world, followed Rose around for a few weeks to capture the life of the superstar off the field. An attractive woman about Rose's age, she was a practiced observer of sexual mores in a changing America. The shenanigans of this quintessential male chauvinist amused more than threatened her. Indeed, Rose's reputation as a prehistoric archetype probably attracted her to the *Esquire* assignment. At the Rose home, Klemesrud took note of the proliferation of children's toys: a pool table, a pinball machine, a hockey machine, a bowling machine, and, in the bathroom, a life-size cardboard cutout of the superstar himself in dress uniform. She followed him around town, appreciating how he looked "awfully good" in his form-fitting clothes, noticing how he drove naturally with one hand on the wheel and the other hand on his crotch, how enthusiastic he was about a braless girl on the street, and how he joshed his hairdresser.

"You're married, aren't you?" Rose asked the coiffeur, noting her wedding ring. When she affirmed it, he wondered out loud if she messed around. Then he broke into his gap-toothed grin.

Klemesrud's portrait was of a narcissistic man-child who had never grown up and felt no need to do so, especially because the press continued to celebrate his childishness—it was as if the perfect professional baseball player was really a boy in a man's body. He was at the top of his game and that was all that mattered. He projected an extraordinary single-mindedness and evinced no vulnerability. Was it possible, Klemesrud wondered, that Pete Rose had no weakness whatever?

"Well, I'm not too good a base stealer," he began, missing the point, perhaps deliberately, "and I don't have the strongest arm in the world. . . . But I compensate for it by charging the ball fast and getting rid of it fast." He paused, and Klemesrud no doubt wondered whether he was speaking metaphorically or putting her on. "But, hell, those aren't weaknesses. I don't have no weaknesses."

While she preened her image of a hard doll and superwife, Karolyn Rose was left to raise her children alone. Her husband's disinterest in their daughter, Fawn, was profound. Even the girl's tomboy athletic ability embarrassed her father. Girls, at least his notion of girls, were not meant to be strong and athletic. On one rare occasion when he played baseball with her, he hit a pop fly into a tree above her. The ball bounced off a limb and slammed into Fawn's nose, causing the girl to cry. Her father said she was a sissy. Later, he found out that her nose was broken.

During her teenage years, Fawn had the misfortune to become overweight. This too embarrassed Rose and provided a further excuse for inattention. He was ashamed to take her out in public with him and told her that her appearance did not square with his image. Later, this childhood snubbing made Fawn deeply ambivalent toward her father. She loved him, she would say, but she did not respect him. Outspoken like all the Roses, she called him the worst father in the world, yet she would be there behind home plate with her mother, urging him on, and rummaging through the stadium trash between innings for additions to her beer can collection.

Toward his son, Petey, Rose's attitude was only slightly different. It was not that Petey embarrassed his father. There was simply no time for the boy. There were the showy moments of public relations, when the father would be photographed or filmed with the son, playing pepper or horsing around in the locker room or roughhousing at a children's party. But Pete Rose was too focused on his own career to become a real father. In 1976, there was a mild contretemps with Sparky Anderson about bringing the boy into the locker room. In that context, Rose was asked if he wasn't pressuring six-year-old Petey to be a ball player.

"Let's face it," Rose said, "because of all the travel and all the selling of the game that I do, I don't get to see my kid that much. He loves playing baseball, and he's real talented, so all I try to do is expose him. I'm not forcing him to do anything, 'less he wants to.

'Course it's gonna be tougher for him than most kids 'cause he's got me to follow."

Inevitably, all this wore thin on Karolyn. "When I married Pete, I was his third love," she would say later. "First there was baseball, second there was his car, and third there was me. That was okay because all I wanted to be was a good wife and mother. Then our daughter, Fawn, was born, and I was relegated to fourth place. Then our son, Petey, was born, and I was in fifth place. Fifth place was too low in the standings."

In fact, into the late 1970s, she knew she was lower in the standings than that. From the beginning of their relationship, she worried about baseball Annies. Even before their marriage, Karolyn called him on the road when she had not heard from him for a few days.

At her very first spring training, holed up in their traditional room at the King Arthur Motel in Tampa, Karolyn answered the phone, and a girl from Miami asked for Pete.

"This is the maid," Karolyn said. "He ain't here."

In Cincinnati, their telephone number was unlisted, but it still had to be changed regularly, given the volume of enterprising callers. The calls often came late at night, when Pete and Karolyn would be in bed, sipping soda and munching potato chips as they watched the late, late movie. On one such occasion, the phone rang and Karolyn answered.

"I love Pete Rose," the Annie cooed on the other end.

"Tell him yourself," Karolyn said and handed Pete the phone.

In March 1979, when the marriage was unraveling, Karolyn published a generally affectionate memoir—affectionate because they were as alike as two peas in a pod. Its original working title had been "Wife of a Switch-hitter," which hinted that she would provide at least a glimpse at the seams of the superstar's life. About the "baseball Annies" who had been the bane of her existence from the beginning, she confessed that over the years it had been difficult to control "her jealousy." She meant her anger. She had accepted his babes as the fate of the good baseball widow, knowing that her husband had his girlfriends in five or six cities and that the ball players squired their girls around during away games.

Rose, however, had become more and more flagrantly indiscreet. He flaunted his affairs openly, took his girlfriends on the team plane, stepped out in public with them in Cincinnati, gave Karolyn's game tickets to them, and even took his own children out to lunch with them. This behavior became a matter of increasing concern to the Reds management, especially when these women came to the ballpark and tried to pass themselves off as Mrs. Rose. Between the small town gossip of Cincinnati and the carefully groomed conservative image of the ball club, the chances for a scandal were alarming.

At spring training in 1976, Rose met a twenty-two-year-old, olive-skinned brunette named Terri Rubio, whose husband was an itinerant musician. She enjoyed the raucous company of star ball players, and Rose began to slip her into Cincinnati on frequent occasions during 1977. To their dismay, she became pregnant that summer. Karolyn knew of the relationship, as did the Reds front office. In the spring of 1978, a girl was born, and Rubio named her Morgan, a dubious honor for Pete's friend Joe Morgan. At first, Rose sent money to support the child, but the checks stopped in December 1978. Two months later, Terri Rubio, now divorced and desperate with no means of support, filed a paternity suit.

"I learned a lot from Pete," she was to say. "One thing was when you hold a strong hand, you play it to the hilt and don't fold. I knew what I was doing when I was his mistress for three years. He doesn't owe me a thing. But he does owe Morgan. She looks so much like him. . . . I look at her and I almost cry. He's making so much money now that he thinks he doesn't have to play by the rules."

When the paternity suit was reported in the *Tampa Tribune*, the reporter wrote, "Rose is thirty-nine and is known as Charlie Hustle." Before long, a fan in San Francisco picked up the theme, painting a huge slogan on a banner and stringing it along the railing of the empty right-field bleachers in Candlestick Park when Rose took his position. It was the one action by a fan, in all the years of boos and garbage hurled at him, that truly got under Rose's skin. The banner read: PETE ROSE LEADS LEAGUE IN PATERNITY SUITS.

Rose, however, refused to change his ways. That became all too clear to Karolyn as she was driving home one day in the family Rolls-Royce. Suddenly, she spotted her red Porsche being driven by another woman. It was Carol Woliung, a blond barmaid and Philadelphia Eagles cheerleader, who had become the number one pretender. Karolyn did a fast U-turn, caught up with her Porsche at a stoplight, jumped out, and tapped on the window. When the blond rolled it down, Karolyn punched her in the nose.

On another occasion, Karolyn took her daughter to the apartment of another of Pete's girlfriends, rang the doorbell, and again delivered a punch when the woman answered. Yet another time, she got word that her beloved Porsche was being driven by a Rose girlfriend in Philadelphia. Karolyn called the Philadelphia police and had the woman arrested for driving a stolen car.

Amid all this personal turmoil, Pete and Karolyn Rose separated in April 1978. The remarkable aspect of all these events is that they did not cause any trauma at all for Pete Rose. He spoke of his appetites as if they demonstrated his virility. "If a guy doesn't like women, he's queer," he would say, "so if you want to say I'm not queer, I'm not queer." Heading toward divorce, his advice to others in his situation was, "Hey, just give her a million bucks and tell her to hit the road." Was he upset? "Nothin' bothers me," he said. "If I'm home in bed, I sleep. If I'm at the ballpark, I play baseball. If I'm on my way to the ballpark, I worry about how I'm going to drive. Just whatever is going on, that's what I do."

Others might go out to kick the cat in this situation, but Rose had a better idea. He pursued his baseball goals with consuming single-mindedness. Baseball was his refuge from these messy personal problems. In fact, his personal problems inspired him to even greater accomplishment on the baseball field. Shortly after the Roses separated, the Reds went to New York for a weekend series against the Mets. On April 29, 1978, he hit three homers and two singles, as the Reds clobbered the Mets, 14–7. The talk in the clubhouse was of statistics, not divorce. "I may have had a better day somewhere but not in total bases. Now I know how George Foster feels. After the first one, I asked him, 'You mean you did that fifty-two times last year?' "

The hits put him within five of reaching the historic three-thousand-hit plateau, an achievement accomplished by only twelve other players in baseball history. Sparky Anderson stirred some controversy by announcing that he would not let Rose break into the exclusive fraternity anywhere but in Cincinnati. The excitement in the baseball world was feverish, and it was enough to make anyone forget what was going on in Rose's personal life. He tried to keep busy, to keep his mind off his domestic troubles and on the imminent achievement of a lifetime goal.

His millennium came a few nights later, as he notched his 2,999th hit on a Baltimore chop and his 3,000th with a clean shot over third base. As the cheering in Riverfront went on and on, Rose draped himself over Tony Perez, then the first baseman for the Expos, for a moment. He was close to tears. The accomplishment, wrote the sportswriters, virtually assured his enshrinement into the Baseball Hall of Fame. One writer pointed out all greats of the game who had never achieved 3,000 hits, among them Rogers Hornsby, Wee Willie Keeler, Jimmie Foxx, Mickey Mantle, and Frank Robinson.

After his 3,000th hit, Rose had a letdown. He went 6 for 51 over a stretch of ten days.

On June 14, another quest began. Rose went after the one record that was considered as unassailable as Ty Cobb's 4,191 career hits: Joe DiMaggio's fifty-six-game hitting streak, which the Yankees center fielder accomplished in 1941. Rose had at least one hit in thirty-one straight games by mid-July. The streak nearly ended in Philadelphia, when he went down in the eighth without a hit. For him to have a chance to continue the streak, the Reds had to bat eight hitters before Rose could get another opportunity at the plate. The compliant Reds did just that, and in the ninth, Rose laid down a perfect bunt in front of Mike Schmidt. "If they're going to give me the bunt, I'm going to take it," Rose said after the game.

On July 24, he ventured to the hellpit of Shea Stadium and sliced a single to left to tie the National League mark, held by Tommy Holmes at thirty-seven games. Shea Stadium gave him a schizophrenic ovation: New Yorkers clapped and booed at the same time. The following day, against the strong fastball of Craig Swan, he went three for five to break the record. Ahead of Rose lay Ty Cobb's streak of forty games and George Sisler's forty-one. Las Vegas put the odds of Rose's catching DiMaggio at 116–1.

Rose wallowed in his glory and scoffed at the notion that he had been lucky so far. "I haven't had any luck at all," he insisted. "I've been getting the meat of the bat on the ball a lot. There were maybe fifteen shots I hit that could have dropped." Gracelessly, he said that Henry Aaron's topping of Babe Ruth's 714 home runs was a more impressive accomplishment than DiMaggio's hitting streak. Rose even had the brass to question the credibility of the Yankee Clipper's record.

On the day DiMaggio was one game away from tying Wee Willie Keeler's forty-four-game hitting streak, he sent a tricky chopper to third during his last time up. The Red Sox third baseman, Jim Tabor, charged the ball and threw wildly past first base, while DiMaggio scampered to second base. There was a long pause, then the official scorer ruled it a double. That was the questionable call to which Rose had alluded. He brought the matter up again when he passed Cobb and Sisler and arrived at the very same point as DiMaggio, one hit away from Wee Willie Keeler's 1897 record. Pete said, "All my hits have been clean hits. There wasn't one off somebody's glove."

The beat went on. On July 28, in a doubleheader with the Phillies, he faced Steve Carlton, against whom he was 0 for 11 in their last confrontations. Rose laid a perfect bunt down the third-base line in the sixth to extend the streak to forty-one games. That tied George Sisler for the second-longest streak in twentieth-century baseball history. On July 31, under the threat of a downpour, in front of forty-five thousand fans in Atlanta—three times the Braves' average crowd, especially for a team that was coming off a 19–0 loss in Montreal— Rose got his hit on a grounder to right field. That tied Keeler's National League record.

The following day, August 1, Rose rolled out of bed at 12:30 P.M. and had a steak and cheese sandwich, salad, and iced tea. After a brief foray to a plant in Atlanta that was producing a new chocolate drink called "Pete" (40 percent milk and good for you), he arrived at Fulton County Stadium three and a half hours before the start of the game. The newsmen around his locker pressed hard upon him, until he asked the throng to move back. Then he laid two towels along the boundary of his locker and George Foster's, declaring it to be the Rose-Foster line. In general, he had been unfailingly cordial and endlessly patient with the press throughout the streak, answering the same questions over and over, while quipping at the stupid questions.

"Would you like to break the record in New York?" No answer required.

"What will it take to continue the streak?" Answer: "A damn hit every day."

"What will end the streak?" Answer: "When I go 0 for 2, 3, 4, or 5."

"Are the pitchers just laying cookies up there for you now?" No answer, contain the anger.

"Isn't it a credit to the other managers that they're not intentionally walking you?" Answer: "No, it's a credit to Ken Griffey who hits behind me."

Now, relaxed and jovial, clothed only in undershorts and a red T-shirt bearing the words Hustle Makes It Happen, he patiently endured the familiar ritual with the press. The boosting was everywhere: from the entire Montreal Expos team, in a message scrawled on a blackboard; even from the tycoon Ted Turner. When Rose was finally dressed and on the field for batting practice, a Braves bat boy came up to him to ask about a bruise the boy had suffered fielding ground balls.

"Spit on it, rub it in the dirt, and get back out there," Rose advised.

Shortly after six, he went for an interview with former Braves pitcher Ernie Johnson, who was now a radio announcer. Rose asked about the starting pitcher, Larry Williams, a twenty-four-year-old rookie who had been pitching in Richmond when the streak began and would be making only his fourth major league start.

"He's been known to wet up a few on occasion," Johnson confided.

"That's okay," Rose replied. "So did you."

The night began auspiciously. Rose walked, and Bench homered. In the second inning, Rose came up again. This time he lined a screamer toward the mound, but the 6 foot, 5 inch rookie pitcher reached behind his back and speared it at his ankles before falling to the ground. It was a spectacular play.

On his third trip to the plate, Rose again met the ball well, but this time the Braves shortstop threw him out on a routine play. By the time Rose came up to bat in the seventh, Atlanta had begun to run away with the game. Nevertheless, Gene Garber, a bearded side-winder with an impressive 1.56 ERA, came in to pitch. He got Rose to line to third, into a double play.

By the ninth, the game was a rout, with Atlanta ahead 16–4. Rose had one final chance to get a hit. As he stepped to the plate for his last at-bat, thirty thousand fans rose to cheer him for a solid minute. The crowd included Lewis Grizzard, the self-styled redneck columnist of the *Atlanta Constitution*, who was forever evoking his deceased, alcoholic father and speculating on what the sentimental old sot might have felt in situations of moment. "My father would have said, 'Look at the way that man moves,' " Grizzard now imagined. " 'He doesn't waste a motion. He has speed. He has strength. He has determination. That's the kind of man you want in a foxhole with you.' "

On the first pitch, Rose attempted a drag bunt and fouled it off. Behind the plate, the young catcher for the Braves, Joe Nolan, grunted in contempt. A drag bunt when your team is behind 16–4? "I bet Joe DiMaggio would never have tried such a bush thing," Nolan said to himself.

Two straight balls followed. They were moving the ball around on Rose, in and out. This was baseball: pitcher against batter, *mano a mano*, with nothing at stake but history. Garber was bidding to stay out of the history books, and his juices were flowing as if it were 0–0 in the ninth with a man on third. It became a World Series situation for both players. Rose expected the pitcher to challenge him with his best. Garber had only one thought: I don't want to walk the son of a bitch. He threw a good sinker. Rose took a fluid swing and fouled it off: 2 and 2.

Garber looked in for the sign. Rose readied himself for smoke. For sixteen years, he had boasted that he was not a guess hitter, but now, in this situation, he primed himself for the challenge that was coming. Garber was not Phil Niekro, who the night before had fed him a rare fastball down the middle rather than his wicked knuckle ball. It would be Garber's specialty, a sinker or a slider, Pete thought, thrown with everything the pitcher had.

Nolan flashed the sign, wiggling his fingers and pointing to the outside. Garber wound up with an intense motion, his arm whipped around at his waist, and the ball . . . floated lazily toward the plate—a shocking, totally unexpected balloon that meandered languidly toward the outside corner. It was too close to take and too slow and outside to hit. Rose swung mightily through it, nicking it, but the ball lodged firmly in Nolan's mitt for strike three.

Rose stayed in hot fury for hours afterward. Had the press seen Garber leap up in triumph, as if he'd just won the World Series? If that had been Phil Niekro pitching, he would have challenged Rose by making three out of five pitches fastballs, not his knuckler. To Rose, it was as if Garber had broken some sacred, gladiatorial code.

Garber, by contrast, was nearly unrecognizable in the fray. Even Rose did not recognize him when they met the press in their street clothes. "I wanted his streak to continue, but I wanted to get him out too," Garber said. "That's what I get paid to do." His catcher, Joe Nolan, was more effusive. Still nagging at him was a game from the year before, when the Big Red Machine had posted twenty-three runs, and Rose and his friends had jeered and cackled from their dugout at the lowly Braves. This was sweet revenge. "The changeup Geno threw was just a great pitch," Nolan said.

In the stands, Lewis Grizzard slipped away to write his column. "What Pete Rose did—hit safely in forty-four straight games—wasn't a man on the moon," he wrote that night. "I reminded myself, as the stadium lights dimmed, it wasn't a lonely flight across the Atlantic or the first heart transplant. But it was a good and honorable thing, a fierce man with a bat in his hand, playing a boy's game as it was meant to be played. I'm thankful I had a chance to witness a part of it, even the bitter end."

For Rose, the game had to go on. The next night, behind Tom Seaver's three-hitter, Rose went four for five, including a double and a homer.

The end of Rose's hitting streak was reported in ninety-six-point headlines on the sports pages of American newspapers. The beginning of Bart Giamatti's presidency was of no less interest to the editors on the other side of the newsroom. *Life* magazine called to propose an intimate cover story on the Giamattis at home, but the president-elect demurred. His staunch, Italian sense of privacy remained in force, even as his public self became nationally known. His hearth would remain inviolate, although to turn down *Life* required very high principles.

In accepting the presidency, Giamatti had asked not to assume the post for six months. Romantically, Giamatti wanted to complete a full academic year of teaching, but practically, he knew he had a lot of learning to do. His own past words could be turned back on him now. To the senior class at Ezra Stiles College years before, he had said that they were typical of Yale students: either brimming with pragmatic idealism or idealistic pragmatism, and that it would be interesting to see which instinct brimmed in each of them as a dominant strain. To make himself over from a Renaissance scholar into a corporate executive would require considerable effort. He realized that "he had a mortgage and one suit, but no policies." Yale and its new president needed a corporate strategy and management goals. He needed to know about flow charts and spread sheets, about budget projections and computer models. At the same time, he wanted to bolster the magic of the place.

It was as if Giamatti were moving from being a promising minor leaguer to becoming a beleaguered rookie manager in the majors during a rebuilding year. As he pursued his teaching duties through the spring semester, he did a good deal of listening to the lions of corporate affairs. Among those he consulted was Henry Rosovsky of Harvard. Rosovsky had written Giamatti a congratulatory letter in which, as a professional economist, the Harvard dean offered his advice about Yale's fiscal ill-health. Giamatti responded enthusiastically, but wondered if their meeting could be clandestine. It would be unseemly for him to venture into Harvard Square to pay court on his old rival. So Rosovsky booked a room at a Logan Airport hotel, and Giamatti slipped in for a four-hour session.

To outsiders, the combination of Rosovsky and Giamatti might have seemed odd. Yet they got along well, partly for the undercurrent of their mutual ethnicity, partly for their shared wit, and partly because they both loved the Boston Red Sox.

In Rosovsky's professional opinion, the situation was not entirely the disaster it had been portrayed. Old-fashioned austerity measures could solve Yale's financial problems. Moreover, Rosovsky approved of Giamatti's expressed goal to use the Yale presidency as a platform from which he could speak to a host of national issues, not simply the issues of quality higher education. Graciously, Giamatti invited Rosovsky to his inauguration in July. Politely, Rosovsky declined.

Through the spring, Giamatti lurched uncertainly toward a program. In early April 1978, perhaps not coincidentally with the opening of the baseball season, he found himself one night in his garage in his modest Westville house. There, betwixt the snow tires of the off-season and the lawnmower of the All-Star break, he had an inspiration. He drafted a memo that was issued on his first day in office.

> To the members of the University Community:
>   In order to repair what Milton called the ruin of our grand-parents, I wish to announce that henceforth, as a matter of University policy, evil will be abolished and Paradise is restored.
>   I trust all of us will do whatever possible to achieve this policy objective.

The memo was met with bemusement, as intended, but it achieved surprising national attention. The *Wall Street Journal* greeted it grimly: "What we need is not more talk about evil, but some decent courses in the practice of arbitrage." The columnist George Will pounced on the memo and matched the fluid stroke of Milton with the power of Montesquieu, Thomas Aquinas, John Locke, and, at first base, Ernie Banks. Even William Buckley, the professional Yale man and professional Catholic, heaped scorn—and ponderous verbiage—on the memo and its Congregationalist author, as he also mistakenly supposed Giamatti to be a liberal: "Milton is all very well, but it is typical of President Giamatti and his ilk to cite secular authority on evil as if, of course, those who have passed any time down in the agora or out on the Rialto needed an authority to know the palpability of evil in all its camaraderie and liberal camouflages." The *New York Times*, the newspaper of record, printed a box on the memo and misspelled Giamatti's name. The *Washington Post* scooped the *Times* by reporting that Giamatti's idea was nothing new: an attorney for the Federal Drug Administration had proclaimed the abolition of evil three years earlier and had printed the regulations in the Federal Register, even though the technicians in the FDA lab had determined that evil was not that bad for your health.

It was one thing to abolish evil, quite another, to restore paradise. Giamatti moved to surround himself with strong-willed administrators who had ideas about twenty-two-million-dollar deficits.

"I'm listening to everyone," he said a few months after his selection. "I am the Aeolian harp of Woodbridge Hall. The impulses of the vernal woods sing right through me."

From the Massachusetts Department of Welfare, he tapped Jerald L. Stevens to be his director of finance, his "moneychanger," as

Kingman Brewster had thought of the role. And from the Yale Law School, he chose the hard-nosed Abraham Goldstein to be his provost. With these forceful voices around him, he nevertheless invited an easy fellowship, referring to the members of his inner circle as "the brothers." But he did not want to share the limelight. He was to be the sole visible spokesman for Yale. In his administrative style, he opted for the one-on-one approach, compartmentalizing his staff and sharing confidences individually, but never collectively. In these individual sessions, he had a remarkable ability to invite confidence. "He sucked things out of you and appeared to give a great deal in return," said Lance Liebman, the Yale trustee and Harvard Law professor who had been with Giamatti at Saybrook College and who had championed him for the presidency. "As a result, he had passionate relationships with a broad range of people." All told, he developed a cast of perhaps three or four dozen people, each of whom was quite sure that he or she was Giamatti's best friend.

Giamatti finally took office seven months after his selection, but he did not receive his formal inauguration until three months after that. On October 14, 1978, however, the Blues turned out in force and in regalia. A distinct giddiness marked the occasion, as they celebrated this cultivated man of wit who was so much a part of Yale and so much a product of intellectual pursuits, who understood so well what a university should be and what kind of citizens it was trying to create. In his floppy, tasseled cap, Giamatti strode down the aisle of Woolsey Hall, acknowledging the ecstatic cheers of his friends and colleagues, even flashing a peace sign to cheering students in the balcony. At age forty, he was becoming the youngest president of Yale in two centuries. When he was seated among the fifty or so university presidents in attendance, as well as New York City mayor Edward Koch and his former babysitter from South Hadley, Ella Grasso, who had gone on to become governor of Connecticut, suddenly, high in the balcony, someone turned on a tape of children singing, "Hail, Hail, the Gang's All Here," to a round of laughter.

The difference between Giamatti's style and his predecessor's was quickly noted. Next to Kingman Brewster's mint green jaguar, his Jose Melande cigars, his taste for pâté de foie gras, his elegant J. Press suits, and his aloof regal manner were Giamatti's yellow Volkswagen, his construction boots, his endless Benson & Hedges menthol cigarettes, his wrinkled sports jackets, his diet of junk food, and his gregariousness. "A human being as president of the university? My God! What will that be like?" asked Giamatti's friend, history professor Don Kagan.

Brewster had made Yale into a great university, and he had nearly bankrupted it. Now, Giamatti was called upon to restrict the expansive vision of the past twenty years. His duty appealed to the punitive side of his character. His mandate was to abolish the evil of extravagance and restore the paradise of sound economic health.

Not long after Giamatti officially became president of Yale, the Yale football team took on Harvard in Cambridge in their annual set-to. Giamatti was in attendance. Festivities and gracious self-congratulations were planned for halftime between Giamatti and Derek Bok, the stiff and undemonstrative president of Harvard. For Bok, the occasion was important, because some of his university's wealthiest benefactors would be on hand for the fun. In Harvard stadium, however, it was no fun at all, at least not for the spectators. With temperatures dipping into the teens and a howling wind coming off the river and the bay, it was a frigid day.

To his further discomfort, Giamatti was seated in a section reserved for Bok's biggest givers, and that percolated his Mediterranean passions. In the second quarter, the Yale quarterback faded back and lofted a marvelous pass that was caught splendidly for a Yale score. Giamatti leapt to his feet.

"Take that, Derek Bok!" he screamed, punching air. "Take that!" His aides whispered to him to remember himself, while the Harvard benefactors turned and gazed in amazement. "I don't care," he snarled and continued his thoroughly disgraceful behavior. When halftime came, he had collected himself and found the dignity to be generous and praiseworthy to both Harvard and Derek Bok. It helped that Yale went on to win the game, 14–0.

Winning, Giamatti would say, had a joy and a "discreet purity" to it. Winning was not everything, but "it is something powerful, indeed beautiful in itself. Something as necessary to the strong spirit as striving is essential to the healthy character."

Because Giamatti was a baseball nut, it might have been expected that the new president would be a great booster for the Yale athletic program. Not only his singular obsessiveness about sports might sway him, but universities throughout the United States had long since discovered how big-time university sports could allay budgetary distress. Moreover, his athletic director was Frank Ryan, who had brought the last NFL championship to the Cleveland Browns in 1964, when he threw three touchdown passes to upset the powerhouse Baltimore Colts. Ryan, however, was not your typical ex-football player. He had a Ph.D. in mathematics, taught in the Yale math department, and was to be responsible for computerizing the voting system in the U.S. House of Representatives. These accomplishments notwithstanding, he liked to win football games.

Early in the Giamatti presidency, the reverse of the predictions proved to be true. In April 1980, Giamatti chose an occasion before the Association of Yale Alumni to address the subject of Yale and athletics. It was like President Jimmy Carter choosing a convention of the Veterans of Foreign Wars to address the subject of amnesty for Vietnam draft evaders. Like any other university alumni, Yale alumni found their connection to their alma mater through its varsity sporting events; but Yale was not Auburn or Oklahoma, with a redneck contingent screaming for sports to overwhelm everything else.

Before he addressed the proper place of athletics at Yale, Giamatti provided an erudite preamble on the nature of sports itself. He evoked the Greeks, a novel from nineteenth-century England, and the Persians of Xenophon who learned to ride a horse as they learned to speak the truth. The proportion of athletics to university life was the central question, and he signaled his view early by warning of how overconcentration on sports could "deform" the development of students as thinking and feeling human beings. Nor could the university be allowed to deform its primary mission by "exploiting" students as athletes in order to enrich its coffers. Yale, he felt, was drifting into big-time athletics, allowing its coaches (whom he regarded essentially as teachers) to spend too much time in the "demeaning" process of recruiting. Athletes were spending too much time on the playing field rather than in the classroom.

Why couldn't Yale athletes hope to test themselves against the best athletes in national competition? "Yale students are among the best," Giamatti replied to his own question. "They are tested and will be tested with the best all their lives. It is to misconceive a Yale education, however, to think that education is interested simply to be the setting for a national-level athletic career in anything." Later, he would say the same thing more trenchantly, "There is in the world an unholy, fallacious belief that there's a correlation between big time sports and big time excellence," he said. "If that were true, then the University of Nebraska would be the greatest university in America."

The hammer blows came in the proposals: strict limits on recruiting by coaches, the elimination of postseason competition at national championships, the elevation of intramural sports, shortening the season in basketball and hockey, and the requirement for coaches to teach more than one sport.

Athletes, administrators, coaches in the Ivy League howled in protest. Yale's own hockey coach called the proposals naive. Others scoffed at Giamatti's plan as idealistic, impractical, and unfair, nothing more than an attempt to transform varsity sports into a sort of esoteric intramural league.

The proposals went nowhere, but the speech itself was prophetic. It would be remembered well into the 1980s, when intercollegiate athletics got completely out of hand, as television deals became insidious and drugs, laughable SAT scores, and flagrant recruiting violations became pervasive. Besides, it was demeaning to have to beg a teenager to come to your highbrow school, even if that was the only way such a school could win ball games.

In the lean years ahead, Giamatti never wavered from his position, even in 1982 and 1983, when the Yale football team posted dismal records. In fact, in 1983, the team was 1 and 9, the worst record in 111 years of Yale football. "Western civilization is [not] going to come to an end because of one lousy football season," Giamatti said. He did not change his position when Yale was invited to play Columbia in the "Mirage Bowl" in Japan. Giamatti vetoed the trip, much to the disappointment of Frank Ryan.

"It's a mirage, Frank," the president said.

"If we don't do it, Harvard will," Ryan protested.

Giamatti would not relent. The following year, Harvard played Penn in Tokyo.

Not only did Giamatti not waver, but he was to strengthen his statements as time passed. "To exploit our students as a source of revenue is a scandal and a shame," he would say two years later. "It is foolish because anybody who thinks that by filling a football stadium you are going even to start to balance the budget is either kidding himself or trying to kid the rest of us."

His critics charged him with programming mediocrity in Yale athletics. Giamatti had one powerful argument in his defense. That was an All-American pitcher on the Yale baseball team named Ron Darling. Without question, Darling was the greatest pitcher ever to take the mound on Yale Field.

Given the pressure Giamatti was under, he might well have thought of the Yale star as Noble Darling, for this prince of part Chinese-Hawaiian blood from Worcester, Massachusetts, had been a late bloomer. In high school, he had been, like Pete Rose, small and wispy, a mere 5 feet, 10 inches and 150 pounds. It was unimaginable then that he had big league promise. The collegiate powerhouses of the Southwest, such as Arizona State and Southern California, where the sun always shone and where the baseball seasons continued for sixty games, did not beckon. Darling was offered only one full athletic scholarship: to the University of Connecticut. But Yale had accepted him (as had Amherst College), and his parents, neither of whom had gone to college, were flattered. Yale was a school without athletic scholarships, without a winning baseball season in thirteen years, without a tradition of preening athletes for the Bigs. It was not until his sophomore year that such a thought even entered Darling's mind. Over the summer after his freshman year, he grew four inches and gained twenty-five pounds.

As an advertisement for Yale, and for Giamatti's position on recruiting, Darling could not have been more tailor-made: "If I was going to get a college education, why not the best?" Darling would tell *Sports Illustrated.* "I was going to have to work to get through, and my father would have to pay part of the tuition. He said, 'Don't worry, Ronnie. We'll get the money somehow.' I've never been sorry for my decision."

Yale and its president could scarcely contain their joy. Darling lumbered along the academic road with a C+ average in his major, history. Even that was important to the Giamatti credo. Good as Darling was on the diamond, it was important to Giamatti for Darling to be defined as a student first and an athlete second. "I believe a kid suffers if he's brought to any institution as an athlete," Giamatti would say. "If his initial contact is athletics, then the fundamental reason for the student to be at the university is obscured."

In his sophomore year, when Darling left his books at the Sterling Library and trundled over to stodgy old Yale Field, with its Romanesque arches and cement dugouts, he set the place on fire. In 1981, he was 11–2 with an ERA of 1.31. When he was not on the mound, he was in centerfield or was used as a designated hitter. At the plate, he had a .384 average and a .589 slugging percentage. Behind him, Yale had its first winning season since the mid-sixties, posting a 24–12–1 record. (The tie was a wind-aided fiasco against the University of Central Florida in Orlando, which was called because of darkness after seven innings with the score at 21–21. Darling did not pitch.)

For all the fuss over Giamatti's reputed campaign for athletic mediocrity, Ron Darling was not the only quality player on the team. At shortstop was Bob Brooke, who later played hockey for the New York Rangers and the New Jersey Devils. In center field, there was Rich Diana, who was drafted by the Miami Dolphins and played in the 1982 Super Bowl team before he quit to become a surgeon. And also in the outfield was another well-rounded All-American, Joe Dufek, who had come to Yale instead of the University of Michigan, because Michigan demanded that he play only one varsity sport, football. At Yale, he could play baseball as well. He went on to play in the NFL for the Buffalo Bills.

In 1981, Yale went to the Eastern Intercollegiate play-offs for the first time since 1956, and there, in a classic matchup, Darling faced another college superstar, Frank Viola of St. John's University. St. John's had gone to the college World Series the year before, and also showcased another pitcher of promise named John Franco. In a pearl of a game, the noble Darling pitched no-hit ball into the eleventh inning, striking out fifteen. Even his adversary, Frank Viola, admired the performance. It was "the best pitched game I ever saw," Viola said later.

To his profound disappointment, Giamatti was unable to attend the championship game, but he had Frank Ryan phone him with a report after every inning. Had he been there, Giamatti might have had a special seat. At the outset of his presidency, he wistfully told Joe Benanto, the Yale baseball coach, that he had always longed to sit in the dugout with the players. Benanto issued him a standing invitation that Giamatti accepted at least once every year, through his presidency and beyond.

With time, Giamatti was to be both sentimental about Ron Darling and disappointed in him. In a move of which Giamatti disapproved, Darling entered the major leagues after his junior year without graduating. Giamatti's hope had been that Darling would be able to resist the temptation. Still, Giamatti kept after the pitcher in the years ahead to finish his Yale degree.

Their touchstone was the Red Sox. Darling would say, even when he stood tall in his New York Mets uniform in the locker room of Shea Stadium, that he had always been and still was a Red Sox fan. He and Giamatti kibitzed about their heroes. Giamatti did not like Yaz much after the down years of the 1970s, and Darling would reply, speaking with authority, that when a team has down years after successful years, the big stars are always blamed. And they would talk about Bobby Doerr, Giamatti's childhood hero.

"Doerr always got the clutch hit," Giamatti proclaimed.

"Always?" Darling questioned.

"Yes, always."

In June 1981, after commencement, Giamatti had no more Yale baseball to admire, nor any baseball at all for that matter. The major league ball players had gone on strike. His equilibrium was distinctly unsettled, and he was moved to boo in print. He published a lament in the *New York Times* that was quintessential Bart and quintessential fan. He deplored the way the "princelings and sovereignets" of baseball treated the game as an industry. To suspend baseball was "deny-side economics," he protested. "Call it the triumph of greed over the spirit of the garden. Call it what you will, the strike is utter foolishness," he wrote. "O Sovereign Owners and princely Players, masters of amortization, tax shelters, bonuses and deferred compensations, go back to work. You have been entrusted with the serious work of play, and your season of responsibility has come. Be at it. There is no general sympathy for either of your sides. The people of America care about baseball, not about your squalid little squabbles. Reassume your dignity and remember that you are the temporary custodians of an enduring public trust." He was writing to the baseball players collectively and individually.

"You play baseball, so that we may remember the future we want for our children," he wrote.

It was his clearest statement yet about the superiority of the fan. To Giamatti, the fan was ultimately the most important person in baseball.

· 7 ·

Two Trades

IN CINCINNATI, amid the splendor and triumph of the three-thousandth hit and the forty-four-game hitting streak, the Reds management soured on Pete Rose. His streak had been wonderful for baseball, glorious for Rose himself, and bad for the Cincinnati ball club. For four full months during the 1978 season, the media hung on Rose's every word. When the team lost and Rose hit, there were cackles and joyous commotion around his locker, while the other players moped around theirs. After one particularly tough game, Rose was whistling cheerily in the showers, prompting Johnny Bench to come in to remind Rose that the Reds had lost. When the team won, the heroics of its other stars were ignored. The circus around Rose was particularly grating on the other leading lights—Seaver, Morgan, Foster, and Bench. Arguably, their contributions were as important to the success of the ball club. Seaver won sixteen games in 1978 with a 2.87 ERA. Bench and Morgan had downturns in their averages and run production, but Morgan remained the most complete player in the major leagues. Foster hit forty homers, hardly a terrible drop-off from his fifty-two the year before. The Reds finished behind the Dodgers of Ron Cey and Tommy John for the second year in a row.

With the close of the also-ran 1978 season, Rose's contract was also running out. For all the history and the excitement he had provided during 1978, it was not his greatest season. He finished barely over .300, at .302, and under his usual two hundred-hit plateau, with 198 hits.

A year and a half earlier, indeed while he dressed for the Opening Game of the season in the coaches' room of the clubhouse, Rose
had uneventfully signed a two-year contract worth $365,000 a year, a
figure that in 1977 and 1978 was near the top of the salary scale. Even
with that contract, all signs pointed toward hard sledding the next
time around. From the business standpoint alone, the Reds might
have wished that instead of the three-thousandth hit and the streak,
Rose would have joined Bench and Morgan in a slight downturn. Free
agency had created a whole new ball game. Rose had acquired a
lawyer for a superagent. He was Reuven Katz, on the surface a courtly
gentleman who wore his Harvard Law School credentials comfortably and promotionally, and who appreciated what free agency
would mean for a client who was already a legend. When the Reds
general manager presented the 1977–78 contract to Rose, Katz advised against signing it.

"I wouldn't take that," Katz snapped contemptuously at the
$365,000-a-year offer. "This club has fucked you long enough."

On the field, Rose was the pride of Cincinnati. Off the field, he
was fast becoming an embarrassment. He was a scandal waiting to
happen. The front office knew about his women, knew that Terri
Rubio had become pregnant, knew that the local press was protecting Rose but probably could not do so indefinitely. In 1978, the club
was still clinging to its prewar morality. The stiff rules about dress
and comportment remained in effect after the club's management
passed from Bob Howsam to his protégé, the dour, square-jawed
German-Irish Nebraskan, Dick Wagner. As committed to the old traditions of the Reds as Howsam, Wagner knew that the transition
ahead for all of baseball was going to be difficult. With Wagner and
the other executives, the disciplining of Pete Rose was becoming a
greater and greater preoccupation. They began to feel as though they
were running a detective agency as well as a ball club. When Rose
would check into the team's hotel with strange women, it was noticed. Not only did the hotels ask embarrassing questions, but the
other players were beginning to complain to the front office. When
"Mrs. Rose" turned up at Riverfront Stadium in so many different
shapes and sizes, the wives of other players were offended. When the
real Mrs. Rose took it upon herself to punch out the girlfriends and
have them arrested, the sympathy for her as the popular Big Momma
who had been so good for the Reds organization remained great. At
one point, during spring training in 1978, a player came directly to
Dick Wagner to talk about a serious clubhouse problem. According to
the player (who was of considerable stature both as a player and a

team leader), Rose was talking loudly in the locker room about how he wished his wife and kids would fly home and that the plane would crash on the way. With real sincerity, the player spoke of how upsetting Rose's talk was to the younger players and wouldn't Wagner do something about it? Wagner had the player talk to Sparky Anderson.

Scandal was brewing in another quarter. It came to the attention of management that Rose was gambling heavily, even compulsively. Frequenting the race track was no sin—the track was a favorite off-day preoccupation of many players and managers—but Rose's behavior there had become bizarre. When he went in the company of other players, it was so vital to him to win and lord the winning ticket over his buddies that he was given to betting on every horse in a given race. His runners started turning up in the clubhouse. More than once, Dick Wagner personally had to shoo one of them, Mario Nuñez, out of the locker room during spring training. Dubbed by Rose as "The Cuban," Nuñez was the maître d' at George Steinbrenner's racetrack in Tampa, known as Sunshine Park, and he adored the company of ball players. "He'll bet you tomorrow is not Friday if you'll lay him two to one," Rose would say of Nuñez, "but he'll only bet you two dollars." Nuñez's thrills were vicarious. He enjoyed placing big bets for the high-rolling baseball stars. Rose and Nuñez had been introduced to one another by Sparky Anderson.

More disturbing were the reports that Rose was betting heavily with illegal bookmakers across the river in Newport, where slot machines and roulette wheels and prostitution flourished openly. In the fall of 1977, it became known that Rose was not only betting with bookmakers but was bragging about how he stiffed them when he lost. To Rose, bookmakers were crybabies who were always whining about not collecting their juice. But they could not complain too loudly, certainly not about the great Pete Rose, for he might just send them to jail. As he would say in a different context, he had a lot of pull around town.

All this was mainly talk, until a report reached the Reds front office of a threat straight out of *The Godfather*. It was said that Rose owed $80,000 (the figure would later rise to $500,000) to Newport gangsters, and that they had made a threat: they would do nothing about Rose's gambling debts, so long as he was still playing for the Reds. But when he stopped playing, if he still had not paid up, he could fear for his limbs. To underscore the threat, Rose received a dead fish in the mail, a classic message from the underworld. Rose laughed off the threats. He was a roughneck. Nothing could scare him. He was Pete Rose.

Shaken by these reports, the Reds management asked Baseball Commissioner Bowie Kuhn for help. On two separate occasions, the director of security for major league baseball flew into Cincinnati to confront Rose with the reports. He denied them. The investigators could not prove them. And the situation remained unresolved.

There were other annoyances that contributed to the general sourness. Rose was an enthusiastic user of greenies—the "diet pill" that deluded journeymen into thinking that they were performing like heroes. While the use of greenies was reasonably widespread in baseball in the late 1970s, for the team captain to be a promiscuous user and promoter of the illegal substance caused the management a special problem. It was another scandal waiting to happen, and it would become a bona fide scandal a year later in Philadelphia.

Rose's polyester suits and Prince Valiant hairdo and bellbottom trousers and braggadocio were another source of contention. Perhaps he was right: this flamboyance off the field sold tickets, even though bizarre exhibitionism was the very kind of thing that the Cincinnati organization had tried for years to discourage in its players. He remained much beloved (and much protected) by the Cincinnati press, largely because he was so wonderfully quotable about baseball. If the writers wrote bad things, he would surely cut them off for future interviews. Moreover, in his outside appearances to Reds booster clubs, he began to develop a pitch that was personally offensive to the Reds general manager, Dick Wagner, because it was racial. He was, Rose proclaimed to his audiences, the most famous white athlete in America, and he should be the highest paid athlete in America because he was white. "A lot of people don't realize that I'm not the same as other ball players in the game. They're not as well known as I am everywhere," he told *Playboy* magazine.

Rose would make this racist argument even more graphic. He boasted about his incomparable marketability in commercials.

"One of the reasons you are considered so marketable is that you're a white athlete?" *Playboy* needled.

"Look, if you owned Swanson's Pizza, would you want a black guy to do the commercial on TV for you?" Rose responded. "Would you like the black guy to pick up the pizza and bite into it? Try to sell it? I mean, would you want Dave Parker selling your pizza to America for you? Or would you want Pete Rose?"

To Dave Parker, Rose's comment was flagrantly racist. It had angered him then, and it still angered him eleven years later, when he sat late one afternoon in the dugout at Baltimore's Memorial Stadium, with a large gold cross studded with ten diamonds planted in his left earlobe, before a game when he hit a tremendous line drive that kept rising and rising until it hit the last row of the right-field bleachers.

"He's a 'neck,' " said the mammoth "Parkway." "It was a racist statement from a racist guy, and his racism has been proven subsequently."

The hardening of Pete Rose had been setting in for years, but the difference in his *Playboy* remarks was that he was not covering it up with reams of boyish enthusiasm about the game. In the privacy of his hotel room, where he spoke to the interviewer with the television blaring in the background, it was not a boy but a man who was talking—a man who was selfish, self-centered, immature, money-mad, resentful, and driven. If he got along fine with most fans, he had ceased to believe that he owed them anything except a hard day's work at the ballpark. He had come to despise the constant imprecations and solicitations and intrusions and importunities that came with his celebrity status: the sloppy drunks who breathed all over him in bars and then bragged to their friends about how they had been out carousing with Pete Rose all night, even the kids who swarmed like Lilliputians with their silly programs and scuffed baseballs. What did he owe them? There was nothing in his contract that demanded he be nice to the fans. In fact, he had come to feel that he had been too nice, too solicitous, too accommodating to everyone, including the Reds management. He had begun to feel like the exploited rather than the exploiting, and no doubt his superagent, Reuven Katz, encouraged this sentiment.

Abruptly in his *Playboy* interview, Rose evoked the 1973 playoffs with the Mets as the emblem and referred often to the time a fan, using a rubber band, shot a paperclip that hit him in the neck, causing him to bleed for three innings.

"What if the guy had put my eye out?" he wondered aloud. "What's the guy gonna get? A twenty-five-dollar misdemeanor? And me? My career is over. Guys threw bottles, chicken bones, garbage. I don't classify them idiots as fans. . . . If people go to the ballpark, they think they're supposed to get an autograph. You're supposed to give them a bat. They think it's all part of a four-dollar ticket."

"Maybe there are some people who still don't think you're worth it," the *Playboy* interviewer prodded.

"I don't give a shit what people think. I used to really worry about that too. I really did. When I used to hold out for more money every year, I used to worry about that because I wanted everyone to like me. Playing hard, being nice, signing autographs. I used to give in to the Reds a lot, because I didn't want to hold out. But when you start getting letters like I get and phone calls and stuff like that, and people being idiots, I say to hell with them. I'm not going to worry about anybody."

It annoyed him that people were always making cracks about how much money he made, when he felt it was not nearly enough, and sympathetic interviewers such as Phil Donahue were constantly referring to him as the "most exciting player in baseball." A time stuck in his mind when he was getting in his car with his suitcase and nearby a lunk was getting in his truck, packed with his beer-swilling buddies, and the guy yelled out, "Hey, Rose, got all your money in your suitcase?"

"I can't get it all in there, asshole," Rose shouted back.

He did not seem to appreciate that his own taunting attitude toward money was inviting this petulance from the fans. While his streak was still going on, he made an appearance on "Donahue," where the subject of money came up immediately.

"I'm gonna make enough next year, you can stack it up and a show dog ain't gonna be able to jump over it," Rose said.

Donahue shoved the microphone in front of a pert, well-scrubbed young woman. "Could money lure you away from Cincinnati?" she asked.

"How much you got, honey?" Rose quipped.

If the *Playboy* interview showed the ugly private thoughts of the man-child, "Donahue" in late July 1978 showed his immense popular appeal. It was a remarkable situation: Donahue returning to Cincinnati where he too began his road to stardom and where his parent company, Multimedia, still made its headquarters. The show was held in the Cincinnati Coliseum, next door to Riverfront, and twenty thousand fans filled the place to hear their native son. Rose might have been Billy Graham in Jakarta or Michael Jackson in the Hollywood Bowl or Muhammad Ali in Louisville. Dressed in a three-piece, wide-lapeled, blue pin-striped suit and somber dark blue tie, Rose came forward to the raised dais, with its single chair in the middle of the throng. His mop of hair was now so thick and long it looked like a wig.

The performance was extraordinary: the single guest on a national talk show, with a live audience of 20,000 hometown folks. With no trace of nervousness, Rose was brilliant as the wisecracking superstar, joshing the ladies young and old, regaling his fans with his wisdom on education and headfirst slides, negotiations and fist fights, age and money. He played the themes of his image deftly, in the same way that Bart Giamatti could evoke baseball or his Italian Americanness when he needed it.

On his perpetual youth: "I was raised here, but I never did grow up."

On his intelligence: "I'm living proof that you don't have to be smart to make a lot of money. If I had dug school, I probably would have went to college and played football, and you wouldn't be looking at me here today."

On his "philosophy" of education: "You can have all the money in the world. They can take your money from you. Take your car from you. Take your house from you, but they can't take what's in your head . . . less they cut your head off, and then you ain't gonna need it anyway."

On his slide into Harrelson: "I made him a star."

It was hard to dispute what Rose himself would say a few minutes into the show: "If I'm worth a million somewhere else, I ought to be worth a million and a half here in Cincinnati." No doubt, his superagent in the front row nodded approvingly, not only to Rose's statement but to his client's overall performance. Pete Rose was a commodity. This was, in a sense, the opening round of his fall negotiations for a new contract: the management had to know how good Rose could be at negotiating a contract through the media. How many other celebrities in all of America, in politics or show business, let alone other major league baseball players, could pull twenty thousand people into an arena for a simple talk show and entertain them so effortlessly?

To the Coliseum crowd, Rose said he saw no reason why he shouldn't be in Cincinnati a year later, nor why he would lose his boyish enthusiasm for the game anytime soon. "If you can't get enthusiastic about playing with Bench, Morgan, and Foster, you oughta get a lunch pail and get another job," he said. Sparky Anderson, moreover, was the best manager in baseball; Rose would walk "through hell in a gasoline suit for Sparky." He would soon get his chance.

A month after the 1978 season, following a seventeen-game promotional trip by the Reds to Japan, Anderson was summarily fired. It seemed certain that coaches would also be leaving wholesale after the 1978 season, including Ted Kluszewski because of ill-health. Rose wanted to show them his gratitude and his affection. After the team landed at the airport following the flight from Tokyo, Rose threw a lunch for the coaches at a nearby Holiday Inn and presented each with a brand new Jeep as a token of appreciation. Sparky Anderson did not get one. Later, the Rose-bashers would say that was why the manager was fired.

Only Johnny Bench had been willing to hint at the real reason for the dismissal: the manager had ceased to communicate with his awesome players. "Our manager is too low-key," Bench had said after the Reds fell seven games behind the Dodgers in September. "Sparky has withdrawn from it all. Intimidated is not exactly the word, but it's close. He's too nice, perhaps in awe of us."

Low-key or not, communicative or not, Anderson's record in modern managing was unassailable. In his nine seasons in Cincinnati, the Reds won five championships in the National League West, four National League pennants, and two World Series; in seven of his nine seasons, the club had won more than ninety games. These were figures that Rose would invoke often, in bitterness, in the coming year. But Dick Wagner and the Reds front office were concerned with the present, not the past. For the second straight year, the aging dynasty had finished out of the play-offs. Next season, six of the eight starters would be more than thirty years of age if no change was made. Rose himself was thirty-seven years old.

Uppermost in Wagner's mind was to hold off as long as he could what he regarded as the scourge of free agency: the guaranteed contract for the aging superstar. He saw the guaranteed contract as a trap. It ossified a club and prevented it from promoting young prospects. Eventually, Wagner considered it the road to bankruptcy, especially because he had three future Hall-of-Fame players in Seaver, Bench, and Morgan, and he had to be concerned with his team's overall salary structure.

That May, Reuven Katz had attempted to exploit the hysteria of the three-thousandth hit by trying to maneuver Wagner into a guaranteed contract. Wouldn't it be a perfect gift to the people of Cincinnati, Katz suggested sweetly to Wagner, to present Rose with the guaranteed contract on the Pete Rose Day that was thrown for the player after he reached the milestone? Wagner demurred. He did not negotiate contracts during the season, certainly not with superstars.

During the World Series, a fitful series of contacts ensued between Wagner and Katz, but they went nowhere. Before the team left for Japan, Wagner made his final offer of $470,000 a year and told the press it was the highest offer in the franchise's history, decidedly competitive with what was being offered to other superstars, such as future Hall of Famer Willie Stargell. Prodded by Katz, Rose was offended. The offer would make him only about the eighteenth-highest-paid player in the majors, merely in the top 10 percent of salaries. He wanted to be the highest paid.

What salary range was Katz talking about then? Wagner inquired.

"The sky's the limit," Katz replied.

On October 18, Rose declared himself a free agent and named three teams in the National League and five in the American League to which he would consider a trade. For a story in *Sports Illustrated*, he happily consented to being photographed, doffing the hat of each team on his list and mugging for the camera in a series of quizzical snapshots. The largest picture in the layout had him in his familiar Reds hat, with his fingers crossed, as if to indicate (to Katz's delight) that he hoped to remain a Red. During the World Series, he did some commentary for CBS and got in trouble with the baseball commissioner's office for an interchange with the oddsmaker Jimmy the Greek, when Rose suggested that the odds were best that he would end up with the Philadelphia Phillies.

This was called negotiating your contract through the media, and in his captive town of Cincinnati no one did it better than Rose. He was resorting to this unique procedure for the second time in two contracts. In 1977, he had told his side of the story so often to the fawning press about the intransigence of the Reds management that the front office took out an advertisement in the Cincinnati newspapers to explain its position. As Dick Wagner was to put it, "When no Cincinnati reporter would write our side of the story, we simply paid to have it told."

Wagner's talks with Rose and Katz were suspended while the Reds flew off to Japan to play seventeen exhibition games. In Rose's case, he did not go solely as a goodwill ambassador of Major League Baseball. There was another prodigious inducement. While there, he signed a contract with Mizuno, the Japanese sporting goods company, for $600,000.

Upon the team's return home, a new, frightening allegation found its way to the ears of the Reds management: Pete Rose had smuggled his hefty downpayment in cash into the country. A gambling crony of Rose's would later say that the scheme had been perpetrated by carrying the money in a small blue purse. The adventure led to some snickering within the Rose entourage. As the story was told to the front office, a traveling companion of Rose's had actually carried the money on the team plane and through U.S. Customs. The Reds officials were slipped a copy of the Mizuno contract, but there was no way for the Reds front office to confirm the smuggling allegation.

Eventually, through a tip from a confidential source, the Customs Service got onto Rose. A three-year investigation between 1983 and 1986 into suspected currency violations uncovered three separate occurrences in which Rose transported large amounts of cash into the country from Japan: $15,000 in 1979, $60,000 in 1980, and $46,197.54 in 1981—a total of $121,197.54. After one of these trips to Japan, Rose had reportedly bought a Mercedes Benz for a girlfriend in San Francisco. In January 1984, when Rose again went to Japan, the U.S. Customs Service was treating him as a suspect. Rose was tailed from San Francisco to Tokyo and back, but the Customs agents uncovered no evidence of wrongdoing on that trip. In December 1986, the government agreed to a compromise: Rose was allowed to pay a fine of $23,098.77, one-half the amount allegedly smuggled in 1981. The 1979 and 1980 offenses were not prosecuted because the statute of limitations had expired by the time the Customs Service instituted its civil claim against Rose in 1986, and because the evidence was unclear about Rose's intent. (He did not seem to have the usual criminal intent of drug trafficking, money laundering, or tax evasion.)

Pete Rose barely escaped the curse of a criminal record in 1986, largely because the Customs agents had been unable to catch him in the act of smuggling and to seize the actual cash, and because the statute of limitations had run on the first two counts. If he had been charged and convicted criminally for his currency violations, he would have been sentenced to jail for a considerably longer time in 1990 under the federal sentencing guidelines on his 1990 tax evasion conviction.

Upon Rose's return from Japan, the sports pages were trumpeting the news of Tommy John's stupendous three-year contract with the Yankees for $1.4 million. The deal was not quite as stupendous as that of Catfish Hunter four years earlier, the contract that touched off the revolution of free agency, but it was handsome nonetheless. Early word from his handlers was that Rose might top Tommy John's contract easily. Ted Turner in Atlanta was hinting at a "tremendous contract." The Mets had shown intense interest, given their customary problems at third base, and the Phillies, who were well endowed at third base with Mike Schmidt, but short on leadership, were expressing real enthusiasm. John Galbreath, the Pirates owner, had invited Rose for a visit to his Columbus, Ohio, farm; his problem was fan apathy. And Auggie Busch wanted to see the player in St. Louis, even though the Cards owner was on his way into the hospital for a hernia operation.

Reuven Katz had a good idea. Why not an auction? Not just an auction but a public auction. Not just a public auction but a showbiz barn-burner such as baseball had never seen before. If Katz used the dignified term of an auction, others were saying that free agency was turning baseball into a meat market.

While Rose was away in Japan, Katz set out to plan a traveling roadshow. Four more teams beyond Rose's original eight wanted in, but a call to Katz from Ted Turner made the Atlanta tycoon into the stalking horse. Turner had a lowly team and a fledgling superstation in a nascent cable television industry. Cash, a lot of it, was his only inducement. He had good reason to be especially grateful to Rose. At the end of Rose's hitting streak, more than seventy thousand fans filled Fulton County Stadium in two nights, while his superstation, TBS, had beamed the historic moment to forty states.

On the Sunday before Rose and Katz hit the road, the negotiations with the Reds were declared dead, once and for all. Buried deep in the story in Cincinnati, Dick Wagner expressed the real reason: "What we have here is a dispute over values. Our values don't go along with Rose's."

The next day, with considerable noise, the dog and pony show opened in Atlanta, where Rose and Katz dined over steak and shrimp cocktail at the Stadium Club with Turner, his Braves manager, and the general manager. A tour of the superstation followed the talks, before the parties delivered their reprise to the press. Turner confessed to the worry that the Phillies had the inside track because they were a pennant contender. "I feel now we are more in contention than we were when the whole thing started," he said.

Rose turned up with a copy of Turner's book, *The Man Behind the Mouth,* tucked ostentatiously under his arm at Hartsfield Airport for his departure flight. He was mobbed for autographs. In the crush, the arresting thought was expressed that, after his interesting week, Rose might just become the highest paid athlete in the world, except for the Brazilian soccer great, Pelé.

"What did Pelé make . . . something like a million a year?" Katz wondered stagily.

"Why exclude him?" Rose grinned.

"Yea, why should we?" Katz echoed.

"See you in Philadelphia!" someone shouted out.

"Don't bet on it," Rose shot back.

When the serious questions came from the press, Katz revealed his strategy. "Ted Turner will be a hard act to follow," he said importantly.

"Now I have a real idea of what I'm worth," Rose chimed in.

It would be several days before the figure of what he was worth to Turner emerged. The offer was virtually to write his own ticket. A million dollars a year for as many as five years, or for as long as he wanted to play, and $100,000 a year for life after that. Inconceivable. At one point in the conversation, Turner had said to Rose, "Join me for two years at a million a year. By then, Dick Wagner will be fired and you can go back to your hometown."

"I didn't know whether to wind my tail or scratch my watch," Rose said later about the offer, invoking his favorite gag about happiness.

Back at Hartsfield Airport, Rose turned to Katz. "Where do we go next?" he asked, his head swimming.

In Kansas City the next day, the Royals general manager met Rose's private jet, and the player was whisked to the Marion Laboratories, where the Royals owner, Ewing Kauffman, was waiting with his spread sheets. "My buddy [George Steinbrenner] over in New York wins the pennant every year in the free agent draft. I gotta try to do the same thing," Kauffman told Rose at the outset. "I never expected to find a player with your credentials in the draft."

By then, the barnstorming was settling into a pattern. Rose rolled a twenty-five-minute videotape of his career highlights, which included segments of his best television appearances. They were selling not so much a mere baseball player but a multifaceted product, which included the capacity to be a spokesman for baseball. Then they sat back to listen.

"We're a little embarrassed," Rose would say disingenuously, "because we don't know what to ask for. You have to help us."

The Royals had become the only American League team under serious consideration now. With its expansive AstroTurf, splashy Royals Stadium was perfectly suited to this slap hitter, and the team needed a leadoff hitter badly. Behind George Brett and Rose's former teammate Hal McRae, the team was a contender. The designated-hitter rule in the American League offered an additional inducement to pursue Ty Cobb's all-time hit record without the strain and the dangers of injury from playing defense.

Rose emerged from his meeting with Kauffman carrying a black bag and a wisecrack: "No, this bag isn't full of money." It might as well have been a doctor's bag, because Kauffman had offered him a pharmaceutical business as part of the deal, as well as a few oil investments for good measure. If he came to the Royals, he would not compete with Brett for third base, Rose assured the press, but would play first, where he would welcome the chance to beat out Rod Carew as the All-Star first baseman in the American League. In fact, Brett had gone to the management himself and offered to move to another position if they signed Rose.

Hours later, Rose and Katz were calling on August Busch, Jr., in his St. Louis hospital room, where the owner was being prepared for a hernia operation. There, the sweetener was beer rather than oil. A Budweiser distributorship was the inducement that had lured Roger Maris to St. Louis after he had broken Babe Ruth's home run record with the Yankees. After his playing days, Rose could be the Budweiser spokesman for life, even if it was true that he didn't drink much of the stuff. Of Busch's impending operation, he remarked, "I probably would have had a hernia too, if I had to carry all the money he was offering me."

One thing bothered Rose about St. Louis, however. The Cards were saying that only one position was open on the club, and that was left field, where Lou Brock played. Brock was then closing in on his three-thousandth hit. That troubled Pete. Someone might try a similar move on him some day.

The following day, the carnival pitched its tent in Columbus, where John Galbreath and his son, Dan, spread out their special treasures. Now it was not oil or beer but horses. The Galbreaths owned Darby Dan Farms, the premier stable for such thoroughbred champions as Graustark, Little Current, and Roberto (the last named for Roberto Clemente), and they knew they were courting a notorious horse player. Their offer was a broodmare with champion bloodlines, and the chance to mate with the great studs such as Graustark. Rose did not have to be told that such a horse might produce as many as ten foals during her motherhood, each worth somewhere between $200,000 and $500,000. As Roy Blount, Jr., was to put it, John Galbreath was proposing to make Rose not only a man of wealth but of breeding.

Rose could scarcely believe what he was hearing. He was a wide-eyed kid again, and who wouldn't have been? "It amazes me how all the proposals are tied in with the way [the owners] make their money," he said. To Sparky Anderson, who as the just-fired manager of the Reds was watching this bizarre tour with morbid fascination, Rose exclaimed: "The offers are getting bigger and bigger. They're offering me the world!"

"If I had been broke, I'd a took the Atlanta offer," Rose proclaimed later. "But if I had been a millionaire, I'd a took the Pittsburgh offer, because he was gonna cut me in on something that money can't buy. I know people with millions who can't get into a syndicate of a Triple Crown winner, but I could have."

On the fourth day of the tour, he popped over to the estate of Ruly Carpenter, the Phillies owner and heir to the duPont fortune, in Montchanin, Delaware, for a pivotal meeting. The groundwork had now been laid: a mountain of cash from Turner, cash plus pharmaceuticals, oil deals, beer distributorships, and thoroughbred horses from the others. In New York, even without a visit from the circus, the Mets board had gathered for the third time to up their offer to three years at $600,000. What would be the response of the Phillies, where Rose really wanted to go, where he had such good friends as Larry Bowa and Greg Luzinski? The whole free-agent process had pointed toward this meeting, and all signals were good.

For three straight years, the Phillies had won the National League East title, only to lose in the play-offs. Their biggest star was Mike Schmidt, but he was sullen and withdrawn, and was not much of a help to the talented younger players when the pressure games rolled around. The team needed a leader who was upbeat.

The executive vice-president of the club, Bill Giles, was a sentimentalist about Cincinnati. He had grown up there, and his father, Warren Giles, kept his office in Cincinnati when he was the president of the National League. In his early career, the younger Giles had even been a scout for the Reds. If Pete was determined to leave Cincinnati, Giles wanted him in Philly. Vivid in Giles's mind were the 1976 play-offs between the Phillies and the Reds. As the leadoff hitter in the first game, Rose had hit Steve Carlton's first pitch for what appeared to be a routine single to right center, barrelled on to second base while the surprised Phillies outfielder made a lazy throw, and slid safely under the tag. Rose's hustle helped to demolish the Phillies psychologically, and the Reds clobbered them in straight games. The Phillies needed a leadoff hitter who exuded that kind of energy.

Moreover, Giles shared with Rose a love of the track and betting, and they had been to the dog track together. With bemusement and a little awe, Giles had watched how Rose would bet five hundred dollars per race. There was another factor. Giles was an admirer not only of Pete but of Karolyn as well. He never forgot the time he found himself in an elevator in Tampa one spring training with Pete, Karolyn, and their son, Petey. Making small talk, Giles had remarked upon what a fine boy Petey was.

"Yeah," said Karolyn, "but he cusses too damn much."

During the preliminaries in Carpenter's hunting box living room, Giles expressed his mixed emotions. "Pete, why don't you go back to Cincinnati and stay where you belong?" he said baldly.

"We've burned our bridges there," Rose replied. "No way I'm

going back." Giles perceived some sort of deep-seated personal antipathy with the Reds management, but the nature of the problem was left undefined.

"Then I'd love to have you in Philly," Giles said.

Katz cued up his promotional tape, but Carpenter and Giles were quickly bored. "We know what Pete can do for us," said Giles, who was a marketing man by training, and the tape was turned off. They were ready to get down to business.

"What kind of money would it take to get Pete to the Phillies?" Carpenter asked.

"Well, we already have an offer in seven figures, guaranteed for three years," Katz began.

There was a pause, as the thought sunk in slowly. Carpenter calculated on his fingers. "My God, that's a million a year," he said, then paused some more. "Let's have lunch," he said. "It's all over."

Rose sat in stunned silence. So it was over, finished. He was not going to Philadelphia. There was no way the Phillies were going to pay a million a year or anything close. As the conversation lurched forward awkwardly, with disappointment on everyone's face, the Phillies best offer came out, if only for the record: three years for $2.1 million, or a mere $700,000 a year. Over Mrs. Carpenter's tasty welsh rarebit and bacon, the talk was mainly about how to break the bad news to the Philadelphia press.

Stricken, Rose fiddled with his food and hinted that he would probably take the Kansas City offer. He wanted to get out of there and wondered if he could take Carpenter's private jet home.

"You can . . . if you pay for it," Carpenter replied.

On the sad trip to the airport, Giles made his last argument. Handing Rose the green book, which contained the records of National League players, he pointed out that Rose was second, third, and fourth in so many major categories. "Pete, I can't believe you would go to the American League," Giles said. "Look at this. You have a chance to set all these National League records. If you go to the Royals, your kids and your grandkids will never see you on top. Listen, you loved my dad, and he loved you. He won't like this. Baseball won't like it. You have to, at least, stay in the National League."

At planeside, Giles tried to be upbeat. They should not all give up hope. He had some ideas, which he would put to Ruly Carpenter. They should stay in touch.

When they were together again, Giles said to Carpenter, "I'm convinced that he'll play for us for less money." But not for as little as they were then offering. A bit of "restructuring" was called for.

Meanwhile, it was announced to more than a hundred reporters in Philadelphia that Rose had rejected the Phillies'—and the Mets'— offers. "The Phils made a tremendous offer . . . much, much more than Cincinnati offered," Rose told the press. "But I've had offers this week that are tremendous, tremendous, tremendous. All my headfirst sliding, all the gut busting is paying off." He could not resist baiting his former team and gloating. "I thank God every morning for being alive. Then I thank Dick Wagner. He made all this possible."

On a Saturday, Rose and Katz tooled over to Lexington, Kentucky, to look at horseflesh. The Galbreaths had spent sixty-five years building the bloodlines of their Darby Dan horses. As he stood by the paddock and the great horses were paraded before him, Pete was impressed.

In Cincinnati that night, Katz confessed to Rose that he had heard back from the Phillies. They were prepared to go higher, because they had gone to WPHL-TV, the television station that broadcast the Phillies games with a simple argument: contribute directly to the deal that will allow us to sign Rose, and your audience will be greater and your advertising revenues will be higher. WPHL kicked in $600,000. Moreover, the Phillies thought they could justify a higher offer to Rose because he might raise the number of season ticket holders by as much as three thousand and improve considerably upon the modest 1.6 million fans that the Phillies had drawn on the road in 1978.

Rose and Katz settled on a figure to ask: they wanted a fourth year guaranteed, the year Rose would turn forty-two years of age. It was a demand Kansas City had already met. "But if I get our figure, you got to go," Katz told Rose. "We can't say we'll get back to them."

On December 5, in a packed Orlando hotel ballroom, where a handful of big league managers looked on in awe, Rose, flanked by Phillies officials, stepped forward to announce his deal: $800,000, guaranteed, for four years, or about $3.2 million. Again, the assemblage heard his favorite remark about the difficulty of a show dog jumping over his stacks of money, but a few sentences later, he was disparaging the offer as the lowest of four final offers. It was as if he had made a noble decision. The press was as awed as anyone. In the typical overblown prose of sports writers, Tom Boswell of the *Washington Post* compared Rose's week to Caesar inspecting gifts.

In the wake of Rose's blockbuster deal, much was written about its "ripple effect," but tidal wave would have been a better image. In courting Rose and losing him, the Pirates had jeopardized their relations with their hulk, Dave Parker, whose negotiations had been put on hold while the Pirates pursued Rose. Parker was clearly the best player in the National League. He had won his second straight batting title in 1978, with a .334 average, while adding 30 homers, 117 RBIs, and 20 stolen bases, and had been voted the National League's MVP. But he was slated to be paid $225,000 for the 1979 season, a sum that suddenly looked like a slave wage. Compared to Rose, Parker was the wave of the future rather than the ripple of the past. He was only twenty-seven years old. "If they pay a singles hitter $800,000, they have to pay an ordinary home run hitter a million plus," was Parker's attitude. His contract had to change.

The contract of the Most Valuable Player in the American League loomed as well, and Boston's Jim Rice was only twenty-five years old. Most significantly of all, seven-time batting champion Rod Carew of the Twins had become a free agent. His agent told the press immediately after the Rose deal that Carew's asking price had gone up significantly.

When the winter meetings opened with the announcement of Rose's signing, Commissioner Bowie Kuhn voiced again his concern that big contracts, offered by teams in large media markets such as New York, Philadelphia, and Los Angeles, would push baseball toward a class structure of haves and have nots. The influence of television on the signing of Pete Rose had been the most direct in baseball history.

If money was the only standard, Rose was to stay the number one player in the game for all of four weeks. On January 9, 1979, Jim Rice signed a seven-year guaranteed contract for $4.9 million. Three weeks later, big Dave Parker became baseball's first million-dollar-a-year player. In their chagrin over Rose and race horses, the Pirates first offered an incredible nine million dollars for ten years, but Parker turned up his nose. Pittsburgh was a lousy baseball town, and "Parkway" wanted to keep his stay there mercifully short. He signed a five-year contract for $5.4 million (although the deal included no thoroughbreds). Two weeks after that, Rod Carew went to the Angels and into the stratosphere.

As baseball fell into the grip of this salary escalation that he had initiated, Rose prepared to leave his hometown. There were roasts and toasts and farewell dinners. One local broadcaster tried to have Rose declared an endangered species, as if he were an exotic snail-darter. Another wanted him made into an historical landmark. As Rose navigated his way through this pampering, he peppered the Reds front office with bitter remarks about his ill-treatment as well as that of Tony Perez and Sparky Anderson. It had been no fun to play for the Reds ever since Tony Perez was traded two years earlier, he said. Dick Wagner, the general manager, was his special villain. On "Donahue," Donahue asked if Wagner had attended Rose's most recent farewell banquet.

"I didn't expect him to show up at my farewell dinner," Rose replied tartly. "I won't be at his."

The first two years of Bart Giamatti's presidency at Yale were, by his own description, no bowl of cherries. His arrival as a public man had been abrupt, even radical, and in many ways, he was unprepared for it. The rhythms of administrative life took considerable adjusting for him. At first, the exercise of power excited him. For ten years, he had been a young Turk on the Yale faculty, relishing the role of the biting critic on the side. Now, he was the Sultan, and the young Turks were snapping at *him*. In the beginning, he enjoyed the fencing and the struggle to outwit them. He did so with affection and with sympathy, for he wanted to bolster and encourage younger faculty. His bent was to promote within his own organization, as if it were a kind of farm system, rather than go outside for the big-salaried free agents.

His romantic impulse applied to the university just as much as to baseball. It too was a garden and a refuge and a Renaissance city that was the embodiment of civility and respect for diversity, where the best minds could compete within set rules of the civilized order. To his friend Peter Brooks, Giamatti painted the university as a cross between the Roman Catholic church and a poem, although, heaven forbid, that sounded a bit hierarchical . . . like Harvard. Harvard, after all, stood only for truth, whereas Yale stood for truth and light. It was a repository of national hope and a source of national leadership. But it needed to practice what it taught, and it needed leadership, because to Giamatti, American universities had many competent managers, but very few true leaders. "If its goals are noble, so must be its acts," he wrote.

To the students, Giamatti nurtured this sense of a noble quest by accenting their privilege to be at Yale. Yale was liberal education, and liberal education was "a process of self knowledge for the purpose of shared civility." It was like . . . a puritan village. "If you come here questioning your election, that too is in the spirit of the place. You will know you are truly of Yale . . . when you hear yourself indulging in that oldest puritan pastime—talking about how hard you work. One of the deepest pleasures of this place is to spend leisure time expostulating about work."

While the students listened to these lofty sentiments and even, in a few cases, took them to heart, they sensed in Giamatti a president they could kid. The *Yale Daily News* had a field day. In its inaugural issue, the *News* reported that Giamatti had no favorite food [in contrast to the pâté de foie gras and caviar on ice of Kingman Brewster], and no favorite color, but his favorite joke was "the Kansas City Royals." Some time later, the *News* put out a fake issue with the headline: "Giamatti Quits!" and a cartoon, picturing the president sitting astride his memorial moose at Ezra Stiles College, exclaiming, "How many times do I have to tell them! *Non ho mai voluto essere il presidente d'altro che la societa americana di baseball!*"* Two years into the presidency, while Giamatti was focused on improvements to the physical plant of the university, the *News* published a cartoon on the reconstruction of Giamatti's face. The drawing featured Giamatti before and after and was entitled "Bartshead Revisited." The cartoonist had the Lilliputian workers of the New Haven Historical Preservation Society deployed upon scaffolding around the face, with orders to halt the receding hairline, putty wrinkles, eliminate the worried expression, reduce the jowl sag, replace the teeth, whitewash the dark circles, and supplant the tie with something livelier, but leave the distinguished gray streaks around the temples.

Behind this cartoon was the sober fact that the president had aged frighteningly in his first two years on the job. Gone was the youthful, energetic look of his inaugural pictures. Without complaint, he confessed that he was often fatigued and was having difficulties with the physical demands of the job. Eleven months into his presidency, he had been smitten with pneumonia and became bedridden for several weeks. "I don't think I had fully appreciated the depth and the breadth of the university," he later told the *New Haven Register*. "I was not prepared for the pace."

It took him some time to understand what he could and what he could not do. Continuing his unhealthy pattern of little sleep from his days as master of Ezra Stiles College, he worked late into the night, often on the some two hundred speeches he gave during his first two years in office. Wistfully, he insisted on trying to teach a course, as if he was, against all odds, trying to hold on to his first love and his true calling. It was a seminar on Dante and Thomas Aquinas, taught with his friend, the Sterling Professor of History, Jaroslav Pelikan. (Out of this course, Pelikan developed a small book on Dante as a theologian, which was published twelve years later.)

Predictably, the pool of applicants was huge, so huge that Gia-

---

* I never wanted to be the president of anything but the American League.

matti and Pelikan required each to write a small essay on why the student wished to attend. Ever the undergraduate professor, Giamatti was eager to have a broad range of students from each class, not simply a grim collection of Phi Beta Kappas. He worried that his presence might intimidate the shy and the less articulate, so he discussed with Pelikan how to tease the timid and the taciturn into a contribution. To Pelikan, more the stern teacher of graduate students, this quaint concern for the sheepish was "almost pastoral."

Giamatti tried to maintain an open door to students at first, setting regular office hours, but inevitably that practice was scrapped. He knew he was undergoing a very real change in his professional life and was not sure it was the right thing. There was no sense of completion to administration. In teaching, he would say, one started a line of inquiry and three years later, one had something with shape and contour. "When you are an administrator," he said, "you start out in the morning to make a pot, and at the end of the day, if you've made an ungainly plate, you're lucky."

In his first year in office, Giamatti faced two difficult and painful and enervating episodes over personnel. The first dealt with Robert Brustein, who had been the dean of the Yale Drama School for twelve years and the artistic director of its adjunct theatre, the Yale Rep. A stormy, passionate man, he had transformed the Yale Rep into one of the finest professional theatres in America. Many of the experimental, avant garde, and radical plays he produced were critically acclaimed and commercially successful. Promising professionals such as Henry Winkler and Meryl Streep had trained as actors under Brustein, as had playwrights Christopher Durang and Wendy Wasserstein. But the Yale faculty derided Brustein's plays. Many, including the Giamattis, were offended by his approach.

While turning the drama school into a training ground for the professional stage, Brustein had downplayed the role of the conservatory as a school to educate and amuse undergraduates. That process put Yale at the center of a classic debate in regional theatre: whether the paramount mission of university-based theatres should be professional or educational. Brustein considered the educational role to be decidedly secondary.

The question was whether to renew Brustein's contract. Brustein sensed he was in trouble, even more so when the choice of Giamatti as president occasioned a headline in the *New Haven Register:* GIAMATTI'S ASCENSION ENDS YALE DRAMA. Could it be prophetic? Brustein wondered.

During the spring of 1978, in three meetings, the two men

jousted, apparently over policy questions. The president worried about the "academic justification" for the drama school, and the dean argued for it as a trade school for actors, not for teachers of the theatre. Giamatti wanted more involvement for undergraduates, and Brustein thought this would deprofessionalize the school. Giamatti wanted to restore such courses as the history of costume, an offering that existed when Toni Smith was in the Yale Drama School before Brustein's tenure. Brustein brushed aside this idea as inessential to the nurturing of the professional actor. Between men of good faith, these were honest disagreements. Brustein himself would acknowledge later that Giamatti was naturally more interested in the future of Yale University than the future of the American theatre. They spoke their lines about policy, but the real plot was in the subtext: their meaningful glances, the inflection of their voices, their true dislike for each other.

Along the way, Giamatti remarked more than once about how alike they were. Implicit in the remark was that they were both theatrical and stubborn. In the general fashion of theatre people, their interchanges became increasingly overdramatic and nasty and, finally, petty. Giamatti informed Brustein in late June 1978, that the next academic year would be his last as dean. To the press, Giamatti portrayed the decision as a simple case of a deanship coming to an end. The normal tenure for a Yale dean was ten years, and Brustein would have lingered for thirteen. It was time for a change of managers, despite the championship seasons. Brustein responded with their disagreements over policy. He cast himself as the symbol of professional theatre and the victim of a Philistine. To fire him was to downgrade professional theatre at Yale. Giamatti denied any shift in policy and anticipated no reduction in quality.

If Toni Giamatti had been a factor before the decision, Brustein's wife, Norma, became a complicating factor afterward. Norma Brustein was a leading actress in the Yale Rep and had a considerable reputation of her own. After Giamatti's decision, she became deeply depressed and bitter and tried to work her way through it, partly by working on a novel whose prime villain was a sinister university president named V. Standish Gambino. In the fall of 1978, only five months after her husband was discharged, she had a massive heart attack and died. More than once, Robert Brustein was to intimate that Giamatti had killed her.

The second traumatic episode of Giamatti's first year in office hit much closer to home. As one of Giamatti's first and most important appointments, he had tapped a strong-willed Yale law professor named Abraham Goldstein to be his provost. The appointment was widely applauded, for Goldstein was perceived to have the kind of robust toughness and bluster and decisiveness that some felt Giamatti lacked. Married to the novelist Ruth Tessler Goldstein, the new provost was a friend and an early booster of Giamatti. Upon his selection, Goldstein spoke of his excitement to be part of Giamatti's administration and of Giamatti's dynamic quality.

In the summer of 1978, the Goldsteins took possession of the university-owned house reserved for Yale provosts and proceeded to make the house over with major renovations. This was entirely in the Yale tradition. Up until the budget crunch of the late 1970s, it was expected of a new master or a new executive to redo his university house. It would be odd not to. But under Giamatti, it was a new time. Besides substantial structural changes, such as a new screened porch, the interior of the provost's house was painted—and then expensively repainted when Ruth Goldstein was displeased with the color. The bill mounted up.

In the spring of 1979, the sleuths at the *Yale Daily News* broke the story, stating that, in this era of budgetary austerity, more than $67,000 of the university's money had been spent to indulge the provost's taste. It quickly became a scandal. Stung by the reports—he felt Giamatti had given him the authority for the renovations—Goldstein turned to the president for support, and Giamatti turned cold and distant, leaving the provost to fend for himself. It became a question of public appearance and public morality. Angered and frustrated, Goldstein resigned.

To the Yale faculty, Giamatti had hung Goldstein out to dry, and there was much whispering. Notwithstanding Giamatti's conservative bent and his principles about appearances, it was widely known that the Giamattis were themselves engaged in a major redecoration of the president's house on Hillhouse Street. That redecoration was estimated to cost Yale's operating budget as much as three times what the Goldsteins had spent. This awareness would linger for years in the background and would become potential ammunition for Yale's clerical union when, four years later, Giamatti found himself in a bitter labor dispute.

While the Brustein and Goldstein flaps were awkward, they did not wound Giamatti's presidency, although they tortured him personally. Like most public men, he desperately wanted to be loved. He adopted an urbane and sardonic exterior, as if he were impervious to criticism, but he was thin-skinned and was disappointed that all his friends on the faculty did not agree as one with his decisions. As his friend and mentor Maynard Mack would put it, Giamatti conveyed the impression of having a walrus hide, but inside he was "tender as a glowworm."

How would he grade himself? he was asked after his turbulent first year in office. "The semester's not over yet," he replied.

On the larger issues, however, his charm and wit and charisma carried him through. The presidency of Yale was not unlike a southern governorship after Reconstruction: its powers were gutted and distributed among committees and lower fiefdoms. The Yale Corporation had the real power. The power of appointment rested with academic committees, and the provost was in charge of the finances. The president of Yale, Giamatti was to say, was an "ambulatory bureaucratic icon." As a consequence, the president had to govern largely through his personality and his power of persuasion.

Where style was everything, Giamatti excelled. When he wanted something done, he projected sincerity and caring along with warmth, and it was hard to deny him. Style became substance. And he knew how to play a role. "I paint myself as this besieged, weak creature trying to get through the day—the Wimp of Woodbridge Hall," he confessed, and then added with some astonishment: "It is not ineffective."

The focus of his early years as president was, of course, the financial situation of the university. By the school year of 1980–81, Yale had its first balanced budget in a decade. He had cut the size of the student body and the size of the faculty, and he had begun to address the problem of the dilapidated physical plant that was referred to bureaucratically as "deferred maintenance." Uninspiring as that prosaic activity was, Giamatti went about it cheerfully, making self-deprecating jokes along the way. He was a president who had "all his ducts in a row," he announced. His presidency represented "the golden age of infrastructure." "Call me Bart the Refurbisher," he suggested. "I will only be remembered by people who like to go through steam tunnels. If my name goes on anything, it will be the Giamatti Memorial Wiring System."

As Giamatti traveled the country promoting a $370 million fundraising campaign for Yale—a goal that would be exceeded by more than $3 million during his tenure—the glory of "liberal education" was the heart of his message. Liberal education, he told his audiences, had its roots in liberty, the freedom of the mind to explore itself, and to connect with other minds in the quest for truth. Its product should be the whole person, intellectually discerning but flexible, tough-minded but open-hearted.

To Giamatti, liberal education had nothing to do with "relevance" or indulgence or open classrooms. It was rooted in classical training and required a solid foundation. When a seventh grader named Kempton Dunn wrote to him, asking if the study of Latin still had value, Giamatti replied: "Ask not, noble Dunn, what prompts us to study a 'dead language,' for the language is not dead. We study Latin because without it, we cannot know our history and our heritage. And without that knowledge, we cannot know ourselves. *Nosce te ipsum*,* brave Dunn. If one can read that, one can—in one's life— begin to do that. The link between Latin and our lives is deep and abiding."

The United States, west and south of the Hudson River, was, for Giamatti, a new experience. He knew little of the larger country. In his Massachusetts provincialism, the rest of America had a boring sameness to it. Still, at Yale Clubs and other gatherings everywhere, he more than realized his potential as a promoter. Preaching his message in Atlanta in the spring of 1981, he told his audience why liberal education mattered: "If you don't have a sense of history, there's no way for you to draw yourself out of yourself. You simply end up a little solipsistic twit." That made his audience perk up. Being a solipsistic twit did not sound like a good thing to be.

In baseball, Giamatti had a passion that could break the ice with any crowd. It was the touchstone, the font, the refuge. It made him approachable and accessible, as it made nearly every American of any class, from any walk of life, accessible to him. He was a baseball nut, and everyone could relate to that. He could talk it low, and he could talk it high. Undoubtedly, he knew and enjoyed the joke about intellectuals and baseball: it was the only sport slow enough for them to understand.

Whereas his promise as a proselytizer for Yale and liberal education was quickly realized, his hope, expressed privately to Henry Rosovsky before his inauguration, to use Yale as a platform for national issues beyond education was not realized. Giamatti knew instinctively that arcane problems of higher education bored general audiences. Moreover, as president of Yale, elitism was always a danger for him. His job was the education of the able, privileged few, not the masses. How big could his problems be anyway? Everyone, it seemed, wanted to attend his school. Once, at a national meeting of college presidents, Giamatti had to fend off the president of a land-grant college who whispered to him that his daughter was applying to Yale the following year, and was there anything Giamatti could do?

* Know thyself.

He spoke of how a new college president learns to talk a language he called "high institutional." High institutional is noncontroversial, necessarily bland speech; its rhetoric is always lofty, but its statements are always qualified, because its practitioner is forever juggling so many ambiguities that he can scarcely keep them all straight. Talking high institutional means that its purveyor ends up with no personality whatever and can barely understand himself what he is saying.

"Tell me about the Boston Red Sox in high institutional," Edward Fiske of the *New York Times* prodded him.

"Okay: Impelled by a high sense of their traditional mission, the central organizing force in that northeastern part of the United States—which, of course, is not the only part of the United States but nevertheless is, for our purpose, the part we are talking about—the Red Sox have both fallen upon hard times and, in their own terms, achieved a significant grandeur. . . ."

"As President of Yale, what did you think about Luis Tiant leaving the Red Sox and signing with the Yankees?" Fiske interrupted, having had enough of high institutional already. But Giamatti was warming to the task.

"Luis Tiant, on the one hand, knowing full well the ravages of time—as of course we all as human beings come to know them—but on the other hand ever mindful of the need to advance the human spirit, played the part of a traitor and left Boston for the asphalt pastures of New York."

"Asphalt pastures?" Fiske said.

"You see, that's where you save yourself from the rest of that sentence. You give them 'asphalt pastures,' and the only thing they get out of it is asphalt pastures, because those who are listening are so tired of this prose that they look for any kind of help."

On August 31, 1981, in a speech before the entering freshman class, Giamatti finally touched a live wire. Titling his speech "A Liberal Education and the New Coercion," he took out after Jerry Falwell and the Moral Majority. At the time, Falwell was riding high with the new administration of Ronald Reagan, even though his rhetoric was still intemperate and mean. The kinder, gentler Jerry Falwell had not yet arrived on the American scene. At this point, he was still a firebrand, complaining when the girls from Sweetbriar College—the Sweetbriar lesbians, he called them—drifted over to Lynchburg. With purple rhetoric that his associates knew only in private, Giamatti lashed out. "Cunning in the use of a native blend of old intimidation and new technology . . . angry at change, rigid in the application of chauvinistic slogans, absolutistic in morality," these "new Savanarolas" believed that they and they alone possessed the truth. "There can be no debate, no discussion, no dissent. They know. There is only one set of overarching political and spiritual and social beliefs. Whatever view does not conform to [their] views is by definition relativistic, negative, secular, immoral, against the family, anti-free enterprise, un-American. What nonsense. What dangerous malicious nonsense." It was "resurgent bigotry." Its source was a "meanness of spirit," the same spirit that motivated the Ku Klux Klan, anti-Semitic groups, and terrorist organizations.

The reaction was instantaneous. Major television programs perceived the chance for a marvelous freak show: Falwell vs. Giamatti, Yale vs. Liberty Baptist College, aristocratic New England ecumenism vs. plebian Southern fundamentalism. "Donahue," "60 Minutes," the "Today Show" all phoned, wanting to orchestrate a debate. The Political Union at Yale was eager to provide the forum. The *New York Times* played the story as an "ancient battle of creeds," and *Time* carried a report headlined "A Humanist Hits Back."

Giamatti, however, turned down all overtures to protract the dispute. "I've said what I want to say on this topic and see no reason to pursue the issue any further at this time," he wrote to the Political Union. Meanwhile, the fundamentalists seethed. Cal Thomas, the spokesman for the Moral Majority, tried to bait him into the open. "I think he is chicken and I would be happy to call that to his face," said Thomas. Giamatti chose to remain silent, even though from the "maw of this morality" arose a good many ideas that he despised.

The maw of the budding Reagan revolution dismayed Giamatti no less. It was not so much a question of politics as intelligence. That a man with so little evidence of intellectual substance could be president of the United States astonished Giamatti. He had been down on Reagan, in fact, ever since a moment in Littleton, New Hampshire, during the 1980 presidential campaign. The president-to-be had done the unforgivable when he told an ethnic joke-cum-slur about a Polish-Italian cock fight.

"How can you tell who the Polish fellow is at the cock fight?" Reagan had asked. "He's the one with the duck. . . . How do you tell who the Italian is? . . . He's the one who bets on the duck. . . . How do you know the Mafia is there? . . . The duck wins." Then it dawned on Reagan that he was out of line. "Uh oh. There goes Connecticut," he added.

Certainly the Connecticut of Bart Giamatti.

"There seems to be a lot of idle time on the Reagan campaign, idle time that apparently allows the candidate to tell ethnic jokes that mock our fellow citizens," Giamatti said of the Reagan joke. "I think he owes everybody an apology, including the ducks."

Nothing infuriated him quite like Mafia jokes, but his reaction was part of a complicated, emotional schema. Even far tamer stories, such as one told by a Yale alumnus about how safe his son had been at a Brooklyn party where the son of a Mafia boss was present, could send Giamatti into a frenzy. And yet, recognizing the Mafia as part of the Italian-American lore, he was fascinated by the Black Hand, fascinated, for example, to hear the tales of lawyer friends, who represented mob clients. He could find humor in evoking Mafia phrases in mock-toughness. When a chemistry professor kept referring to the residential colleges of Yale as "dormitories," Giamatti threatened to break his kneecaps if he didn't cut it out.

To Giamatti, his immigrant countrymen were not so much criminal as underachieving. Toward those who did attain prominence, like, say, Mario Cuomo, Giamatti was supercritical, as if he held them to a higher standard. At the same time, a major objective of his presidency was to improve relations with ethnic New Haven. At a reception at the president's house early in the Giamatti presidency, the U.S. Congressman from the district, Bob Giaimo, was to say, by way of a compliment to Giamatti, that during the fourteen years of the Brewster regime, he had never set foot in the house of the Yale president. No newspaper article had quite wounded and appalled him as much as his very first interview after he assumed the presidency, when the *Washington Post* Style section's Sally Quinn described him as looking like a Mafioso don and the man with him like a consigliere.

George Bush, he of Andover and Yale, was a different fish from Reagan. Giamatti and Bush had served together on the board of Andover in the early 1970s, and they often found themselves in agreement on educational directions for the school. When Giamatti's name was put forward for the Yale presidency, Bush had been consulted and had provided a glowing recommendation.

By 1981, Giamatti was already restive in his job. The life of the significant administrator was just not him, he had decided, especially not in an era of retrenchment. Living in the president's Georgian mansion on Hillhouse Street, with its vast, formal spaces for entertaining on the ground level, loaned Oriental rugs covering the floors, borrowed Hoppers and Remingtons on the walls, made him feel uncomfortable, as if he were merely the housekeeper of a public memorial, as if he were a character in *Rooms for Tourists*, the Hopper painting on his wall. He made jokes about the ducts and steam pipes and wiring of Yale, but they were bittersweet and acknowledged the limits on bold and imaginative initiatives. After he was upbraided for using a cuss word early in his presidency, he could see the dangers of blandness. His friends also noticed unwelcome changes: Giamatti had begun to suffer from creeping stuffiness.

Not long after Reagan and Bush took office, Giamatti attempted to escape. He called his friend from Scroll and Key, Steve Umin, who had become a powerful attorney in the Washington, D.C., firm of the Baltimore Orioles owner, Edward Bennett Williams. Could Umin make a private, confidential inquiry of the new administration about the ambassadorship of Italy? It was the job he wanted more than anything in the world.

Simultaneously, Giamatti got in touch with Eli Jacobs, another Yale man, who would succeed Edward Bennett Williams as the principal owner of the Baltimore Orioles and who was somewhat better connected politically than Umin. Could Jacobs make a feeler to the new administration about Giamatti as ambassador to China?

Umin and Jacobs were astonished by the requests, but both tried to help. The word came back, however, that the serving ambassador, Max Raab, was quite satisfied in Rome, and a new ambassador, Arthur Hummel, had already been chosen for Peking. Giamatti had expressed his interest a little too late.

Bart's disappointment was evident and profound.

· 8 ·

The Strike and the Hit

EVEN BEFORE the 1979 season officially opened in Philadelphia, Pete Rose had already earned his keep. In the bluster and chill of January, the Phillies sent a maroon-and-white bus on a four-day caravan through eastern Pennsylvania and New Jersey with Charlie Hustle as its ticket barker. It would not be long before any conveyance carrying the new Phillies would be called Pete Rose's World Series Express. "I feel like a man playing seven card stud with nine cards in my hand," the Phillies general manager, Paul Owens, would chortle along the way, as he reveled in season ticket sales going up from four to nineteen thousand. With the acquisition of Rose, the handicappers put the Phillies as the odds-on favorite to win the National League title.

Rose set the tone by betting the loquacious Larry Bowa, while they were having a last fling at the gambling tables of Las Vegas before the start of spring training, that he would be the first ball player in the clubhouse in Clearwater.

"Do you want to win as bad as Pete Rose?" Rose had asked his new teammate. Bowa was as much a home-grown symbol of the Philadelphia Phillies in the 1970s as Rose was a symbol of Cincinnati, and being first to work was his treasured reputation. Bowa was about to be supplanted on both counts.

Rose won the bet, arriving on a red-eye from Vegas to Tampa and standing, sleepless and grinning, in uniform when Bowa arrived forty-five minutes early.

"I guess I don't want to win as much as Pete Rose," Bowa said in mock disappointment.

"No," replied Rose consolingly. "You want to win just as much."

He liked being a "happening," Rose told the throng of expectant reporters the next morning. Then, as he pounded his fist into the claw of a first baseman's mitt, he was fitted with a wireless microphone, so that history could capture every unexpurgated detail of his first day at Carpenter Complex.

With all the hype of Rose's arrival, his teammates watched his work habits keenly. First in the clubhouse, he was also longest in the batting cage and the last to leave after a practice. Because he was moving to a new position, his fourth in the majors, he had the hitting coach fungo him endless grounders a good hour after practice, so that he could feel comfortable and competent at first base. In the games, he exuded an energy and an appetite for hitting that the team had previously lacked in its leadoff hitter—and would not have again until 1990, when Lenny Dykstra projected the same physical energy and hunger.

Despite the merchandising of Pete Rose, 1979 was to be a frustrating, injury-riddled, disappointing season for the Phillies. At the All-Star break, Rose was mired in a 3 for 32 slump. Greg Luzinski's knees were uncertain, and the team was faltering. In late August nobody, not even Pete Rose, was talking about the World Series Express anymore. When the team fell below .500, Manager Danny Ozark was fired and replaced with a company man, Dallas Green. Now, here was a person who knew disappointment. Once he had been a fire-balling right-handed pitcher of great promise, but an injury while he was in the minors transformed him into a mediocre hurler during his four seasons with the Phillies. The organization had been good to him afterward, however, and he was devoted to it.

Under the difficult circumstances of his promotion from director of the Phillies farm system to manager, Green would need all the help he could get, not only to get the team to finish out the awful 1979 season like professionals but to evaluate the situation over the winter. His managerial experience consisted of two years in the minors, and many questioned whether his big stars would respect him. With players such as Rose, Luzinski, Schmidt, and Bowa, how could any team finish fourteen games out of first place?

The new skipper perceived in Rose a different way of winning, and it became difficult to decide whether Rose was helping more as a player or as a psychological boost. To the other Phillies, Rose was a baseball warrior who did things on the playing field that they would never dare to attempt. At the beginning of the work day, Rose's custom was to take a prominent seat in the lockerroom near the door, where he could watch his teammates arrive one by one, and deliver an opening commentary on the player's deportment as he came through the door. Green began to think of Rose as his great agitator. If players weren't putting out the way Rose found satisfactory, Pete badgered and cajoled. More than once, he came to Green's aid when the new manager had a problem with one of the other players.

Green did his own share of badgering and baiting. He was lousy at praise but great at criticism. Whether by design or not, this set up an "Us against Him" mentality on the team and unified it, first against its own manager and then against the opposition.

As a commodity as well as a ball player, Rose was a good deal. The press continued to dote on him. "Rose has never been the best player in baseball, but he may be the best thing this game has to offer," Tom Boswell of the *Washington Post* wrote in a valentine. "Defense, speed, power—Rose lacks those. Humor, character, generosity—Rose is always on a streak in those areas. Best of all, Rose truly is what he seems. For most baseball fans, he captures the best of their game's traditional values." It is hard to know if Boswell really believed all that, or was simply pandering to his sporting audience. There was a certain cartoon quality about Rose which made him good copy: the wise cracks, the braggadoccio, the ribald jokes, the memory for his own statistics, the bad grammar, the ardor and the single-mindedness, the elemental, balls-scratching primitivism. Perhaps that really was the best of the game's traditional values—values that were as real as AstroTurf for an audience that cared to know very little about the true character of their performers. The truth is that for the fans real values are irrelevant, until a player does something so horrendous that it touches on "the integrity of the game." The press fell in with the merchandising of Pete Rose. He became a joke figure who laughed along as people laughed at him.

In the pre-Rose 1978 season, the Phillies had finished first in the National League East and sold 2.7 million tickets, 200,000 less than the year before. In 1979, with Rose, the team finished fourth and drew 3 million fans. That alone translated into an additional $3 million in gate receipts. The team was simply more exciting to watch. And Rose did the expected: a .331 finishing average and 208 hits. He was, however, far from the magical missing link that could ensure a World Series appearance for the Phillies, not in 1979 anyway. In April, Rose had said, "I'd say the Phillies are the best team in the league now because they have me. If the Pirates had me, they'd be the best team."

In October, the Phillies finished fourth, and the Pirates, behind Willie Stargell and Dave Parker, went on to sweep the Cincinnati Reds in the play-offs and win the World Series with a Stargell homer in the seventh game.

The work ethic, the magnet for the press and the fans, the mature spokesman for the team, especially in the bad times, the increased gate—that was enough to endear any star player to his front office, and Rose's relationship with Bill Giles, the Cincinnati native who was the Phillies executive vice-president, deepened. Giles had come to think of Rose as the greatest baseball player of all time, largely because his accomplishments had come with such ordinary skills. He had never forgotten the scouting report about Rose to the Reds in the early sixties: "He has heavy legs . . . and if he ever makes it in the big leagues, it will be as a catcher."

Besides the game, they shared the love of the bet. Having spent more than forty years in professional baseball, Giles liked to think of himself as a fierce competitor, every bit as aggressive, every bit as intent on victory as any of his players. He lived for competition. It was important to him to think that he was competing at some activity every day of his life—in the front office, on the golf course, at the track.

Before Rose came to Philadelphia, the Phillies front office happily made the arrangements to have a special table set up for him at the harness track at Brandywine, Delaware, when he came to town. It was something like professional courtesy. Now, Giles and Rose could pick the dogs at Derby Lane together, and they did so regularly. That Rose generally bet five hundred dollars a race, which was quite a lot of money, engaged Giles's curiosity, but because the Phillies were paying their new star $905,000 in 1979, Giles figured that Rose could well afford this level of action. Besides, Giles did not think too much about it. Gambling was in the baseball culture.

Giles and Rose often joked about their gambling exploits. Rose once bragged to Giles in 1979 that he had been changing planes in Las Vegas with little more than an hour to spare, so he went to the tables for a little action. Within ten minutes, he was down $9,000, at the baccarat pit, but he won $17,000 in the next fifteen minutes. Rushing to be on time to Philadelphia, he came home $8,000 ahead. Rose's biggest night gambling did not take place until several years later, however, when he was the manager of the Reds. In the company of Giles during spring training, he won $212,000 at the dog track between Clearwater and Plant City.

The only time Giles ever thought there might be something sinister about Rose's gambling was when he made paid personal appearances for the Phillies. "Make sure they pay me in cash," Rose would say to Giles, "because Reuven has got me on an allowance." Giles understood that this cash was Rose's play money for the track and asked no questions. Like others, he thought of Rose as a little kid who expected a unique entitlement: Rose believed he could get away with anything, simply because he was the great Pete Rose.

About Rose's personal life, however, Giles had to ask a few questions. Rose and his wife, Karolyn, had made a few attempts at reconciliation, but in 1979, the marriage was in the end stage. Rose continued to flaunt his affairs, and Karolyn continued to battle. On several occasions, she stormed into Giles's office at Veterans Stadium, demanding that some girlfriend be thrown out of the ballpark. Giles tried to calm her and get her out of there, but refused to enter the domestic quarrel. Despite his affection for Karolyn, the most he ever did was to ask Rose one day, "Pete, why do you play around like this? Why do you have to flaunt your women like this?"

"Aw, c'mon, Bill, don't you lecture me," Rose snorted. "There are four vices: women, booze, gambling, and drugs. I've only got two vices, but you've got three."

The day Karolyn filed for divorce, Pete Rose went 5 for 5.

Ironically, the way Rose disregarded his messy personal life increased respect for him among his teammates. The other stars on the team—Bowa, Schmidt, Luzinski, Carlton, and Garry Maddox—were all about the same age, and before Rose arrived, they were contentious and jealous of one another. No one was ready to step forward and claim leadership, and none were prepared to allow someone else to assume that position. But Rose was older. He came to the team with more records than those players could ever hope to achieve. It took a year of watching Rose grind it out every day, despite his tumultuous off-field situation, for him to earn the respect of these more gifted players. It took a year for them to allow him to assume the leadership. Pete Rose was genuine: he was what his reputation claimed.

The effect on Mike Schmidt was particularly profound. A kid from Dayton, Ohio, who had grown up during the heyday of the Big Red Machine, Schmidt was instantly drawn to Rose because he had idolized the Cincinnati star from childhood. But Schmidt was a brooder. When he was booed, he went into a shell (whereas Rose was energized by being booed). He had a stormy relationship with the press, partly because his talent was so prodigious that his stellar play looked effortless. When his play was less than stellar—he had an especially high strikeout rate—the fans and the press thought he was slacking off. At first glance, Rose saw Schmidt as the best player in the league . . . for four days a week. Rose befriended Schmidt and worked with him, developing almost a big brother relationship with the third baseman, given the eight-year difference in their ages. Schmidt began to grow. Into the 1980 season, that growth became apparent, and Schmidt's performance rather than Rose's became the centerpiece of the Phillies success. He transformed himself into the best player in the league, not for four but for seven days a week. In an interview with Tom Baldrick of WCAU-TV in Philadelphia ten years later, Rose would say that he did not set out purposely to make Schmidt into a more mature player and person. He was simply doing what he had always done. He had been taught to win. He had won more than anyone around him. He expected to win. And he knew what he could and what he could not do with the talents he had. To Schmidt everything came easily, and that was part of his problem, whereas Rose was playing every game as if it was his last, because he knew that each game could indeed be his last. For six weeks of the 1980 season, he played with a broken toe, cutting open his right shoe to make room for the swollen member. For two months that season, his elbow was hyperextended after a runner crashed into him at first. Only the trainer knew the extent of his pain. "I don't let nobody but the trainer know when I'm hurt," Rose said. "People will use it for their benefit."

One ugliness marred the otherwise glorious 1980 season for the Phillies, and it might well have been related to the physical pain that Rose was suffering. In July, around the All-Star break, the *Trenton Times* broke the story that the physician for the Phillies farm club in Reading, Dr. Patrick Mazza, was under investigation for distributing amphetamines to Phillies players, including the stars: Rose, Bowa, Schmidt, Luzinski, and Tim McCarver. The scandal rocked the baseball world, for it was the first bona fide tempest over drugs in modern baseball history.

Neither the Phillies management nor the league officials knew how to handle it. The inclination of Dallas Green was to believe his players when they looked him in the eye and told him the allegations were untrue. (In the years ahead, Green would learn to be more skeptical.) The normal charges and denials followed the breaking of the story, with Larry Bowa and Mike Schmidt, most notably, flying into a rage at the press over the allegations and promising never to talk to another reporter, ever. The scandal became known alternately as the Reading Connection, the Phillie Eight, and Pillgate. While the

Phillies management publicly denied any knowledge, Bill Giles knew that Rose's use of greenies was chronic, and that he taught younger players how to use the uppers, sometimes in concert with coffee. In the age of cocaine, the management had adopted a tolerant attitude toward "diet pills."

Again, Rose considered himself above the law, and he seemed to be right. He denied the use, denied knowing the doctor in Reading, even denied having a doctor of any kind in Philadelphia. At the same time, he was on the record in his *Playboy* interview from the year before as having admitted to using greenies: "I might have taken a greenie last week. If a doctor gives me a prescription of thirty diet pills, because I want to curb my appetite, so I can lose five pounds before I go to spring training, I mean, is that bad? A doctor is not going to write a prescription that is going to be harmful to my body."

"But would you use them for anything other than dieting?" he was asked.

"There might be some day when you played a doubleheader the night before, and you go to the ballpark for a Sunday game, and you just want to take a diet pill, just to mentally think you are up. You won't be up, but mentally you might think you are up."

"Does it help your game?"

"It won't help the game, but it will help you mentally. When you help yourself mentally, it might help your game."

"You keep saying you might take a greenie. Would you? Have you?"

"Yeah, I'd do it. I've done it."

He did not say, however, that he was doing it nearly every day, and that he was teaching younger players how to do it. But when federal narcotics agents came calling at Veterans Stadium, that was the understanding of Bill Giles.

The tempest passed. Dr. Mazza was not formally indicted until the season was over. When his day in court finally came, the Phillie Eight denied the allegations of greenie use and refused all cooperation with either side. In anger, the attorney for Mazza said in his closing argument, "What we have here is a bunch of ball players who call themselves the world champions, but who are also champions in the art of lying." And Dr. Mazza himself said, "[The prescriptions] were made at the request of the ball players and were done in good faith. Pete Rose was having trouble with his weight and he needed some help with his thirty-eight-year-old body." The criminal charges against Mazza for illegally prescribing amphetamines were eventually dismissed.

By then, the Phillies were World Champs. Unlike the previous year, they stayed in contention in 1980, hovering six games back and winning so many games in which they were down in the early innings that they became known as the "come-from-behind gang." Then in September, they made their move, with especially brilliant relief pitching from Tug McGraw. With the pennant on the line, the press gave Rose the credit for bringing the team together. Mike Schmidt agreed. Rose was, despite a subpar year in which he hit .282, "the straw that stirred the drink." It was a gracious thing for Schmidt to say, but his own forty-eight homers that year, which led the majors, and his 121 RBIs, which led the National League, made up the drink itself. The Phillies took the Eastern Division championship, finishing ahead of the Montreal Expos.

Then, in the most exciting play-off series since the divisional play-offs had been established eleven years earlier, the Phillies topped the Astros three games to two, with four of the five games decided in extra innings. That series belonged to the Bull, Greg Luzinski, to Shake and Bake McBride, to the Tugger, McGraw, who had been untouchable down the stretch, and to Lefty, Steve Carlton.

Rose had his signature moment, along with his 8 for 20 at the plate. In the tenth inning of the fourth game, he singled. With two outs, Dallas Green called for Luzinski to pinch hit, even though the Bull had gone 0 for 5 the day before. Luzinski promptly lined a double into the left-field corner, and here came Rose, barreling around third, as if he were twenty-nine rather than thirty-nine years old, as if it were the 1970 All-Star Game all over again. He crashed into Bruce Bochy, the Astros third-string catcher, and jarred the ball loose to score the winning run. "I know Pete Rose and I know what kind of runner he is in that situation," the third-base coach for the Phillies, Lee Elia, would say. "It was a gamble, but we really needed to get the run." Bochy, at least, did not suffer the same consequences as Ray Fosse.

After the Phillies won the deciding game in ten innings on a Garry Maddox double, Rose provided the quote of the day. "I think these guys just got tired of losing."

By contrast to the fabulous play-offs, the World Series against the Royals of George Brett were flat and anticlimactic. Behind Mike Schmidt's .381 hitting, his two homers and 7 RBIs, the Phillies triumphed in six games. Rose put on a poor performance through five games, batting a pathetic .150. He protested that he had a "tradition" of hitting well in the play-offs and poorly in the World Series, largely because he was unfamiliar with the tricks of the American League pitchers. Then, characteristically, in the last game, he stole the show. He went 3 for 4, including a perfect bunt to load the bases in the third that set the table for Schmidt. Going into the ninth, the Phillies were ahead, 4–1, but McGraw had a lapse, yielding a walk and two singles to load the bases. Second baseman Frank White came to the plate with one out. By this time, policemen with dogs had moved onto the field to control the hometown crowd in the event of a Phillies victory. White got under a pitch and sent a high foul that sliced toward the Phillies dugout. Rose and the catcher, Bob Boone, converged on the ball near the steps, close to a policeman with a nervous German shepherd. Though it was clearly Rose's ball, Boone waved him off, found himself out of position, and at the last moment, lunged for the ball. It hit off the heel of his mitt—his steel mitt, he would later call it—and fell toward the ground. Rose leapt for the deflection, however, and snared it just before it hit the ground. That hustling play would remain the single most vivid memory of the 1980 Series.

Two days later, the World Champions climbed onto flatbed trucks and began a six-mile parade through downtown Philadelphia. A half-million fans lined the streets, some on rollerskates. Others in wheelchairs were said to stand up and walk at the miracle. In sunglasses, a floppy beach hat, and a T-shirt that read "Phillies Phantastic #1," Rose stood between McGraw and Bowa, who himself doffed the Stetson of an urban cowboy. The executives, Bill Giles and Ruly Carpenter, flanked them, seated, for it was the players, not the owners, who deserved the attention. The parade inched toward Kennedy Stadium, where eighty thousand people waited to hear the remarks of their heroes. In the stands, Schmidt and Carlton were put forward as candidates for president. More to the point, one sign read: "The Phillies Are Like Sex: We Never Get Enough." When the time came to speak, Tug McGraw, the discarded New York Met, got the most applause when he said, "All through baseball history, Philadelphia has taken a back seat to New York City. Well, New York City can take this world championship and stick it!" Tug for President! . . . or at least for mayor.

In the Philadelphia press that day, the prophets looked into the future and saw trouble. To repeat a world championship was one of the hardest challenges in all of sport. One needed only look at the Big Red Machine of the 1970s. There was speculation that the tempestuous Phillies manager, Dallas Green, would now move to the front office, where he had always wanted to go. If that was so, the columnist Sandy Grady of the *Inquirer* had a suggestion: let Rose replace Green: "He may lack Green's talent for handling pitchers, but he knows the nuances of baseball cold. He has the mental toughness to control players. The Phils to the man respect him. And Lord knows, Rose has the candor and the humor to deal with newsmen."

Respect, Rose would learn, can be fleeting, when lies replace candor and when jokes turn sour and stale.

While the Phillies of 1980 were melding as a championship team, Bart Giamatti was preoccupied with a longtime nuisance to his university. Four times in the past twelve years, Yale had suffered through increasingly bitter and traumatic strikes of its blue collar workers. The cycle began in 1968, when the workers went out for six days in an unorganized expression of anger. From the Federation of University Employees' standpoint, that action had been a fiasco, producing nothing but a humiliating surrender to the tycoons of the Yale Corporation. The result was that an insurgent slate of union leaders gained control of the local union, a slate that included a young, beefy 1967 graduate of Yale named John Wilhelm. In 1971, when their contract came up for renewal, the workers went out for seven weeks; three years later, for ten weeks; and in 1977, with the tough-minded and sometimes high-handed Hanna Gray as the adversary, for twelve weeks. With each strike more bitter and longer than the last, with the concessions less substantial with each succeeding strike, there was a sense that this sorry condition might just go on indefinitely every three years. As the contract neared its expiration in 1980, there was a strong willingness on both sides to establish a semblance of peace with a semblance of justice.

In Giamatti, the union perceived a president who was the epitome of Yale values, and that was precisely his problem. The new president spoke the old language of decency and reason, of respect for the working man and his dignity, of the coziness of the Yale family. Indeed, he seemed to do it even more eloquently than Kingman Brewster, their old nemesis who had set himself magisterially above the fray, and upon whom the union had never been able to lay a glove. Toward Brewster's upper-class liberalism, the union leaders were forever shaking their heads and saying: "If Kingman only understood!" knowing in their hearts that Kingman understood full well. By contrast, Giamatti seemed to be more of a regular guy, and he offered the opportunity for a new beginning.

The blue-collar force at Yale numbered only about a thousand workers. The only way to gain significant concessions over time, the union felt, was to widen the labor pool. Beyond its food service workers and its janitors, the university employed close to three thousand clerks and technicians. They were mainly intelligent and independent women, many of whom were related to professors. A lot of them worked part-time. Most were deeply loyal to Yale. And they were widely dispersed across the campus. If there was any hope of organizing them, it lie in the women's issue of equal pay for equal work. Initial efforts to organize in the 1970s had been unsuccessful.

Some months before the three-year contract was due to expire, John Wilhelm and his union offered Yale a deal: if the university would work to change its hostile stance toward the workers and establish a "healthy" relationship, the union would accept the cheapest economic deal and negotiate an early settlement. This was accomplished. In May 1980, Giamatti and Wilhelm held a joint news conference, where the tone was hearts and flowers. They announced an interim agreement for twenty months rather than the full three years, which included modest cost of living increases. The parties also agreed to "concentrate their time and efforts" to resolve the old antagonisms. Giamatti heralded "the start of a new era in constructive labor management relations at Yale," while Wilhelm announced "a different tone and a different approach" to labor problems in the new administration.

If the year and a half of this patchwork agreement concentrated the time and the efforts of the parties on anything, it was not on harmony but on the likelihood of eventual war. The union began its campaign to organize the clerical workers in earnest, while the university retained a law firm from Hartford that was notorious for union busting. Whether Giamatti was acting as a union buster or was simply carrying out the orders of the Yale Corporation is not clear, for he operated behind closed doors and staunchly refused to enter the public debate. May 1983 was set as the time for the clerks and technicians to vote on whether or not to unionize. As the climax approached, the posture of the university became more openly anti-union, but in a precious, even scholarly way. The university meant to win, but thought victory would come by arguing its case in elegant prose, complete with footnotes and asterisks, and with talk about raising the debate to a high level. The union did not play that way.

To some, the question was whether the administration was doing everything it could to win, particularly Giamatti himself. Was he tough enough? Did he really know how to play hardball? Giamatti was torn—more torn than he wanted anyone to know. He had to follow the lead of the corporation, and yet he fancied himself a man of the people.

In any case, he made one well-meaning but strategic error: he delayed the union vote until the school year was over, not wanting students to become embroiled in the labor dispute. But that gave the union the time it needed to consolidate its support.

Amid the hoopla—balloons in Battell Chapel, street rallies, genteel signs, such as "Geology and Geophysics Rocks to the Union Tune!"—the struggle remained civilized. Indeed, a civil tone was central to the union strategy. It worked. After the paper ballots were counted one by one in Strathcona Hall, the union won by thirty-nine votes.

A confrontation appeared to be inevitable. John Wilhelm and his two locals now represented nearly four thousand Yale workers rather than one-fourth that number. He was duly constituted as their sole bargaining agent.

A strike in the offing became even clearer when the Giamatti administration fired its local strike-busting lawyers and hired a Chicago firm with a national reputation for union decertification. It was a law firm whose senior partner boasted that he came from the "bomb-them-into-submission school of labor relations."

For a while, Giamatti stayed in the shadows. Even when the labor negotiations got under way in the fall of 1983, Giamatti receded behind the lawyers. To some on the faculty, he seemed to have the habit of disappearing in a crisis. An officer of Yale said reflectively, "You could kick the university in the groin, and you would get back a careful, considered, well-documented response. Bart would write an elegant 'Dear Colleagues' letter."

To the union, these initial "negotiations" were a joke. With pickets on the street and a one-day work stoppage called "59¢ Day"—a reference to the disproportionate low worth of women on the dollar compared to men—another partial agreement was signed so that the talks could go on. That twilight phase dragged on for a year, with two strike deadlines coming and passing. Then, in September 1984, the university made its final offer, an offer that Giamatti represented as going beyond the economic limits of the university. The union gave up and called its inevitable strike.

To call a strike against an aristocratic American university created special problems and special opportunities for the union. With no product to boycott or plant to shut down, there was no way to beat the university economically. Moreover, the institution was nonprofit and was run by a faceless and formless board called the Yale Corporation, which was difficult to attack. This was the fifth strike in sixteen years, but the first that would take place during the school year. For the university it was to be traumatic beyond description. The business of education would go forward regardless, but the pleasure of education would be significantly affected. At Yale, the core of that conviviality was the dining hall at the residential colleges, and they were shut down. Before long, the faculty and students stridently took up sides.

"Going to Yale is an experience," John Wilhelm was to say, "and that experience was wrecked by the strike. The fabric of the place was torn apart." Better than anyone, this Yale graduate cum labor leader knew precisely the pain he was inflicting. Wilhelm knew there was a natural reservoir of sympathy for the workers—the very thing that infuriated Bart Giamatti: rich kids trumpeting the rights of workers.

Upon the announcement of the strike, Bart Giamatti at last stepped forward as the spokesman for his administration. By stepping forward, he immediately made himself the target and the villain to the union sympathizers. "Bart Buster" T-shirts began to pop up all over New Haven, and pickets sang songs that were directed at Giamatti personally. With apologies to Little Eva, the union adapted her tune, "The Locomotion," with this verse:

> Other presidents can afford to be creeps,
>   *now come on, A. Bart, do negotiations . . .*
> But the president of Yale should be top of the heap,
>   *now come on, A. Bart, do negotiations . . .*
> If Yale can be a leader in the world at large,
> Why can't you act fairly in your own frontyard,
>   *so come on, A. Bart, do negotiations right now.*

Or in a "Yale Solidarity" song, there was the verse:

> It is Bart who hires the lawyers, it is Bart
> who calls the shots.
> He treats his women workers like a
> bunch of timid tots.
> It is Bartlett who has tied this university in knots.
> But the union makes us strong.

As in Giamatti vs. Brustein and Giamatti vs. Goldstein, it became yet again *mano a mano.* Now, it was Giamatti vs. John Wilhelm.

To Wilhelm and his advisers, it was not immediately clear that Giamatti had done the union a tremendous favor by stepping forward. The traditional ritual in industry was for the director of labor relations to take all the heat during the strike; then, with the settlement, the aloof CEO stepped grandly forward and embraced the union leader in a gracious display of harmony. As a result, Wilhelm's strategy was to focus attention on the Yale Corporation, if he possibly could, not on its tool. To make matters more difficult, the Yale president was formidable and articulate. His statements carried a genuine tone of moral outrage. Most important, he could control the media.

Accordingly, the union leader vetoed certain ad hominem measures that were available. One of them involved the renovations to the president's mansion. Even though Wilhelm knew that the Giamatti renovations had cost three times the amount that had drummed provost Abraham Goldstein out of office four years earlier, he demurred to use this information. It was enough for the president to humiliate himself in public.

For Giamatti, the strike was unspeakably traumatic. Upon the union bargaining units sat his second and third cousins from ethnic New Haven; they peered at him as a traitor to his own people. In the faculty council, a resolution of no confidence in the president was introduced. While it failed, this distressed Giamatti beyond measure, as if it were a personal betrayal rather than a disagreement over social policy. He tried to continue his practice of walking to work from his mansion on Hillhouse Street, only to pass through cordons of angry and profane demonstrators who hurled epithets about his intelligence and his manhood. At one point, someone spat in his face. It became necessary for him to have a bodyguard. One day, pig's blood was splattered across the steps of Woodbridge Hall.

Amid the crowds that followed him with such signs as "Bart, Bart, Have a Heart!" and "Boola, Boola, where's our Moola?" were faculty friends who hurled outrageous and hysterical accusations at him. For a man this private and this sensitive, the toll was great. He could not disengage himself.

"Bart, they're not attacking you personally," a history professor said to him once. "You're just a symbol. They're attacking the president of Yale."

"But I am the president of Yale!" Giamatti exclaimed.

Perhaps the most upsetting moment came when several hundred protesters gathered in front of his house in a candlelight vigil, chanting, "Bart Can't Sleep, because Yale is Cheap!" Being called a fool may have hurt the most because in his own mind he was a supremely intelligent man who was merely trying to protect the place he loved. The Corporation had mandated in 1977 that by 1980 there be a balanced budget, and Giamatti had accepted that as law. Now, the union was making wage demands that would throw Yale back into the red.

No doubt Giamatti longed to handle this major crisis of his

presidency with a fine Italian hand. He would bring warring parties together with such Machiavellian deftness that they would be almost unaware of what was happening. During the bitter strike of 1984, however, people ceased to talk about Bart Giamatti as a Renaissance prince. In his dominance of the press, he sounded like the typical, embattled company executive who mouthed shop worn phrases.

Was there discrimination? he was asked.

"Of course there's discrimination in America," he replied to the *New Haven Register*. "But the fact that so-called women's work is inhabited by women who have come into the marketplace late as a function of having married and raised families may well also be a reason why certain areas are underpaid and may not be claimed as discrimination." When he uttered a phrase caustically like "so-called women's work" in the midst of a bitter strike by women workers, it could have a bad effect. The union seized upon such lapses and chewed Giamatti up. "Because [Giamatti] personalized it, the strike became nasty," Wilhelm was to say later. "He sounded arrogant and disrespectful of the strikers' position. The rank and file of that strike were really together, truly vibrant, and he came off as contemptuous of women."

In early November, the nation got a glimpse of this struggle when Giamatti and Wilhelm agreed to appear in separate segments on "Donahue." For Giamatti to agree to appear was in itself a concession. He had refused to be interviewed by "60 Minutes." Along with an articulate registrar at Yale named Lucille Dickess, Wilhelm went first and realized immediately that the union had been snookered. The live audience for the show was stacked against it. As the minutes rolled on, the allegations of the union about incomparable pay, low wages, and poor benefits were met with vocal derision from the audience. At one point, Wilhelm was charged with being in the struggle only for personal gain, an old and often used charge against labor leaders.

That set the stage for Giamatti, as the show's producers segued from the first segment to the next with pictures of pickets carrying signs "Lux & Veritas?" and music of bow-wowing and barking to "Our team will never fail." The president came on looking elegant and commanding.

"You look like a rock-ribbed, blue-suited businessman whose color drains from his face at the very mention of the word 'union.' " Donahue tried.

The audience twittered and waited for an angry retort. This was big-time television—debate as show business—and Giamatti understood perfectly what the game was. He had the perfect rubbery face for it, and now his face became that of a deadpan comic. "No, no, that's not true," he said with a hurt expression, and went on with solemn expressions about working in good faith with a duly elected and certified union.

What about binding arbitration? Why was the university refusing to submit to it. "It doesn't make you look good," Donahue intoned. "It looks like you're afraid of something." But, on national television, Giamatti did not look like a man who was afraid, and he let the laughs of the audience answer the question.

Giamatti was serious and earnest. This was no time for frivolity. The questions to him from the audience were charged with emotion, often hostility, and that impression alone cut against the university position. While he handled the questions competently, Yale came off as a troubled place that had for years been paying its clerks slave wages, and whose own president, powerful personality though he might be, was uncompromising and even dictatorial.

By prior agreement, union and management got one minute to sum up. It was a measure of his difficulty that Giamatti proceeded to do something he had never done before in public: he became earnestly personal.

"My father didn't speak English when he went to grammar school," he began, shaking with powerful emotion. "His parents came from Italy. When he finished high school, he had one of two choices: go straight to the factory or go to the local college . . . which happened to be Yale . . . on a full four-year scholarship.

"That means an enormous amount to me. That capacity of access to this place on one's merit, talent, and hard work is a very important principle. That seems to be a very important principle in this dispute, not because we disagree about it, but because we must maintain it."

The effect was electric and winning, even if his personal comments were somewhat beside the point.

By Thanksgiving, the workers had been out for nine weeks. That duration itself undermined Giamatti's credibility because he had promised that the conflict would be swiftly over. As week followed week, the president was increasingly blamed for the strike dragging on, as if he himself were the obstruction to settlement. That was only partly true. In negotiations, he was stubborn and inflexible, and this very stubbornness, in the view of such a practiced negotiator as Cyrus Vance, was prolonging the strike. The Corporation itself was split in its judgment of how well Giamatti was handling the crisis.

In the meantime, the union enlisted Cesar Chavez and Bayard Rustin to lend moral weight to its cause. Chavez came to Yale to tell of the wicked machinations of Yale's union-busting law firm in the struggle to unionize the farm workers of California. And Rustin, who the previous May had been given an honorary degree at Yale, allowed himself to be arrested in a peaceful demonstration in front of Giamatti's house, where, only months before, Rustin had dined in gracious splendor. The union singled out the liberal members of the Yale Corporation, such as Eleanor Holmes Norton and Bishop Paul Moore, and harassed them unmercifully in Washington and New York. John Wilhelm too evinced stubbornness and inflexibility in the negotiations, seeming to promise his workers more than he could deliver. But he had one overarching advantage: "Yale's behavior toward labor was absolutely at odds with Yale's ideals," he would say. "The university was totally vulnerable on that score."

When the students went home for the Thanksgiving holiday week, the canny union sent its workers back to their jobs. If there was no settlement, Wilhelm announced, the workers would go back on strike when the students returned. Meanwhile, the university was compelled to pay the union members during this strike moratorium, for working the very days they were not needed. The Thanksgiving ploy was wicked and totally effective.

By December, the situation had become intolerable. It was the university equivalent of garbage piling up on city streets. The situation had to be resolved.

At length, the strike was finally settled over Christmas. Yale surrendered unconditionally. The terms were substantially in excess of what the union expected. It got the gesture toward the women's issue of comparative worth that lent national significance to its struggle, and the settlement was treated as a great victory for the flagging union movement. It also launched John Wilhelm upon a national career as a union leader. In the 1980s, he would go on to negotiate major contracts for the hotel and restaurant workers in Boston, Los Angeles, San Francisco, and Las Vegas.

Sitting one day in a coffee shop in Las Vegas and in touch, by beeper, with his pickets outside the major casinos, Wilhelm reflected upon Giamatti. "I felt sorry for the guy," he said. "He tried to carry out Corporation policy, and he was scapegoated for it. The strike required Bart to move on."

As for Giamatti, he told his closest friends after the strike was over that he felt like a "cinder." This may have been more than the artful phrase of a burnt-out man. His medical profile would later show that he had suffered a mild heart attack during this period. The generations were repeating themselves. His father, Valentine, had suffered a heart attack at about the same age, but Val's had been massive, a clear warning that he heeded. He changed his ways and lived another twenty years.

Bart's mild heart attack was not enough of a warning to him.

In December 1970, Harry Rose, Pete's father and mentor, had died prematurely of a massive heart attack. He was fifty-seven years old. Harry had seen his son win two batting titles and play in a World Series, but he had missed the best of the career. When Pete Rose heard the news, he wept, and in the years to come, the mere mention of his father made Rose maudlin. He was, he liked to think, no more than his father made over and carried on, the fulfillment of a spirit, the realization of a potential, in the next generation.

Ty Cobb's father was a professor rather than a bank clerk, and he too had been essential to his son's relentless striving. The professor had disapproved of baseball, regarding it as trivial and indulgent and unrespectable, as well as pandering to his son's worst instincts. "Be good and dutiful," Cobb's father had written him in 1902. "Conquer your anger and wild passions. Be guided by the better angel of your nature, not the demon that lurks in all human blood and is ready and anxious and restless to arise and to reign." Cobb's father had wanted his son to be a lawyer or a doctor, and thus, to pursue baseball was for Ty Cobb to violate his father's fondest hope. It was an essential disobedience that led to estrangement. "My overwhelming need was to prove myself," Cobb was to write. "My father held me down, withholding acceptance of me as the man I yearned to be." No amount of accomplishment in baseball could allay the essential disapproval Cobb's father felt for sport as a career.

If this produced the energy of anger, there was also ambivalence. For Cobb's father had also died early, turning him, like Harry Rose, into a spirit that hovered in the imagination and goaded the son. Only three weeks before Ty Cobb entered the major leagues against his father's will, his mother shot him dead, as the professor ignominiously crawled through the window of the family house. Mrs. Cobb had mistaken her husband for a prowler. But then, she was having an affair with another man.

The obsession with Ty Cobb became greater as Pete Rose's decline set in. "I probably know more about Ty Cobb than any living player," he would say in the strike-shortened season of 1981. "I've studied his statistics. I know how he played. I know all the Ty Cobb stories." Yet he was caught between the past and the present. When people spoke of him as a legend, even if it was as a living legend or a legend in his own time, it implied that his career was nearly over. To Rose a legend was Jesse James or Bat Masterson, maybe Babe Ruth. "There aren't too many guys who can look at you and say, 'I've got a little girl fourteen years old. I only failed to hit .300 one time since she was born.'"

When Fawn Rose was sixteen years old, Rose could make the same statement. Still, he knew instinctively that he was not a true legend yet, not until he surpassed Cobb's mountainous record of 4,191 career hits. To have a chance to surpass that record would require another three seasons of playing regularly, of avoiding injury, and of coaxing a forty-one-year-old body to respond in competition with players half his age.

How would he like to be remembered? he was often asked. In truth, he wanted to be a figure of the morning sports pages rather than the history books, but still he answered: "I just want people to say: there is a guy that worked the hardest and the longest to become a switch-hitter, the best switch-hitter that ever lived, plus the guy who no matter where he played, he was a winner."

From his cumulative statistics alone, Rose in 1981 could lay claim to being the best player in National League history. During that season, he passed Stan Musial's National League record of 3,630 hits, and only Cobb lay ahead. At that point, the odious comparisons began in earnest. Rose had worked out the mathematics. In mid-season 1982, he pointed out that a player could have two hundred hits for twenty seasons, and he'd still be nearly two hundred hits short. Still, Cobb's record could be broken by a guy who played every day, hit from both sides of the plate, and played for an offensive team. But could he play every day, or nearly every day, until he was forty-two?

Fate had entered the picture ominously in 1981, with the seven-week baseball strike in June and July, which cut into Rose's customary hit production by sixty hits. Bill Giles considered the 1981 Phillies to be an even better team than his world champions of the year before, and Rose was still part of the equation: he finished second to Bill "Mad Dog" Madlock with a .325 average and led the league in hits (140). In the new play-off format created by the strike, the Phillies "won" the first portion of the split season, thereby ensuring their place in a postseason play-off. But with that insurance, the team lost its zeal, and even Rose could not pump it up. The Dodgers went to the strange Series instead.

Two river rats. With Bernie Wrublewski, a pretty good pitcher at Bold Face Park, who later became a priest in Riverside.

Number 55 at Crosley Field with Harry, September 1962.

Spring training, 1963. Big future in a few years.

June 1963. A slow, jerky pivot to first.

The competitor.
Against the Mets,
July 1968.

Collision at Home Plate. Hitting Ray Fosse in the 1970 All-Star Game.

The Arab look. With
Sparky Anderson, January
1972.

One of many gift cars, 1975.

Tom Seaver and the Hickok
belt, 1976, which Rose later
sold after dejeweling it.

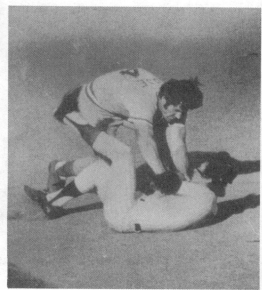

Johnny Bench with Reds general manager Bob Howsam, who assembled the Machine. After the NL division title, October 1976.

The fight with Bud Harrelson. NL play-offs, 1973.

Clouting the second of three homers against the Mets, April 29, 1978.

With first wife, Karolyn, and daughter, Fawn. Spring training, 1976.

The litigious girlfriend, Terri Rubio and daughter, Morgan, March 1979.

Second wife, Carol, April 1984.

As a Phillie . . .

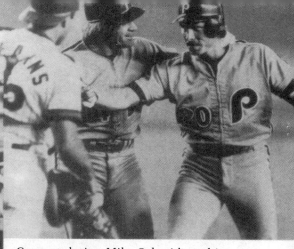

Congratulating Mike Schmidt on his three-hundredth home run.

Still running like a scalded dog.

With manager Dallas Green.

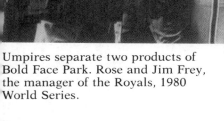

Umpires separate two products of Bold Face Park. Rose and Jim Frey, the manager of the Royals, 1980 World Series.

World Champion Phillie, 1980.

Player-manager, 1985.

An audience with Pope Pius XII, April 1948. Bart would not kiss the ring. With sister, Elria; father, Valentine; and mother, Mary Walton.

Capri, 1955. "Angie" and friend.

Valentine Giamatti, 1960.

The Tomb, where the mysteries of Scroll & Key unfold.

The Master of Ezra Stiles College, 1972.

Abbie Hoffman during the troubles, May 1970. To Giamatti, Hoffman's rhetoric was "corrosive as acid."

The Rivals. Henry Rosovksy of Harvard and the young "Sforza" of Yale.

The president is inaugurated, October 1979.

Toasted after the 1980 Ivy League football championship.

Halloween 1980, with friends.

The agony of the 1984 strike.

The king at his last human chess game, Yale, 1986.

The Renaissance fan.

Inducting Carl Yastrzemski into the Hall of Fame.

The end prefigured. Giamatti turns down Rose's appeal on the thirty-day suspension.

The accuser, Paul Janszen.

The bookie, Ron Peters.

The protégé, Tommy Gioiosa.

The purloined betting slip, in Pete's handwriting, with his fingerprints.

The superagent and counselor, Reuven Katz, spring 1977.

The fall of Pete Rose, spring training, 1989.

Bart Giamatti
on integrity,
Martha's Vineyard.

To jail, July 1990.

Memorial, the Yale campus.

Ironically, Giles would come to feel that, had it not been for the strike of 1981, Rose would have finished his playing career in Philadelphia. By 1983, Rose was clearly over the hill and not close enough to Cobb's record for Giles to justify holding on to him for sentimental reasons. His bat was slowing down, as were his legs. Over the winter of 1981–82, he hurt his back playing tennis, and he was forced into excuses. After all, he protested, he was hurt because he was preparing for Cobb. "It wasn't because I was bending over to pick up the garbage or something. I was all warmed up, and it was the fifth time I played that week. . . . I've been hurt before. When is the last time that a guy forty [years old] played every game and almost led the league in hitting?"

To the public, the Phillies put up a brave front. "He's got the kind of body that doesn't wear down," Paul Owens, now the director of player personnel, professed. "He's got so many intangibles. He's proud. He works hard. He's a leader. And the son of a gun can still hit." In private, Owens (also known as the Pope) was more skeptical. Rose's contribution to the Phillies was becoming marginal. Weak grounders to second were becoming more the rule than sharp shots through the gap. To hold on to him or to release him became a business decision, having to do with his drawing power rather than his hitting skill. Moreover, there was nothing intrinsically exciting about the accumulation of singles, except for the accountants of baseball.

In August 1982, when he broke the major league record for the most career at-bats, Rose was hitting a mediocre .280 and dropping. Giles now gave serious consideration to releasing him at the end of the season. The legend had ceased to be a good leadoff hitter who could be counted on to get on base regularly. During the home stretch in September, the Phillies collapsed. Rose, hobbled by a bad heel, finished the season with a prosaic .271.

Still, Giles, the Cincinnati sentimentalist, overruled Owens and others in the front office who wanted to drop Rose. Instead, Giles signed him to a hefty one-year extension worth more than a million dollars. Thus, Rose had another personal record: he had been the first singles hitter to reach both the hundred-thousand-dollars-a-year and the one-million-dollars-a-year plateaus. Not only that. Giles added a few more reliable and durable parts of the old Big Red Machine to the Phillies. He traded for Joe Morgan and acquired Tony Perez in the free agent market in January.

In the 1983 season, Rose's statistics continued to bear out Owens's skepticism. From May 30 to June 7, he went 0 for 20. Once during this period, his pride was bitterly wounded when a batter in front of him was walked intentionally with men on base so they could pitch to old man Rose. A few days later, the million-dollar legend was benched for the first time since his rookie year. Trailing Cobb by 272 hits, he grumbled to the press: "It's obvious I can't catch Cobb if I'm not playing regularly."

Ironically, Rose was replaced not by youth but by age. Tony Perez took over first base and had a burst of productivity, driving in eleven runs in twelve games, while Rose warmed the bench. Rose reentered the lineup in mid-summer, only to be benched again in September, replaced this time not by the great Perez but by a rookie hulk named Len Matuszek. Rose posted an embarrassing .245 average for the season, but the Phillies had nothing to be ashamed about. They took the pennant and entered the Series against the Orioles.

During the World Series of 1983, Rose was to suffer one last humiliation. In the first two games in Baltimore, the Phillies hit weakly but managed to stay even at a game apiece while Rose went 1 for 8. On the off day before the Series resumed at Veterans Stadium, a press conference was staged for the copy-hungry reporters. Inevitably, Rose was offered up as the supreme authority to analyze the state of things. That led to another round of fawning articles. Paul Owens, "the Pope," had taken over as manager toward the end of the season, and he contributed his benediction: "He exemplifies class. It's no wonder we all love him—not just because of his records, but just to be associated with him."

Hours later, Owens excommunicated Rose from the lineup for the third game. Rose's superagent, Reuven Katz, was in the stands when he heard about it, and he stormed into Bill Giles's office to appeal the decision, but Giles refused to intervene. Tony Perez again replaced Rose, because Owens considered Perez, even at age forty-one, to be the best breaking-ball hitter in baseball.

Rose was furious. "Sure it hurts. And it's embarrassing," he sounded off to Howard Cosell. "This just isn't the way baseball should be played. The two most surprised guys in this ballpark are myself and Tony Perez. I was the one who told him he was playing. That's not the way baseball should be conducted, but it's not the first time it's happened this year."

After the season, on November 15, the Phillies released him. The team softened the blow with a $350,000 "buyout bonus," which was something like a bonus in reverse.

By all accounts, Rose should have quit. He was old, slow-footed, slow swinging, overpaid. That he was a legend had no bearing on winning ball games any longer. Had he been virtually any other ball player in baseball, the decision would have been clear. Johnny Bench chose to retire after the 1983 season, quitting when he was still a producer rather than an embarrassment. But Bench had achieved all that was within his grasp. Rose, 201 hits short of Cobb's record, still had Ty Cobb ahead of him. If he were to be used only as a substitute and pinch-hitter, it would take him at least two seasons more to close the gap—if he could get a team to take on Rose and his huge salary.

First signs were discouraging. The Angels expressed a bit of interest, only to re-sign Rod Carew instead. The Seattle Mariners looked at his drawing power but decided on a general policy of re-building through youth. Ted Turner in Atlanta called a few times, undoubtedly thinking of the extravaganza he would stage at the breaking of the Cobb record, but the price of petrified wood was too high. In Cincinnati, which finished in last place for the past two seasons, one had to be on the inside to read between the lines. That old dealmaker, Bob Howsam, had been lured back to the Reds after three years in retirement and was now the president of a club that bore no resemblance to his Big Red Machine. He had already picked up Tony Perez and Dave Parker. "After getting Parker and Perez," Howsam said, "I didn't have the thing [Pete] needed. There was no sense in me blowing a lot of smoke. Sometimes situations don't fit. I wish they did."

Surprisingly, the Montreal Expos came into the picture, as the club president, John McHale, and the team's manager, Bill Virdon, flew into Cincinnati for a talk. The problem for the Expos in 1984 was not unlike the Phillies' in 1979. A perennial contender (except in 1983) that had come within a few games and a few innings of winning the pennant in 1979 and 1981, the team was loaded with talent: Andre Dawson in center, Gary Carter behind the plate, Al Oliver at first, and Steve Rogers as their premier ace. Reuven Katz trotted out the 1978 arguments once again. The team of young superstars needed a leader, someone to look up to, a stabilizing force, someone who would not allow the youngsters to relax, especially in pressure games. His client was the missing link, the extra ingredient. No longer a spry thirty-seven, Rose was pushing forty-three years old, which was pos- itively ancient. It had taken a year for the younger Phillies to respect him, and respect had come from Rose's performance on the field. Suddenly, Katz's arguments sounded hollow. "Montreal is where he really wants to be," he told the press with a straight, counselor's face, as if Rose really had much choice.

For his part, Pete Rose was annoyed that his benching in Philadelphia had given him the reputation as a part-time player in the future.

"How many games do you want to play," Virdon had asked in Cincinnati.

"Every one," Rose replied unhesitatingly.

"That's the attitude," said the skipper.

Through the winter, Rose changed the habits of a lifetime. For years he had shunned the weight room, relying instead on good eating habits, and playing tennis and basketball in the off season to keep in shape for Cobb. Now, after his pathetic season, he put himself in the hands of the trainer for the Reds, Larry Starr, and ventured into a forest of Nautilus machines. ".245 will wake anybody up," he told *Sports Illustrated.* "My way doesn't work anymore." He ventured to Ohio University, where the chairman of the Zoology Department, Dr. Fritz Hagerman, treated him as an anthropological specimen, subjecting him to a battery of tests and designing a conditioning program to shore up the relic's bones and sinews. After weeks of hour-and-twenty-minute workouts every day, of shunning red meat for chicken and fish, he transformed himself.

Starr declared after the program that Rose might be in the best shape of his career. Shedding his paunch and thirteen unneeded pounds, Rose looked positively svelte. There was, however, no Nautilus machine to improve a batting eye.

There were other changes in his personal life that winter. To keep from getting bored, he sued the IRS for $36,303 in back taxes. That was the cost of the jeeps he had given his coaches on the Reds after the 1978 season as a token of his gratitude, an amount he had claimed as a necessary business expense but which the IRS saw as a gift. The Rose team trotted out the Reds coaches—local personalities all—who wowed the local jury and won the case. The IRS would get its revenge seven years later. Meanwhile, he was engaged to be married to Carol Woliung, the comely blond and former Philadelphia Eagles cheerleader, who was fourteen years younger than Pete and was an ornament that fit Rose's image of himself. (The couple talked about being married at home plate at Riverfront Stadium.) In the swank Indian Hills section of Cincinnati, a neighborhood of quiet, understated wealth, with horse trails meandering through the estates, he had acquired a spectacular, slant-roofed modern house, whose spacious garage fairly burst with his automotive toys and whose den, with its gigantic television screen, had become a private sports betting gallery.

Around the Indian Hills spread, he had his houseboy, a stocky,

thick-headed kid from southern Massachusetts named Tommy Gioiosa, who doted on Rose like a puppy and was ready to do any chore
to please his master. Gio had lived with Rose ever since his marriage
with Karolyn went on the shoals. It was a most pleasant form of
indentured servitude: Gio never wanted for money and had a spiffy
little jeep to drive around; he paid no rent, and he got to meet sports
heroes and even movie actresses. To be Pete Rose's pal gave him
goosebumps. The two had met in 1977 during spring training, when
Gio was an aspiring, All Cape Cod infielder for a junior college team,
with ambitions to be a big leaguer.

Gio had entered the dazzling world of the superstar in the most
innocent way. In Florida, a small boy had approached him with a
Norman Rockwellian question, "Will you toss with me?" and Gio, the
most compliant of teenagers, readily agreed. The next day, the same
request came and was granted. Gio invited the kid to be the bat boy
for the Massasoit Junior College team, thinking it might be a thrill for
the kid. That was when Gioiosa learned the boy's father was Pete
Rose. By being nice to Petey, Gio ingratiated himself with Karolyn
and then with Pete Rose himself. One thing led to another: an invitation to visit Cincinnati for Christmas was extended to an invitation
to move into the Rose home, and finally, Rose personally requested
that Gioiosa receive the Pete Rose baseball scholarship at the University of Cincinnati.

In everything he did, Gio emulated Pete Rose. At UC, he wore
number 14 on his uniform. He slid headfirst. He cut his hair the same
way and copied Rose's conversational mannerisms. Rose got Gioiosa
a tryout with the Orioles in 1982. But poor Gio, still skinny at 155
pounds, was cut, and he was devastated. His standing with his mentor was lowered, he was sure. For Rose, the attachment was clear: in
Tommy Gioiosa he saw himself. To the extent that Rose possessed
any charity whatever, it was toward those who came from his own
background: poor, white, hardworking, modestly talented.

At spring training in West Palm Beach in 1984, Rose was to
make the acquaintance of another Massachusetts character from the
same area as Gioiosa. He was an avid baseball fan named Joseph
Cambra. By all appearances, the contact was of the innocent kind
that had happened thousands of times in Rose's career: the chance
contact, the kibitzing about baseball, the offer of a signed bat that
Rose was using in the batting cage. Cambra professed to be a Yankees
fan who loved to tweek the nose of the Red Sox fans around his home
near Fall River. (Why he was in West Palm Beach rather than in Fort
Lauderdale, where the Yankees trained, remains a mystery.) From

this first contact in the spring of 1984, the relationship was to deepen over the coming five years. Cambra was a bookie.

During his brief tenure as an Expo, Rose had other outlets close by for his gambling passion. Through the grim vigil, before the Fall of Pete Rose in 1989, a Montreal hotel manager named Rene Longpre would tell *Sports Illustrated* that he had placed bets for Rose on hockey and basketball games. Some of them from phones at Montreal's Olympic Stadium.

As the season opened in Montreal, Rose reached another plateau of achievement in a tapestry that was becoming as complicated and as glorious as Dante's Paradise. On April 13, the twenty-first anniversary of his first hit in the major leagues, he stroked a double off Jerry Koosman of the Phillies for his four-thousandth hit. Inevitably, he was asked what it meant to him, and he had genuinely run out of things to say. "All the hits are the same to me," he grumbled. After that, the season settled unhappily into part-time play on a team going with youth. By midsummer, he was batting a mediocre .259. The thrills on the field were few.

In July, his relationship with Joseph Cambra had become business as well as pleasure. But of what nature? On July 5, Rose wrote two checks to Cambra, for $10,800 and for $9,000. Four and a half years later, the so-called Dowd investigation in behalf of Commissioner Bart Giamatti found these checks highly suspicious, especially because they were written at the height of the baseball season. In his interview with an investigator, Cambra portrayed the checks as part of a real estate venture between him and Rose, but he could provide no details and no supporting documents. In his sworn testimony, Rose was also hazy about the deal. It might have been raw land, he wasn't sure, he had never seen it. "He [Cambra] just told me it was a good opportunity to double my money. I said fine." But the "deal" fell through.

Dowd's suspicions lay in his questions. "Have you ever bet with Mr. Cambra?"

"Bet with him?"

"Yes, sir."

"No, sir."

"Have you ever gone to the track with him?"

"No."

"Has he ever given you any money?"

"No."

"Has he ever loaned you any money?"

"Well . . ."

"Go ahead. Take your time."

"He gave me the return of my money."

"He returned the 19,000-dollar check?"

"19,800 dollars."

"Did he return the check that you sent him?"

"No, he returned it in cash."

"And when did he do that, sir?"

"I don't remember. I know he brought it to Montreal, is all I could tell you. So it had to be in '84 sometime. . . . It probably was a couple months after he got it."

But Pete Rose was not in Montreal several months later.

On August 15, 1984, he had been traded back home, to the Queen City of his upbringing, to the Reds, as a player-manager. Ulysses had returned home, sore right shoulder and all, after having been cast upon the sea and having wandered for five years. The negotiations had been tense and highly secret. Despite the signing of the awesome Dave Parker as a free agent over the winter, the club was 50–70 in mid-August, next to last in the division, and unhappy with its manager, Vernon Rapp.

Howsam, now president of the Reds, knew all the old dirt on Rose, but under the present desperate circumstances, with the Reds on the bottom rather than on the top, the risk of the move seemed minimal—at least for a while. Business was business. With a brand-new wife, it was a decent bet that Rose's domestic life would be reasonably tranquil for a time. Howsam wanted Rose only as a manager, but Rose (and Reuven Katz) would have none of that. The pursuit of Ty Cobb had to continue. That was a given, an obsession. It was nonnegotiable. Rose would come only as a player-manager. Reluctantly, Howsam agreed and made the offer good through the 1986 season—but at a salary of $225,000, less than half of what Rose was making in Montreal. Rose was 129 hits short of Ty Cobb. He accepted.

Rose was joining a grand but outmoded tradition, which imparted further history to the move. Greats of the Old Game had also been player-managers: Tris Speaker, George Sisler, Rogers Hornsby, Lou Boudreau. Cobb himself had done the same toward the end of his career. "I am going to rub the boys the right way, and I'm not going to do anything to discourage them," said Cobb when he took over the Tigers in 1921, at a salary of thirty-five thousand dollars. "When I feel compelled to apply vile names to them to get them to take action, that is the time to clear them off the club. What I want is a hustling ball club." Soon enough, a framed picture of Ty Cobb would be placed on Rose's manager's desk at Riverfront Stadium as a daily reminder.

Headlines in ninety-six-point type greeted his return to Riverfront. It was "Pete Rose against the Chicago Cubs" that night to a local newscaster, as the reporters groped for language equal to the moment. Making his entrance into the clubhouse, he was relaxed and jovial. He asked Dave Parker how the club normally handled infield practice. "I liked that," Parker would say. "It was like a new guy in town asking where the best restaurants are." To his leadoff man, Gary Redus, Rose had not vile epithets but simple advice. "Run your tail off," he said.

Cramming a little history overnight, the reporters discovered poor records for the other greats who had tried to manage. Would Rose too be impatient?

"I tell young guys, 'Hey, everybody makes outs.' I've made nine thousand of 'em, more than anybody in the history of baseball," Rose replied.

Would he expect too much of his players? Would he set for them the goals he had set for himself?

"Why would I expect someone else to do that?" Rose was quick to answer. "Only one other guy done what I done."

His first order of business was to call in his first baseman, Nick Esasky, and close the door. The manager would be starting himself at first base that night.

"It's better for the people," the skipper said. "They're not coming out to see me change pitchers."

Esasky was willing . . . for one ceremonial night. Minutes later in the locker room, sporting a "Pete's Back!" T-shirt, Esasky was gracious. "I can give it up for Pete tonight," he said. "I'll be in there tomorrow."

In front of thirty-five thousand jubilant fans, more than double the normal crowd, Rose singled his first time up, driving in Redus, who had singled and stolen second. The next batter singled as well, and Rose motored around second and slid safely—headfirst, of course—into third base. He came home on a single. His first minutes back were a distilled essence of Pete Rose.

But nothing is perfect. On his next trip to the plate, he hit into a double play, then grounded out in the fifth. In the seventh, with the Reds up 5–4, two outs and a man on second, he singled again, bringing in the man on second, and he kept going toward second. The throw was way wide of the bag, but still Rose hit the dirt headfirst. The old hot dog from 1963 had returned. Why had he done it?

"My damn legs were so sore I thought it would just be easier sliding that way" was his first, insufficient explanation. But he had another motive. "Get 'em out here once," said the company man of his clientele, "and you might as well try to get 'em back."

Pete Rose appeared in twenty-five more games that season as a Red. Compared to his .259 average in the alien north, his average for his hometown was .365.

On November 12, 1984, about an hour and a half before the Seattle Seahawks took on the L.A. Raiders in a Monday Night Football game, Rose's acquaintance from Massachusetts, Joe Cambra, called his boss, and the boss was annoyed.

"Keep that guy down, Joe. Christ, twelve hundred times on one bet!"

"That's good action," Cambra replied. Twelve hundred times, at five dollars a time, meant six thousand dollars.

"No that ain't good action. . . . I mean if this guy is gonna, you know, this guy is gonna give you more than just one piece, it ain't bad. But try to keep him down a little bit."

"All right. I'll keep him down if you want. . . . Hey, if you don't want it, I can call him back and call it off."

"No, no, it . . . this guy is just one bet, ain't it?"

"He called last Monday, just bet, he bet Boston over and under."

"Yeah, but that's two separate bets though."

"Yeah."

"Yeah, they're eight hundred times a piece. Well that ain't bad."

"Well, a thousand times is the limit. I mean, hey, if you don't want it, I'll call him back now and tell him."

"No, no, it's already in, but . . . keep it down, because if . . ."

"You're the boss."

"What's gonna happen is, you know what I mean."

"He wants to play now every week."

"We haven't heard from this guy all season!"

"I know. That's what I told him: Where you been?"

"I don't want him to come in, you know, take a shot at us and then we don't get nothing more."

"He said he was at the [inaudible]"

"In the what?"

"In the instruction league . . . in the minors down in Florida, teaching the kids. He's the manager now, you know."

"Give a thousand. Like today, let it go."

"As much money as these guys got is their business."

"The guy's gotta be nuts, you know."

"I can see Pete Rose. He makes millions, you know what I mean."

"Yeah, but we ain't gonna get it."

"Hey, we'll knock him out. We're gonna knock him out."

"So let it go. If he gives you a thousand times take it. If he gives you . . . whatever he gives, take, but I mean don't let him get ridiculous."

"All right, I'll tell him the limit is a thousand."

"Yeah, take a thousand times a position. If he wants to be a thousand on over and under. . . ."

"Well, I told him, it's no bet until I call you back. I'm gonna call him back, say, okay, it's in for twelve hundred now."

"The twelve hundred we took already."

"But my partner says from now on a thousand times the position is plenty."

"Cause we gotta figure on who . . ."

"Manny, I don't want you to be mad."

"No, I'm, not mad . . . I says, we haven't heard from this guy all season. It scares me like that."

"I'm here I am laying in the bed, and the phone rings, he says, JC? you know who this is? I knew right away. I says, Yeah. Pete Rose. He says, How the hell do you know. I says I knew it's your voice. He says, Ah, you never let me know. . . . I says, Don't tell me. I say I wrote to you. I says, I gave you my numbers for football, and he says, You never let me know if I got the money, I says, you must've known I got the money. He's full of shit."

"Of course he's full of shit. . . . What did he take, Seattle?"

"He took Seattle."

"What's the, ah. . . ."

"L.A., three."

"L.A.'s three?"

"No, Seattle's three. We're getting three. The Rams are going to beat 'em."

"It don't make no difference to me, Joe."

"I never expected Pete Rose."

"But try to keep him down to a thousand a position. That way, it gives us a little more leeway with the other people too."

"Me, I says, You wanna wait till after the Rose Bowl? He says, Oh, no, I wanna work every day, like tomorrow. I says, No, that's too much trouble. I says every week. Our week starts on a Monday and ends on a Sunday. Monday we mail you the money or you mail us the money. So that's it. So in other words, one week is the limit."

The following day, having wiretapped the above conversation, the Massachusetts state police raided Joseph Cambra's house and arrested him as an illegal bookmaker. The raid at Cambra's was only one of thirty-eight locations, involving more than 120 state policemen. The district attorney in charge would say that the gambling combine had a handle of $500,000 a week and underpinned the drug operations of a Providence organized crime family. Among the items seized at Cambra's house were copies of the two checks from Rose to Cambra totalling $19,800 from four months earlier. Two years later, in 1986, Cambra was convicted of illegal bookmaking.

And three years after that, in his sworn testimony before major league baseball, Rose was asked about Cambra's line of work.

"[During spring training in 1984] what was Mr. Cambra's occupation?"

"Baseball fan," Rose replied.

"Did he have any other occupation?"

"Not to my knowledge."

"Did you know that he was a bookmaker?"

"Not to my knowledge."

"How about in 1985? Did you know that he was a bookmaker?"

"No."

"How about 1986?"

"No."

"Did you know that he had been convicted of bookmaking activities in Massachusetts?"

"I read that in the paper about two weeks ago."

For his part, Cambra was also interrogated by Giamatti's investigators. Protected by his lawyer, Cambra was nervous about certain bookmaking charges from the 1984–86 period that were still outstanding and for which he could still be prosecuted. He had never *seen* Rose bet or gamble, he told the baseball investigator, and he never talked about baseball with Rose. With an air of authority, he asserted that bookies in his area did not take baseball bets because they couldn't make money on baseball. In any event, Rose had never bet on baseball with him.

Other sports?

"My impression," Cambra replied, "is that the baseball commissioner's office is only concerned with Pete Rose betting on baseball."

As Rose entered the 1985 season—the season he expected to break Ty Cobb's hit record—the sportswriters groped for the link that would bind Cobb and Rose together. The differences seemed more profound than the similarities. On the playing field, where the opponent was the enemy in a life and death struggle, where losing required revenge, Cobb was mean and terrifying, the personification of rage. Rose's competitiveness pushed the outer limit of competitiveness but was within the rules, and that was why, until the end, he was the perfect advertisement for the game, the perfect role model for every modestly talented youngster in America. Cobb was chasing no one except his phantoms in his quest for the records. Rose had this slavering stalking horse. Without that, his career as a player would have ended two years earlier, and his transition to managing—essentially a sentimental business decision by the Reds, occasioned only because they were a losing team—would never have taken place.

Off the field in public, Cobb could be graceful and articulate, comfortable with presidents and senators, whereas Pete Rose was the essence of tackiness, whatever its charms. Yet Cobb was also a rabid, flagrant, fire-eating racist who was given to calling Babe Ruth a nigger because of his dark complexion and his moon face. Cobb, in fact, had leapt into the stands and throttled a spectator who called him a "half-nigger." Except for his lapse in his 1979 *Playboy* interview, in which he had painted a racist image of Dave Parker, Rose was colorblind way ahead of his time.

"The only thing you ever hear about Cobb is that he was a bad person," Rose was to say. "It's always easy to exaggerate after a guy's gone, because he can't defend himself." And then he would add something that in the light of later events was touching. "When people read what's on my plaque at Cooperstown or on my tombstone, it's not gonna have that Pete Rose was a good person. I am. But that's not going to carry on. A hundred years from now, people will just remember me as the guy with the most hits."

There is nothing in Rose's career, certainly not the vicious collision with Fosse in 1970 or the flagrant slide into Harrelson in 1973 that approaches the ugliness of the episode in May 1915, when Dutch Leonard was persistently moving Cobb back off the plate with inside pitches, until at last, he hit the batter. Cobb seethed and bided his time. On his next trip to the plate, Cobb laid a bunt down the first-base line that the first baseman would have to field, requiring Leonard to take the throw and make the play at first. As Leonard crossed the bag just ahead of Cobb, Cobb leapt toward him viciously, spikes high, anger and blood lust in his distorted face, and slashed across Leonard's ankles, ripping his stockings.

"He never threw another beanball at me," Cobb justified himself later with satisfaction.

Hatred never motivated Rose. As a consequence, he never inspired the sheer terror that Leonard was to feel after that episode with Cobb. To the contrary. Rose's headfirst slides were fundamentally dangerous to himself rather than his opponent. Had he encountered, at any point in his twenty-two years of playing, an infielder with a fraction of Cobb's anger and revenge, he could have been maimed in an instant.

"Do you think Ty Cobb is up there looking down at you as you chase the record?" Rose was asked during the 1985 season.

"From what I know about the guy, he may not be up *there*," Rose replied. "He may be down *there*."

Nevertheless, Cobb's devil spirit inspired and sustained Rose. In addition to the picture of Cobb that Rose kept on his desk at Riverfront, he had traded his precious 1975 World Series ring—the ring with its diamond and its personal engraving and its tie to the greatest World Series in modern baseball history—for a huge bust of Ty Cobb. There was only one other copy of the Cobb bust in the world. Besides, Rose had two other World Series rings.

As Rose approached Cobb's record, the comparisons were an endless source of heated discussion and amusement among fans, with Rose throwing himself into the debate with relish. With spitballs and dead balls, baseball, in Cobb's day, was a pitcher's game, and, before Babe Ruth, there were few home runs. But then the playing surfaces were inferior; spring training was a nightmare; the mitts were grotesque; and some of the top players in the nation, those who happened to be black, were barred from the majors. In Rose's time, the specialists, especially the relief pitchers, had arrived; most games were played at night, when it was harder to see the ball; the travel on the road was more taxing; and the pool of talented black players changed everything. "I had Willie Mays and Bobby Bonds chasing my stuff down," Rose said, resting his case.

In the end, he was right: you really could not compare the old with the new. Yet when he tried to diminish Cobb, he diminished his own accomplishments. He asserted blithely that Cobb's lifetime average in the modern era of night baseball, relief pitchers, and black superstars would be only about .330. Who could know? Rose's statement drew attention to the fact that his own lifetime average was way down the list, a respectable but scarcely historic mark of .305. More than a hundred players were ahead of him in the column. It was true that the few years at the end had drawn down his mark considerably. However, Cobb's average in his last season was .323. He was forty-one years old when he quit.

On the day in 1923 that Ty Cobb passed Honus Wagner for the most hits in the young history of baseball, little was made of the occasion, and the ball continued in play. That had been a different time. In the months before Rose approached his chance to tie and exceed Cobb's record, it was a time of promoters and self-promoters, of kitsch and Diamondvision, of a baseball card that could sell for thirty-nine dollars. In those months, Rose's imagination was obsessed with the staging of THE DAY, his day. Before the 1985 season, he had predicted that it would happen on August 26.

That inspired the astrologers and meteorologists and astronomers to put their heads together. They predicted that August 26 in the Ohio Valley would be cool and cloudy, and Halley's Comet, that fuzzy, dark snowball of a celestial body, would be making its first appearance in seventy-five years in the night sky. But August 26 would come and go, with weather cool and cloudy all right, temperature at 62 degrees; Rose was still twelve hits short.

By mid-August, the anticipation was tremendous; it was better than the consummation. Rose held twice-a-day press conferences for the professional observers on the Rose Watch. He did so with a tone of apology, expressing his sympathy for those working stiffs of the press who had to write the same old story day in and day out. He hoped for them that the milestone came sooner rather than later, "So you guys can get on with the rest of your lives." He ranged afar, trying to keep his banter entertaining and seemed never to run out of material. His favorite Cobb story, he told Tim Sullivan of the *Cincinnati Enquirer*, was the time Cobb was sitting in the Yankees dugout before batting practice, when a sour Yankee approached him and told him, "Get the hell out of our dugout." That made Cobb sore. During batting practice, he responded by hitting fifteen straight shots into the Yankees dugout. To Rose, that showed Cobb's bat control. Rose even spun a speakeasy tale of 1920s in Chicago, when some New York Yankees found themselves awestruck in the company of Al Capone. It was a story about autographs. If the ball players treasured a signature from the Big Guy—and their lives—they should not reach into their pockets for a pen, Capone's goon warned them. Rose wished he had been there that day: "He'd have to give you a tip on a horse or something, wouldn't he?"

Rose and his mouth were not enough, of course, and the reporters resorted to unusual methods to keep the story going. Tim Sullivan engaged a medium in St. Louis in a worthy attempt to talk to Ty Cobb about Rose. In the seance, Cobb was indulgent. Rose was great but not that great. And the shade predicted that a player then in the minors was going to surpass them both. His name? Bob something, said Cobb, and he was eventually going to play for the Giants.

The event itself was simply a point on a continuum, a simple number, and there was nothing intrinsically interesting about that. In the march toward the number, in the numbers beforehand, the real interest lay. Still, Rose made the process more bearable by addressing the final achievement in original ways. He had no set speech, no standard lines, even though the questions were always the same. He had changed his mind that Cobb was probably burning in hell. "You can't be that bad a guy and get 4,191 hits." The statement was vintage Rose, a sentence so simple yet full of meaning, suggesting if not divine intervention, certainly divine notice and even blessing on so heavenly a game.

In the memory of Cobb as sour and vicious, Rose had a clear advantage as an upstanding representative of the game. In this endgame, he presented himself as a picture of integrity. Two hits short of the record, with the Reds in Wrigley Field, Rose went 0 for 4 in a Saturday game. Had he done it on purpose, just to save the record for Cincinnati? A left-hander, Steve Trout, was scheduled for the Sunday game, and Rose was not hitting right-handed these days. He inserted his old friend, Tony Perez, against left-handed pitching. But on Saturday night, Trout fell off a bicycle on his left shoulder and was scratched for the Sunday game, in favor of a right-hander, a junk pitcher named Reggie Patterson, who had been called up from the minors only five days before. Rose penciled himself back into the lineup. With a three-hit performance, he could break the record on foreign ground. "I had thirty thousand people yelling here," Rose said after the game, "and one lady sitting back in Cincinnati kicking her dog every time I got a hit." This was a reference to the new owner of the Reds, Marge Schott, and her companion, a St. Bernard named Schottzie.

On the first pitch of his first at-bat, Rose slashed a single to left center, bringing him one short of the record. "Don't do it," big Dave Parker growled at his manager. "Don't do it."

It was a dilemma, perhaps even in the constellation of baseball, a moral dilemma. Rose's agent, his owner, his wife, and even his new child, Ty—"I already have a son named Pete," he had explained—had not expected him to play. Didn't he owe it to Cincinnati to make the hit there? But the game was tight, and he was the manager who was supposed to win. And wasn't baseball a national game anyway? His record was for the nation now, not just for his hometown.

In the fifth inning, Rose got his second hit, to tie the record. Wrigley Field swelled with the roar of approval as he stood on first base. The Cubs first baseman, Leon Durham, tried to freeze him. "Don't move," Durham said. "I need the TV exposure." In the dugout, the scraped and bruised Steve Trout kept trying to get Rose's attention by pointing to himself, as if he were responsible for this historic moment.

In the ninth, with the game knotted at 5–5 and two men on, Rose again came to bat. Now, the issue was truly joined. It had become a measure of his stature as a ball player that the baseball world assumed—and perhaps Pete Rose believed—that he could choose to hit now, if that was what he really wanted. The choice transcended the pitcher he faced—it was the towering fastballer, Lee Smith—and the conditions—it was late, and the Chicago sky was dark and foreboding. A hit could win the ball game. But Rose struck out. Back in the dugout, his son Petey asked him if it wasn't hard to see, being so dark and all, as if only the gloom of the afternoon accounted for this failure. The pitch "sounded" like a strike, his father replied with true wit, so he had swung at it.

If there was a script for all this, it was hard to know who was writing it: Rose or Marge Schott, the mayor of Cincinnati or the Heavenly Father. Minutes later, the skies opened up and the rains came, delaying the game for two hours, before it was suspended altogether for darkness. There would be no more at-bats for Pete Rose that day. The game in which Rose officially tied the hit record of Ty Cobb was never completed and never recorded as an official game.

Before Rose's next game, there was a session with a press corps that had swelled to four hundred.

"Where do you get your strength, Pete?" a reporter shouted out. Slowly, mischievously, Rose unbuttoned his jersey and yanked it apart to reveal his T-shirt: "Wheaties—Great out of the Box," the slogan of Rose's major product endorsement that year.

As the Reds took the field, a plane flew over Riverfront, trailing a streamer that read: "Latonia is betting on Pete." That was amusing in 1985, for Rose's "hobby" was well known. Latonia was his favorite racetrack in Cincinnati.

On the mound for the San Diego Padres was Eric Show, who had the unusual distinction, for a ball player, of being a member of the John Birch Society. Show was not well liked by his teammates, not because of his politics but because he was a loser and a whiner. The wily old veteran Graig Nettles, who was finishing off his career in San Diego, put in his dig about the likelihood that Show would give up "the big one." If it happened, Nettles said, "the Birch Society is going to expel Eric for making a Red famous."

Before the game, Show was sour as he contemplated his acquisition of a third negative distinction. "I guess it doesn't mean as much to me as it does to other baseball enthusiasts," he said. "In the eternal scheme of things, how much does this matter?" Not many in the ballpark that night were given to such Zen thinking.

The Padres went down in order in the top of the first, and the Reds came to bat. With Rose in the on-deck circle, testing his fat-handled, thirty-four-ounce black bat, fashioned in Japan of Kentucky ash, Eddie Milner popped out, and Rose strode to the plate. He was a beefy, almost portly figure now. In his mind was a simple formula, and it had been there for months: See the ball. Hit the ball. And it will come. Occasionally, he had an addendum: and don't get hurt. But he had arrived at his moment, unhurt, and after tonight, all was denouement.

Show's first pitch was high, a fastball. Rose saw it clearly and didn't like it. He swung at the next pitch, fouled it off, and took another pitch low. The count was 2 and 1, a hitter's count. It came. He saw it and hit it, stroking it to left center.

Above the field, in the lights of the Goodyear blimp, on the dazzling Diamondvision screen of Riverfront, in the fireworks bursting over the Ohio River, in the license plate of the Corvette that emerged from right field, in the official removing of the base from beneath his feet, and in the ball, seized as if it were the Moonstone diamond, the news was conveyed: 4,192 hits. In the eternal scheme of things, the event did matter: in the words of the Padres Steve Garvey on first base next to Rose, "Thanks for the memories"; in the embrace of Reds coach Tommy Helms, who had roomed with him in the minors, had followed him three years later as the National League Rookie of the Year, and who would take over as manager of the Reds when Rose resigned; to Tony Perez, who had always hovered, ever so slightly and unfairly, in Rose's shadow; to his son Petey, now sixteen years old, a poignant figure who had a decent chance to become a big leaguer himself; to the disgruntled Eric Show, who sat on the mound while the festivities went on and on and on. It mattered to baseball, and baseball mattered to America, especially at a time when both baseball and America were depressed with reports of drug trials and talk of hero-criminals and sports junkies.

What would Rose say? No doubt, in the months beforehand, he had thought a lot about that, just as another technical man, Neil

Armstrong, had thought a lot about what he would say when he set foot on the moon.

Rose was a simple man: "Clear in the sky, I see my dad, Harry Francis Rose, and Ty Cobb. Ty Cobb was in the second row. Dad was in the first."

And he cried—and later, he tripled in the seventh, scored both runs in the 2–0 victory, and ended the game with a defensive dive at first.

· 9 ·

Hanging Spikes

IN 1983, with the resignation of Bowie Kuhn, the search for a new baseball commissioner got under way. Giamatti's now-famous aside about yearning only to be president of the American League had been enjoyed—and remembered—in the baseball world. Baseball was flattered. After Giamatti became president of Yale, the president of the American League, Lee MacPhail, had offered to swap jobs.

Now, the search committee, chaired by Bud Selig of the Milwaukee Brewers, wanted to test Giamatti's seriousness. That June in New York, Giamatti and Selig had dinner together. They had never met, but there was an instant rapport between them, and after dinner, they spilled out into the streets of Manhattan, wandering aimlessly until after 1:00 A.M., talking baseball with the intensity of two fanatics. Joyfully, they replayed the summer of 1949 . . . before it was fashionable. Soon after, Selig committed his thoughts—and his recommendation—to paper. Giamatti understood the sociological ramifications of the game better than anyone he knew, Selig wrote his colleagues, perhaps better even than he himself.

Beyond question, Giamatti was tantalized. Apart from the powerful fact that this would be a boyhood dream come true, the Commissioner of Baseball made considerably more money than the president of Yale, and money was becoming important to Giamatti. The role of the Commissioner of Baseball was really the role of a great educator, he could say to himself by way of justification. As yet, however, he did not have the spine to chuck the Yale presidency. The abuse and scorn from the academy would be too intense. He had served only four years, and he had promised seven. The labor situation remained to be settled. To leave would seem cowardly, especially to leave for such a seemingly trivial reason. Just in case Giamatti was really serious about this whimsy, Cyrus Vance, in his capacity as a Yale trustee, had a word with him.

"I hope to hell you won't take it," Vance said half-seriously, but with the serious element firm enough to register. "There are lots of other things you can do where your talents can be usefully applied. This is no time for a flight of fancy. You have a special, God-given opportunity to lead the university during a difficult time." Coming from Vance, that was powerful discouragement. With some regret, which no doubt became even stronger as he moved into the searing strike months later, Giamatti removed his name from consideration.

Nevertheless, in January 1984, fully a year before the Yale strike was settled, Giamatti decided to resign, and so informed the Senior Fellow of Yale, J. Richardson Dilworth. The president had predicted in 1978 that he might serve seven years. He gave his notice in five. The travel, the begging for money from rich people, the sharp criticisms of his once boon companions, who accused him of contemptible things, had exacted a price. He longed for some more purely joyful pursuit. His health had suffered, as had his family life. At the age of forty-six, he was beginning to look twenty years older. Even fencing with the Young Turks had ceased to amuse or excite him, and he knew that as he lost the ardor of battle, he was put at a disadvantage. More than most public men, Giamatti had been asked continually throughout his presidency if he was having fun in the job. The question was part compliment, for it implied a man with a great zest for life, to whom having fun, even in the most serious work, was important.

"Fun is not a word I would use lightly in regard to this kind of thing," Giamatti had said before the Yale strike. "If you take on a presidency of an education institution in these times on the assumption that you're going to have fun all the time, then you will engage in a tragedy of sinking expectations."

To such friends as Dean Don Kagan, however, there had never been joy in the presidency of Yale for Giamatti. It had always appeared to be a burden. Kagan ascribed the emotion to Giamatti's "sardonic appreciation" of the initial offer, when he was his beloved university's second choice after a Harvard man with no affection for Yale, a fact that imparted an element of bitterness to the presidency. Kagan had never shared the concern of some at the outset that Giamatti was too "Mediterranean" to be president. Rather, his concern was that his friend would be too reluctant to fight out the tough battles.

Ultimately, Giamatti's disappointment in his faculty friends who had turned against him during the strike hardened into a distaste for academic pettiness in general. He viewed their criticisms as an act of betrayal and an act of institutional disloyalty to Yale. And there remained in Giamatti an element of insecurity in his job, despite his effulgent public persona and despite the fact that he had grown in his work. This was manifest in the way he snubbed Kingman Brewster when the former president returned to New Haven from the Court of St. James. The word spread from Woodbridge Hall that Giamatti frowned on senior faculty socializing with the Brewsters. The situation got to the point where Louise Brewster, trying to be generous in her dismay, remarked that to be an ex-president of Yale was like being a 1927 Chevrolet.

Giamatti knew he had to remain in place until the labor troubles were resolved. The month after they were, in February 1985, he again expressed to Dilworth his intention to leave, and Dilworth agreed, because, as Giamatti would state it later, "the poor guy had no choice." Giamatti offered to stay an additional year, however, as the search for a new president went forward. On April 22, 1985, Dilworth and Giamatti held a joint press conference to announce the resignation, effective in fifteen months, or June 1986. That would make eight years in office, one more than he had imagined at the outset, but then there was nothing magical about the number seven. (Only threes, fours, and nines were magic to Giamatti; three strikes, four bases, and nine innings.) He had set certain goals in 1978, he told the gathered press, especially stabilizing the fiscal situation and affirming the tie of the university to New Haven. While it was not for him to say whether those goals had been met, he knew he had done what he could.

In the coming months, in other places, he was more forthcoming. "The great trick," he told the *New Haven Register*, "is to develop enough scar tissue so that you can continue while at the same time not developing so much that you become insensitive to what's going on. When one feels one's epidermis thickening into a dinosaur's and, therefore, losing one's capacity to be thoughtful, to be flexible, then you ought to cease for the good of the place."

He was even more candid with the Yale magazine called *The New Journal.* "I never want to be one of those people of whom they're saying in parking lots and hallways, 'When's he going to go?' " Giamatti said. "Because that's too late. And I didn't want to come to a point where I had a feeling of defending what I had done."

To the outside world, privy to none of Giamatti's inner doubts and ambivalences, the initial surprise over the resignation gave way to an air of mystery. The strike had not been his finest hour, to be sure, but it was over, and Yale could look forward to a period of tranquillity. If his presidency had been unenterprising, the university, now on a solid financial footing, was in a position to look beyond its ducts and its wiring. If Giamatti had bridled under the housekeeping quality of his administration—"the head janitor and custodian" had become his phrase—he could afford now to become visionary and creative, perhaps even to assume the role of spokesman on a broad array of national issues, the role he had always coveted. What better platform could he find than the presidency of this great university?

Indeed, what was he leaving for? He had no set plans for the future and no specific job in mind. "When you're president of Yale, if I may say so, you don't go out looking for another job," he said smugly. "It's not honorable nor necessary." But to his chagrin, Giamatti was to find that it was necessary—and not dishonorable. Unsolicited offers did not swamp him, as he had anticipated. The problem was partly cultural. In decades past, one became a university president as the capstone of a career and left only to go into a quiet and distinguished retirement as an elder statesman. But Giamatti was only forty-eight years old. What did the nation do with an ex-university president of such youth and apparent vitality? William Fulbright had gone into politics, Kingman Brewster into diplomacy, and many others had become foundation heads.

Inevitably, Giamatti resorted to baseball talk in discussing his situation. "I can still run and catch the fly ball in center field," he said. "You leave when you're feeling good, and the institution is in good shape." Ironically, the only job he ruled out was to become Commissioner of Baseball, because now, regrettably, Peter Ueberroth was already installed in the job.

Giamatti's closest friends on the faculty—Maynard Mack, Peter Brooks, Don Kagan, Jaroslav Pelikan, and William Brainard—got busy in trying to devise a way to lure Giamatti back into teaching. They designed a remarkable package: a year in Italy at full presidential salary, followed by two years as a DeVane lecturer, before he resumed teaching regularly as a chaired professor. Giamatti toyed with the idea of doing a big book on the influence of Italian Renaissance literature on the English Renaissance, a notion his friends encouraged. Bart was the perfect person (perhaps the only person) to do the study, they said. Kagan wanted Bart to turn himself into an old-fashioned literary critic, attacking the scourge of deconstructionism that taught the relativity of literary texts and argued for the uselessness of language.

Giamatti took this flattering possibility under advisement, but he had his doubts. He had been out of scholarship for eight years, and he had fallen behind. He had missed the critical period of a great scholar's life, in which promise develops into international authority. In his heart, he knew there were those who did not consider even his early work to be that impressive and still others who regarded his sociability and this baseball silliness to be evidence of an unserious mind. His academic articles, he was later to confess in a sworn deposition, were of no academic value whatever.

"I'd like to do it," Giamatti said to Kagan, "but I think I've lost my fastball."

Kagan, himself briefly an athletic director at Yale when he took a sabbatical from the Peloponnesian Wars and his biography of Pericles, gladly picked up on the analogy: "Go away, read yourself back into shape. Your arm will get strong again, and you'll be ready to pitch."

But scholarship had become too narrow and scholars too frivolous and parochial for him. He had become less tolerant of the dark campus conspiracies that once fascinated him. Now that he had dined with presidents and Wall Street magnates, deconstructionists paled in comparison.

In the summer of 1985, as Pete Rose was about to overtake Ty Cobb, the Republicans of Connecticut came to Giamatti and asked him to run for the U.S. Senate the following year against the incumbent Democrat, Christopher Dodd. They savored the idea of a candidate who could be Angelo in Bridgeport and Bartlett in Fairfield. Lowell Weicker, Connecticut's maverick Republican in the Senate and the titular head of the party, was thinking about running for governor in 1986, and the Republicans saw Weicker for Governor and Giamatti for Senator as a dream ticket. The representative of the Republicans who came to call was the state party chairman, Thomas J. D'Amore, Jr., a second-generation Italian like Giamatti, from northeastern Connecticut. A graduate of UConn, D'Amore was not sure what to expect when he arrived at the imposing mansion of the Yale president, but it was not what greeted him. Giamatti's regularness struck D'Amore immediately. The political boss could scarcely believe that Yale had had the good sense to make such a real person its head.

D'Amore had come to talk earnestly about the duty of public service and about Giamatti in the U.S. Senate. Giamatti, however, opened their talk by asking if D'Amore wouldn't consider going to Baseball Commissioner Peter Ueberroth instead and persuading him to run for the Senate in California—there was talk of a Ueberroth candidacy at the time—so Giamatti could have Ueberroth's job.

The political overture was serious, and Giamatti took it seriously. For years, he had regarded himself as a political independent who had voted for Richard Nixon but hated Nixon's Vietnam War, who cherished civil rights but despised the intrusion of big government into local affairs. Asked why he would consider associating himself with the Republican party of Ronald Reagan, he had a simple answer: "Because they came to the door." This could not be so lightly waved aside, however, for he maintained an abiding contempt for Ronald Reagan. That Reagan's English could earn him the moniker of "The Great Communicator" was personally offensive to Giamatti. He turned to withering sarcasm. "I'm not sure on a lot of big issues I like him at all," he said about Reagan. "In fact, I know I don't. But it's become irrelevant. Who cares? Reagan is a remarkable president. Carter was always worried. Carter was always running. Reagan walks. Reagan is not worried. If he's not worried, why should we worry? People say, 'Well, my gosh, I think it's terrible I'm out of work . . . that my kids can't go to college . . . that we are a landlord in Central America.' I don't know who told him he could cut taxes and spend money and not have us in the worst deficit in the history of the universe. But he's not worried, so why should I?" He put himself forward as a Republican in the mold of John Sherman Cooper, Jacob Javits, Charles Mathias, Jr., George Bush, and an academic politician in the mold of Daniel Patrick Moynihan or, better yet, Woodrow Wilson.

After some months pondering a political race, Giamatti finally decided against it. Senator Dodd was a formidable opponent, but Giamatti had found, to his embarrassment, that he was essentially in agreement with Dodd on most issues. That took away the necessary fire in the belly. Moreover, he was not sure he liked being around those Republican types. They were not his kind. In the Yale community, as the possibility of a Giamatti candidacy was gossiped around, many doubted that Bart had the inner fortitude for the rough and tumble of politics. Lowell Weicker's decision to stay in the Senate clinched Giamatti's decision. Without Weicker as his ticket-mate, there was no chance of victory. Giamatti withdrew his name from consideration in November 1985.

The academic year of 1986 drew to a close wistfully for Giamatti. On the Cross Campus green, he competed in his last town and gown chess game—a human chess game, that is, with huge squares carefully laid out with bed sheets upon the green. The president of Yale was the white king, and the mayor of New Haven, Biagio Delieto, was the red king, while students and townies with a dramatic flair were their knights and pawns. Giamatti did not seem to mind the nasty placards about the need for Yale to disinvest in South Africa that ringed the game. Having been trounced the year before at its own game, Yale triumphed, at last, on the field of cerebral battle.

Giamatti had reason to feel mellow. A few days later, Peter O'Malley of the Los Angeles Dodgers sought him out as the representative of the commissioner's search committee for the new president of the National League. To O'Malley, what came through immediately was Giamatti's respect for the institution of baseball and understanding of its unique place in American culture. "Many people say they love baseball," O'Malley would say later, "like they say 'I Love Lucy' but Bart had respect as well as love. We were sold on his ability to communicate what he believed." The search committee was to interview a score of candidates, but it quickly narrowed the candidates down to Giamatti and James Baker, then the Secretary of the Treasury under Reagan.

Two more meetings with Giamatti followed before he became the unanimous choice of the committee. As Giamatti's selection leaked to the press, a baseball official wondered revealingly if the job was big enough for "someone of his stature." Could Giamatti be slumming? The salary was certainly big enough: $200,000, the same as the president of the United States, although not quite as big as the salary of the manager of the Cincinnati Reds.

Immensely flattered, the baseball world rejoiced. A bit out of its depth, the baseball press found itself asking unprecedented questions. Why would a man of literature be interested in such a job? the reporters asked him at his introduction in the Starlight Room of the Waldorf-Astoria.

"Men of letters have always gravitated to sports," he mused. "Witness yourselves." The reporters groaned. "I've always found baseball the most satisfying and nourishing pursuit outside literature."

Inevitably, he got a question about what Dante's attitude would be toward him taking the job. It would become the most asked question of his next two years.

"Dante would have been delighted," Giamatti imagined. "He

knew very well the nature of paradise, and what preceded it. He would have approved of a game that was first played in 1845 on the Elysian Fields of Hoboken, New Jersey."

The truth is that Giamatti considered *himself* to have arrived in Elysium after a long wandering since childhood. The next day, in the sports pages, this ungainly, plumps, urbane man stood alongside Tim Teufel of the Mets, who had just hit a pinch-hit homer to beat the Phillies, and Dave Winfield, who was safe at home when he swiped the mitt of the Tigers catcher, Lance Parrish, with the ball in it during a close play at the plate. Following his Manhattan press conference, he returned home to New Haven and spoke to the waiting reporters about baseball as it had never been spoken before. "The pace is such that the fan can enter the game and decide what he or she should do," he said. "It's a game whose weave is open enough to let everyone in. That's why it reflects the country. That's why it's so much a part of the country's history." He meant to be the fans' president.

New Haven greeted his selection—and his acceptance—with part astonishment, part mortification, part delight, and part envy. Some of the faculty's Walter Mittys were overjoyed. Others felt that Giamatti's decision was degrading, a rebuke to them personally and a rejection of their own lofty values. A few took the stance of superior bemusement. How fitting. Just like old Bart.

Maynard Mack, the Shakespearean scholar, understood perfectly: Bart saw baseball as a paradigm of what life might be. In idealizing the game, invoking the Odyssey and the concept of Nostos, Giamatti had given the parallel of baseball to life its most elaborate development. Jaroslav Pelikan, whose only childhood fantasy was to direct Beethoven's Ninth Symphony with a full chorus at Tanglewood, needled Giamatti.

"Think of all the things you hated as president of Yale: the travel . . . dealing with rich people . . . unions." Pelikan grinned. "Now you'll be traveling all the time, fighting with unions, and the millionaires will all be twenty-five years old."

The inevitable round of farewell dinners followed. At one, a luncheon given by the chemistry department, Giamatti was presented with a thirty-year-old baseball mitt, inscribed with the magical name of Zeke Zarilla, the star outfielder of the 1952 Bosox. Ceremonially, a chemist gave him a dollar bill. The rumor that Giamatti would be making exactly the same salary as President Reagan interested the academics mightily.

"Now, if reporters ask you whether you make more than the

President of the United States, you can reply, as Babe Ruth did in the 1920s—"

"Yes, but I had a better year!" Giamatti's voice boomed, beating the chemist to the punch line.

With a certain bemusement of his own, Giamatti observed the heated reaction at Yale to his decision. "One group thought it was nifty. The other thought it was the ultimate proof of my essential unsoundness," he chortled.

From a distance, far away in Cambridge, Henry Rosovsky watched Giamatti's leavetaking with interest. Rosovsky had not been an admirer of the Giamatti presidency, though it would not do for him to say so, but he felt the intimacy that only old rivals can know. After Giamatti had announced his intention to resign, Rosovsky had written him a letter—a letter that was never answered—urging him to return to academic life as a professor. Rosovsky was sentimental about what he called the John Quincy Adams principle: the president who leaves the White House, only to run, surprisingly, for the U.S. House of Representatives. That was, to Rosovsky, the essence of American democracy, the dignity and self-confidence to trade down after one has been at the top. Now, as Giamatti left Yale to go to baseball, the Harvard dean perceived a bitter element. After all of Giamatti's troubles as president, Rosovsky thought he was saying to Yale, "You think you're so great. I'll show you."

Others thought the same thing. When William Brainard, Giamatti's provost during the bitter strike of 1984, stood in the line at his local New Haven supermarket, the check-out girl turned to him and said, "I knew Giamatti would make it big some day."

Pete Rose was getting old and could not accept it. He had excelled for twenty-three years in a sport where the average player was lucky to stay for five. Now that he had broken Ty Cobb's hit record, his statistics argued that he was the best person who ever played the national game. As a result, he had come to believe that he possessed superhuman powers.

"There's nothing I can do about the date I was born," he was to say with a certain annoyance. "I wish people would forget how damn old I am. I don't feel old. I don't act old. And medical experts have told me, my body isn't old."

Off the field, he had become an idol of monumental dimensions. If he didn't act old, his adolescent behavior was central to his charm and appeal. The baseball writers knew all about his escapades at the track and in the bedroom and treated them as amusing peccadillos.

They added to his aura. They made him more interesting, more of "an original." Some reporters had gambled with him. A few had even borrowed money from him and still owed it.

Under these circumstances, it is not surprising that Rose believed that he could play the game of life by his own rules. Everything he did in public was applauded. He lived the way he wanted to live. He was above criticism.

Part of the problem was that Rose had no real friends. His relationships with players and baseball people were short and fleeting. His fans did not question his behavior, but rather cried for greater excess. His acquaintances, such as his errand boy, Tommy Gioiosa, were in no position to confront him. As his skills waned, his wife found him even more aggressive and difficult to deal with. His stooges and flunkies sponged off him, and yet that satisfied his need for constant adulation.

There was only one man with whom he had a continuing, close relationship over the years. That was the genial and cosmopolitan Harvard man, Reuven Katz, his lawyer, agent, and all-purpose adviser. Theirs was, however, essentially a business relationship. What socializing they did generally took place on the tennis court. But because this was Rose's only true friendship, he came to idealize it, just as he had idealized his relationship with his own father. Katz evolved into a father figure to Rose, and, in turn, Rose became something like an adopted son to Katz. The adopted son did not want the surrogate father to know about his vices any more than the real son would have wanted his real father to know about them. What Katz did know, he treated as the actions of a prodigal son who was now too old to be scolded. A father simply did not disown the black sheep of the family.

At the center of Rose's greatness as a player and of his difficulty as an adult was his compulsiveness. Like a child, he had trouble controlling his impulses. What was he to do with his kinetic energy as he played baseball less and less? What in life was equivalent to the thrill of stretching a single into a double or sliding headfirst into third base? How was he to sustain the thrill of major league competition, or the daily challenge of winning and losing before a huge, cheering crowd?

The answer was gambling.

To the extent that Rose was ever questioned about his gambling before 1985, his response was always the same: with a smile and a twinkle, he would say he was betting no more in 1985 than he had bet in 1975. He meant no more proportionally to his income. He could afford it. He made a lot of money, and it was his business how he spent it. It was not the grocery money he was betting but money he had earned with his sheer, dynamic determination. He loved to gamble, sure. It kept him interested in sports of all kinds.

By the agreement of virtually everyone later, including his own advisers, the district attorneys who prosecuted him, and eventually Rose himself, Pete Rose's gambling had become pathological by 1985. People stopped his lawyers on the street to tell horrifying stories of the huge and crazy bets Rose was placing and to say how the man's life was out of control.

If his gambling was pathological, it was also poorly done. He lost dizzying amounts of money and needed a way to finance those losses so that Reuven Katz would not find out. While his gambling was getting much worse, requiring more and more cash, his official earnings were going down. His salary from Montreal to Cincinnati had been halved, but Ty Cobb saved him. Now that he was the all-time hit leader and probably the most engaging personality in all of sport, his outside endorsements picked up the slack for a while. That too was tightly controlled and managed by a cadre of other advisers who organized the official portfolio and planned the Rose estate. Rose was given a comfortable allowance, but he came to think of it as a leash. Katz tried to disabuse him of this notion of constraint.

"Pete, it's your money," Katz would say. "If you want a million dollars, say so."

Rose knew he could not reply honestly. How could he say that he was losing a ton on gambling, that he owed some bookies hundreds of thousands of dollars, and that a few of them had ties to the mob.

He needed cash—and a lot of it—that he could hide . . . if not hide, at least to avoid confrontation. During one period, he began writing bad checks. When they were presented and bounced, Rose's accountant would be called, and he would simply transfer funds from another account. After a while, the accountant became expert at these "sweeps." The point was that by writing bad checks, Rose did not have to ask Reuven Katz for money, but knew the staff would cover them automatically.

Rose found the answer in the baseball card mania and memorabilia craze. This once benign hobby of collecting baseball mementos was becoming a megabuck business enterprise. With his historic achievement in 1985, Rose was near the top in demand and in value (behind José Canseco). As a result, he was besieged with offers to make personal appearances at card shows.

When the memento business was moving into telemarketing,

the price of balls and bats, posters and cards that bore an authentic Rose signature skyrocketed. In a single appearance on cable television, hawking Pete Rose items—the price of an official baseball with a Pete Rose signature was thirty-eight dollars—he could sell more than a million dollars of merchandise in a few hours.

His old pattern of demanding only cash now began to mean something: for several hours sitting at a table and signing whatever was put before him, he could make more than $20,000. And he was good at it. Compared to a sour, aloof, unresponsive Canseco, who sat glumly and did the minimum for his maximum, Rose kibitzed with the clientele, cracking his coarse jokes, taking the time to have his picture taken, and seemed to enjoy the situation. After all, his signature was worth nine dollars a pop.

The card show deals were all made in advance, with the promoters guaranteeing him a set figure. A flunky would collect the cash, often in a simple paper bag, and give it to Rose later. Rose would fly in on a private jet, do his gig, fly home, and stuff his cash all over the house, in places where even a show dog couldn't jump over it. This was play money, free money. Because he lost most of it anyway, he did not have the criminal intent—or so his lawyers would later argue—to cheat the government out of its taxes.

To deceive his family and his advisers and, implicitly, the government of the United States about this play money, Rose went to considerable lengths. When certain promoters insisted on paying by check instead of cash, Rose insisted on a series of blank checks, sometimes made out to fictitious names, all in an amount under $10,000, because under IRS regulations, banks had to report to the government checks only over $10,000. His runners presented these checks at the windows of racetracks, where Rose and his cronies were known, and they were accepted with a wink. The authorities later considered these elaborate deceits to be powerful evidence of a guilty mind and of criminal intent.

As a bettor, Rose was a whirlwind of activity. Once, when a particularly big payoff was at stake at Churchill Downs in Louisville, he had himself helicoptered onto the infield. For less conspicuous outings, he preferred the tracks of Florida, where it was said he was good for $10,000 a night, and Turfway Park outside Cincinnati. For years, he had endured the annoyances of the public dining room at Turfway, where fans hounded him, asking him for a tip on the fifth race, assuming that a Pete Rose would always have inside information. "They think everytime somebody like Pete Rose goes to the window, they know [what horse] is gonna win," observed Arnie Metz, a Riverfront groundskeeper who was Rose's favorite runner in Cincinnati and took 15 percent of Rose's winnings for his trouble. "If they follow him enough, they know that's not true."

When major league baseball came to investigate his gambling in 1989, Rose had to teach the commissioner's investigator, John Dowd, about the "sport of kings." They were talking about the sad state of betting at Tampa Downs.

"When I say you can't bet money there, you understand what I'm saying? Whenever you go to a track and there's no handle. You know what handle is?"

"No, I don't," Dowd confessed.

"Handle is money bet through the window."

"Okay."

"The odds are made based on how much money is bet through the window. Now if they're only handling three hundred thousand dollars for the day, and you go up and bet a thousand dollars on a horse, it will go from twenty to one to one to five. So you're betting against yourself."

"Uh huh."

"Now if you go to Hollywood Park or somewhere where they're handling five or six million dollars, then it doesn't matter what you bet. You don't affect the odds. But if you wanted to, you could make the favor in every race by betting a thousand dollars on a horse. So it's just crazy."

A perplexed John Dowd moved on to another area.

But Rose was intent that Dowd understand. Did Rose ever bet $5,000 on a Monday Night Football game? Dowd wanted to know.

"No. What you do on Monday night is according to what you did for the weekend. You know, if you're plus for the weekend, then you can sponge your bet a little bit. But if you're minus, then you fall back a little bit."

"Oh, I see," said Dowd. "So it depends on . . ."

"Right."

"Now when do you place the bet for the weekend?"

"Probably Sunday morning. Sunday noon."

"When do you have to have the bet in? Before kickoff?"

"Yes," said Rose smugly, on solid ground now. "I wish it was the other way. I wish they could kick off first. That would be nice."

By 1986, Rose had his own personal handicapper, a Runyonesque figure of the track named Bruce Battaglia, who was a professional oddsmaker and picked the favorites for the newspapers and the racetracks. Rose and Battaglia would speak at night after the oddsmaker had pored over his racing form. When a Battaglia pick won a race, he would receive a third of Rose's winnings. Rose had an adviser even closer to home in Rob Murphy, his middle-inning relief pitcher, whose hobby was horse breeding and who ran a computerized horse-breeding business on the side. It became a common sight in the clubhouse to see Rose and Murphy giving one another high fives an hour before a Reds game. The reporters would smile, shake their heads in amusement, and joke that so long as Rose was manager, Murphy would never get traded, no matter how badly he pitched.

During the off-season, according to another handyman, Chuck Beyersdoerfer, Rose would sit in his first-floor den, in front of his forty-inch television screen, with two nineteen-inch televisions on the side, watching three basketball or football games at once. "He'd be sitting there with the TV sets, keeping track in spiral notebooks of who was winning and who was losing," Beyersdoerfer said. "Pete would bet on anything, with anybody who was in the room. He would bet on the coin toss. He would bet on who would score the most points in the first half . . . Pete always had a wad of money, a stack of hundreds you would not believe."

Another crony, Paul Janszen, pictured Rose as a study in constant motion, when he was betting: "He was always active, always doing something. If there was a good play or if his team won, he'd jump and give Tommy [Gioiosa] and me high fives. Pete's wife would just stay in the kitchen. If Pete lost on a game, he wouldn't be bothered unless the game was lost by a real dumb mistake. Then he'd be upset for five minutes. Otherwise, it was always, 'Don't worry, we'll get even on the next game.' "

Extending back to 1979 and earlier, Rose had always had his gaggle of flunkies and parasites to make his wagering reasonably anonymous. Tommy Gioiosa had moved from being a starstruck, poignant, dreamy charity case to being a professional leech: Rose's runner, errand boy, and bodyguard. He had moved from covering up Rose's liaisons with women to making the arrangements and providing the place. Where once Rose tossed Gio a few hundred dollars when the boy needed it, in 1981, Gio was entrusted with a mission to fly to San Francisco and pick up $50,000 in cash from "Cappy" Harada, the U.S. representative for the Mizuno Sporting Goods company, which had Rose under contract. From running Rose's bets to the window at the track so that Rose could avoid the autograph seekers, Gio was now Rose's link with illegal bookies. By 1983, Gio was not only getting handsome gratuities from Rose for his courier and car washing duties but getting a 10 percent kickback from bookies on

Rose's losses—which amounted to thousands of dollars—because the bookies were so grateful to have Rose's action. Once a 155-pound weakling, Gio took a job as a bouncer in a downtown Cincinnati bar called Sleep Out Louie's, and after the other bouncers made fun of him, he started to work out with weights at a local gym.

Inevitably, in that nether world of narcissistic musclemen, Gioiosa began to take anabolic steroids to bulk up. Eventually, his habit became so pronounced that he was injecting himself five times a week. His body took on the shape of a human balloon that was blown up with an air pump. With his horse-strength dose of steroids, his personality also underwent a change. He became aggressive and confrontational, irritable and reckless. He was unable to engage in extended conversations, unable to sleep, and delusional about his manly invincibility. Once, while he was driving, he grew enraged when the car ahead of him was slow to make a turn. Leaping out of his car at a stoplight, he ran up to the slow-moving car, grabbed the partially rolled down window and smashed it with his fist, all the while heaping abuse on the terrified driver. Formerly the sweet jock with a choirboy look, Tommy Gioiosa had become a freak.

In 1985, as Pete Rose approached Ty Cobb's record, Gioiosa found employment as the manager of a gym in north Cincinnati called Gold's, at a salary of $500 a week. "The first thing I know, he starts looking like a million bucks," Rose would say of Gioiosa, in the tone of childlike surprise. "Geez, I said, you know, is this business that lucrative? And the guy who was his partner, Mike Fry, did the same thing. He had a new Ferrari, Rolex watches, gold everywhere. I didn't ask them where they got their money. It wasn't none of my business." Gio's new job was a convenience for Rose because the player-manager had swung over to the modern fashion of weight training. Gio invited him to work out at Gold's Gym "for nothing."

Rose soon found himself in the midst of a thriving cocaine ring. The local kingpin was a thug named Donald Stenger, who, together with his girlfriend, was making substantial buys of cocaine in Florida and distributing in greater Cincinnati. Stenger used Gold's as a front for respectability, which he needed because he was a body builder of national reputation, having won a national title in 1983.

Stenger had become a major drug dealer in the usual fashion for a muscleman: he had moved from using steroids to improve his physique into cocaine, and then to dealing in order to support his habit. At Gold's, he found a kindred spirit, Michael Fry, the owner of the Gold's franchise, who took Stenger in as a partner in body building and in cocaine trafficking.

Rose's presence, Stenger and Fry quickly discovered, was good for business. Before long, the baseball hero lent his name to the establishment for its advertising. Gold's Gym became "the home of Pete Rose."

If Rose was good for business, his patronage also expanded the nature of the underworld activity at the place. Gioiosa talked loudly and openly about placing big bets for Rose. These boasts seemed to puff up his importance around the Nautilus machines. Soon enough, the other weightlifters were drawn into the intense activity of their resident celebrity. Gold's thus became a nest of illicit gambling as well as of steroid and cocaine trafficking.

In due course, Stenger joined the covey of Rose cronies. A familiar figure in the Reds clubhouse, he hung around to watch Rose hit in batting practice, attended a celebration dinner for Rose after the Cobb record was broken, traveled to several baseball card shows with Rose, went to the racetrack with him, ran Rose's bets to the window, and watched sporting events in Rose's living room, as Rose placed his "dime" ($1,000) bets.

It would often be said later of Pete Rose that his best quality was his street smarts. Yet as he became more involved with the hoodlums at Gold's, he was, at minimum, extraordinarily naive. Naivete was his best defense, but at the sight of Gio with wads of cash stuffed in his knee-length socks, driving fancy cars, sporting gold and Rolex watches, all on a $500-a-week salary, it strains belief that Rose did not know what was going on.

In 1985, when Rose's gambling had become wild and uncontrollable, and when he needed secret cash to pay his debts, he sold Stenger his M-1 model BMW for $70,000 cash, even though its engine was blown. The very fact that these cocaine dealers had stacks of ready cash drew Rose to them. It was not their drugs but their cash that interested Rose. Who else in today's America but drug dealers has that kind of money? Who else would be willing to plunk it down for such toys with no questions asked and no document trail? Stenger later testified to baseball that his cocaine business was "generally" known to Rose.

To satisfy his immense appetites, Rose expanded the web around him. In the early eighties, through Gioiosa, he put down "nickel" bets ($500) with a bookie across the river in Kentucky, but it was not enough. He then switched to another bookie who was willing to take a dime on an event, but that became too confining. With Cambra in Massachusetts, he had been able to move higher than $6,000 on a single bet, but Cambra got busted along with his ring that was doing a $500,000 handle a week and was tied to a

Providence–based mob family. Through his associations at Gold's Gym, Gioiosa was able to come up with an outlet in Franklin, Ohio, a bookie named Ron Peters. In that quaint small town midway between Cincinnati and Dayton, Peters, once a golf pro, had a restaurant, but he was also dealing cocaine and making illegal bets on the side. Starting in 1984, Rose was able to put as high as $5,000 down with Peters on a single event. When troubles developed with Peters, Rose started betting with Richard Troy, also known as Val (because he parked cars for a restaurant as a valet). Troy had been indicted on gambling violations twice in 1985 and was a low-level operative for the Bonano crime family.

Taken together, over the period from 1984 through 1987, when his passion for gambling huge sums seemed to have no bound, Rose's associations with drug dealers and low-level mobsters and illegal bookmakers had become broad and deep. He was using Gold's Gym not only as his betting parlor but as his bank to borrow and to launder money. These characters from Gold's were turning up at the ballpark and in the clubhouse, and they were noticed and disapproved of. Johnny Bench, who had become a television announcer for the Reds games, found these cronies highly distasteful. More than once, Bench turned away from Rose's office, not wanting to discuss the joys of baseball in the presence of such unsavory characters. In 1985, after the trial of Pittsburgh Pirates players on cocaine charges, the Commissioner of Baseball, Peter Ueberroth, issued an edict banning all "nonessential" personnel from the clubhouse. Rose flagrantly ignored the ban. When Ueberroth got wind of this disobedience, he summoned Rose and issued a formal warning about the undesirables.

Perhaps Rose *was* totally blind to what was happening all around him. Perhaps he was an innocent, abroad in a world that was dangerous and sure to destroy him sooner or later. Perhaps he was simply a sick man, caught up in a maelstrom beyond his control, or just oblivious, due to his own blinding fame, to the motives and activities of others, so long as they could help him fuel his desperate need for cash. Whatever it was, he was consorting with sharks and snakes, who would turn upon him with a vengeance when things began to go awry. After selling his BMW to Donald Stenger, he turned to another drug dealer, Mike Fry, for a loan of $30,000 and used the Corvette he had been given by Reds owner Marge Schott on the night he broke Ty Cobb's record as collateral. Meanwhile, Fry was getting into the business of selling other Rose memorabilia.

While all this was happening, Rose wanted to become formal business partners with Stenger and Fry in Gold's Gym. Negotiations got under way. Floating around in it all was his purported adopted son, now the bloated, reckless, muscle-bound Tommy Gioiosa.

Gioiosa had entered the Stenger drug conspiracy in late 1984 by investing several thousand dollars in cocaine loads that Stenger was bringing into Cincinnati from Florida. In the summer of 1985, as the hysteria over Rose's chase of Ty Cobb was reaching its climax, Gio undertook his first "mule" operation. In Cincinnati, Stenger handed Gioiosa $70,000 in a UPS package and set his courier on the road, while the kingpin flew ahead to Fort Lauderdale. There, Stenger took back his $70,000 and handed Gio two kilos of cocaine. Gio put this in a shoulder bag and headed back to the Queen City, one terrified ex-Oriole who was "sweating bullets" as headlights trailed him in his rear-view mirror. Back in Cincinnati, the mule turned over the load to Stenger and received $3,000 for his terror. A month later, with his mentor now the all-time hit king, Gio undertook another run for Stenger, but he was more relaxed the second time around. The same modus operandi obtained, except in this second mission, the money was $100,000, and Gioiosa took the time to pay a farewell visit to Riverfront Stadium before he left for Florida.

There in the manager's office, behind closed doors, Gioiosa opened the suitcase to show off the stacks of cash to Rose. According to Paul Janszen, who claimed that both Rose and Gioiosa had told him the same story later, Gio boasted that he was going for five kilos. Rose marveled at the mother lode.

"You better watch out the DEA doesn't nail you, Tommy," Rose purportedly said. By Janszen's account, Rose had exclaimed to him after the mule was on the road, "Boy, you wouldn't believe how much money Tommy showed me. That Stenger! He must be making a million bucks a year."

During the summer of 1986, as the Cincinnati Reds plodded along in last place of the National League West, the president-elect of the National League threw himself into his new work. He wondered aloud whether this old bow could take a new string, but he was playing to his audience as he proclaimed that the National League owners were taking a bigger risk than he was. At long last, it had become a professional requirement rather than a pleasing avocation to read about baseball history, to study its regulations, and to ponder its current health. He spent hours soaking up the wisdom of the outgoing president, the cigar-chomping, Roman-nosed Charles Feeney. Now his duty in Elysium was to attend baseball games as well, to converse with great players past and present, to manage those secret heroes of the game, the umpires. In July, he attended his first All-Star Game in an official capacity, where the sight of Roger Clemens of the Red Sox squaring off against Dwight Gooden of the Mets was more than thrilling to Giamatti.

"It transcends rooting," he was to say of the experience.

Giamatti was a preeminent conversationalist. Presidents and students, Washington wives and South Hadley coaches had remarked upon the quality: to sit next to Giamatti at dinner was the high point of their lives in society. With his fertile mind, his astonishing range, his sharp wit, and his common touch, he could transfix any listener. "I like to talk. It's what I do best," he said once. Now, he had entered a world where talk was everything.

"Baseball is profoundly oral," he said in the summer of 1986. "The people around it, the youngest and the oldest, love to tell stories. The swapping of tales . . . the telling of stories . . . it's so much a part of the game. It has this oral tradition. When baseball people get together, there's always this constant talking. I like that. It's so available, such an available history . . . even if it's not true."

And yet, Giamatti knew how to listen as well.

There were serious issues. With the cable superstations bringing televised games to every corner of the land, the national pastime was becoming national as never before. "What will come out of the welter and farrago of this," Giamatti said, as baseball people scratched their heads, "remains to be seen." (If *welter* and *farrago* confused them, Giamatti was soon to refer to a strikeout record as "an *auto-da-fé* that has never been bettered.") With their astronomical revenues, the superstations—and the teams they represented—threatened to create a class structure of aristocrats and peons in the National League. It would be Giamatti's job to see that this revenue was fairly distributed to the smaller franchises, such as Cincinnati, so that no teams had an unfair advantage over others when it came to bidding for high-priced players.

In connection with this issue, Giamatti first uttered his concerns about "the integrity of the game." Television degraded integrity. From the beginning of his days in baseball management, Giamatti would speak of his role in protecting the "public trust."

With the spreading epidemic of drug use, he had to address the question of mandatory drug testing, and he came out against it. A drug policy for professional athletes could not be simply punitive, for he understood the dangers of adulation. The groupies and hangers-on of baseball put temptations before the star players that were hard to avoid. Sympathetic in the abstract to players who went astray, he expressed a principle about player mistakes, which he would have to test in searing, specific concreteness two-and-a-half years later with Pete Rose. "Athletes are sheltered and idolized like a special breed," he told the *Vineyard Gazette*, as he vacationed on Martha's Vineyard in July 1986, with a book on the cruelty of Roman games nearby. "You don't get to the top of your profession without having lived a life where a lot of people are taking care of you. It's an adulated, isolated life, and you're vulnerable. These people who have developed their physical gifts haven't necessarily developed the rest of themselves. They think they're immune." The rest of themselves. The moral component. The instinct to responsibility. There could be no better definition of Pete Rose's vulnerability in this very period.

At last, Giamatti could become himself again and express opinions that were unconventional . . . in their quaint old-fashionedness. He came out against AstroTurf and the designated-hitter rule, a bit late perhaps, but his passion on the subjects defined him as a purist. The DH was the creature of crass commercial television and the ratings crunch, he contended for the sake of argument, but it did not make the game more interesting or more watchable for a fan such as himself. Perhaps it did extend the careers of old and lame hitters, but it shortened the careers of younger pitchers who were left on the mound too long, when they should have been removed for a pinch-hitter. Most of all, it robbed the game of strategy. As one who wanted to enter "the weave" of the game as a fan and could only do so through his mind and imagination, it cheapened Giamatti's pleasure in the watching. Moreover, it violated a fundamental rule of liberal education: "This is a game where all nine guys are supposed to be able to play both games, offense and defense."

If the All-Star Game in July was pure art for Giamatti, the World Series in October was like the cry of Clytemnestra. Now, Roger Clemens and Dwight Gooden were competing against one another, and the outcome meant something. For Giamatti, the thrill that transcended rooting in July turned to an agony that was below wailing in October. Surprisingly, his beloved Red Sox made it as far as the Series, and he was duty-bound to root for their opponents. O Pain and Lamentation! Through the late season, he had joked of how he would cheer for the Red Sox until September, and then they were on their own. Implicit was the certainty of seventy years that the Sox would choke at the end, as they always did. But as the bean-and-cod boys closed in on a division championship, he tried to find refuge in Greek mythology: "In the World Series, I will try to remember, like Aeneas, what my obligations are as opposed to my preferences."

When Greek literature failed him as the Sox triumphed, he turned wanly to love and to aesthetics. One always remembered the first girl he fell in love with, he said, but then "passions change and mature." Maybe. "You might come to love art portraiture through Velázquez, and then you discover Ingres and become a devotee of his work. But what you really love is portraiture, painting, art." Perhaps. Luckily, Ron Darling of Yale was pitching for the Mets. When noble Darling won in noble fashion, that was some kind of reed to hold on to.

Nevertheless, when Bill Buckner let Mookie Wilson's pathetic grounder dribble through his legs, and the Mets won the sixth game of the Series, Giamatti was genuinely furious and said so. Sometime later, he calmed down and settled back into his role as the Dantista who knew well the nature not of Paradise but of Purgatory. The calendar had simply shifted later into the season for the Red Sox and their tragic, long-suffering fans. The punishment had merely shifted from the upper to the lower Hell.

"If the Red Sox won the World Series, nobody in New England would know what to do with themselves all winter long," he proclaimed later. "People would be in despair if they couldn't say to each other, 'I remember what happened on the twelfth of July [or the twenty-seventh of October].' I know. I've been doing it for forty-five years. New England is eccentric that way, bound together in common suffering. It's the most Calvinistic part of the country, the part that would feel guilty about winning."

On January 16, 1987, Pete Rose was in his familiar perch in the Rose Room, off the press area at Turfway Park in Kentucky, and looking forward to a big night. During this period he was at the track nearly every night, but this night was special. The Pik Six jackpot had rolled up to more than $200,000. A Pik Six, where a bettor tries to pick six winning horses in a row, was his favorite kind of bet. If only one bettor picks all six, he gets the entire pot. If no one picks six winners, the pot rolls over to the next night and continues to build until there's a winner. For years, Rose had been attentive to these opportunities; he would win on a half dozen occasions. Memorable moments in Pik Six land for him had been the time a pot reached a half million dollars at the Tampa Kennel Club, and Rose's runner in Florida, Mario Nuñez, had put $7,500 down for him on the dogs, and lost. A winner finally turned up when the pot rose to $750,000. Only two months earlier at Churchill Downs, Rose had hit on a Pik Six ticket worth more than $94,000, and there had been high fives all around.

In his box at Turfway were the usual supernumeraries. Besides

Rose and his wife there were his chief Cincinnati runner, Arnie Metz, the groundskeeper at Riverfront and his personal oddsmaker, and the portly and pasty mumbler, Bruce Battaglia. They picked the horses. Also present was the newest addition to the Rose circle, Paul Janszen, a tall, sallow bodybuilder who was inveigling his way into Rose's affection and pushing the faithful puffball, Tommy Gioiosa, aside as he did so. Tensions had not yet developed between the two. Rather, Janszen and Gioiosa were a Mutt-and-Jeff-like team.

Gioiosa rolled in around the fifth race, fresh from an assortment of jewelry scams, fights with bookies, juggling multiple girlfriends, forging Rose's signature on balls and bats to be sold, and small-time drug deals. The poor fellow looked a little dejected. Rose greeted him with warmth and locker room jive. They were only a few winners away from hitting the Pik Six, and this was no time for a long face. Didn't Gio want to go in on the ticket? Gio demurred, unenthusiastic. He knew this game. He had enough cash problems of his own then, as well as a few debts of Rose's that were riding on his shoulders. Rose kept after him, baiting him, chiding him.

At last, Janszen offered Gio to buy into half of his $1,000 share of a $4,800 ticket. Reluctantly, Gio agreed, largely to get Rose off his back. He reached into his knee sock and peeled off $500 from his roll. With five winners in a row now, they needed only this last race, old number 7, and old number 7 won by fifteen lengths. The Rose Room erupted in bedlam, yelling and screaming "the way guys will do," as Janszen would later describe it in Federal Court. The two ladies, Carol Rose, sometimes called the Princess, and Janszen's girlfriend, a blond bodybuilder, shared in the ecstasy. Four other bettors had hit the Pik Six that night, making each winning ticket worth $47,646.

When the shouting was over, Rose, who always held the tickets, turned to Gioiosa. "Tommy, you go cash the ticket," he said, proffering the winning stub with an air of generosity. "You need to show some income." He was referring to the IRS. By having Gioiosa present the winning ticket at the window, as if he had forked over the full $4,800 cost himself, the track would automatically take out income tax from him. To Gioiosa, that sounded like a good idea because his current income did not come from honest work and he needed to have something to put on his tax records.

"I paid enough to the IRS," Rose grumbled. "Why should they get my winnings?"

Gioiosa bounded off to the window and returned with $36,000, which he handed to Rose. Rose counted out a generous $10,000 to Janszen, who in turn counted out $5,000 to Gioiosa. Everyone seemed happy, even Gioiosa, who eventually reported $47,646 in taxable income for the calendar year 1987.

A few months later, Bart Giamatti journeyed south to Lynchburg to give a speech at the inauguration of his former associate provost at Yale, Linda Lorimer, who had been chosen as president of Randolph Macon College. Giamatti and Lorimer were close, and he had been instrumental in her being chosen by the Virginia college and in her acceptance. Together, they had suffered through the Yale strike, with Lorimer taking her fair share of abuse on the streets of New Haven. Perhaps the most disgusting and vulgar lapse of Yale civility in Giamatti's eyes—worse even than his being spat at or shoved—had come when angry students and professors hissed at Lorimer and called her a "whore." Now she was being swept into the presidential ranks of higher education, and Giamatti was pleased and proud.

He was still caught between two cultures. As National League president, he was giving high-flown speeches at educational conferences and at college commencements, speaking not to the estate of baseball but of the American university, invoking not Casey Stengel and Joe Garagiola but Emerson and de Tocqueville. For Lorimer's inauguration, he led a legion of Yale blues who had come down for the celebration. Baseball, however, was never far from his mind. Scanning his guidebooks, he discovered that the Lynchburg Red Sox of the Carolina League would be playing while he was there, and he got in touch with the owner, Calvin Falwell, who happened to be the first cousin of his old antagonist, the Reverend Jerry Falwell.

In his academic robes at the college, Giamatti spoke of the American university as a free and ordered place with moral contour. When he turned to the difference between a leader and a manager, however, he brought education and sports together and signaled what he himself intended to be as a leader of the greatest American game. "Leadership," he said, "is an essentially moral act not, as in most management, an essentially protective act. Leadership is the assertion of a vision, not simply the exercise of style. It is the moral courage to assert a vision of the institution in the future, and the intellectual energy to persuade the culture of the wisdom and validity of that vision. Leadership is much more a rhetorical than a fiscal or strategic act. Leadership must define institutional shape, define the institution's standards and purpose. And such assertions of leadership, by speech, by deed, by decisions large and small, have been largely missing." He was talking about American universities, but he was unwittingly defining his philosophical credo as he approached his collision with Pete Rose a year later.

After his speech, switching roles and costume, Giamatti buoyantly led the Yalies to the county ballfield to see the small-size Red Sox perform. For the president of the National League to be there was a real event, but he insisted on attention for the new president of the local college. She had to throw out the first pitch. It was a tradition. As Lorimer scaled the mound, Giamatti whispered to her to try to throw the ball over the catcher's head, then it would land just right. "It's a strategy that's worked well for me over the years," he confided.

The autograph seekers flocked to him with their programs. One brought an official National League ball with Giamatti's signature printed on it. With joy, Giamatti spoke of how in the major leagues canned mud from the Delaware Valley was shipped to the ballparks to rub the balls down before each game. The thought appealed to him.

He fell into easy conversation with the players and the coaches, especially the pitching coach for the Lynchburg club, the towering and talkative Jim Bibby, a solid performer once upon a time for the Pittsburgh Pirates, whom Giamatti knew had been traded from Cleveland to Pittsburgh for the great Gaylord Perry in 1975 and who had won nineteen games in 1980. He insisted as well upon a chat with the umpires and repaired to their cramped, isolated dressing room. They were his special band of cherubim, to whom he conveyed a special blessing. They were the keepers of the rules, the ones who controlled the fire of competition and made sure the contest was a fair and legal test of athletic skill. Their job was nearly impossible: to judge whether a ninety-mile-an-hour missile had passed millimeters within or without an imaginary zone; to decide whether a foot in a cloud of dust had arrived at its goal before or after the tag; and, in the majors, to be second guessed by the technology of television.

What a way to live! Isolated, lonely, abused, anonymous, laughed at as joke figures in bloated costume. To yell at the umpires was as much a part of the fan's game as to drink beer and eat hot dogs, and Giamatti enjoyed all three as much as anybody. Who could love an umpire? Giamatti could, desperately. He identified with their work. In the National League, he was their boss and manager and, yes, disciplinarian. He always went out of his way to consort with them.

As he sat in the stands, dressed in his J. Press blazer and open-collar white shirt, the brim of a Lynchburg cap pulled down over his Ray-Ban sunglasses and looking decidedly Upper East Side, he re-

galed his Yale friends with stories of his exotic new job. His sentiment about the game was evident. It was meant to be as it was there
in Lynchburg: a decrepit park in a small town, a quiet evening,
lengthening shadows, the crack of the bat, the magic of threes and
nines. If only he could bring it back to what it had been when he was
a boy: the radio in Gene's gas station in South Hadley, trading in the
schoolyard five cards for one DiMaggio—good wholesome fun that
made life's everyday problems vanish.

"Baseball gives the image of the past . . . one which probably
never existed . . . as a rural pastime," he had told the local paper.
"Baseball is in the business of selling tradition."

Beneath the good-fellowship, there was a serious undercurrent
to his drift. His role, he seemed to be saying, was to purify the game
of baseball. As much as it was within his power, he wanted to clean
up the national pastime. Baseball was for the family. It was about
tradition. There was the old question of deferred maintenance. He
wanted to improve the ambience of the ballpark. Just as he had been
concerned with the ducts and the wiring of Yale, so he was now
concerned with the rest rooms and the seats and the food of the
ballpark. Bart the Refurbisher had simply moved to a different arena.

The reality of the modern fan and the modern player was cutting across that rural romance. With drugs and foul language and sex
scandals, with huge contracts and bizarre off-the-field behavior, the
heroes of the game had changed, and Giamatti did not like it. The
sports pages read like the police blotter or a legal brief or a corporate
trade magazine or a supermarket rag. Because he was an educator at
heart, he understood full well the power of example, especially famous example, for good or for evil. Coarse behavior, even beyond the
hearing of the crowd, offended Giamatti.

Midway during the 1987 season, in a game involving the Cincinnati Reds, a rookie umpire made a questionable, fair-foul call
along the outfield line, and Pete Rose rocketed out of the dugout to
argue. The crew chief was John McSherry, an Faustian figure with a
tremendous girth, small expressionless slit-eyes, and a hoarse grav-
elly voice. He came to the defense of his rookie.

Rose shifted his attention to McSherry, lacing him up and down
with one epithet after another about his judgment and his manhood.
To the experienced McSherry, it was just another day at the office,
but when Giamatti heard about it, he wrote his first, full-bodied
reprimand to Rose. Such language and behavior had no place in the
game of baseball, Giamatti wrote to Rose. When he got a copy of the
letter, McSherry was a tad chagrined. He appreciated Giamatti's ges-

ture, all right, but he felt the new president was still a little naive about what was standard and what was unusual in an umpire's life. Giamatti had yet to understand what was really tough about an umpire's job.

Nor did Giamatti like the bad eggs in the stands. He worried about the drunks and the vulgarians.

"You get the guy wearing a T-shirt with profanity written on it sitting next to the grandfather with his grandson," he said in Lynchburg. "How do you accommodate both of them?" Ironically, Giamatti's concern about bad fans was not too different from Pete Rose's. In a book called *Charlie Hustle,* published some years before, Rose had said, "These people in the bleachers are sick. And they're getting a little personal, stuff about my mother and the like. The owners have to be worried about this. There are women and children up there. Not twenty feet away from a guy who's shouting obscenities at me is a man and his wife or girl. I think I'd have to get myself punched if I was in the stands. I'd be damned if I'd let anyone shout words like that if I was there with my wife and kids. Okay, a ticket gives a fan a right to yell and scream, but you can go too far. We are human beings out there." Those were words that would come to haunt Rose.

Giamatti preferred not to accommodate the guy in the T-shirt at all, but the problem was worse than that. Baseball was entering the age of fan violence, where the specter of the gruesome and bloody fan riots in the antiquated soccer stadiums of Britain's steel cities loomed. In his first year as National League president, there were a number of ugly incidents where fights broke out in the stands and spread, and the security reacted with nasty counterviolence. Oddballs and exhibitionists were forever popping onto the field and interrupting the game. Crowd control, Giamatti had come to believe, was the number one problem in the game. In his meetings with the National League owners, whose minds were naturally focused on television deals and player contracts, Giamatti was constantly dragging their attention back to the game itself, the nature of entertainment at the ballpark, the enjoyment of the true and civil fan. The owners could do a better job of cleaning up their ballparks, and remembering that children represented the future of the game.

There was something biblical about Giamatti's attitude. A battle was raging in heaven. He was Michael, the avenging archangel, the guardian of paradise, whose mission, nearly military in character, was to drive the bad angels out of heaven. The outcome was uncertain, for the forces of Lucifer were strong and pervasive. They were on the field in the costume of players and even umpires, or in the stands, or in the owners' board rooms. Paradise was in jeopardy of being lost.

In the winter of 1987, Giamatti preoccupied himself with a major area of responsibility: to decide upon the complexion of his umpire crews for the season and to set their schedule. This was his closest touch with the game on a daily basis. It was his way to enter the very "weave" of baseball he had always talked about as a fan. In that connection, he had a special case in umpire Dave Pallone, a stormy and abrasive loner who had entered the major league during the umpire strike of 1979 as one of eight minor league umpires willing to cross the picket lines. Ever since, the union men had isolated and ostracized him as a scab and did what they could to undermine his credibility. Pallone had maintained a turbulent relationship with Giamatti's predecessor, Chub Feeney, for the National League supervisor of umpires, Ed Vargo, was, of course, a union man and a former umpire himself. Complicating the situation were rumors about Pallone's personal life, but they were the very kind of rumor that might be spread about a strike breaker, and Giamatti knew he had to be careful. From personal experience, he knew all about the slurs of labor strife. He was in the union snakepit once again.

During spring training, in a misunderstanding, Pallone missed several games he was expected to umpire, and it fell to Giamatti to discipline him, even though it was unclear whether Pallone was really at fault. Giamatti sided with the interpretation of his supervisor of umpires, without giving Pallone much chance to make his case. Nevertheless, in their first talks, Giamatti won over Pallone, even as the umpire manfully took his $200 fine. Talking to Giamatti, Pallone would write later in his book, *Behind the Mask*, was "like talking to your father and your favorite teacher at the same time." It was a bit more complicated than that: Giamatti was trying to ease Pallone out of the game.

"Dave, do you really want to umpire?" he said paternally at one point in a conversation. "I don't mean you don't love your job. It's obvious you do. But is this the life for you?"

Standard ploy as it was for a manager of people, Pallone took the question to be an expression of concern by his newfound father.

"It's funny, but I've been thinking about that a lot lately. I'm not sure," replied Pallone. Giamatti was encouraging an honesty that was not necessarily in Pallone's interest.

"You should go to school," Bart continued. "You're too intelligent not to continue your education."

Pallone left the Park Avenue office of the National League in a trance. It seemed as if, for the first time in his baseball career, after all the snubs and dirty little rumors, someone really cared about him. "If he's any indication of where baseball's headed," Pallone thought to himself, "maybe there's hope for the game after all."

That fall, Pallone found himself selected to umpire the National League play-offs between the Cards and the Giants. It was as if he was performing first and foremost for Bart Giamatti. In the second game in St. Louis, Giamatti called Pallone over to the president's box, pointed to a speck of wood on the field, and asked Pallone to pick it up. "Giamatti was a perfectionist," Pallone would say. "To him a wood chip on the artificial turf was an imperfection." One game later, Pallone was behind the plate, where he noticed another wood chip near the batter's box and had a bat boy take it over to Giamatti in the stands as their private joke. Before the seventh game of a taut series, Giamatti was, as usual, with his angel-umpires, when Pallone strode in, resplendent in his latest Hugo Boss suit with its wide Italian lines and heavy shoulder pads.

"They can definitely hear you coming, Pallone," Giamatti quipped in admiration, ". . . and not by your footsteps." Pallone now put a well-honed taste in high fashion among Giamatti's other admirable qualities.

"Pallone, shut up, sit down, eat your pasta, and listen to my wife praise you for the great series you're having," Giamatti growled. It was as if he was back on the streets of New Haven, as a Yale freshman, acting like Sal Mineo.

Into the new year, the rumors about Pallone persisted and even intensified—rumors that Giamatti, no doubt, had known all along. In January, the umpire again paid a call on the National League president, and he was greeted with the usual warmth and apparent caring. Passing along a compliment from Whitey Herzog, the Cards manager, about how Pallone had given the performance of his career the previous October, Giamatti allowed that Herzog did not suffer umpires lightly.

Then, again with surprising abruptness, Giamatti said, "David, you strike me as a person who wants to do more than just umpire for the rest of your life. I've mentioned school to you, but you didn't go this winter like I suggested, did you?" Pallone hung his head. "God damn it, Pallone, you're too intelligent not to be in school. I just don't think baseball is for you anymore."

Pallone was no dummy. He said he was thinking about retire-

ment, but he wanted to round out his ten-year career with an assignment to the World Series.

"I can't promise you anything," Giamatti said coolly, "but if you
come to me during the season, and you tell me you're really ready to
retire, and if the opportunity presents itself, I will do everything in
my power to help you round off your career with a World Series."

Saturday night, as every actor and ball player knows, brings out the
toughest audience. Loaded for bear, they dare the performers to entertain, demanding to be shown that this theatre was worthy of one's
precious night out instead of something else. April 30, 1988, was a
downright cold Saturday night in Cincinnati, temperature dipping to
the mid-thirties. Yet, with the first trip of the hated Mets to town, a
hardy crowd of forty-one thousand flooded into Riverfront Stadium,
swept up in early season enthusiasm about Rose's young and gifted
team. On the mound for the Reds was Rose's control pitcher, Tom
Browning, and for the Mets, Bob Ojeda. Dave Pallone was umpiring
at first. Pallone, by his own admission, had a longstanding animus
toward the Reds. It extended back to a 1983 incident with Dave
Concepcion, when the umpire had called Concepcion out at second on
a close play, and Concepcion had risen from the dirt screaming, calling Pallone a scab and spitting in the umpire's face. The animus
deepened toward the Queen City as the rumor was spread in Cincinnati that Pallone had once tried to pick up a young man in a Cincinnati bar. Pallone believed that Pete Rose was spreading the insidious
rumor that he was gay. Ever since, Pallone had gone out of his way to
make life difficult for Rose and the Reds.

Umpiring behind the plate was Eric Gregg, a beefy and cheery
Othello with a decided love for a king's banquet. There was some
good-natured joshing before the game, as Rose promised to stake
Gregg to a free meal at his riverside restaurant if Gregg called a
perfect game.

"Now to buy Eric a meal . . . baby, I've got to call the owner to
get his permission," Rose quipped in an appreciation.

In the early innings, the game itself was good, wholesome fare.
There was a close and exciting play at the plate in the third inning,
where Gregg called the Reds left fielder, Lloyd McClendon, out as he
tried to reach home on a double by the pitcher, Browning. Rose
darted out to argue, opening his case by saying, "Well, Eric, it's
obvious to me you're not very hungry." At first base, Pallone watched
"one of baseball's ritual dances" with only mild curiosity. Rose appeared enraged as he got into the meat of his case, but he retreated

quickly to the dugout, where he watched the television replay confirm the correctness of Gregg's call. "Hey, Eric, if the next call goes for me, I'll send you some champagne at dinner," the now-mellow Rose was shouting out to the plate.

But the following inning, with two out, Mookie Wilson tripled for the Mets, and Tim Teufel came to the plate. Teufel already had two hits and had scored twice. He had gotten nine hits in his last sixteen trips against Browning. Browning went into the windup. Unexpectedly, Teufel stepped out of the box without calling time. Browning stopped his motion. Umpire Gregg called a balk. Mookie Wilson trotted smugly home. Rose was instantly in Gregg's face. No more joshing now. It was a true dispute over the rules, and the issue rested with what was in Teufel's mind. If Teufel had deliberately tried to provoke a balk by stepping out, the umpire should overlook Browning's aborted windup. If Teufel was free of guile, the balk should stand. There was no doubt in Pallone's mind, as he watched from first base: Rose was more furious at Teufel's "pussy" baseball than at Gregg's blown call. Getting no satisfaction from Gregg, Rose marched to the mound to hand down an order. The next pitch hit Teufel squarely in the small of the back. The Mets bench emptied, led by Darryl Strawberry. No punches were thrown, but Strawberry and Browning were ejected.

The threads of the game were garish and misshapen: blown calls against the home team, fan anger, Reds miscues, deliberate drilling, ejections, close score, a Saturday night's huge lubricated crowd. The outlines of violence were taking shape. In the top of the ninth, the score was 5–5, when Mookie Wilson of the Mets came to bat with two out and Howard Johnson on second. Wilson hit a hot smash into the hole, but the Reds shortstop, Barry Larkin, made a fine stab and swirled to make the long throw to first. It was wide, and Nick Esasky stretched to reach it. As umpire Pallone hovered over the base, he saw Esasky's foot pull off the bag as the speedy Wilson swept across it. There was a split-second delay before the ump delivered his verdict.

"No!" Pallone screamed, pointing to the foot. "Safe!"

Esasky turned in disbelief, forgetting that the action was still live, and the alert Hojo was scooting around third and heading for home. Had Esasky been concentrating, he could have easily nabbed Johnson at the plate. Instead, he spat out his protest at Pallone.

Rose raced onto the field, now genuinely livid. His focus was Pallone's delay in making the call, which would grow by ages in the retelling. It was Pallone's fault that the run had scored. No, Pallone retorted, he couldn't help it if Rose's first baseman had fallen asleep.

They were chest to chest, chin to chin. Pallone towered over Rose, and Rose tried to bring him down to size. Rose's finger came up near Pallone's face, jabbing, as he argued that the umpire blew the call. It was a test of wills, where appearances were everything. With lessons ingrained from umpire school, Pallone had to argue just as vehemently, lest he appear before forty thousand hostile fans to be losing the argument. "Stick that finger up your ass," Pallone shouted at Rose. But then, he brought his own finger up to underscore his point. His finger was very, very close to Rose's cheek.

"It's your fault! You stole the goddamn game from us! You waited too goddamn long!" Rose was screaming. His face was distorted with rage.

"Get your fuckin' finger out of my face," Pallone yelled back, but he had to trade epithet for epithet, gesture for gesture. His own finger was just as menacing now.

With that, Rose gave Pallone a tremendous shove backward with his forearm. Pallone ejected him instantly and turned his back to walk away, when Rose shoved him a second time from the rear.

"You're in a lot of fuckin' trouble, Rose," Pallone said, now more in amazement than anger.

In the broadcast booth above, the Reds announcers, Joe Nuxhall and Marty Brennaman, heaped scorn on the umpire. To Nuxhall, Pallone was a liar and a scab, a rotten umpire who didn't belong in the league and deserved anything he got. Brennaman called him an incompetent, a terrible, terrible umpire, and reported that in the battle of the fingers, Pallone's finger had grazed the face of the saint of Reds baseball. Garbage poured down on the field: golfballs, coins, cigarette lighters, marbles, hot dogs. A whiskey bottle from the upper deck exploded on a seat near an usher. When toilet paper fell near Pallone, the incendiary broadcasters remarked upon the aptness of the symbol.

The situation was terrifying, the most terrifying moment of fan riot since the Rose-Harrelson incident at Shea Stadium in 1973. Ironically, in the Mets dugout, Bud Harrelson, now the Mets third-base coach, watched in fear, gasping when Rose shoved Pallone, shrinking from the scary aftermath, guessing in his mind that Rose would get a two-week suspension—if any of them got out of there alive. In a bizarre twist, Joe Cocker's song "You Are So Beautiful" began to waft over the angry mob from the stadium public address system. When a boom box landed near the on-deck circle, the umpires departed the field.

Fifteen minutes later, the "game" resumed, minus Pallone, who fumed alone in the dressing room but had the good sense to stay safely in the catacombs. The Mets first and third basemen, Keith Hernandez and Howard Johnson, took the field in batting helmets, as the bottom half of the ninth inning was quickly completed without further score. In the Reds clubhouse, Rose appeared before the press with a strange and suspicious abrasion near his eye, which Pallone would later claim was self-inflicted for effect. He had only pushed Pallone, Rose proclaimed, because Pallone had jabbed him near the eye. It was self-defense. Why, the umpire could have put his eye out!

That did not explain the second shove from behind . . . or did it?

"If you're somewhere on the street, that's usually how a fight starts," Rose suggested, and then abruptly, he thought of his father, Harry. Harry Rose was always there watching him, judging him, egging him on. "If my dad was there, he probably would have gotten mad at the way I reacted," Rose said. Mad because the shove was not enough. Harry Rose was never satisfied.

With real fear for his life, Pallone made his way to his car under the stadium, through crowds that waited to jeer him. As he pushed his way through, the image of Jack Ruby in Dallas came to his mind. Later, in his hotel room, he listened to a few death threats before he disconnected his phone.

Early the following morning, Giamatti finally reached his umpire.

"I really feel bad about it," Giamatti said, as he told Pallone of the league officials who were then on their way to Cincinnati. "We've all agreed that you should not work home plate today, as scheduled. We'd like you to work second base." In other words, second base was the farthest point on the field from the crowd, but Pallone might have viewed it differently, as the longest run to the safety of the dugout.

"Whatever you think is right," Pallone replied.

But the umpire's colleagues did not think that was right. If anyone worked home plate that day, it ought to be the scab who caused the trouble in the first place. Pallone himself was beginning to have second thoughts about Giamatti's order, for it would cause him to lose respect of the players on the field. It was a macho world out there, and they might think he was a sissy. At the ballpark, the other umpires were putting forward an ironic argument to Pallone: it was important—to the union!—that he work home plate that day. Pallone was willing, for his own reasons, and called Giamatti back to insist bravely on his rightful place at home plate.

"I don't want you to do that," Giamatti repeated himself. But when Pallone insisted, he gave in.

"All right," Giamatti said, "if you feel that strongly, go ahead. But I want it absolutely clear that the union made you work home plate, and I was firmly against it." The ironies multiplied. If nothing else, Pallone had guts.

On the day after the riot, he called two balks, one during an intentional walk, on Reds pitchers, as New York drubbed Cincinnati, 11–0. "I felt good that it [the balks] happened," Pallone wrote in his book, "because it screwed the Reds." He was paying back Concepcion for the spit and Rose for a rumor.

The next day, President Giamatti suspended Rose for thirty days and fined him $10,000. This suspension ultimately prefigured the collision between Rose and Giamatti in 1989 in a number of significant ways. It focused Giamatti's mind on Rose's unique position in baseball. To Giamatti, the unique hero bore special responsibility, and he had to be held to an even higher standard. His transgressions could be more damaging to the game than the same transgressions by lesser figures. To Rose, Giamatti revealed himself as an inflexible moralist, who was sure to side with the prosecutors over the accused. And the process of adjudication revealed itself. There would be no due process, no equal protection of the laws, no Fourteenth Amendment in baseball, only an amorphous concept of "natural justice" and "fairness" that was vague and left to the commissioner or the league presidents to define. Baseball was a private employer. It could not be held to the standards of governmental justice. The league official had only to meet the standard that he was not operating in an arbitrary or capricious fashion.

Rose's suspension was the stiffest reprimand since Commissioner Happy Chandler suspended Giants manager Leo Durocher for consorting with gamblers in 1947. The penalty was double the suspension of Bill Madlock in 1980 for shoving his glove into the face of an umpire. In his statement, Giamatti called the incident "extremely ugly," "disgraceful," "unprofessional," and "one of the worst in baseball's recent memory." "The National League will not tolerate the degeneration of baseball games into dangerous displays of public disorder, nor will it countenance any potentially injurious harassment, of any kind, of the umpires. A tiny minority, of fans or others, cannot be allowed to disgrace the vast majority of decent individuals who truly care for the game."

It was quintessential Bart Giamatti. In this second warning to Pete Rose, the old hero was hanging spikes on the field as well as off, upon which to impale himself.

Cincinnati reacted with a novel argument to explain the penalty of Maximum Bart: Rose's sentence was longer precisely because he was Pete Rose. There was something to this position, but not as it was stated in Cincinnati. If the manager had been, say, Dave Bristol or Tommy Helms, the crowd might not have turned into the angry and dangerous mob it became, even if the umpire did graze the manager's face with a finger. Pete Rose was not just any manager. He had a special place in baseball. He had, therefore, a special responsibility, especially where he was deified. When he stepped beyond the bounds of normal decorum, he took the whole stadium with him as no one else could, and the consequences could be catastrophic. A slightly different trajectory for a radio . . . another set of nuts in the stands . . . a wider fight . . . a stampede . . . and the face of Wembley Stadium yawned before baseball.

Rose appealed through his lawyers and the Cincinnati press, protesting that he had not been given due process and that he was entitled to equal protection of the law. Technically, he deserved neither under the rules of baseball, but it made a good argument. Even Johnny Bench came to his defense. To Pete Rose, thirty days away from baseball was akin to life imprisonment, Bench said.

With Reuven Katz alongside, Rose went off to New York, decked out in a shiny, light-blue, double-breasted shark-skin suit and leaning on a cane, because he had seized the opportunity of his suspension to have surgery on his knee from a tennis injury. They took with them the television tape of the episode, slowed down frame by frame, as if it were the Zapruder film, to show that Pallone's finger had actually made contact with Rose's face. In a sense, the procedure was a dry run of what would happen a year later with the gambling allegations. Rose and Katz were trying to remove Giamatti as the sole judge and jailer, for in this case, they knew his reverence for umpires. Now they got their way, as a three-man executive council of the National League gathered to hear the Rose side of the story. But the panel was not convinced by Rose's argument and let the suspension stand.

Before the hearing, Giamatti and Rose had met together, alone. "I gathered from Giamatti's vibes that it is sacred to touch an umpire," Rose said about their tête-à-tête.

Giamatti also met with the announcers for the Reds, Nuxhall and Brennaman. While he took no action against them, he let them know firmly and succinctly that inciting a riot was not part of their job description.

A month after the Riverfront riot (and a day before Rose resumed managing the Reds), Giamatti and Pallone met again. Before they got down to business, they conversed like two old paisans. About Pallone calling that balk during an intentional walk the day after the Rose episode, Giamatti had watched that game with his wife. "That's the Italian in him," Giamatti had remarked to his wife. "He's got to show them. 'See, I called a balk.' He didn't have to call it."

Then they rolled the tape of the actual episode. Pallone conceded that he had lost his temper. He should not have pointed back at Rose in kind. He should have simply walked away. Giamatti had a way of extracting concessions painlessly.

"I like your style, Pallone," he said, as he proposed to fine the umpire $100.

That would be a political mistake, Pallone surprisingly objected. What would the owners think? If there was to be a fine at all, it should be a real slap rather than a gentle rap. Pallone was just trying to look out for Giamatti's best interests—and his own. His generosity cost him another $900.

As the subject of Pallone's education arose again, the umpire had the forwardness to wonder if Giamatti couldn't help him get into Yale. If not Yale, perhaps into the World Series that fall.

"Pallone, get that out of your head," Giamatti replied. "You're not working the World Series this year." Not with a $1,000 disciplinary fine on his record.

"That means I'll have to stay another year," Pallone said. "And I honestly don't know if I can take it."

"Tell me why you feel that way."

"My personal life is in a shambles."

"What about your personal life?"

"I'm gay."

Reading between the lines of this conversation, which Pallone reproduced in his book, it is clear that Giamatti had known all along. Until there was an incident, however, he could do nothing about it. Now there was an incident on the field, an incident that resulted in an official reprimand, an incident that had an umpire losing his temper in a volatile situation. Still, while Pallone's competence had been questioned, it was not enough to get him out of baseball. At Pallone's confession, Giamatti made the proper noises about the need for Pallone to be discreet and all that. It is true, that as president of Yale, Giamatti had dealt with gay rights—and wrongs—before. That very thing had made him miss the great matchup in the college playoffs in 1981 between Ron Darling and Frank Viola, precisely because an outsider was found to be buying favors for butch Yale athletes, and there was a question of perversion. And Giamatti had to worry about the attitude of the NCAA.

Yale was one thing, baseball another. Giamatti was now the

keeper of the image, the trustee of a national institution. Like Rose, Pallone was a scandal waiting to happen, and Giamatti was determined to get the umpire out of the game before the matter became public. A gay umpire in the Grand Old Game? That would not do.

Two months later, Pallone and Giamatti met again in New York. This time, Giamatti brought along the director of security, Kevin Hallinan. Giamatti's compassion seemed to be wearing thin.

"I know a great Italian restaurant called Oggi," Pallone said cheerily, as they pondered lunch. "It means 'today.' "

Giamatti turned slowly and fixed Pallone with a steady stare.

"Pallone, I know what that word means," he said icily.

It was not *oggi* but *domani* that was on Giamatti's mind. A few weeks later, in Sarasota Springs, New York, Pallone's name was mentioned in a sex scandal involving teenage boys, and Giamatti forced him to take a leave of absence while the matter was investigated. As it turned out, Pallone was cleared totally of any involvement in the matter. His name had been thrown into the investigation falsely and maliciously. He was completely innocent. And yet, the allegations, false though they were, gave Giamatti the pretext he wanted. Not fairness or justice but image transcended all.

Firing the umpire in November 1988, Giamatti told him flatly, "We just don't feel that you can handle the pressure from all the negative publicity."

The following day, Pallone got his official letter of termination from the league's attorney. It cited negative publicity from false rumor, including the unproven rumor that Pete Rose had started about Pallone picking up a man in a Cincinnati bar in 1986.

Neither fairness nor natural justice marked Pallone's firing, but neither, in the image-conscious baseball ethos, was it arbitrary or capricious.

· 10 ·

Squeeze

IN THE WINTER OF 1988, the FBI began to focus on Gold's Gym as a warren of cocaine trafficking with ties to a major Florida-Colombia drug operation. To the Bureau, it was just another dope ring, no different from thousands of other operations across the country. The agents proceeded to crack the case in textbook fashion. Running their investigation through the grand jury and the drug task force of the U.S. Attorney's office, the FBI cast about on the periphery of the Stenger-Fry conspiracy for vulnerable minor players who would have knowledge and access. With the conspiracy centered in a body shop, the investigation was made easier by nature of the beast—and the beasts. To enlarge their curves and folds, bodybuilders throughout the nation are heavy users of anabolic steroids, a drug whose uncontrolled use is technically illegal, but which is not a dangerous narcotic on the banned-substance list. To government agencies, steroid use is essentially a health concern rather than a police concern, unless steroid trade could be used as a lever to recruit an informer.

The FBI focused on the burly Paul Janszen and began to develop information about his sideline of illegally selling steroids on a broad scale. From 1984 to 1986, his business had involved perhaps seventy-five people, and that could be made to sound grander and nastier than it really was. The money Janszen made was modest, perhaps less than $20,000 a year, because steroids are not the cash crop that cocaine is. Naturally, Janszen had not declared his earnings on his income tax.

In March 1988, the FBI agents came calling at Janszen's door. They found a figure who was strong in body but weak-faced and weak in character, and that was in his favor. He was a small-time crook whose value to authorities lay in his access to bigger crooks. Though he had no moral fiber, he was articulate, having gone to the University of Cincinnati for three years, and he was clearly terrified. When the agents told him he was under investigation for drug trafficking and tax evasion, he saw years in the penitentiary yawning before him—unless he became a cooperating witness in a wider federal investigation.

For Janszen the knock on his door in March 1988 was only a bottoming-out point at the end of a year-and-a-half slide, a slide that began when he met Pete Rose in the fall of 1986. In the interim, he had gone into cocaine deals with Tommy Gioiosa, then supplanted Gioiosa as Rose's head leech. He had quit his job of thirteen years in a family-owned barrel company to become Rose's contact with his bookies, to babysit Rose's son Ty, to cover for Rose's womanizing, and to be general houseboy, gofer, all-purpose playmate, and strong-arm bruiser. In 1987, he accompanied Rose to baseball card shows, where by Rose's account his main duty was to keep the line of autograph seekers straight. The role was more important than that. He also had to deal with the promoters and to take their brown-bagged cash for delivery to Rose. At times loud and aggressive, at other times whining and maudlin, he was one of Rose's undesirables whose presence in the Reds clubhouse was unwelcome to the other players and to management, and about whom Commissioner Ueberroth spoke to Rose.

But it was a mutual exploitation society. Janszen was the flunky Rose wanted and needed, more imposing and more worthy somehow than the absurd Tommy Gioiosa. Rose, in turn, was Janszen's entrée into a world of glamor and fortune that he could not achieve on his own. To be around Pete Rose made the 6-foot, 4-inch Janszen feel like he was a big man. His hints to Rose about his drug dealing made him feel as if he was on the same level with Rose and that, as a result, the great player respected him. For about seven months, they were happy enough with one another. In the spring of 1987, their relationship was at its most intense, when Rose's betting was going badly and he was seeking new ways to turn his fortunes around. His streak of bad luck began with the Super Bowl in January, when Rose lost $34,000 on a single bet. It continued with college basketball, a sport in which he was clearly out of his element, and into the NCAA Final Four tournament, where he lost more. On average, he was losing $30,000 a week. By the time the baseball season of 1987 approached, Rose was in deep trouble with his bookies.

As a convenience, Rose had invited Janszen (and his girlfriend) to spring training that year, largely to train Janszen to be his "writer" with the bookmakers. Janszen had arrived. He was Pete Rose's house-guest, and that conferred considerable status upon him around the spring training field and at the track. The two men spent hours together in confidential, revealing conversation, much of which would later be held against Rose in the court of baseball. Toward the end, the vacation developed its sour side for Janszen. Rose's bookies were increasingly upset with his negative balance, and they were beginning to lean on Janszen. Had the worry been solely with his local connection, the golf pro cum cocaine dealer cum bookie cum restaurateur, Ron Peters, this might not have been such a problem. All bookies were whiners and liars, Rose felt. It gave him distinct pleasure to stiff them on a regular basis.

"They all moan and bitch and complain about being paid on time," Rose confided to Janszen, "but they never ever really expect to be paid on time."

But Rose had taken to doubling and tripling his bets, wagering with Peters in amounts up to five thousand dollars a contest at home, while he bet even larger sums with Richard Troy, the Mafia bookie in Staten Island, as well as with another New York connection, a fatso named Mike Bertolini. Bertolini was from Brooklyn. He loved Pete Rose, promoted his baseball card show appearances, and took his bets on the side. If you doubled or tripled up and lost, Rose believed, at least, you didn't owe it all to one person. With Troy, the Mafia bookie, however, unpaid debts might have real consequences. By Janszen's account, the heat was such that he was having to draw on his own modest savings to cover Rose's debts.

"I didn't have the money if he came back to me and said I only lost ten thousand that night, not fifteen thousand," Janszen would tell the baseball investigators two years later. "It was never laid in front of him every night. Days went by when he called in and we never discussed what he lost the night before. He would just say, yeah, I took a bath last night. We'll get him tonight. A whole week would go by when he did not even know what his figure was at the end of the week. At first it didn't bother me, until I realized that the man did not have the money that I thought he had. Then it started to scare me. He was like a runaway locomotive."

Besides, Rose did little to conceal his betting. He bragged loosely about it to friends and strangers alike. He refused to employ the normal number code that bookmakers generally use to mask the identity of their clients, or he insisted on using number 14. In time, Janszen began to think of himself nobly as Rose's protector. It was particularly noble because he was using a considerable amount of his own money to cover Rose's debts.

"I covered for him very well," Janszen said. "Pete did not think of covering himself at all. If I wasn't around, Pete would have probably already dug himself a nice-size grave right now. He thought nothing of calling from the clubhouse. I told him not to do that, to get somebody to run up to a pay phone at the stadiums he was at. He would talk about his gambling in front of people. And his answer was always, 'they can't get me.' He put himself above everything. They can't get me. What have they got? What are they going to prove? How are they going to prove it?"

In the end, Janszen was how they were going to prove it.

On the day that the FBI came calling and his life came crashing down around him, Janszen was broke, in trouble, in need of a lawyer, desperate and frightened. In his first interrogation, the FBI warned him to be 100 percent truthful or face the consequences of perjury as well. By the by, they asked him about his relationship with Pete Rose. At first, Janszen turned their questions aside. Even if Rose was involved, he told the agents, he could not talk about it. As he heard himself say that, he sensed the agents making a calculation that he was being only 80 percent truthful. He was getting deeper and deeper in trouble.

But Janszen did not have quite the motive for protecting Rose now. Only a few weeks before the FBI came, Janszen's friendship with Rose had been shattered in a most unfortunate way. On a snowy day in February, Rose had called to invite Janszen to drive with him to a baseball card show in Cleveland. As they started out of Cincinnati, Rose made an unscheduled stop at a house, and out came a young woman whom Janszen knew. The threesome proceeded happily to Cleveland and checked into adjoining rooms in a Holiday Inn. A half hour later, there was a bang on the door, and there stood Pete's wife. Long-suffering and often cheated upon Carol Rose had finally put a sleuth on her husband's tail.

Janszen described what took place next: "Pete is frantic. 'Paul, would you please take the blame. If I put the girl in your room, we'll lock the middle door. I'll tell my wife you are with the girl.' So he lets Carol in, and they are fighting and arguing, you know. And she thinks there's two girls. He finally throws her out of the room. I said, Pete, why don't I take this girl to the airport. Just get in there with your wife. . . . Carol was going crazy. . . . Pete, I said, just have Carol come in the room, stay with her, and I'll take the blame. Hell with that, he says. I didn't drive 200 miles to sleep with my own wife!

"So his wife is in the hallway crying. She finally gets a room. I go down and find out what room she's checked in. I am down in her room. She is crying. I'm upset, trying to explain to her, I am with a girl that I'm not with. And Pete is up in the room, having sex with this girl."

The upshot of this farce was that Carol Rose banished Janszen from the Rose house. To her, Janszen had become a "bad influence" on her husband. This provided Rose with a perfect excuse to avoid Janszen and his annoying questions about some supposed gambling debt.

A week after his meeting with the FBI, Janszen went to Reuven Katz for help. If he ever got into trouble, Rose had once told him, he should go see Katz (and if Katz couldn't help, "I'll call the governor," Rose had joked). Now Janszen needed two things: a lawyer and the $44,000 Pete Rose owed him for past gambling debts. For nearly a year, Janszen told Katz, Rose had been promising to repay this debt. If he had not paid it by December 1987, Rose had said to Janszen, he would sell the black Mizuno bat that had stroked the hit that broke Cobb's record and would pay Janszen from the proceeds. But the bat had been sold, and Janszen received no money. The excuses had gone on and on. At one point, Rose said he couldn't pay Janszen just then, because his wife was overspending on their second home in Florida. What could a fellow do?

From the specific demand for money, Janszen laid out the full scope of Rose's gambling habit. Katz listened impassively to the narrative until the end, when he professed shock and surprise. To Janszen, it was as if all Katz's fears and suspicions were turning out to be true, that finally someone was telling him face to face the full scope of Pete's problem. At length, Katz leveled a steady stare at Janszen and asked him if Pete Rose had bet on baseball. When he heard the answer, he put his head down in genuine hurt.

"That's it," Katz groaned. "It's over."

In this netherworld of con men and low lifes, one man's debt could be another man's extortion. From a man under federal investigation for drug trafficking and tax evasion, the demand for $44,000 sounded to Katz like extortion pure and simple. Katz was no different from many who wanted to think the best rather than the worst about their baseball hero. Besides, people were always trying to shake Pete down for money. At this point, Katz was still inclined to accept his client's word over Janszen's. When he confronted Rose, Pete denied owing Janszen a nickel. If Janszen was due any money, it must be from a bookie, not him. Perhaps Janszen was placing bets of his own and using Rose's name. Katz did not push him.

Somehow, the matter got turned around. Rose would not pay Janszen $44,000, but he would *loan* him $10,000 as an act of charity and friendship. Perhaps that would be enough to assuage Janszen just then. When Janszen came for his money a few days later and opened his envelope, he was stunned and infuriated. He was being given less than one quarter of his supposed debt, and it was being labeled a loan. After all the joshing with Rose about stiffing bookies, now he was the one being stiffed.

From this moment sprang Janszen's fury against Rose. The following day, he began to cooperate fully with the FBI, answering all their questions about Pete Rose—with the passion of Judas.

To Janszen's disappointment, however, the FBI was only mildly interested in his tawdry stories about the baseball king. Historically, gambling had been downgraded in the Bureau's priorities since the Nixon presidency, when the Bureau found that to bust mom-and-pop gambling operations all over the country might help statistics, but made no dent whatever in organized crime. With the legalization of lotteries in America and the attendant promotion of gambling by politicians as nearly a civic duty, gambling had almost ceased to be prosecuted as a vice. The drug trade had become the area of greatest interest during the Reagan presidency. In Cincinnati, it was the activities at Gold's Gym that attracted federal attention. The gambling stories only spiced the tale. If Pete Rose was financing drug deals, the agents were interested. If he was gambling and losing a lot of money with bookies, so what? They did not have the energy or time to pursue it.

They did listen to his stories about Rose's gambling, however. Even if the Bureau had little intention to pursue Rose's gambling as a criminal matter, it was an area that could test Janszen's credibility and reliability. By the by, a federal agent remarked, offhandedly and with a coy chuckle, that it sure would be helpful to Janszen's believability if he could come up with some actual baseball betting sheets belonging to Pete Rose. Shortly after, dutiful Paul let himself into Rose's house when no one was home—he still had a key—and found what he and the FBI were looking for. He also found and took collector's coins, a Mizuno bat worth $500, and a stack of signed Pete Rose lithographs, just to offset some of the debt that Rose owed him. To his disappointment, he could find no cash.

By July 1988, the training of Paul Janszen as an effective informant had progressed to the point of providing him with a telephone recording device and entrusting him with an undercover cocaine buy. The target of the sting was Ron Peters, not for his bookmaking operation so much as his cocaine activity. That operation was carried off smoothly. Janszen made his purchase with marked bills and led the FBI not only to Peters but to his supplier. One by one, largely based upon Janszen's leads, solid cases against the other figures in the Gold's Gym conspiracy, including Stenger, Fry, and Gioiosa, were developed. When the FBI knocked on the door of Michael Fry with a search warrant, the agents discovered a kilogram of cocaine, twenty pounds of marijuana, two scales, close to $10,000 in cash, and two pistols. Just to show that Fry meant business, one of the pistols was fitted with a silencer. All but Gioiosa were to plead guilty without the expense and hassle of a trial.

Once the FBI had developed its cases against Peters and the Stenger-Fry ring, it began to close the books on the Gold's Gym conspiracy. Over a period of a year as an informant, Janszen had proven himself to be diligent and reliable and articulate, and he had an excellent memory. Other witnesses corroborated his information. At no point was he caught in lies or exaggeration. Of course, he was vindictive toward Pete Rose, but revenge was so common an instinct for cooperation that the agents knew how to put that in perspective. He had also been overzealous, especially in entering Pete Rose's house without permission and stealing betting slips. The attitude of the prosecutors was that so long as Janszen had done that on his own initiative and not at the direction of any government agency, the stolen material could be used as evidence.

As a reward for his good work, Janszen's cocaine transactions and other assorted crimes were ignored. He was allowed to plead guilty to tax evasion on the proceeds from illegal steroid sales for one pre–Pete Rose year, 1985. His sentence was six months in a halfway house.

Unresolved was the matter of Rose. Although Pete's awareness of—and interest in—drug operations was clear enough, the authorities discounted any Rose involvement in drug trafficking per se. With particular relish, Janszen had told and retold a story of traveling to New York in the Rose entourage in December 1986 to do a card show for Bertolini in Brooklyn. Mickey Mantle was going to be there, and Janszen was looking forward to it. Their private jet landed at Teterboro Airport outside New York, where two limousines waited for the party. As if he were the host, Rose set the seating arrangements. He, his wife, and Janszen's girlfriend would get into the first limousine. Bertolini, Gioiosa, and Janszen were to get into the second. (With his special brand of showing off, Gio had lifted his pant leg for Janszen's perusal earlier, to reveal about forty thousand dollars stuck in his boot.) According to Janszen, he got in the car and found himself face-to-face with a fierce-looking guy with a big nose, a butch haircut, and an Italian name. He was introduced only as Tom. Once they were on the main road, Tom the Nose pulled a brown bag from his side, extracted a kilo of cocaine, and dropped the brick on Janszen's knees. Gioiosa was excited.

"Hey, look at this, Paul." Gio whistled. "Take a look. Is it good? If it is, we can get as many as we need!"

Janszen was horrified, or so he later professed to the authorities. He was not, however, especially surprised, because Gioiosa had talked to him about needing another source that could provide more cocaine for less money than he was having to pay in Cincinnati. Janszen was afraid at this open display, afraid that the limo drivers were federal agents, and that he had fallen into a trap along with fat Mikey, Tom the Nose, and crazy Gio. Moments later, as Janszen remembered it, the phone in the limousine rang, and the receiver was handed to Janszen.

"Is it any good?" the flat voice of Pete Rose was asking from the lead limousine.

On that occasion, Janszen let out a stream of invectives at Rose, telling him this was insane, he was nuts. To Tom the Nose, he shouted that if the dealer did not put his paper sack away, he was going to put Tom's head into the highway wind, roll up the window, and he could ride that way all the way to Brooklyn. With that, the less-than-happy caravan proceeded to the Catholic elementary school in Brooklyn for the card show.

"Pete was real excited," Janszen recounted. "As soon as we get to a show, I usually walk right next to Pete in case guys start really crowding him, just to help him get through the crowds. And I was saying, Pete, is this for real? I said, Pete, this guy just got out of the limousine, and he's right now carrying a kilo of cocaine and walking about three steps behind us. And [Pete says] 'Who is going to know? Nobody is going to follow him. Nobody is going to know what is in that brown bag. You know, is it any good? I can come up with some money. I'll get some money, Paul. I'll get some money together, if it's any good. I'll buy a bunch of them, if it's any good.' " The episode ended with Tom wandering around the card show, with his brown bag under his arm, looking over Rose's shoulder as Rose signed autographs for the kids.

Intriguing though that story was—Janszen would again tell Rose he was nuts three months later, when Rose repeated his interest in investing in kilo-sized cocaine deals—there was not much the federal agents could do with it. So far as the agents could determine, Rose's interest in cocaine had never been consummated. Nevertheless, Janszen had provided enough information to justify a major federal investigation into large-scale, illegal gambling operations that stretched from New York to Chicago to Las Vegas. In the Peters operation alone, the nexus between gambling and drug-trafficking was evident. To pursue Janszen's leads might take the authorities to much larger operations of the same character, some of them mob operations.

To target a well-known figure in America has its up-side and its down-side. Nailing someone such as Rose might address a widespread concern that the rich and famous always get away scot-free while the common and coarse go to jail. Because there was a possible tax case against Rose, an indictment of him—and the accompanying publicity—could send the right message to the public, especially if the indictment came at tax time. But prosecutors know that if you're going to target a famous figure, you have to shoot him through the heart. To shoot and miss was worse than not shooting at all.

Because gambling had become such a low priority for federal law enforcement, the FBI had to ask: Was it really worth the effort? Higher authorities in the FBI looked at the Rose case and decided not to pursue it—to the considerable disappointment of the local Cincinnati field office.

The case of *United States v. Peter Edward Rose* was turned over to the IRS as a mundane tax evasion matter.

The transformation of Bart Giamatti into a professional baseball man had been brief and reasonably uneventful. In his six months' tutorial with Chub Feeney, before he had officially taken over the National League presidency, he had learned the nuts and bolts of baseball administration and found much that was similar to academic administration. He was the impresario to the gifted and talented who were in intense competition with each other. His job was to ensure that the competition was fair and encouraged talent to reach its full potential freely. The stiff suspension of Pete Rose and the delicate easing of umpire Dave Pallone out of baseball had been the most difficult problems of his early presidency, but they were not his only problems.

Next to the Rose suspension, the enforcement of the balk rule was probably the most visible issue to confront him. The rule states that the pitcher must come to "a single, complete, and discernible" stop in his stretch, before delivering the pitch to the plate. For decades, the language had been open to interpretation. What was a "discernible" stop anyway? National League presidents as far back as Warren Giles (1951–69) had struggled with the problem, and the rule's enforcement had swung cyclically between the loose and the literal. Suddenly, in the 1988 season, umpires were enforcing it tightly again. This resulted in an inordinate number of balk calls. Fans turned on Giamatti, as if this professor, this man of Latinate words, had found some obscure etymology in the word "discernible" that required free gifts to the base runners and tilted the game against the pitchers. Blame for Giamatti was unfair, since he was only one member of the Rules Committee, but he made an easy target. His professorial air, ornate language, even his dark and evil complexion made him the perfect villain for the bleachers.

In late July 1988, on a muggy afternoon at Shea Stadium, the depth of fan feeling about the balk rule burst into the open. The Mets were throwing a party for Tom Seaver, Giamatti's special hero, as the club retired number 41 ceremoniously. Around home plate, the heart of the game, folded chairs were set up for the baseball brass, who were introduced one by one. When the public address announcer came to Giamatti, the packed stadium erupted in a wave of hearty boos. Giamatti was flattered, and he strode to his chair with a smile. That 50,000 fans cared enough, one way or another, to react emotionally to a man in a gray suit—well, that was gratifying. "All people in suits get booed at ballparks," Giamatti said later. Because he was seen as the "prime mover" of the balk rule, he understood and appreciated the depth of feeling, momentary as it was. A few minutes later, the real emotion filled the stadium as Tom and Nancy rode onto the field in a convertible, the Adam and Eve of the franchise. Disembarking at the plate, Seaver trotted to the mound, dressed for the occasion in coat and tie and bathed in the pure adulation of the stadium. Reverently, his number was placed on the outfield wall next to Casey Stengel's 37 and Gil Hodges's 14. Seaver especially liked his proximity to the latter. Gil Hodges taught him "how to conduct myself as a professional," Seaver would say. To Giamatti, it was one of his most vivid baseball memories. He and Tom Seaver were at last joined on a nearly even playing field.

Other issues were to test his traditionalist instincts. Wistful though he was about this antebellum institution, he acceded to the installation of lights in Wrigley Field without much protest. The appropriate use of the huge video screens in the modern ballpark was another area of concern. For a time, the screens were occasionally used to undermine the credibility of the umpires. Like his predecessor, Chub Feeney, Giamatti made sure that umpires occasionally sat with video-screen operators to dictate when a replay could and could not be shown.

However, it was not the fine-tuning of the rules in the modern age or even the containment of violence but cases of a quasi-moral nature that truly engaged Giamatti. His thirty-day suspension of Pete Rose was a straightforward proposition of safety and civility. Similarly, in May 1988, when he suspended the Dodgers' Pedro Guerrero for four days after he had flung his bat at David Cone of the Mets, safety was again the issue. Serious and reprehensible though these dangerous episodes were, they did not strike at the integrity of the game. They were violent acts that extended unacceptably the physical exertion that, to Giamatti, was the glory of the game. "Regulation and discipline seek to contain, not expunge, violent effort in sport," Giamatti was to write.

When Billy Hatcher of the Astros was caught with a corked bat, however, or pitcher Jay Howell was caught using pine tar on his glove in the 1987 National League play-offs, or Kevin Gross of the Phillies was caught with heavy sandpaper implanted in the heel of his glove and pine tar on the thumb of his glove, Giamatti's moral sensibility was engaged passionately. That was cheating. Premeditated, covert actions were meant to gain an unfair advantage. The violations offended Giamatti morally. "Such acts are the result not of impulse, borne of frustration or anger or zeal as violence is, but are rather acts of a cool, deliberate, premeditated kind," Giamatti wrote in the Kevin Gross case. "Unlike acts of impulse or violence, intended at the moment to vent frustration or abuse another, acts of cheating are intended to alter the very conditions of play to favor one person. They are secretive, covert acts that strike at and seek to undermine the basic foundation of any contest declaring the winner—that all participants play under identical rules and conditions. Acts of cheating destroy that necessary foundation and thus strike at the essence of a contest. They destroy faith in the game's integrity and fairness; if participants and spectators alike cannot assume integrity and fairness, the contest cannot in its essence exist. . . . Cheating has no organic basis in the game and no origins in the act of playing. Cheating is contrary to the whole purpose of playing to determine a winner fairly and cannot be simply contained; if the game is to flourish and engage public confidence, cheating must be clearly condemned with an eye to expunging it."

In all of the above cases, Giamatti's fines and suspensions were considerably stiffer than any league president had ever imposed previously. These issues and problems were scarcely earth-shattering, however. Giamatti was simply biding his time, trying not to make any mistakes, and letting the sheer warmth of his personality win him admirers, until the icy and widely disliked Peter Ueberroth stepped aside as Commissioner of Baseball. Giamatti had the clear understanding that he would be the obvious choice, perhaps the sole choice for commissioner after Ueberroth, so long as he did not alienate the owners with some stupid decision.

Little noticed in his first year as National League president was a matter with considerable importance to Giamatti's future. During his first year as league president, the umpires' labor contract came up for renewal. It would have been easy enough for Giamatti to cease to be the surrogate father and to become the recalcitrant management tool. But Giamatti seemed to lean over backward to be accommodating. In 1987, the new contract was negotiated without much difficulty, unlike 1979, when the umpires went on strike. More money came to the umpires for their travel on the road—a significant grievance to them—and they were grateful. In Giamatti's manifold sympathy and understanding for their demands, the perception that he was a friend at contract time did as much as all his cordial visits to their dressing rooms to endear him to the umpires.

Nevertheless, the quick contract negotiation yielded a hidden but significant benefit to Giamatti. The baseball world was only vaguely aware that he had experienced labor troubles at Yale and had suffered through some sort of a strike. For the National League presidency, such difficulties were almost irrelevant; but not for the commissionership. A difficult contract negotiation with the players loomed in 1990, and the commissioner would be the prime negotiator for the owners, if it came to a strike or a lockout. The umpire negotiation of 1987 seemed to show Giamatti as adept, and even skillful, with labor questions: it wiped the labor slate clean. No doubt, Giamatti knew exactly what he was doing. He had a tremendous stake in his first labor test. Success had a way of making people forget prior failure.

"If they had looked carefully at the Yale strike," said a Yale man who became a baseball owner after Giamatti became commissioner, "they never would have chosen him commissioner."

Not that, in 1988, there was no warning at all as Giamatti became the heir apparent to Ueberroth.

"You should never choose him," a former president of Princeton told Bill Giles, the owner of the Phillies. "He collapses in crisis."

No one was paying attention to his past record for good reason: Giamatti's personality was dazzling the world of baseball. As a celebrant of the game, there had never been anything like him. By the summer of 1988, he was experiencing all the high points of the game and enjoying his participation tremendously. An insider now who could speak eloquently to the wider world about the institution of baseball, about its history, and its value to American life, he elevated the game. When he spoke about it as a national treasure, his words were entirely sincere and heartfelt. By contrasting baseball to other American institutions, he could be insightful about how the game mirrored the society and the culture, not only the greatness and uniqueness and striving of America but also its deep social problems, such as racism and drugs. People listened as Giamatti taught. He had the standing and the stature to teach. He found lessons in the game that were worth learning.

In August 1988, only a few weeks after the first night game was played at Wrigley Field and only two weeks before the owners unanimously chose him to be Commissioner of Baseball, he went off for his annual vacation on Martha's Vineyard. There, he agreed again to an interview with the *Vineyard Gazette*, in which he placed baseball in a larger context: "Baseball reflects issues of social justice, affirmative action, the role of minorities, issues of substance abuse, financial issues, municipal issues. These are all American issues. If these games, and baseball in particular, were somehow viewed by the culture as so completely separate from these issues, no one would be interested." While he celebrated the fact that baseball had integrated itself racially before the U.S. Army did and well before the Supreme Court handed down its landmark decision in *Brown v. Board of Education*, he lamented the fact that black Americans were underrepresented in the stands and still did not feel entirely welcome in the ballpark. "Baseball is not unlike a lot of other American institutions which have racist pasts and have to expunge whatever vestiges that remain. Baseball is no different."

The people who played the game *were* different, however. "The fact is that sports heroes are among the only authentic walking-around heroes, that's just a fact," he told the *Gazette*. "When someone does something that is better than anyone else in the world can do, yet that person is alive and in all other outward respects looks like you and me, but has this capacity to do things that you know are virtually superhuman because your humanity can't do them, and who picks you up out of yourself because he can do it, that person is treated with a kind of awe."

What of the person with those gifts and achievements who violates our admiration and awe, as he brings shame to himself and the game? "Nobody ever said that because we treat them with this awe that they also aren't human," Giamatti continued. "That's, of course, one of the reasons for the awe, that they are human. Most people aren't astonished when human beings have human frailties. What astonishes us is the capacity to do something that most people frankly can't do. What happens on the sports pages—America's love of sports, its worship of sports—should not amaze us in a culture that has always admired the individual who can reach farther than anybody else." One did not go to the ballpark to get away from the world but to witness a better one. "People who say politics ought to be kept out of sports have misread the history of sport."

Inevitably, he was called away from Martha's Vineyard on business. At the airport, he was stuck in a delay as fog hovered over the island, and he had to wait several hours for it to lift. By chance, the writer John Hersey was waiting for the same plane. They shared the common suffering of a Red Sox fan and the adoration of Yale; for five years of Giamatti's Yale presidency, Hersey had been master at Pierson College on the Yale campus.

At a turn in their conversation, with a note of skepticism, Hersey asked Giamatti if he was still enjoying his work.

Giamatti shot a sidelong glance at Hersey. "John," he said. "My name is on 200,000 baseballs!"

Some weeks before Pete Rose broke Ty Cobb's record, the old spitballer Gaylord Perry won his three-hundredth game. After each inning on the way to his milestone, Perry disappeared into the clubhouse to change his shirt. Besides his public glory, whatever that was worth, Perry now had something more tangible: nine items, each of which he could sell for thousands of dollars. Perry also collected a packet of ticket stubs for his historic game, signed them, and mass-marketed them.

This seemed like a good idea to Rose, and he wondered how he might do something similar. Perhaps he could wear three or four jerseys on top of one another on his historic day, but because the jerseys were form-fitting, he might cut a rumpled figure at home plate. More modest than Perry, Rose changed shirts only three times on September 11, 1985. Keeping one jersey himself and giving another to Reds owner Marge Schott, he sold the third holy shroud to a collector for $50,000 cash.

Authenticating such items continued to be a problem. "One of the jokes in the hobby," a memorabilia collector from New York was to say, "is that if you go to a show anywhere in the country and tell a dealer you wanted a game-worn Rose jersey, he could say, 'What year? What size? What color?' "

The bat for *the* hit was even more valuable; Rose had thought that through from the business standpoint as well. As he came within a few hits of Cobb's record, he got hold of one of Ty Cobb's own bats and tried to use it at the plate. What a marketing idea! A bridge to history and a snub to Cobb at the same time. To break Cobb's record with one of Cobb's own bats—think what the bat would be worth! Unfortunately, Rose cracked the relic soon after he used it, and the marketers wept.

A black Mizuno was the instrument that finally accomplished the feat of history. Rose loaned it to his biggest booster in Cincinnati, a sports-bar owner named Willie DeLuca, who put the artifact on display in his memorabilia-filled glass case beneath his cash register and watched the customers flood into his place. DeLuca had been in attendance at Riverfront on the night the record was broken. Accordingly, the clocks in his sports bar were all stopped and frozen at 8:02, the minute his hero broke Cobb's record. In due course, a wealthy insurance man and collector in Cincinnati came forward to inquire if the bat was for sale. DeLuca asked Rose. Rose pulled the price of a half million from the ionosphere, and to his surprise, the insurance man said yes. But clouds developed, and the price started coming down . . . to $250,000, then to $175,000. This was bad news to Rose, who was under pressure from Janszen and the bookies to pay his gambling debts. He finally settled for $125,000. But the memorabilia mogul must have sensed he had Rose on the run. He would only meet that price in installments, and only if Rose threw in his well–broken-in first baseman's glove, some autographed balls and bats, and his favorite sweat-stained Reds cap. Finally, he wanted to be personally introduced. By March 1989, ten collectors claimed to have the bat that broke Cobb's record.

On the spectrum from the bizarre to the fantastic, however, the matter of Rose's Hickok belt stands out. In 1975, Rose became the last recipient of the Hickok Award, which was given to the athlete of the year. During the twenty-six years of its existence, the honor had been accorded to such greats as Fran Tarkenton, George Foreman, and Steve Carlton. The honor came with a fabulous, massive gold belt, studded with diamonds and rubies, embossed with the recipient's name, and worth $30,000. A decade after Rose won the award, the Hickok belt turned up in the hands of a mysterious, moon-faced entrepreneur from Medford, Oregon, named Dennis L. Walker.

In early 1985, Rose had gone into business with Walker, who

had once been a political science professor before he went into international finance and founded an offshore bank in the Kingdom of Tonga in the South Pacific. The International Bank of the South Pacific floated securities that offered a return of more than 30 percent in interest on the investment. But Walker was also a collector, first of coins and jewels, then of sports memorabilia. With the assets of his bank, Walker founded a museum in Medford, Oregon, called the National Sports Hall of Fame. Opening in February 1985, with Pete Rose as master of ceremonies, the exhibit was spread over 6,000 square feet of floor space and was valued at more than $14 million. Among its special items were a uniform worn by Babe Ruth, a 1927 New York Yankees World Series ring, Willie Mays's 1954 World Series ring, a Ty Cobb bat, as well as a snakeskin cane used by Cobb in his later years, and other rings belonging to such luminaries as Willie Stargell, Frank Robinson, and Harmon Killebrew. Pete Rose was the best represented of the famous ball players. Among his mementos were a 52-ounce pure silver bat for winning the National League batting title, his first spring training uniform, and twelve rings, including one that carved out the number 3,631 in diamonds, for the time when he became the National League's all-time hit leader, and a sequel with the number 4,000.

"I've won three silver bats," Rose said at the opening. "What am I supposed to do? Put a sign on my basement door, 'Hey you want to come in and see my bats?' I've got sixteen All-Star Game rings and six World Series rings. I've only got eight fingers, and I'm not Mr. T."

But Walker wanted the Hickok belt most of all. Rose acceded, but only after he took the belt to a jeweler, had the precious stones removed and replaced with fake stones, and had the real diamonds transplanted into a pendant for his wife. Walker paid $30,000 for the de-jeweled belt, put $20,000 down in cash on the belt and the other Rose items, and gave Rose the balance of $50,000 in securities from his bank in Tonga. The securities were to mature in two years, in the spring of 1987.

The National Sports Hall of Fame stayed open for ten-and-a-half months and then closed abruptly, as the enigmatic Dennis Walker dropped from sight. A few months later, the U.S. Comptroller of the Currency issued an all-points bulletin to U.S. banks about Walker's International Bank of the South Pacific, asserting that it was nothing more than a shell bank operating illegally by selling unlicensed and unregistered securities. No more than a Ponzi scheme, Walker's operation was paying high returns to a few investors (mainly members of his Mormon Temple in Medford, where he had been a bishop) as a means of attracting new investors, whose money in turn footed the bill for the earlier payoffs. In February 1986, the Oregon attorney general filed a $6 million civil racketeering charge against Walker and named the Sports Hall of Fame in the complaint. If the sports collection could be seized and sold, the proceeds would be used to pay back the depositors who had been duped. But neither the valuable sports collection nor Walker could be found.

Rose knew nothing of Walker's wayward path until spring training in 1987, when he looked forward to the maturity of his Tongan securities, worth $75,000 on paper, just at the time when he needed the money to pay off his gambling debts. When he heard from his attorney that Walker's securities were worthless and that Walker had disappeared along with his entire memorabilia collection, Rose flew into a rage and set Janszen to the task of trying to recover his valuable mementos, especially his phonied Hickok belt. He had cheated Walker, but Walker, it now seemed, had cheated him twice over.

Dennis Walker was too clever by half. In July 1987, he registered at a seedy motel off the strip in Las Vegas in the name of Charles Lee. Four days later, his body was discovered in the motel room, so badly decomposed in the desert heat that the authorities had to resort to dental records to make an identification. The police suspected a professional homicide, for the toxicology report found no drugs or poison in the system. The logical deduction was that Walker had been either electrocuted or suffocated. To the FBI, the motive lay in Walker's memorabilia collection, rather than in his offshore financial fraud. "Sometimes an attachment to the memorabilia can be more powerful than the money it was worth," an FBI agent in Las Vegas was to observe. The case remains unsolved.

After Walker's death, pieces of his baseball collection turned up in New York in 1989. The FBI was alerted, for it was stolen property now. As the FBI reopened its Walker investigation, agents in Cincinnati interviewed Rose. It would be the only time the Bureau would formally interview Rose about any of his alleged crimes and misdeeds. He complained that Walker owed him more than $70,000, not only for the Hickok belt but for the bat that broke Ty Cobb's record.

There were only so many special bats and game-worn jerseys, Hickok belts and World Series rings to market, and only so many collectors like Dennis Walker around to purchase them. But Rose had developed another sideline that was a continuous, free-cash machine. A bottomless demand existed for bats and balls, photographs and posters bearing Rose's signature, but it was not as if a Sotheby appraiser was there to certify the authenticity of each item. Only Amer-

ican children were the appraisers. Rose was understandably bored
with the constant signing, as Janszen's girlfriend routinely wheeled a
garbage can full of official baseballs into the manager's office at Riverfront. Because Rose had a short attention span for autographing,
Tommy Gioiosa relieved his mentor of the pain. By all accounts, Gio's
rendition of Rose's signature was nearly perfect. He, in turn, trained
the cocaine dealer, Mike Fry, to forge, although Fry was only good at
flat items, not rounded surfaces. When Janszen came into the picture
and got into the sports memorabilia game himself, he ran the atelier.
Before long, there was a regular little cottage industry at work in
Rose's home or in Gold's Gym, and nobody was the wiser, certainly
not the kids who were the victims of this duplicity. Later, it would be
rumored that two little old ladies in southern Indiana were Rose's
chief forgers, but it was never confirmed.

When Rose attended baseball card shows, however, he had to do
the work himself. As the popularity of these events grew in the 1980s,
even the Baseball Hall of Fame was in the business of staging extrav-
aganzas with its living legends. In 1985, the year of the record, Rose
was a number one draw. By Janszen's estimate, he made $200,000 on
card shows alone that year. In 1986, his drawing power dropped off
slightly to about $175,000, and in 1987, next to Jose Canseco and
Mark McGwire, he faded to $125,000. Through these years, he aver-
aged fifteen shows in a year. It did not take long for him to reach six
figures.

Given Rose's passion for betting, the manner of payment was as
important as the amount. Cash was the tender, and you could annoy
Pete Rose considerably if you tried to present him with a check. The
business settled into a routine. A promoter—anyone, even Paul Janszen and the fat man, Mike Bertolini, could be one—would guarantee
Rose a set figure, usually somewhere between $8,000 and $12,000.
Rose would jet in, sign for two or three hours, while a television set
blared a sporting contest nearby to keep him from getting bored. The
kids or their starstruck dads ponied up their six dollars, lined up, and
were hustled for a few seconds into the presence of greatness. At the
end, the promoter gave Rose's flunky a brown sack, with his guaranteed money inside, plus 90 percent of the kids' money. When Rose got
home, he stacked his lucre on top of his television set or shoved it in
the kitchen cabinet next to the Tupperware. From the hands of babes,
the money went to the hands of bookies.

For unreported income on card shows and memorabilia sales,
not for gambling, Pete Rose had started down the certain road to the
penitentiary. Through 1988, Janszen was able to reconstruct these

card show appearances for the FBI and the IRS in fine detail. Because his duty had been to collect Rose's fee and count the money, he could provide close approximations of the money Rose had made. It was a simple enough matter to check these figures against Rose's tax returns. Moreover, Janszen could give testimony of Rose's criminal intent. He told the authorities about Rose's annoyance on one occasion, when his appearance at a card show had been reported in the press. "Now I'll have to declare the income," he said. On another occasion, Rose grumbled to Janszen that he was declaring a small proportion of his card show income just to satisfy the IRS.

Significantly, Rose's superagent, Reuven Katz, was on to the possibility that he might be cheating as early as the spring of 1987. After the Reds packed their gear in Tampa and pointed toward home, the team detoured to Nashville to play a final exhibition game. Because Johnny Bench, another of Katz's blue-chip clients, was beginning his new career as the television commentator for Reds games, Katz flew to Nashville to witness Bench's inaugural commentary. Coincidentally, a major baseball card show was being held at the Opryland Hotel, where Rose was featured along with Carl Yastrzemski, Joe DiMaggio, and Tommy Helms. Paul Janszen came along to carry the bags. Once there, he was given the additional duty of shooing the press away from Joe DiMaggio.

Katz entered the huge ballroom of the hotel to see scores of tables set up with the famous and not-so-famous ball players scribbling away on anything that was shoved in front of them, scribbling as fast as they could. Some had ceased to render a legible script in the interest of speed; others shortened their name to hurry the process. (Whitey Ford in these days was signing "Ed Ford.") The money over and under the table nauseated Katz. The place had become a veritable zoo. Back in Cincinnati, when the time was right, Katz asked their accountant how much income Rose had listed for the Nashville show. The answer was zero. This was a clear warning to Katz, and he made sure that Rose reported his earnings from the Nashville show. But policing Rose would not be easy.

In 1988, fully a year before Giamatti and baseball began the investigation into Rose's gambling, Katz was informed that the FBI and a grand jury were taking a hard look at Rose's finances. Officially, Katz promised full cooperation, while Rose promptly filed an amended tax return for the years that the IRS investigators were looking at, amended to reflect a certain amount of income from card shows and memorabilia sales.

To the prosecutors, there were two ways to look at the amendments: as evidence of good faith, or as a consciousness of guilt. In any event, Rose was in deep trouble for federal offenses that were likely to send him to jail.

By the fall of 1988, the avenger, Paul Janszen, was getting frustrated with the slow pace of the federal investigation. His snitching had closed down the cocaine ring in Gold's Gym, but he was not satisfied. Pete Rose still remained unshaken upon his steed, and Janszen was determined to unhorse him. For a while, Janszen seemed to be in conflict. At times, he acted the part of the spurned friend, trying to get mutual acquaintances to smooth things over with the Roses. At other times, he acted the part of the thug, issuing violent threats, directed primarily at Carol Rose, either to blow out her brains or to blow up her cars, unless her husband paid up the $50,000 he now claimed Rose owed him. To the authorities, he presented himself as the remorseful crook who was cleansing himself of all the bad things he had done in the past few years, who wanted only to pay his debt to society and to get on with his life.

The real motive all along was money. He wanted to be repaid the money he lent Rose, not money from honest labor but dirty money he had saved from his illegal steroid business. The reforming criminal wanted back the money he had made during his life of crime.

Late in 1988, a new threat came from Janszen. If Rose did not pay up, Janszen was going to the commissioner with the charge that Pete Rose had bet on baseball.

In early 1989, only a few weeks before Commissioner Peter Ueberroth and Commissioner-elect Giamatti focused on Rose, the ultimate danger of this connection between gambling and superstardom was realized. At Trop World Casino in Atlantic City, a three-day baseball card show took place. It was promoted by Mike Bertolini and hosted by Pete Rose. Rose's New York connections had finally brought their boy into line, and they wanted to be paid. But how much? In the conversation Janszen taped with Bertolini in April 1988, Janszen's real purpose was to extract from Bertolini on tape how much Rose owed his New York bookies.

"Did you ever get settle up with Pete?" Janszen asked.

"About what?"

"The money."

"Fuck'n, we're working it out and shit. I don't know, the fuck. Did you ever?"

"He still owes me about twelve grand."

"So he paid you about thirty-eight?"

"Huh?"

"Did he pay you anything yet?"

"No, well, he signed a bunch of autographs for me."

"I hear you."

"Plus he wrote some checks that I had cashed that I had sent up to the guy."

"Yeah."

"So he's into me for about anywhere from . . . I don't know . . . once you figure out all the autograph stuff . . . he probably owes me about anywhere from like $10,000 to $12,000." Then Janszen asked, "He was up to you for how much total?"

"What me or all together?"

"No, the guy . . . the bookies in New York, how much did he . . ."

"Don't talk like that on the phone," fat Mike said. "I hate that."

"All right. How much did he owe you? Owe them?"

"Altogether between me and them about two . . . two and a quarter."

"Jesus Christ."

"But we're forgetting them," Bertolini said. "He's just gonna take care of me."

"What do you mean, you're forgetting them?"

"Forgetting them," Bertolini replied. "They don't get nothing."

"What are they gonna do to him?"

"I don't know. We're not gonna worry about them."

"Oh, my God, Mikey. You're gonna have some people after him."

"This is what he's gonna do. I have no control."

"Doesn't he even give a shit?"

"What are they gonna do, Paulie? They made enough off of him."

But it did not quite work out like that. Rose had been cavalier about stiffing these New York mobsters long enough. Through the show in Atlantic City, they were forcing Rose to make restitution. The show, Janszen believed, was being held for the sole purpose of paying off, or at least whittling down, Rose's gambling debts. But there were grumbles. As Paul Janszen heard it, both Mickey Mantle and Henry Aaron had considered pulling out of the show "because Pete had let organized crime infiltrate the baseball card business."

More than 30,000 people passed through the casino show during the three days. The featured baseball stars all walked away with more than $100,000. Purportedly, Rose pulled in more than $160,000 for the extravaganza, but it was not his to keep.

"In my opinion, they were using Pete," Janszen told baseball. "Instead of paying him, he comes in and does it for free, and that's a way of paying off, of subtracting money from the debt."

If that is true, the ultimate nightmare had occurred. The mob had their hooks into one of the greatest figures ever to play the game of baseball, and the mob did not let go. Rose had put himself at the mercy of the mob.

As the show in Atlantic City took place, Paul Janszen was preparing to begin his six months in a halfway house. Now he delivered his final ultimatum to Rose about his lost drug money. Writing to Reuven Katz about his "personal loan" to Rose in June 1987, he chronicled the various broken promises to repay his shattered relationship with the Roses.

> Because I covered for him with his wife, while he was sleeping his way around town, she no longer wanted me in their house. . . . Carol doesn't have the guts to leave him, so she has to blame his friends for his disgusting behavior. If she ever blamed him, she'd have to leave the lifestyle of fame and fortune behind and she can't do it. . . .
>
> For years I heard the stories that Mr. Rose didn't like paying his debts and had left several people hanging out to dry. I've watched many times as he dug a hole for himself financially, and he always needed someone else to bail him out. Evidently, he's living a lifestyle he can't afford and he's using his so-called "friends" to feed off of. It's really sad when a man making the money Mr. Rose does has to borrow from people around him. But this is nothing new. I've recently spoke with a couple of people who have known Pete for many years, and they told me of similar situations where he abused his friendship with others. They say the same thing, "A great ball player, a zero as a human being. . . ."
>
> I wasn't put on this earth to be Pete Rose's doormat.

· 11 ·

Collision

IN LATE JANUARY 1989, baseball's commissioner-elect, joyful at the consummation of his childhood dream, stood before a packed house at the University of Michigan to deliver the distinguished Cook Lectures. Over the three days of his declamation, the diverse audience—made up of professors of English and little old ladies, of students and softball teammates who had gotten their summer caps out of their closets and turned them around backward—grew markedly. For his lecture entitled "Baseball as Narrative," Giamatti was introduced by the legendary Michigan football coach Bo Schembechler, who pepped the crowd up with a bit of Upper Midwest whimsy. Giamatti had once been president of Yale University, Bo said drolly, which was not the University of Michigan, but nevertheless was a very strong academic institution. The speaker possessed nineteen honorary degrees, one of which was from Notre Dame, but that did not count for much. (The Fighting Irish had defeated the Wolverines on the gridiron three times in a row.) In his special field of Renaissance literature, the coach understood that Dr. Giamatti had written pages and pages in books and even in scholarly articles.

"During the thirty-day suspension of Pete Rose for bumping an umpire," Bo said, not one to sympathize unduly with the men in stripes and chest protectors, "it is my understanding that Pete had to read a dozen of those articles as part of his punishment."

When Giamatti assumed the podium, the romance for sport rolled out of him. He took as his text a line from Shakespeare's *Henry*

V: "If every day were holiday, to sport would be as tedious as to work." In a thought he knew not to be original with him, he observed that more could be learned about a culture by contemplating how it played than how it worked. Sport had a religious quality. It lay in the devotion of the fan. As athletes strove for paradise and perfection, they were offering a vision of "enhanced life" akin to the vision of priests. They shared with actors the talent of the fluid motion, the need for perfect timing, the goal to elevate training and thought to the level of instinct. To witness victory in a game was to make oneself more noble as the observer connected with a "higher human plane of existence."

"I believe we have played games and watched games to imitate the gods, to become more godlike in our worship of each other, and through those moments of transmutation, to know for an instant, what the gods know," Giamatti proclaimed.

Several hundred miles to the south, Pete Rose prepared for a more profane joy. After Super Bowl XXIII—in which he bet and lost—he got ready to travel to the Reds new facility at Plant City, Florida. He was going with his usual ebullience and optimism. For four consecutive seasons, under his leadership, the Reds had finished second, a fine record for a team marked by so many young and inexperienced players. In 1989, there would be no more excuses, although no one could put a stop to clichés. The future was now; they were going for the gusto; no more thinking about the year after next. With the signing of Eric Davis for $1.35 million right before his case went to arbitration and only a few days before training camp opened, Rose had in his arsenal four million-dollar-a-year players. (The other three were the pitchers Danny Jackson, Tom Browning, and John Franco.) Todd Benzinger, a switch-hitter, had been acquired from the Red Sox in the off-season. He provided the team with a solid performer and a likable personality at first base, as well as yet another Cincinnati native.

The debate raged along the Ohio River whether the former great players of the game made competent managers. The great Tris Speaker brought the first world championship to Cleveland in 1920, and was hitting over .300 and finishing second in the standings six years later as the Indians manager. But Rose was interested in comparing himself to Ty Cobb, not Tris Speaker. Rose could boast that his record as a manager was considerably better than that of his old nemesis. In his six years of managing the Tigers, Cobb had only one second-place finish along with two sixth- and one last-place finishes, although in his last year of managing the Tigers, in 1926, Cobb hit

.339. Cobb's lackluster record came from demanding too much of his players, expecting them to perform at the same level and with the same aggressiveness as he had. That took away from them the ability to think and react for themselves.

Rose's problem was the opposite. His method was decidedly laissez-faire. In Tony Perez, his hitting coach, he had one of the most stylish hitters of the modern game, and he let Perez do the teaching. It was beyond a question of delegating authority. Rose was curiously indifferent to the teaching process. He did not even pontificate, as, say, Ted Williams had done when he managed the Washington Senators briefly. Rose did take an interest in Benzinger when the young first baseman arrived in camp, probably because Benzinger was a switch-hitter and a hometown boy. But with the others, Rose left well enough alone. As a result, the fundamentals of the Reds were poor, the discipline on the team was lax, and Rose did not communicate well with his players, especially young and gifted black superstars.

According to opposing managers, Rose had had advantages and disadvantages as he entered management. About on-the-field situations, no one knew more, but good managing was more human relations than strategy. In handling people, Rose had a lot to learn, but he had worked hard at being a good manager, did his homework, and got better every year. If you managed against Rose, Pirates skipper Jim Leyland would say, you knew you were in for a dogfight.

As always, Rose had no trouble communicating with the press. He loved to hold court, regaling the reporters with endless tales of his fascinating playing days of yore and then using reporters to send messages to his players rather than confronting the offending players himself. That was a practice that caused considerable resentment in the clubhouse. No one in Rose's tenure as a manager was more resentful than Dave Parker, whom Rose traded after the 1987 season and then accused behind his back of exerting "negative leadership." To Parker, that was an obvious attempt to make him the "whuppin' boy," to blame the second-place finish on him, rather than for Rose to take the blame himself. Parker felt he had been the leader and a model for the young black players, making sure they did not get "too down . . . or too high."

With this spicy stew, the upcoming season would be nothing if not interesting.

On February 20, the second day of spring training, Rose was inexplicably absent. The Reds public relations office put out a bland announcement that the manager was simply away on "personal business," a statement that was met with grumbles from the press. *Cin-*

cinnati Enquirer columnist Tim Sullivan complained that no major league manager was as lackadaisical as Rose when it came to spring training duties, and that in recent times, Rose had even refused to ride the team bus when the Reds played some distance from Tampa.

Hours later, the real story came out, and Sullivan was even more annoyed. Rose's personal business was actually to meet in New York with the Commissioner of Baseball, Peter Ueberroth; the commissioner-designate, Bart Giamatti; and his designated deputy commissioner, Fay Vincent.

The scene at baseball's office at 350 Park Avenue had been a study in contrast. As Rose strode down the corridor lined with pictures of famous baseball players, including Lou Gehrig, Henry Aaron, and Ted Williams, he was concerned not so much with the danger that lay only a few feet from him as with the fact that there was no picture of him on the wall. Once in the commissioner's wood-paneled office, flanked by his two attorneys, Reuven Katz and Robert Pitcairn, Jr., the famous ball player leaned back in his chair with a certain "prove-it!" expression on his face. Because it was Ueberroth's meeting, the outgoing commissioner sat magisterially behind his desk, his gold Olympic torch nearby and pictures of himself with President Ronald Reagan on the wall. He was the cold, slender, pragmatic technocrat, intensely focused on a single specific allegation. He cared nothing about the other seedy rumors, which to him were irrelevant.

"We have only one purpose here," Ueberroth began icily. "We've heard rumors about your gambling. We don't want to hear about betting on basketball or football. Did you or did you not bet on baseball?"

Knowing full well that his life in baseball depended upon it, Rose denied the rumor strenuously. He had not placed a bet since the Super Bowl, he said with a certain smugness. It seemed as if the meeting would be over in a few minutes. Then, Giamatti began to speak. To Rose's lawyers, Giamatti seemed every bit as unfocused as Ueberroth seemed single-minded. He began to amble around the issue with thoughts that were both romantic and ponderous. To this decidedly unromantic collection of men, his drift was bizarre, rambling, out of place. He tacked into the subject of clubhouse undesirables. With a rising passion, he mentioned the name of Mike Bertolini, whose Italianness particularly interested and offended him. Especially guys like that had to be kept out of the clubhouse, Giamatti scolded. The regrettable behavior of other great players was mentioned, although Giamatti paid momentary homage as he professed to be a Pete Rose fan. It seemed, at least to one of Rose's lawyers, that Giamatti was displaying a deep contempt for the players, while he was expressing a profound love for the game they played. Left to their natural devices, players were the real threat to the game, he seemed to imply, and only executives such as himself could contain their excesses. Fay Vincent, stony-faced and inscrutable by Giamatti's side, his hand on his cane, said nothing . . . and judged.

In the course of the meeting, Rose denied other rumors as well. He had not won a Pik Six for nearly fifty thousand dollars two years earlier, nor had he won a much more substantial Pik Six only three weeks before for more than five times the 1987 jackpot. By Giamatti's subsequent account, the parties were genuinely in the dark at this meeting. The rumors were thick and deeply distressing, but their origin was obscure. At one point in the conversation, Pitcairn cautiously tried to flush the source out by saying he "hoped" these rumors weren't coming from one Paul Janszen. Pitcairn had hesitated to mention the name, for he did not want to put the commissioners onto Janszen. If it was Janszen, this same Janszen was trying to blackmail Pete Rose. In Giamatti's memory, Pitcairn seemed genuinely puzzled about Janszen's demand for money and was trying to get to the bottom of it.

With nothing confirmed and a good deal denied, the meeting broke up, but not before there was one last item of business.

"What should I tell the media?" Rose asked as he was leaving.

"Tell them, I just needed some advice," Ueberroth suggested. "Nothing ominous."

"How about, I bet on basketball?" Rose said helpfully.

"We don't care," Ueberroth replied. When Ueberroth was questioned by the press a day later, he did his part to cover up.

"We asked him to come," he told the *New York Times*. "We didn't order him. There's nothing ominous, and there won't be any follow-through." On the very day Ueberroth's statement appeared in the *Times*, Giamatti was organizing his strike-force investigation.

For Rose, the brush fires were breaking out everywhere. In Cincinnati, it was being reported that three weeks previously, on January 27, he and a local track owner named Jerry Carroll had won a Pik Six for a grand total of $265,669.20, on a ticket to which Rose had contributed only $1,340. Rose vehemently denied the report, while he confirmed that he and Carroll were considering going into a partnership on a San Antonio racetrack, because Texas had just legalized pari-mutuel betting. Not he, but Arnie Metz, the former groundskeeper at Riverfront, had won the ticket. The reporters groaned at that explanation. Metz, Rose's chief clubhouse runner, did not have that kind of money to throw around.

Back in Plant City, the reporters descended on Rose, demanding an explanation for his New York meeting. With Ueberroth's sanction to dissemble, Rose did his best to send them sniffing down false trails. Did the meeting center on his gambling? Specifically on this Pik Six report? Tim Sullivan wanted to know.

"You know why it wouldn't be about racetracks?" Rose said.

"Steinbrenner?" replied the eager Sullivan. It was a good guess, because baseball had acquiesced to George Steinbrenner's ownership of a Tampa track.

"No, no. Because all baseball people are worried about is if you owe somebody a lot of money. How can you owe somebody a lot of money at a racetrack? You don't have a credit card out there. If you want a ticket, you've got to put your fucking cash up. It's not like you can go up there—I guess the owner of the track can charge bets, but I sure the fuck can't. That's why it didn't make any sense. It would have made more sense if he had come up with the theory that he [the commissioner] had me there because my company did card shows at a casino in January. That would make more sense than the Pik Six."

Rose paused and waited to see if Sullivan would bite on this red herring. He didn't. "With a Pik Six, don't you get five or six guys and get syndicate as such. Together, you buy x numbers of tickets?" Sullivan asked.

"I've had a couple of guys."

"They might be 'known gamblers.' I'm not saying that's what it is, but I think that's what the speculation is."

"Let me tell you something. I didn't do it on that one, that Pik Six. I wasn't part of that Pik Six. But a lot of times, you do a Pik Six for one reason and one reason only: there's enough money for two or three guys and you don't want to put all the money up yourself. You don't want to put three thousand dollars up. If the first horse loses, you're out."

"Do you think you have to change your lifestyle because of what's being speculated?"

"Yeah, I have to watch." Then Rose grew bolder, enlarging the lie. "I don't go to River Downs during the season. I go to the fucking ballpark."

"You know you have a reputation for gambling outside of horses."

"I don't know how I can get that."

"You have it."

"Yeah, but that don't mean it's fair."

"I know."

"I mean anybody can say anybody bets on this or bets on that. That's just like I don't believe that guy can come out and say I have a history of betting on college basketball. That's illegal! And no one's ever proved that I bet on college basketball."

"I got a call the other night from a guy. . . ." (At this point, Sullivan did not know it was Paul Janszen who had called him.) "He wouldn't give me his name, and he said that he had evidence that you owed him a lot of money. I don't know if he was looking for headlines or what."

"I bet the guy don't call back."

Instinctively, Sullivan moved to the heart of the issue.

"Don't you think players are tempted to bet on baseball because they know more than the average person?"

"No, you can't do that. That's asking for trouble. There wouldn't be anybody you could trust. No way. I mean you're asking to get a new job. You'd have to be the dumbest son of a bitch in the world to do that." He paused to gauge the effect. "You have to uphold the laws of gambling on baseball because baseball has integrity."

"Have you been hurt by this thing?"

"No."

"Does it bother you?"

"Yeah, it bothers me. Anything bothers me. The first day it happened you insinuated that I didn't like my job because I took a day off." Rose knew how to get a sleuth off-balance, while he maneuvered his way out of a tight corner. It was the way he had done it many times before, the way he had had to do it as far back as his childhood, when his father had him in a tight corner and had his hand raised to slap his son on the back of the head. Inevitably, Harry came into the conversation.

"How do I feel about gambling? Let me tell you something. One thing that my father was was a gentleman, and a banker and a respected citizen. I've got the utmost respect for him, as much as any man I've ever met in my life. When I was this big"—Rose put his open hand close to the floor—"he used to take me to the racetrack for the sport of it. He couldn't even afford to bet. And I take my son, and my son will take his son. That don't mean it's bad. If it was bad, I wouldn't do it."

The sheer enormity of these lies was only part of the chemistry that Rose mixed for himself at the outset of baseball's investigation. To the reporters who had waxed poetic about Rose for years, the fact that Rose now looked them in the eye, face to face, toe to toe, and told them these things created a sense of betrayal. As the lies were revealed, the reporters turned on Rose with anger. That anger was something that Rose never understood.

The first of the lies to be uncovered was the Pik Six jackpot of

January 1989, the big one. The irony lay in the unnecessary quality of the lie, for Rose could have admitted winning on the ticket with Carroll, although it would have been embarrassing. The great Pete Rose and the owner of the track win out on a big Pik Six jackpot, when the big boys from Chicago and elsewhere could not? It had the smell of a fix. The track owner was even more intent than Rose to cover it up. Still, the winning ticket had been fair and honest and legal. Tax time for 1989 had not yet rolled around, so, unlike the Pik Six win in 1987, there was no question yet of hiding the income from the IRS. Rose compounded his difficulties by denying to his legal advisers that he had won on the ticket. When the truth eventually came out, his attorneys came very close—but not quite close enough—to throwing him out of their office and severing their relationship with him.

In due course, Arnie Metz, the base-path sweeper, told what happened on January 25. Carroll made his choices, purchased his ticket for $2,688, and sat back in his box with another horseplayer, Ted Gregory, a local Rib King, to watch the ponies run. The Pik Six races began with the third race, which Carroll won. He had just won the fourth race as well when Rose breezed in with Metz, fresh from a booster event in Dayton for the Reds. Carroll smugly announced that he was 2 for 2.

"Am I in on that ticket?" Rose asked jokingly.

"Oh well, what the hell, if you want in," Carroll said reluctantly, because he liked to win as much as Pete Rose. The owner slapped the ticket on the table, and Rose counted out his half. The Rib King decided he wanted in as well, but Carroll said no.

"The ticket happened to hit," Metz recalled, "and Jerry being the owner of the racetrack and Pete being who he is, Jerry decided it wouldn't be wise for him to cash the ticket. So I took the ticket from Carroll's box down to the money room of the racetrack. I was just going to leave the ticket for safekeeping, so nobody would have the ticket in their pocket and take a chance on losing it on the way home. When I took the ticket to the money room, I signed my name to the back of it, as I was to be the only one who could get that ticket out of the money room. . . . I would be the only one who could cash the ticket."

The winning ticket lay uncashed for two days, until Rose got ready to go to spring training a week early and wanted his money. There was an annoyance. A card show in Boston was on his schedule the day before the family was to leave for Florida. With his Pik Six money, he could avoid the hassle of a first-class commercial flight and rent a jet for $4,000. He avoided the inconvenience of the airport, however, only to find that the show was not in the city of Boston at all but forty-five minutes to the north, and, more annoying, Jose Canseco was going to be there. This put Rose in a thoroughly foul mood, but he did his duty, signed his thousand autographs, picked up his guaranteed $7,500, and flew home. He threw $109,000 of his track winnings in a satchel, which he took to Florida after he peeled off $23,000 to a Cincinnati jeweler for a ring he had bought his wife at Christmas. In Florida, he bought a golf cart for $3,600, took another $24,000 to pay for a tennis court at his new Florida house, and spent the remainder of his satchel on trifles, including losing tickets at Gulfstream Park.

Later, in his official deposition, he was asked why he had lied about all this in the initial meeting in New York with Bart Giamatti.

"Pete, do you recall telling Commissioner Giamatti about the Pik Six of January 25, 1989?"

"No. Recall telling him what?"

"Telling them anything about it."

"No. I think I told him the same thing I told you before, that I wish I won as much money as people say I do. I'm glad I don't lose as much as people say I do."

"Pete, isn't it a fact that after the questioning was over, that you told Bart Giamatti that an example of these terrible rumors was the Pik Six that recently occurred in January that we've just talked about. And that you, in fact, had not won it?"

"I don't remember saying that."

"Do you remember the subject being discussed at all?"

"No. I remember something about the Pik Six. Because I remember Mr. Giamatti saying something like 'We don't care about Pik Sixes' or something. He said, 'I'm just here to ask you about baseball.' That's what he said."

Pete Rose had a way of getting very literal when he was caught in a lie.

Three days after the meeting with Rose in New York and the day after Ueberroth was widely quoted as promising no follow-up on the Rose visit, Giamatti was in Washington, schmoozing around Capitol Hill with the executive vice-president of baseball, Ed Durso. Ueberroth had turned the Rose case over to Giamatti entirely, since Ueberroth was now a lame duck and a short-timer. Late that night from his room in the Four Seasons Hotel, Giamatti held lengthy telephone conversations with Fay Vincent about how the Rose investigation should proceed. It was no longer a question of whether there should be a major investigation, but rather what its shape and character should be. To head the effort, Vincent suggested a Washington attorney named John Dowd, whom Vincent knew personally from their days together at Yale Law School.

On the surface a big, affable, unpretentious Irishman, Dowd hailed from the shoe and leather town of Brockton, Massachusetts. A tough ex-Marine and ex-prosecutor, his early training had been in the tax division of the Justice Department. There, in 1972, he had headed a group called Strike Force 18, which had the authority to search for mob cases to prosecute. The force used the tax laws, and among its targets was Meyer Lansky, the mob's "investment" kingpin. That baseball wanted this former mob prosecutor as its investigator said something about how it saw the Rose case.

Late that evening, in a conference call, Giamatti and Vincent talked with Dowd. He agreed to take the case.

In their first meeting, Giamatti spoke to Dowd in lofty terms. The commissioner wanted the fair play of the baseball field to distinguish this investigation. Let the chips fall where they may, Giamatti told Dowd. "I had in my mind almost the image of wood chips falling in a random pattern that wasn't designed, predesigned, or preplanned," Giamatti was to explain later, "but wherever they would fall according to the best investigation of the truth as possible." Dowd was to search for the truth, while Giamatti remained in charge of the "moral contours" of the investigation. "I did not consider myself in charge of every investigatory act, but I consider myself absolutely responsible and so charged with the responsibility to oversee the overall shape and fairness, what I call the moral contours, the dignity, the impartiality of this thing."

That sounded grand, even noble, but Dowd was about to enter an underworld where Giamatti's personal standards for honor and manners did not obtain. The potential witnesses against Rose were small-time crooks, leeches, racetrack touts, Nautilus queens, artless dodgers, groupies, clubhouse flunkies, petty racketeers, tipsters, and con men. What did baseball have to offer them as an inducement to talk? If they did talk, could they be believed? Unlike an official criminal investigation, the baseball commissioner represented only the owners of baseball and by extension the fans. Therefore, his investigation had no power over anyone who was not employed by baseball. With no subpoena power, it could not compel anyone to testify. The testimony of these hoods would be entirely voluntary. If gambling remained baseball's capital crime, it had ceased to be vice in America. Indeed, with the institution of state lotteries, gambling was being promoted as a virtue and a civic duty in America. "Why Pick on Pete?" a headline in *Time* screamed later.

Moreover, the target of the investigation was the very personification of the game. Baseball had, in effect, targeted itself. If Rose were guilty of the rumors circulating about him, to what extent had the environment of modern baseball, with its big salaries and its symbiosis with the gambling world, encouraged those very transgressions? If the investigation were to go awry, Rose might go free, and the office of the baseball commissioner might destroy its own integrity and credibility and authority.

Giamatti put only one restriction on Dowd. He could not pay for information. "Why did I say that? Because there were rumors that journalists were willing to do that, rumors I couldn't substantiate," Giamatti said, "but I wanted to make sure that we were all in agreement that that is not the kind of thing he would do." Giamatti was absolutely right about the journalistic world. Before long, the mass circulation magazines were reportedly offering as much as $100,000 to the principal accusers, Janszen, Peters, and Gioiosa to tell their story.

Together with fair play, Giamatti wished his inquiry to have the mark of "natural justice." These two fundamental concepts, fair play and natural justice, went back to the inaugural days of the first baseball commissioner, Judge Kenesaw Mountain Landis, and were contained in the original blue books, the baseball equivalent of the Madison-Hamilton papers, which underpinned the Major League Agreement of 1921. Fairness and natural justice were, however, a matter of interpretation. The interpreter was the sitting Commissioner of Baseball, who had been accorded thoroughly dictatorial powers. Giamatti wanted to be a gentle dictator. To him, natural justice was simply akin to the Golden Rule.

"Would your understanding of the meaning of natural justice differ from your meaning of fair play?" he was asked.

He gave a rambling, dense reply. "I can't imagine describing natural justice and leaving out fair play, because this was written in the context of a game, of a sport, of a profession which is sport. For what it is worth, I always assumed that, as a jurist by profession, Judge Landis understood what he meant by natural justice. So far as he was writing this in the context of baseball, fair play would have been a way of encompassing the same kind of symmetrical, even-handed principles for baseball apprehension that perhaps a jurist could take for granted when dealing with jurists or

with other lawyers who are much more at home in the other ter-
ology."

In short, as a Renaissance scholar rather than a jurist, he did not
w the answer to the question, but he knew how to obfuscate it.

As the Rose investigation got under way, Giamatti had been
ing considerable attention to the life and thought of the great
Judge Landis. He had been reading the J. Taylor Spink biography of
the first commissioner, in which the rationale for gambling as the
preeminent capital offense in baseball is made clear. The Office of the
Commissioner of Baseball itself is the child of the Chicago Black Sox
scandal of 1919, where big-time gamblers perpetrated the Big Fix in
order to win a huge wager. Landis assumed his office to purge the
game of this pernicious influence. His passion for purification was
inquisitional. Early on, he had expanded the natural justice of baseball beyond the narrow justice of the court room. A court of law
might acquit the Black Sox players of wrongdoing, but he, of his own
accord and power, would banish them forever from the game: "Regardless of the verdict of juries, no player who throws a ball game, no
player who entertains proposals or promises to throw a game, no
player who sits in conference with a bunch of crooked players and
gamblers where the ways and means of throwing games are discussed and does not promptly tell his club about it, will ever play
professional baseball. . . . Just keep in mind that regardless of the
verdict of juries, baseball is entirely competent to protect itself
against the crooks both inside and outside the game."

In Landis, Giamatti had his mentor. The judge's love for the
game of baseball, not his bent for punishment, provided Giamatti
with his attraction. Landis was the commissioner of the fans. Baseball greats were his first heroes. This love for the game had brought
him like Giamatti, to the attention of the baseball world because
Landis doted on the Chicago Cubs as much as Giamatti ever doted on
the Boston Red Sox. Landis was a familiar figure in a box along the
first-base line in the old West Side Park, where Mordecai "Three
Fingers" Brown dueled with Christy Mathewson, and the double
plays went from Tinker to Evers to Chance. Like Giamatti, Landis
was chosen partly for the classiness he could bring to the game. As
Will Rogers had put it, "Somebody said, 'Get that old boy who sits
behind first base all the time. He's out there every day anyhow.' But
don't kid yourself that that old judicial bird isn't going to make those
baseball birds walk the chalkline." When Landis accepted the job,
with the cloud of the Big Fix hanging over the national game, he had
said, "The only thing in anybody's mind now is to make and keep

baseball what the millions of fans throughout the United States want it to be."

Landis's obsessive views about gambling have lasted as the essential credo of modern baseball. Extending his reach retroactively by two years, the commissioner permanently banned a Cardinals first baseman named Eugene Paulette for accepting gifts in 1919 from St. Louis gamblers. Paulette "offered to betray his team and put himself in the vicious power of gamblers," Landis wrote. "My only regret is that the real culprits, the gamblers, can not be reached by this office." From his days in the 1890s as an attorney for the Pinkerton Corporation, when horse race fixing became a national scandal, the judge had a visceral contempt for the track and all who hung around it. Betting on the ponies must never be allowed to infect the game of baseball. "There are too many questionable characters around a track," he said. "Gamblers, touts, racketeers, men who wouldn't know how to make an honest living." Racetrack types "would sell out their mothers or the Virgin Mary," Landis said. They had almost destroyed baseball in the Black Sox case.

According to Landis, "These vermin no doubt got so double crossed by other crooks on the track that it no longer was profitable, so they tried to entwine their slimy fingers around baseball. But by God, so long as I have anything to do with this game, they'll never get another hold on it." Consequently, he barred the crooner Bing Crosby from acquiring a professional baseball club because Crosby was a horse player. In another action, he forced the manager of the New York Giants, John McGraw, to drop his plan to invest in a Havana racetrack. The manager had to choose; McGraw chose baseball. Late in his commissionership, Landis drove the president of the Philadelphia Nationals, William Cox, from the game after Cox, who had been a catcher at Yale University in his college days, was found to have made "sentimental" bets on his own team.

From the literature, Giamatti could see that the federal courts had uniformly supported Landis whenever his absolute authority was challenged, even when the puritanical commissioner had restricted the freedom and the rights of ball players off the field. In a federal court decision in 1931, a federal judge wrote in Landis's favor that the clear intent of the commission's founding fathers was "to endow the commissioner with all the attributes of a benevolent but absolute despot and all the disciplinary powers of the proverbial paterfamilias." To join organized baseball was to divest the traditional rights of American citizenship and cede them to the commissioner. A ball player who was acquitted of car theft, for example, asked to be reinstated to the game, in the illusion that a legal acquittal wiped his slate clean. But Landis read the transcript and decided otherwise. For Landis the trial itself had sufficiently compromised the character and reputation of the player. "Your mere presence in the lineup would inevitably burden patrons of the game with grave apprehension as to its integrity." The player, Benny Kauff, "could not be restored to good standing without impairing the morale of the other players and without further injury to the good name of professional baseball."

Undoubtedly, in his reading, Giamatti paid close attention to Landis's behavior when the judge's abhorrence of gambling brought him into collision with the great players of the game. Landis had warred constantly with Rogers Hornsby, who loved to bet on the horses. Landis denied Hornsby a share of his winnings in the 1932 World Series because of betting, and indubitably, the judge's influence over baseball management had something to do with Hornsby losing his job as a big league manager in 1937. Hornsby simply could not stop betting. "That fellow never will learn," Landis said of Hornsby. "His betting has got him into one scrape after another, cost him a fortune and several jobs, and still he hasn't got enough sense to stop."

If Giamatti identified with Landis, Rose might have found inspiration in Hornsby's response: "No one ever accused me of a thing in baseball. As a player I hustled with the best of them, and as a manager, I made every effort to win. I don't drink or smoke, never did, and racing is my recreation. I enjoy it and get a kick out of it. Racing, and betting on races, is permitted by law in many of the states, so I was doing nothing illegal. I always gave full time to my baseball jobs, and if I bet money on races, it was my own, honestly earned. I could see no difference from betting a horse to win than a lot of club owners playing the market and betting a stock would go up or down."

In the famous case of alleged gambling and fixing against Ty Cobb and Tris Speaker in 1927, however, Giamatti could see Landis's pain at judging great players. In investigating the great ones, harm could come to the game if they were judged unfairly, especially in 1927, when the memory of the Black Sox scandal was still fresh. In the Cobb-Speaker case, though, Landis's natural justice showed its gentle side: to absolve rather than to punish, to restore rather than to banish, especially if it were a close call. With borderline evidence against great stars of the game, the best interests of baseball were better served by vindication than banishment.

The facts of the case were these: Late in the 1925 season, with only three games to play, Speaker's Cleveland club had clinched second place, but their opponents, Cobb's Tigers, needed to win one more game to finish third and garner the bonus money for a third-place showing. (Fourth-place finishers were out of the money altogether.) According to Dutch Leonard, a pitcher on the Tigers, a meeting took place under the stands before the September 25 game, involving Speaker, Cobb, Leonard, and Smokey Joe Wood, a former pitcher for the Red Sox, but then an outfielder for the Indians and later the baseball coach at Yale University. Leonard charged that Cobb and Speaker conspired to fix the game in the Tigers' favor and to make some money on it besides by laying down a wager. The Tigers won, 9–5.

Landis later came into possession of two letters, one from Cobb to Leonard and one from Wood to Leonard, that showed a wager had indeed been made, but not that the game had been fixed. From the Cobb letter, his intent to bet on the game was clear, but it appeared that time had run out before he could get the bet down. Speaker was mentioned in neither letter, but Leonard had made incriminating statements about Spoke. Dutch Leonard had every motive for revenge (and exaggeration) against both Cobb and Speaker. Cobb had put Leonard on waivers after the 1925 season, and Speaker had failed to pick him up in Cleveland.

The question for baseball's legendary disciplinarian was this: Would Landis be true to his statement after the Black Sox scandal that no player who entertains proposals or promises to throw a game, no player who sits in a conference with a bunch of crooked players and gamblers where the ways and means of throwing games are discussed will ever again play professional baseball? Was there a double standard in baseball—one set of rules for its greats and another for its mediocre players? How absolute was his post–Black Sox morality to be?

Speaker and Cobb, both better politicians than Pete Rose, knew how to mobilize their natural constituency—and their legal defense. Both threatened major law suits against major league baseball if their names were not cleared, and both cooperated with the commissioner in his investigation. (Their accuser, Dutch Leonard, refused to attend the commissioner's hearing.) Speaker emphasized that there was no evidence whatever to show that the game was fixed, as he deemphasized the evidence that a bet had been made and won. Moreover, in his losing cause, he had the reasonable alibi of having collected two triples and a single in the questionable game, just as

Smokey Joe Wood could protest that he had not even played in the game. For his part, Cobb issued a powerful and effective statement: "I have been in baseball twenty-two years. I have played the game as hard and square and clean as any man ever did. All I have thought of was to win, every year, every month, every day, every hour. My conscience is clear. I have had very high ideals in this game of baseball and I have carried them out from the beginning of my career until the end. I will rest my case with the American fans."

If Rose had had the wit to make such a statement as Giamatti's investigation got under way, he might have been more effective in steering the course of the inquiry.

In the Landis biography, over which Giamatti pored as preparation for his commissionership and reviewed as the Rose case began, the biographer Spink had written that Landis "sweat blood" over the Cobb-Speaker case. It was the toughest decision of the judge's quarter-century in baseball. He understood the far-ranging consequences full well. His eventual decision, rendered after several agonizing months and announced in January 1927, was that "no decent system of justice" could find that the game in question had been fixed. He left it at that. The baseball world heaved a sigh of relief, as Ty Cobb and Tris Speaker escaped being declared ineligible.

The question had been close enough, however, that Landis was to recommend certain formal rules to govern betting on baseball. On December 27, 1927, eleven months later, they were formally adopted. Because the Cobb-Speaker case, as well as a case against Swede Risberg for purportedly slacking off in a game in 1917, had come six years or more before these cases were adjudicated in the court of baseball, Landis proposed a statute of limitations for past offenses.

More applicable to the Rose case for Giamatti were two rules on gambling: a one-year ineligibility for betting on any game of baseball where the bettor had no duty to perform, and permanent ineligibility for betting "any sum whatsoever upon any ball game in connection with which the bettor has a duty to perform." Landis wanted a harsher penalty for the first rule, betting per se, but did not prevail.

"I feel some of these players got into these difficulties because there were no specific rules covering such conduct," Landis remarked. "But we learn as we go on." From that day forward, the rules about betting were posted in the locker rooms of all major league teams. The warning was a part of every major league contract. And each season, in spring training, league officials and the FBI lectured the players on this capital crime of baseball.

As Giamatti bonded with Landis, with the Landis legacy, and

with the Landis mentality, he could take note that despite their brushes with the commissioner over gambling violations, Rogers Hornsby and Ty Cobb and Tris Speaker were icons of the Baseball Hall of Fame in Cooperstown. But so too, he could note with even more pleasure, was Kenesaw Mountain Landis.

Within a day of his official hiring, Giamatti's super-investigator, John Dowd, was in Cincinnati, interviewing Paul Janszen. With the relief of a man whose conscience was torturing him (although he still wanted his steroid money back), Janszen unburdened himself. No matter what was going to be written about him later, Janszen said, "I can walk out of this door today and feel good about everything."

In the next two days, the whole tawdry tale rolled out of him, from the soup of his drug dealings to the nuts of Rose's baseball betting. Soon enough, they focused on the spring and summer of 1987, when Janszen's personal and business relationship with Rose had been at its most intense, and where Janszen spoke directly to the capital crime of baseball. Without hesitation or haziness, Janszen accused Rose of betting two thousand dollars a game and of betting seven games almost every night between April 7 and May 13. Rose's bookie in that five-week period had been Val, the Mafia book in New York, through a Florida bet writer named Steve Chevashore. Janszen, now the expert stoolie, presented Dowd with a clandestine tape of a conversation between himself and Chevashore, in which they discussed how Val had cut Rose's betting off on May 13 because Rose would never settle up on Monday, the way an honorable bettor should always do with his bookmaker, no matter what.

"Pete wound up winning about ten that night," Janszen told Chevashore about Rose's last night of betting with his New York–Florida connection, "and he called me up the next day to place more. I said: Pete, I didn't even get in the action the night before. He asked why. I said: because I've been telling you, the guy won't take anymore 'til you get cleared up with him. He says: Well, if he's going to treat me like a baby, fuck him."

"Yeah."

"That's how it ended."

"When I spoke to Pete," Chevashore said, "I says, Pete, we keep falling behind, and they won't take any more action. The figure was maybe fifteen or sixteen. He said, Stevie, I stopped betting when we were in New York on the last trip. I'm not betting any more."

"I'm so frustrated," Janszen said. "I have my life's savings sitting over there with some son of a bitch. You know what his attitude is now? You know what he says to me? 'What money?' "

"What? He's crazy. What's the matter with him? He's got the money. He's not broke. Jeez, he cost me money. He caused me nothing but problems."

"I'm going to the Commissioner of Baseball," Janszen announced.

"Oh, wait a minute, Paulie. Aren't you going to get yourself in trouble for that?"

"No."

"Well, you're looking to expose the guy, aren't you?"

"Yeah. I'm going to ruin the motherfucker for doing this to me. He has taken my life's savings now."

"Yeah."

"And I was his friend."

"Yeah."

"I went over and busted my ass for a whole year doing all kinds of little odd jobs for the man. Never got a penny for it. Just because I thought he was my friend. Not because he was a famous ball player, because he was my friend."

Val was not Rose's only New York avenue for betting baseball, Janszen told the investigation. Fat Mike Bertolini was taking two to four dimes a baseball game independently through this period, although Janszen knew that only because Mike had told him that Rose's gambling debt to him was into the hundreds of thousands of dollars. As for his own direct knowledge, Janszen said Rose had switched to Ron Peters, his old local book from Franklin, Ohio, after Val had cut him off. Between mid-May and the All-Star break, Rose won four out of five weeks and came out forty thousand dollars ahead. Within this critical damning three months, Janszen described Rose's methodology. It was the classic pattern of the inside trader.

"He would call up different managers and ask them how certain pitchers' arms were, and if they were going to play certain players that night. He would try to get as much information as he could about a game, so then he could go ahead and either bet the game or not bet the game. Once, he called up Sparky [Anderson] to find out how [pitcher] Jack Morris's arm was."

Rose had his sentimental favorites. He always bet on Dwight Gooden, Mike Scott, Bret Saberhagen, and Jimmy Key, all of whom would be favorites in anyone's book. He also bet nostalgically on the Phillies, even though the team lost nine out of eleven in late June 1987. About betting on the Reds, however, Rose was principled. He never bet against them, and he only abstained once from betting for them. That was a time when a declining Mario Soto was slated to pitch, and the gambling manager did not like the way his pitcher was throwing in the warm-up, so he did not bet on the game. In fact, Rose was downright mad at Soto: the pitcher had cost him money in the past. Soon enough, Soto was sent down to Triple-A ball. "Rose didn't want to put money down on a guy when he didn't know if [the pitcher] really still had it," Janszen told baseball.

But his principle about betting the Reds to win had its price, too.

"If I had enough money riding on a game," Rose told Janszen, as Janszen now remembered it, "I'd think about throwing the game. There are a lot of easy ways to do it. Hell, Paul, I could pinch hit a guy at the wrong time or hit-and-run at the wrong time."

Therein lay the ultimate rationale behind gambling as the game's most serious offense. It was a mortal danger pointed directly at the integrity of baseball as a fair, honest test of skill. The knife of gambling pointed far more lethally at the heart of the contest than did drug use or child molesting or a host of other tawdry sins. When Giamatti read the deposition, the words of Judge Landis might well have reoccurred to him: "No player who sits in a conference with a bunch of gamblers where the ways and means of throwing games are discussed and does not promptly tell his club about it, will ever again play professional baseball." Premeditated and clandestine, Rose's sin was cheating for personal gain, and no Big Fixer was compelling him to do it.

Within the first three days of its life, Giamatti's investigation had the most compelling testimony it would ever receive. The information came from a witness who had nothing to gain except the supreme satisfaction of revenge. To document his testimony, Janszen had provided betting records from April 7 to May 13 with Val, although he had destroyed his records from the Peters period. More importantly, he provided three of Rose's own betting sheets, which he had stolen from Rose's house "when I began to worry about him reimbursing me for the loan that I made."

These records had to be expertly analyzed. If accurate and authentic, Janszen's records showed that Rose, over a thirty-six-day period, had bet more than $16,000 a day, or a total of nearly $600,000. The records were checked against Janszen's telephone records. Calls to Chevashore in Florida, Val in New York, and Peters in Franklin squared with Janszen's notes. Usually, the calls were made by Janszen only minutes before the opening pitch. Generally, he also made long-distance calls of short duration around 9:30 P.M. to a sports line to check on the night's scores around the league.

Authenticating the three Rose betting sheets was more problematic. Janszen had provided only copies. The originals remained with the FBI, and the FBI had no authority to cooperate with the private baseball investigation. Indeed, the Bureau was intensely aware of its duty not to cooperate because it had its own on-going investigation and its own secret grand jury. If the sheets contained Rose's fingerprints, the FBI was not saying. The handwriting on the sheets might be verified, although in the universe of law enforcement, it was generally more difficult to get an expert to certify handwriting than to confirm a fingerprint.

Because the full-scale baseball investigation remained secret during its first month, Dowd proceeded under orders from Giamatti with the methods of a covert CIA operation. "From the outset," Giamatti would say later, "I believed that the confidentiality of the proceeding was essential in trying to maintain the dignity of it as well as the privacy of Pete Rose, who is a public figure, as well as the capacity of counsel on any side to function adequately in an atmosphere that wasn't bombarded or harassed by the press."

The form that the investigation took in Tampa on March 16 was awe-inspiring. For Rose's handwriting test, Dowd rented a separate bungalow at the Hyatt Hotel and brought in a force of security men with bulging suit jackets and earpieces. Rose was slipped in secretly, and there he rendered samples of his grade-school block letters for the examination of an ex-FBI agent with twenty-seven years of experience as a document examiner. Not only was Rose required to write a sheet with the alphabet and then a sheet with made-up names, such as "Ulysses T. Velez," but then he was asked to copy letter for letter, word for word, the notations of the three incriminating betting sheets. The expert then compared the two sets under his stereoscopic binocular microscope, as well as by using low-power magnifiers and "controlled illumination," in order to determine, he said, "writing skill, letter formation, slant, pressure variations, height ratios, beginning and ending strokes, speed of writing, rhythm, and all of the little subtle movements of the writing instrument which reflect the habitual unconscious writing habits of Pete Rose."

The expert, Richard E. Casey, then made twenty-four points about Rose's childlike handwriting, such as "The numeral 2 has a short initial downstroke, a rounded neck and a small loop formed at the bottom left as the ending stroke swings around to the right. However, when the 2 is used in a fraction, the 2 is shaped like a Z."

The original betting slips, Casey concluded, were written by the hand of the subject, Pete Rose.

In forcing Rose to copy the incriminating evidence, the Dowd investigation ran roughshod over the normal constitutional protections that any ordinary criminal defendant would have had. But Rose was not an ordinary second-story man, nor was Dowd bound by constitutional strictures. Rose's refusal to cooperate would have been held against him. Indeed, Dowd had repeatedly warned the Rose attorneys that any failure to cooperate with his investigation would be considered by Bart Giamatti to be contrary to the best interests of baseball and would, in itself, be grounds for suspension. The Rose attorneys permitted this outrageous handwriting test to go forward, as the affable John Dowd kept representing his investigation as "fair and impartial." Still, the surreal, essentially unfair strike force atmosphere of the March 16 event convinced Rose's attorneys that whatever else might be true, Dowd and Giamatti would spare no expense in an effort to nail their client.

From copies of the original betting slips and through these highly questionable investigation methods, baseball could conclude that the betting sheets had been written by Rose, but that was only half of the equation. The other half was denied to them by the FBI, which had dusted the originals and found Rose's fingerprints on two of the three sheets. This information was never in the possession of the Giamatti investigation. But between the handwriting and fingerprint evidence, the fact that Rose had bet on baseball on at least two occasions is absolutely and incontrovertibly established.

After Paul Janszen's two-day interview on February 23–24, the process went forward to authenticate his story with telephone records and other circumstantial evidence. As these reports tended to confirm what Janszen was saying, at least some members of Giamatti's team concluded by early March that he was telling the truth. Janszen was a felon, however. That undermined his credibility. On March 2, baseball's chief of security, Kevin Hallinan, shared his concern directly with his star witness.

"Your involvement in cocaine is going to be an area that is going to be pounded by the other side." (When this statement was shown to Rose's attorneys later, they concluded that Hallinan, at least, had decided Rose was guilty only ten days into the investigation and was already worried about how to bolster Janszen's credibility.) Hallinan had another purpose on March 2; he wanted to prepare Janszen for a lie detector test the next day.

"We have contracted with a guy who has a good track record as far as polygraph expertise," Hallinan told Janszen. "We're going to meet with him, and try and fill him with as much information as possible, so he will have a good knowledge of the case . . . [so] he is able to pose the questions to you that are direct, and there's only one answer. It is not something that has two answers or a trick question or anything like that."

"Okay," Janszen replied.

"He will try to set the stage with you," said Hallinan and then he gave a hypothetical. "Your birthday is February first, and he will say to you, is your birthday February second, and you say yes. He will watch for that kind of reaction, because you are obviously lying. Then he will ask you, is your birthday, February first, and he will see the reaction, the line. It is a very useful investigative tool. It sorts a lot of stuff."

"Once you take it and you pass, it's just another little piece of the puzzle you can put together?" Janszen offered.

"Absolutely right," Hallinan replied.

The only problem was that the next day, Janszen did not pass. He had been asked nine "relevant" questions:

- Concerning Pete Rose and any major league baseball bookie betting on his part, do you intend to answer each question truthfully about that? Janszen answered yes.
- Is it a lie that Pete Rose personally placed bookie baseball bets with you? Answer: no.
- Would you be lying by saying that during 1987, Pete Rose personally placed major league baseball bookie bets with you? Answer: no.
- Did you personally obtain those betting sheets from any place other than Pete Rose's notebook inside his residence? Answer: no.

On all of the above answers, Janszen, according to the polygrapher, was lying.

The test had a second phase.

- Have you told me any lies today about Pete Rose? Janszen answered no.

- Are you falsely reporting that during 1987 Pete Rose placed major league baseball bets with you? Answer: no.
- Is it a lie that Pete Rose owes you money for handling his bookie baseball bets? Answer: no.
- Would you be lying by saying that you personally saw Pete Rose writing his baseball bet action on a sheet of paper? Answer: no.

To these questions as well, Janszen's answers were "deceptive."

Given the fact that lie detector tests are considered an art rather than a science, Dowd demanded a retest, but his star witness would have no part of it. When the idea of a second test was put to him, Janszen stormed angrily out of the room.

David Griem, an attorney for William Robertson, the original polygrapher, was bothered by the way Dowd handled the investigation. Griem characterized Robertson as "a real pro" who saw his role simply as determining the truthfulness of the witness. Griem told an investigator for the Rose legal team that, following Janszen's refusal to take a second polygraph test, Dowd and Robertson exchanged words over the result of the first Janszen polygraph and it was Griem's opinion that Dowd was interested in confirming his own suspicions. Soon after, Dowd hired another polygrapher who certified Janszen's reliability. Whether Dowd ever shared with Commissioner Giamatti the fact that Janszen had flunked his first critical test is unknown.

The wheels continued to grind nevertheless. Three days later, Pete Rose was officially informed that a major investigation of his possible gambling activity was under way, and that a Mr. John Dowd of Washington, D.C., had been hired to conduct a "thorough and fair investigation."

Meanwhile, Giamatti's investigation turned its attention to the bookmaker Ron Peters. Of the three bookies fingered by Janszen—Val, Bertolini, and Peters—as well as the "beard," Steve Chevashore—only Peters might be persuaded to talk voluntarily. Peters was preparing to plead guilty to two felony counts and was on his way to jail for quite a while, whereas the others could only incriminate themselves by admitting to illegal bookmaking. They had nothing to gain from cooperating with a private investigation that might later become public.

On March 13, the baseball cops turned up at Peters's restaurant. To their embarrassing questions about Rose betting on baseball through him, Peters said nothing. A meeting between Peters and

Dowd was set up for two days hence. Immediately after the investigators left, Peters tried to see what he could squeeze out of the situation. Picking up the phone, he called one of Rose's attorney, Bob Pitcairn. After telling the lawyer of baseball's visit and saying he had told them nothing, Peters said in his best, menacing whisper, "I think it would be in Pete's best interest to give me a call."

Peters and his attorney contacted *Sports Illustrated* to see how much the magazine would pay for Peters's story. They secretly taped the call.

On March 15, the baseball investigators had a busy day in Cincinnati. John Dowd met with Rose's attorney and assured him that the Rose side would be provided all the evidence, pro and con, that was developed. He had drawn no conclusions about Rose's guilt or innocence, Dowd proclaimed, and he would not do so in his fair and impartial investigation.

Meanwhile, baseball's security director, Hallinan, met again with Peters. Peters was now eager to cooperate, if something could be worked out with the U.S. Attorney's Office concerning Peters's sentencing for his felony counts. A memorandum of this offer of a quid pro quo was written. Giamatti was later asked about it.

"Were you aware that members of the security staff of the commissioner's office had met on March 15, 1989, with Ron Peters and his attorney?"

"I can't say that I knew it was on March 15, no," Giamatti replied. "I knew that there were meetings."

"Did anyone report to you that [Mr. Peters's attorney] stated to the investigators that it would be very worthwhile for major league baseball to talk to Peters regarding Pete Rose betting on baseball, if something could be worked out with the U.S. Attorney's Office?"

"I can't say that I was aware of that at the time, no," Giamatti replied.

"Were you subsequently informed that [Mr. Peters's lawyer] had [said] words to that effect?"

"No. Mr. Dowd had said that if he found Mr. Peters's testimony to have been corroborated and to have been sustained by other things, he said that he would seek to ask me to say so to a judge."

On April 5, two days after his agreement to plead guilty to cocaine trafficking and tax perjury, Ron Peters was formally deposed under oath by Giamatti's counsel, John Dowd. (Dowd and Hallinan had informally interviewed Peters three weeks previously.) In the preamble of their discussion, before Peters had uttered a single sentence about Pete Rose, Dowd laid out the devil's compact between them: "Correct me if I'm wrong, but in exchange for your full and truthful cooperation with the commissioner, the commissioner has agreed to bring to the attention of the United States District Judge in Cincinnati the fact that you were of assistance to us and that we believe that you have been honest and complete in your cooperation. Is that the understanding?"

"Yes it is," Peters replied.

"And participating in this deposition today is part of that cooperation?"

"Right."

"Now I've asked your counsel to advise me as soon as possible the name of the United States District Judge who will be handling your plea and your sentence. And I will arrange for the commissioner to communicate directly with that judge and outline, confidentially, to the judge what you've done to assist major league baseball in this inquiry."

With Peters's veracity already established, they got down to the business of discovering the truth. Peters laid out a horrendous set of allegations. Extending back to 1984, Rose had bet $2,000 to $5,000 a game on professional football, college basketball, and major league baseball. At times, his bets were placed four to five times a week, and over the entire period of 1984–87, through Gioiosa and Janszen, the total outlay was about a million dollars. On balance, Rose had lost about $150,000 overall.

On baseball, Rose always bet on the Reds. But more important to Peters, Rose had bet heavily on the play-offs in 1986 and won every game. That had cost the bookie a considerable sum of money. As many as six times, Peters had talked with Rose about baseball betting directly over the telephone, conversations in which Rose made no effort to conceal his identity. Because a dispute over $34,000 developed between them—each claiming that the other owed him about that amount—Peters taped a conversation with Rose and then immediately played it back to him.

"What the hell did you do that for?" Rose had cried out in anger.

"Pete, I just want you to know I got this . . . for obvious reasons," Peters said coldly. "Business is business."

In explaining his insurance policy to the baseball investigators, Peters said, "I'd heard that he stiffed other people, so he didn't have a real good reputation." In the parlance of the bookmaking world, Pete Rose was a dud. His marker was worthless. By contrast, Peters was proud of his own honor as a bookmaker. It would be against the bookmaker's "code of ethics" either to solicit a bet or to try to steal another bookie's client. Gioiosa, said Peters, had no such high moral standards. Not only had he stolen $34,000 of Rose's money that was supposed to go to Peters, but upon occasion, Gio would take one betting line from Peters and give a different line to Rose, removing the risk of the bet and raking off the froth for himself. How did Gio explain his treachery?

"He laughed hysterically," Peters told the strong-arm baseball men. "He said he felt like he ought to make something out of this. I didn't care what he did. What he does to Pete Rose is what he does to Pete Rose. I just like the business." Gio had laughed loudly and hysterically one time too many around Rose, and Rose was put out with Gio. There had been complaints about Gio's loud and offensive behavior at the track. The kid was giving the Rose Room a bad name.

As usual with this set of wilting Rambos and bizarre Dick Tracy characters, there was a touch of farce in what the bookie related to the baseball investigators. Peters told of the time Rose had paid a call on him personally at his restaurant in Franklin, Ohio. Rose's red Porsche arrived in a cloud of dust, and behind it, Gio's black Porsche pulled in with Gioiosa and Mike Fry. Rose brought along a black Mizuno bat inscribed to Jonathan's Cafe, but his real purpose was to collect $36,000 in winnings. His boy, Gio, disappeared into the back office in true gangster fashion, while Rose sat down for lunch. There was quite a stir among the clientele. Depending on whom one believed, Rose had either a bowl of chili (Peters's recollection) or a tuna fish sandwich and iced tea (Rose's recollection). In both cases, their eye for detail was meant to display their credibility. But Peters scored on the point: he had never offered tuna fish sandwiches on his menu.

Peters also remembered a display of Rose's special brand of humor. The ball player told a joke about a blind guy coming up to him with a German shepherd, wanting Pete to sign the dog's collar.

"I'll sign anything you got, but get that fucking dog away from me!" Rose exclaimed as Jonathan's filled with raucous belly-laughter.

The baseball detectives were a little slow on the uptake.

"Was it a big black dog?" one flatfoot asked.

"No, this was a blind guy's Seeing Eye dog."

"Was it a shepherd?" Dowd wanted to know.

"Yeah, I think so," replied Peters, no doubt rolling his eyes at these plodding gumshoes, in whose hands the "integrity of baseball" now rested.

More relevant, however, was the time of year. Peters thought Rose's visit was in the summer.

"Would that have been winnings on baseball?" Dowd asked.

"Well . . ." Peters mumbled hesitantly.

"Summertime," Dowd prompted his witness.

"I believe it was, yes," Peters said. "It most likely was."

As Peters fortified his testimony with betting sheets, including a few master sheets, with notations about Rose's betting, therein lay his "full and truthful cooperation" with the baseball investigation.

Now Giamatti had to fulfill his side of the bargain. The arrangement was Dowd's rather than his, and with the gloss of legality the Renaissance scholar was at a disadvantage. Giamatti allowed himself to be dazzled. Dowd's legal stature as a former Mafia prosecutor impressed Giamatti unduly, and he was too eager to show that he had complete confidence in his counsel. A supportive letter to Peters's sentencing judge was the price of Peters's vital testimony against Rose, Dowd had explained to Giamatti. But such a letter would be required only if Dowd was able to corroborate independently what Peters told him. Such letters, said Dowd, were strictly routine. As it became quickly clear, this was horrendously bad legal advice.

By his own account, Giamatti paid very little attention to the entire matter. He told Dowd to draft a letter to the judge and send it up to New York. There is no indication that he questioned his special counsel closely about whether the lawyer had really corroborated Peters's testimony, by whom, or what was their credibility. Had he asked, the answer would have been, at least so far as betting on baseball by Rose from 1984 to late 1986, that there was no other corroboration except Peters's own assistant bookmaker. Only with Paul Janszen's testimony, which itself had dark motives, was there corroboration of baseball betting for a period of three months in 1987.

When Dowd's draft arrived, the commissioner was being asked to represent that Ron Peters, one of two principal accusers of Rose, a convicted tax evader, cocaine trafficker, drug addict, and bookmaker, had given "significant and truthful cooperation" to the baseball investigation, along with "probative documentary evidence" to support his sworn testimony. Giamatti was "satisfied [that] Mr. Peters has been candid, forthright, and truthful with my special counsel." The request was made that the commissioner's letter be kept under seal, until his investigation of Pete Rose was complete. It was implicit that the judge might consider this cooperation in mitigating his sentence for Peters.

The consequences of committing this sweeping endorsement to paper did not seem to occur to Giamatti. It was one thing to be

persuaded in one's mind by the mounting weight of evidence against
Rose, evidence that was being dribbled to Giamatti drop by drop as
it was acquired. It would have been inhuman for Giamatti, especially
given his sentimentality about baseball and his awe for its great
players, not to have been deeply troubled by the damning testimony
of Janszen and Peters. But it was quite another matter to commit to
paper one's growing conviction, if you were to be the ultimate "trier
of fact." A man of Giamatti's sophistication and intellect should have
known better.

The mistake was deeper than that, however. In a deposition
later, Giamatti conceded that one always made judgments as an investigation proceeded, but "I would insist that the findings be subjected precisely to that grid or cross hatching or test of other
perspectives or other information." Against what grid had he tested
Peters's testimony before he endorsed it? The answer was, no grid
whatever. Later, it would be asserted that Peters's testimony was
corroborated by the bookie's betting sheets, but those very sheets
were in the possession of neither Giamatti or John Dowd when
Giamatti wrote his letter. When the sheets arrived, only one bore the
name "Pete," with the notation, "-41,800," and it would never be
subjected to analysis by the Rose side. Pete who?

In effect, Giamatti had ceded to his own special counsel his
commissioner's role to judge all the evidence before making up his
mind. He had abdicated his responsibility to judge the credibility of
Rose's accusers himself. Instead, Giamatti was simply accepting his
counsel's word as to their credibility midstream in the investigation.

Giamatti told his secretary to retype Dowd's draft on the commissioner's letterhead and send the letter off to Cincinnati. He would
describe his role at this point as nothing more than a "human repro-
ductive xerographer," a considerable confession for the Commissioner of Baseball, who had a solemn duty to perform.

Later, in a legal deposition, Giamatti was asked to explain his
action. "I had been told by Mr. Dowd that if he thought this person's
testimony was credible and truthful . . . that he would want me simply to communicate to the judge that this man had been forthcoming
and cooperative with baseball. I considered that kind of a routine
request, as I understood it. I had, frankly, forgotten about it. It did
not make a big impression on me." He did not show the letter to
anyone else, nor seek anyone's advice.

With a hundred different judges in different places in America,
Giamatti's letter might have been just another unpersuasive letter in
the file, but with Carl Rubin of Cincinnati, it was an affront and an

outrage. Judge Rubin saw the letter as confusing two entirely separate matters: a federal criminal matter and a baseball investigation.
The latter had no bearing whatsoever on the former.

Rubin is a bantam fighter: feisty, independent, strong-willed,
with a hot temper that quickly flares. As the senior judge in the
Southern District of Ohio, he had once flown into a rage when over-
worked and underpaid federal judges were denied a 50 percent pay
increase. Rubin promptly announced that if he was going to receive
only an average salary, he would be an average judge and move into
a slow-down. Once Rubin cooled down, he apologized publicly, but
local lawyers knew to beware. He was also a man of set rituals. One
of them was well known: when it came to sentencing, he would brook
interference from no one.

Upon the receipt of Giamatti's letter, Rubin immediately informed Reuven Katz and then called in the district attorney and the
lawyer for Ron Peters. Reading them the letter as if it were the riot
act, he demanded to know if the district attorney had solicited the
scurrilous letter. "No," the district attorney replied with considerable chagrin. "I wish they had asked us about it first."

"I am offended by this," Rubin said acidly. "I don't believe that
it is of any concern to me, zilch, what this man may have done with
the Commissioner of Baseball . . . I will not take this into consideration in [the] sentence imposed upon Mr. Peters." Moreover, the judge
would not keep the letter under seal. He inquired now of the lawyers
how quickly Peters could be brought in for sentencing before Giamatti's letter became public.

There was a wrinkle. Judge Rubin was an ardent Reds fan who
had enjoyed the spirited play of Pete Rose over the years and had
strong opinions about the Baseball Hall of Fame. Regardless of what
Rose may or may not have done off the field, Rubin felt that it would
cheapen the Hall of Fame itself if a player of Rose's accomplishments
was not enshrined. "I resent the baseball commissioner entering into
what I think [is] a vendetta against Pete Rose," Rubin told the attorneys in his chamber. "It seems to me that whatever cooperation Mr.
Peters gave them on their investigation is totally and thoroughly
irrelevant to any charge against Peters, and the idea of confusing the
two of them I just find very offensive. . . . I'm sort of out in center field
all by myself, and I don't want to be. I don't want to get this whole
business confused, and that's why I want to sentence this man as
quickly as possible."

When Judge Rubin angrily told Reuven Katz about the Giamatti letter, Katz's first thought was: "Pete is dead." But it was not

long before his lawyer's sensibility took over. Why let Giamatti decide the Rose case, when he had already decided it, even before a supposedly fair and impartial hearing? Giamatti was biased. He had prejudged the matter. It seemed to confirm what Katz had been told by a baseball insider when the first rumors about Rose began to circulate. Get your hearing quickly from Ueberroth. Ueberroth is only amoral, but Giamatti is crazy! Now, the commissioner's mob prosecutor had cut a cold-hearted deal with a bookie, a cocaine dealer, a convicted felon, promising a supportive letter to his sentencing judge in exchange for the information that the counsel wanted to hear and had to have: that Pete Rose had bet on baseball. If the felon was truthful, the hero was lying—and Pete Rose had not yet even stated his case or confronted his felonious accusers. Make Giamatti the issue, not Rose. From his first reaction as Rose's friend that Pete was dead, Katz now saw new life. He began to think that Giamatti had handed the Rose side an extraordinary gift: with proof of the commissioner's bias, his whole prosecutorial process was tainted!

For the Rose side, the situation was clarifying. Their client had two chief accusers. Both were drug dealers and tax evaders and felons. Janszen was an extortionist who had failed his first lie detector test and who was consumed with hate for Pete Rose. The other was the bookmaker Ron Peters. When the Rose defense turned its attention to Peters's credibility, they received an affidavit from the lawyer of Peters's ex-wife, who had deposed Peters in the past on a variety of topics.

"Ron Peters can not separate truth from fantasy even if he wished to," the affidavit read. "If Mr. Peters would testify under oath that the sun would come up in the morning, I would take great pains to verify his testimony independently."

In his apologia later, Giamatti explained the reason why he had paid so little attention on April 18 to his ill-considered letter to the judge in support of Ron Peters. Two days hence, on April 20, Rose was to give his deposition to Dowd.

"I was much more concerned to make it very clear, and to have it very clear between Mr. Dowd, Mr. Vincent, and myself that when Mr. Rose came to have his deposition taken, that he be shown every material or key or essential piece of information that Mr. Dowd had that was troublesome," Giamatti would say. "I wanted to make sure [that] nothing be left out because I was concerned that Mr. Rose know what was going on and have every chance to know what was going on."

With that in mind, Giamatti flew off to Columbus, Ohio, to give a talk to a Boy Scout luncheon, not about Pete Rose, not even about baseball, but about the decline in moral values in America. Inevitably, a horde of reporters shouted questions about Rose at him. Giamatti put up his hands in a gesture of truce. "I'm not going to say anything. The fairness and scrupulousness of the investigation must be protected. There's no point in plying your marvelously subtle stratagems. I admire them, but they are not going to work. Believe me, I've seen more moves than Air Jordan in the last six weeks."

Meanwhile, on the West Coast, the Reds dropped two in a row to the Dodgers, both shutouts, as the Cincinnati bats went strangely silent. Afterward, Rose caught the red-eye east. With plane changes and time differences, with road construction and a distant destination, he arrived for his critical interrogation having slept only an hour and a half. He was clearly exhausted and unfocused.

"Someone who gets 4,200 major league hits never realizes he's tired," Rose's attorney Bob Pitcairn suggested to Dowd plaintively as they settled in.

"I know," Dowd said.

The site for the deposition had been chosen to avoid the press. For a month, ever since the major league baseball investigation had been announced by the commissioner's office, the press had hovered over the Rose gambling story with an intensity equivalent to that with which they covered Nixon and Watergate. Rose's every move was watched and noted. The offices of his attorneys were staked out, and Rose's handlers had no delusions about the resourcefulness of the reporters. Therefore, Dowd and Rose's third attorney, Roger Makley, both Catholics, had settled on a Mariological seminary in Dayton, thirty miles from Cincinnati. Makley made sure he left for the deposition from a place other than his office. Both lawyers were reasonably sure that the priests and brothers of the Society of Mary would not turn them in to the pagan press, for this was a search for the truth in a morality tale.

In this solemn setting, during the evening of April 20 and the morning of April 21, Dowd assailed Rose for eight hours with questions about Rose's betting, his relationships with his accusers and assorted bookies, his incriminating betting slips, about tapes in which his betting on baseball was discussed, phony checks he had written, his winning of Pik Sixes, and his suspicious telephone records. Rose told little lies. "I don't go to the track in the summertime. I'm playing baseball." And he told big lies. "No one calls me and tells me I owe them money. Because I don't owe anybody a damn dime." He was as boastful as a schoolyard dude. "How do I keep track? I'm pretty good with numbers. . . . I'm a big boy. I can handle cash." He denied that he was a compulsive gambler, and no doubt believed his own denial. "I don't go overboard. I mean, I'm not out of my means." And he made statements that Dowd could easily disprove. "I can honestly look you in the eye and say I met [Ron Peters] one time and never talked to him on the phone." He went into elaborate explanations about why his accusers were saying such nasty things about him. "I'm guilty of one thing in this whole mess, and that's I was a horseshit selector of friends." Peters was a "coke-head" and Janszen was a "scumbag," Gioiosa and Bertolini were liars. Stenger and Fry were, well, crooks. "Those guys could have a quintet the last three months. Because they're all singing. They're all singing a lot. They have to sing or they'll be in Sing Sing. People have a tendency to say things that really aren't true when their ass is on the chopping block."

Soon after Rose gave his deposition, Giamatti read it. If the commissioner felt himself to be in charge of the "moral contours" of the investigation, it is difficult to know where any terra firma might be found. Rose's flawed word stood against the untrustworthy words of unsavory and vengeful lowlifes, all of whom now hoped to get something out of their confessions. Still, Giamatti insisted in his subsequent deposition that Dowd was not being prosecutorial.

"My reading of the Rose deposition was that most of what Mr. Dowd thought was key and critical were documentary in nature, that he presented it to Mr. Rose, that it was not testimony from people so much as it was checks, it was slips, handwritten betting stuff, tapes, checks. . . ."

"Highly selected, wasn't it?" he was challenged.

"No," Giamatti replied. "It was nontestimonial, if you let me make up a word. It wasn't highly selective."

At minimum, that was naive. Dowd had called his interrogation a deposition, but it qualified as such only in the technical sense that Rose swore to the accuracy of his testimony. It had none of the protections that a real deposition would have had in a normal legal proceeding. Over and over, Dowd had made it clear that a failure to cooperate would be reported to the commissioner. That failure itself, not proof of baseball gambling, would result in permanent suspension. The Ruler's powers were absolute, with absolute authority to determine what was in the best interest of baseball. The Ruler should not be angered.

While Dowd paid lip service to Giamatti's fairness and impartiality, he said nothing about the commissioner's letter to the judge about Rose's chief accuser. Dowd did not feel his inquiry to be bound by the principles of natural justice and fair play. Under baseball's rules, those principles applied only to an eventual hearing, if there was one, not to the investigation itself. Dowd could be the consummate prosecutor, liberated from constraint. In interrogating Rose, his questions were framed with the imputation of guilt rather than innocence. To Rose's attorneys, it was as if the Court of Baseball had become the Court of the Star Chamber. Dowd was councillor to the king, Giamatti was Henry Tudor at the end of the Wars of the Roses, where only royal prerogative mattered.

Had Rose's lawyers had the courage, or the stupidity, to use this medieval analogy to the commissioner's inquiry, it might have angered Giamatti as no modern charge could do. He was accustomed to being called a Renaissance Man, not a Man of the Dark Ages.

Furious activity marked the days that followed Rose's deposition, as sensational headlines filled the press. On the Sunday following the deposition, Reuven Katz released the Giamatti letter to Judge Rubin. Giamatti might have compromised himself as a fair and impartial judge by allowing himself to get involved in his own investigation, Katz told a reporter. Judge Rubin himself criticized Giamatti publicly for taking too long to get to the bottom of the Rose case, and the judge's statement about Giamatti's "vendetta" against Rose made its way into the papers. The press had "tried, convicted, and executed Pete Rose," Rubin said.

A day later, the judge removed himself from the Peters sentencing, and a week after that, he removed himself as the judge for Tommy Gioiosa, who now stood charged with tax evasion and drug trafficking. However well-intentioned its motive, Giamatti's letter had now skewed the judicial process in two federal criminal matters.

Nevertheless, what was transpiring in secret in Dowd's Washington law office was the important thing. The chief investigator was writing his report to the baseball commissioner. Having been told by Giamatti that he was to draw no conclusion, make no finding as to the ultimate issue of Pete Rose betting on baseball, Dowd now wrote, "In sum, the accumulated testimony of witnesses together with the documentary evidence and telephone records, reveal extensive betting activities by Pete Rose in connection with professional baseball and in particular Cincinnati Reds during the 1985, 1986, 1987 baseball seasons."

Later, in tortured reasoning, Dowd protested that this was not a conclusion or a finding at all, but merely an "assessment and evaluation" of the evidence. Worse still, if Dowd was exceeding his mandate from Giamatti, Giamatti had every chance to reinstruct his investigator on the profane and moral contours of the investigation. In the weekend before the report was formally submitted, Dowd went to New York expressly to give Giamatti a draft. For a day, Giamatti pored over the draft. He did not merely read and reread it several times but proceeded to edit it. And he gave it to Fay Vincent to do the same. Later, he would say that his editing was merely stylistic, that his reading was merely for grammar.

"Then you recommended changes to the style?" he was asked.

"Mostly in punctuation," he replied. "But I didn't recommend any. . . . No, I didn't make any substantive changes at all."

As embarrassing and compromising as it is that Giamatti edited and commented on a report that was to be formally submitted to him and about which he had a duty to judge and test fairly against Rose's rebuttal, he had no expectation that this involvement would ever be known. He did anticipate that, at some point, the report itself might be released. The English professor in him wanted it to read well.

Apart from these questions about the methods and the procedures of the investigation, the Dowd Report shriveled the soul of A. Bartlett Giamatti. He was profoundly and deeply and morally offended. This was not what he had entered the great game of baseball to do. He wanted to be its great celebrant, its greatest Romantic poet, the human bridge to its historical past. His bent was to hold its great players up to American youth as icons, as near-godlike human beings who reached a level of perfection that was beyond the scope of most mortals. Great players taught the young by showing the way. A Pete Rose was the rightful successor to the heroes of his youth: Gehrig, Ruth, DiMaggio, Williams. Instead, the Dowd Report was like a fifty-ton load of manure dropped in his lap, and his duty was to dispose of it.

In private, to his closest friends, Giamatti turned on Rose with moral rage. Rose was not godlike but a low life. The terms Giamatti used were not those of the former John Hay Whitney Professor of the Humanities: Rose was a scumbag; he had treated people around him like rodents; baseball was peering into a sewer; the player had defiled the national treasure. That Rose was possibly the greatest player of the modern age made his crime that much more evil.

All his life, Bart Giamatti's view of human existence was Manichean. Life was a primal struggle between the forces of light and the forces of darkness. No gray scale existed for him. He believed in the search for truth and believed that truth could be found at the end of the day. If you could discover truth, why deal? In the Rose case, in the unlikely arena of sport, Giamatti had found his paradigm.

On May 11, Giamatti wrote formally to Pete Rose and informed him that a report on gambling allegations had been received. Pursuant to the commissioner's power to investigate and judge activity deemed "not in the best interests of the national game of baseball," the commissioner intended to hold a hearing in two weeks. The Dowd Report and its exhibits were attached to Giamatti's letter.

Under the charter of baseball, Giamatti had no obligation to hold a hearing. In his absolute power, he could have banished Rose then and there. But it had become not a matter of guilt or innocence, as much as of tactics and public relations. Giamatti needed to go through the proper channels, to give Rose his day in court and provide the appearance of natural justice in a judicial-like proceeding. Had the commissioner banished the hero without a hearing, a firestorm over his unfairness and arrogance would have surely followed and could have hurt both Giamatti and the office of the commissioner.

Not surprisingly, the Rose lawyers were appalled by the Dowd Report. Robert Pitcairn, Jr., wrote the first official response to Dowd:

> In my opinion, [your report] is no more than the bellicose, repetitive arguments of a prosecutor who knows he cannot make his case but is trying to confuse the jury with speculative, tainted evidence. In fact, most of the information you describe as circumstantial evidence is not evidence at all and would never be admitted into evidence in a court of law. . . .
>
> What puzzles me is why you would engage in a hatchet job after you assured us repeatedly that you were conducting a fair and impartial investigation. The Report goes beyond mere bias on your part. It shows desperation to provide support for action Mr. Giamatti apparently wants to take. If this Report is your idea of fair play and natural justice, I feel sorry for you.

Three days later, Pitcairn wrote to Giamatti, demanding that the commissioner remove himself entirely from the Rose case. "You allowed yourself to become involved in a direct conflict of interest when you participated in the investigation," Pitcairn wrote. "Prior to Mr. Rose being given any right of due process, you solicited, received, and pronounced truthful the testimony of a drug dealer."

Giamatti responded a few days later. He declined to withdraw, saw no reason why he should "abdicate" his responsibilities as commissioner, and denied that he had prejudged the case. Efforts to make a commissioner withdraw from a case over supposed bias or prejudice had happened before, Giamatti pointed out, but no commissioner had ever done so. "In my judgment, such withdrawal would be inconsistent with the purpose of the Major League Agreement and the unique authority and responsibilities conferred upon the Commissioner of Baseball." He had every intention to be evenhanded.

Pitcairn replied a day later with his disappointment: "We do not understand how you can seriously believe that the procedures you have outlined [for a hearing] comport with anyone's idea of fair play." He requested a thirty-day delay for the hearing, which Giamatti granted. The new date for the Rose hearing was set for June 26.

That Giamatti suddenly found himself being cast as the villain wounded him deeply. All his life he had prided himself on his fairness, his worldliness, his lack of prejudice, his civility, his precision of thought and word. Now he was caught and trapped by, of all things, an imprecise, naive, and unwise letter of his own making, and he did not know how to defend it. The case was moving into an adversarial proceeding. It was becoming ugly and personal. The issue of Rose's gambling was being set next to Giamatti's prejudice. It was moving toward a showdown, not of issues but of people: Rose versus Giamatti. Why was it that it always seemed to happen that way in his life?

For Rose, the pressure was no less intense. With every passing day, new charges were forthcoming, while old denials were proven to be lies. On the surface, he was the same old Pete: optimistic, never down, seemingly unflappable, always competitive and defiant. He harnessed his enormous ability to concentrate his mind on simply getting through this ordeal. He knew he was neither intelligent nor educated, but he had the extraordinary mental discipline of a superior athlete and he applied that now. With each new revelation in the press, even the reports that were false and misleading, he tried not to pay too much attention. In his own house, his wife, Carol, was going down the drain, in the phrase of one who knew, as she moved into the last trimester of her pregnancy. Over in Maryland, where his son Petey was a struggling third baseman in Double A ball, the crowd derisively waved dollar bills in the stands when Petey came to bat. Rose tried not to let these family troubles shake his resolve. His cockiness was losing its charm in Cincinnati, however. Each bombshell lost him a little more credibility, a little more support.

"I could have gotten out of that situation," a cab driver was to say contemptuously, as he drove across the river toward the stadium.

"Back in the spring, Pete should have apologized, declared that he would seek help, ask for forgiveness and support from the fans. But he wanted to fight it. He made a fool out of the commissioner, a fool out of the fans, a fool out of his own ball club. Then he got caught in a lot of lies. If he had done what I say in the spring, there never would have been a big investigation."

"Pete Rose Way" should be renamed "Gambling Way," people were saying. The popular song "Rambling Rose" was applied boisterously to Pete. When Bob Hope came to town for an event, everyone waited anxiously for his Pete Rose joke. Inevitably, Johnny Carson found the situation irresistible.

"I could be in trouble tonight," Carson greeted his audience, "Pete Rose bet against my monologue."

In the clubhouse, the scandal was wearing on everyone. For the players, it was distracting and disconcerting to have their locker room turned into something akin to the courthouse steps. It would not be long before the tensions affected their play, and the team began to slide in the standings. Every day, the story for the beat reporters was to watch Pete refute the latest charges, and it got difficult to find out who would be pitching the following Tuesday. The sports press began to write the story negatively, not so much out of malice as fatigue. It was regularly called the "grim vigil."

Rose was confused about what was happening to him. He did not understand why his old friends were turning on him. To his closest friends, such as Reuven Katz, he could say, with real sincerity and genuine hurt, "Why are they doing this to me?" As he heard that once friendly reporters were hovering around those disgruntled players, including Nick Esasky and Dave Parker, whom he had traded, he would ask about his former friends in the media, "Why are they harassing me like this?"

Meanwhile, as the story of a possible Mafia connection for Rose's betting appeared, David Letterman offered a list of tips for Rose. Among them was: "Every time you see a baseball bat, be thankful it's not breaking your legs."

As their thirty-day extension began, the Rose attorneys surveyed a set of unattractive options. If Giamatti would disqualify himself, they were prepared to go forward with a hearing, but the commissioner had stubbornly refused and was not likely to change his mind. They bridled under the archaic nature of the original Major League Agreement of 1921, sometimes referred to as the bible of baseball, but it was far from sacred. That charter never envisioned the magnitude of the baseball business. It had been drafted in a day when only a few players could even make a living playing baseball. If Rose were suspended, he stood to lose millions. Staggering property rights were involved. Consequently, his right to due process was that much more important. Yet to his handlers, that right had already been trampled. The former director of the players union, Marvin Miller, described Rose's rights in a hearing wryly. "He has the right to put his head in the guillotine," Miller said.

To file a lawsuit, on the other hand, was not a decision lightly taken. Technical questions of fact and of law were involved, for baseball would surely argue that it was a private business and that Rose's transgression was simply a violation of his contract. Baseball could be defeated only if it could be proven that the commissioner had acted in an arbitrary, capricious, and vindictive fashion. The absolute power of the commissioner had been repeatedly upheld in the courts. The chance of eventual success was slim, while the delay in reaching a decision could only sour Rose's public further, not to mention the hundreds of thousands of dollars that the suit would cost Rose.

On June 19, one week before the scheduled date of Giamatti's hearing, Rose and his lawyers decided to damn the torpedoes, and *Peter Edward Rose v. A. Bartlett Giamatti* was filed in the Court of Common Pleas of Hamilton County, Ohio. Rose sought relief from the threats of "irreparable harm to his reputation" and protection of his right "to be judged fairly by an unbiased decisionmaker." The court was asked to restrain baseball from holding its hearing on June 26. The language directed against Giamatti was harsh. The suit asked "that punitive damages be awarded against Giamatti in a sum sufficient to punish him for his unfair and outrageous conduct in the way he has handled from the outset the proceedings against Pete Rose."

Two days later, Giamatti responded in an affidavit with his oft-stated denials. He added only one new thought. The 1989 season was nearly half over, and it had become the season of the Rose scandal. The matter had to be brought to an expeditious resolution. "Major League Baseball must move quickly to assure the public's confidence in the integrity of the game."

The commissioner's standing in Cincinnati courts was scarcely lofty, however. In that venue, the best interests of a citizen's constitutional rights transcended the best interests of the game of baseball. After three days of court testimony, in which neither Rose nor Giamatti participated, Judge Norbert Nadel granted Rose's request to prevent baseball from holding a hearing for two weeks. If Giamatti's hearing were held on the following day, June 26, as scheduled, the judge said, Rose's reputation would be irreparably harmed. Such a hearing would be "futile, illusory, and its outcome a foregone conclusion."

"The commissioner has prejudged Rose," Judge Nadel declared. That night in Riverfront Stadium, someone hoisted a banner that read, "Pete 1, Bart 0." Stadium security asked the fan to take it down.

Giamatti reacted in anger. Promising to fight the ruling tooth and nail, he said, "The more this kind of thing goes on, the less inclined I would ever be to consider [removing myself]. I have been challenged in my own personal self here. I am not inclined to roll over."

On June 29, Rose's lawyers finally got their shot at their arch villain. They had retained Robert Stachler, a gravel-voiced street fighter with an exalted reputation in Cincinnati as the city's foremost litigator. His first task was to take Giamatti's deposition in their lawsuit. Stachler had grown up rugged on the pavements of Dayton, had played football with Chuck Knoll at the University of Dayton before he had entered the paratroops and served in Korea. Over the years, his reputation in the courtroom rested on his perseverance—and his instinct for the jugular. In his interrogation of Giamatti, Stachler wanted to accomplish three things. Certain things about the Dowd-Giamatti process needed to be discovered, such as how the final report was prepared and how well Giamatti understood legal concepts such as due process and the burden of proof, which were supposed to govern baseball's proceeding against Rose. Stachler's main task was to nail down the central contention of the Rose camp: that Giamatti had made up his mind and could not judge Rose fairly and impartially. But most important, Stachler wanted to take the measure of Giamatti the man. Stachler wanted to probe and push Giamatti, to annoy or anger him, to see how he would react to certain charges, so that he would know how to impeach Giamatti later on the witness stand in open court. Stachler approached the deposition methodically, confidently. How many times in trial practice, he chortled to himself, do you have a damning piece of evidence in the form of a letter, where the key witness is a professor of English? Stachler was looking forward to the day.

Giamatti arrived at the opulent Georgetown law offices of John Dowd in the company of several lawyers. His lazy foot dragged perceptibly, and he looked tired. The dark circles under his eyes had become roiling storm clouds beneath his black eyes, but in the longer range, the low pressure system had hovered stationary within him for weeks. The pressure showed dramatically. He had spent about three hours in preparation for his deposition. Dowd had counseled him about what to expect, and he had refamiliarized himself with a few key documents. It would not be enough.

At the outset of his grilling, as Giamatti lit the first in his chain of cigarettes, Stachler wished to establish that the commissioner was a man of words and a man of letters. They went through the salient points of the distinguished résumé, including his authorship of several books and a dozen scholarly articles.

"I don't think any of the articles I authored were very important, Mr. Stachler," Giamatti said revealingly.

Shortly into the session, they sailed into the Rules of Procedure for Major League Baseball, specifically that any proceeding against a baseball player or manager should be handled "in general like judicial proceedings and with due regard for all the principles of natural justice and fair play." To Giamatti, these were philosophical and aesthetic, rather than legal, concepts. At the first mention of major league rules, Giamatti glanced nervously to his left at his attorneys, and Stachler brought him up short.

"I don't want to be rude, Mr. Giamatti, but if you will kindly look directly at me and turn your chair this way, I would appreciate it."

The scold seemed to fluster Giamatti. He apologized and lit another cigarette as he got down to the nub of the one he was smoking.

A lengthy and interesting colloquy into the principles of fairness and natural justice followed, a discourse to which Giamatti seemed to rise enthusiastically, as if he were the Socratic teacher again, back in a humanities seminar at Ezra Stiles, turning a question over and examining it from every side. He did not seem to appreciate that he was headed into a trap. Playing with the shadings of difference between the two concepts, like the linguist and semanticist that he was, he expressed his desire that any hearing for Pete Rose be characterized by these concepts, as he understood them. He tacked into puzzling digressions.

"When I say baseball, I don't simply mean the activity on the diamond," the witness said. "I mean the whole universe of activities, attitudes that ought to be fair and just that govern the environment of that actual playing of the game which itself, after all, must be conducted according to rules that are meant to level the field, if you will. So I don't see them as separate."

"Would you consider that the investigation that was conducted of Pete Rose, the results of it, to become eventually part of the proceedings before you?" Stachler asked.

"I asked Mr. Dowd, Mr. Stachler," he began and then stopped. "I am sorry, I glanced to my left. . . . Let me look out the window here. . . . I want to think. I want to be clear, and I want to be able to think. I want to be able to think. I don't want to have you sitting there wondering why I am sitting here staring at you. You chided me appropriately. I am trying not to look at anybody."

Stachler peered, fascinated, at the witness in his cloud of smoke and haze of words, as if the litigator were a slugger who had unexpectedly weakened his opponent and had him on the ropes early. Stachler made a mental note: on the stand, alone, before an audience including national media, unable to smoke, Giamatti could never withstand this pounding. This early faltering was surprising. Stachler had a preconceived image of the Commissioner of Baseball. By definition, he would be a man of power and an intimidating presence, a man with nerves of steel. That was not what Stachler saw before him now. The importance was there all right, but it took the form of self-importance that made Giamatti vulnerable. For a literary man, Giamatti was loose on facts, loose on words, and seemed confused and uncertain about the very legal concepts that were supposed to govern his judicial-like proceedings. A cigarette burnt out, and Giamatti's lighter did not work. Ostentatiously, he looked to the right, as he reached to the left, for his attorneys to provide him with a match.

"I'm not allowed to look at you," he said out of the corner of his mouth. Stachler saw the gesture as that of a weak and insecure man.

For two hours, they jousted, with Stachler thrusting and Giamatti absorbing the thrust as if he were a feather pillow. And then they broke for a sumptuous power lunch, which was catered in the fashion of a four-star restaurant. Giamatti was jovial and loquacious. As he ate, he smoked simultaneously, a process that amazed his fellow diners, if only for the dexterity it required.

After lunch, the interrogator honed in on the Peters letter itself. Stachler took up the words of the letter one by one. What did *candid* mean to Giamatti? . . . and *forthright?* . . . and *truthful?* Then he put the words together in a sentence. "Based upon other information in our possession, I am satisfied Mr. Peters has been candid, forthright, and truthful with my special counsel." Did it not stand both to reason and to logic? Peters had testified that Pete Rose bet on baseball. Giamatti had seen that testimony. How could it possibly mean anything other than that Giamatti believed on April 18 as he wrote the letter that Pete Rose had bet on baseball?

Giamatti flatly denied it. It was not his opinion but Dowd's! He was merely expressing Dowd's view. It was his opinion of Dowd's opinion, his view of Dowd's view. He had not paid much attention to the letter.

Stachler was appalled. "Let me ask you as an English scholar, as an English professor, as an English authority, as a doctor of English, are you expressing his view, when you say, based upon other information in our possession, 'I am satisfied Mr. Peters has been candid, forthright, and truthful with my special counsel'?"

"'You, sir, with splendid gifts which I wish I had, have read that to emphasize the first person pronoun, *I*. What I am satisfied is that Mr. Peters has been candid, truthful, and forthright with my special counsel . . . in my special counsel's opinion. *I am satisfied* that is Mr. Dowd's opinion, and that is how I read that sentence." As the lawyers around the table scratched their heads, Giamatti said he was merely engaged in a "ministerial act." The sentence said to the judge that "I am transmitting to you in a kind of ministerial way the views of my special counsel."

For several more hours, the quibbles continued, until at last, mercifully, Stachler moved on, convinced in his mind that he had proven Giamatti's prejudice and that he had the means to destroy Giamatti with his own words later in a public forum. Instinctively, he moved to a theme that was deep in Giamatti's past. Did the commissioner consider himself to be under personal attack? Was he being personally wronged?

"I don't feel a personal animosity or sense of aggrievement against any one person," Giamatti replied. "I recognize that these are terribly difficult, grave, troublesome, awful circumstances. I recognize that people have absolutely every right to pursue whatever recourse that is lawful to them. I have a personal disappointment which is not with anybody but internal to myself. That is that I wanted desperately to have confidentiality envelop what I knew wasn't a secret, but confidentiality envelope an investigation, whether it resulted in a hearing or not, that would allow for a measure of dignity, for fairness, for impartiality to have its play. That, I am sorry to say, will always haunt me, as something that I was not able to pull off."

Five hours into his interrogation, the wreckage of Bart Giamatti was clear to both sides. At times, he seemed ready to shake. He did shake with anger when the suggestion hung in the air that he was an essentially unfair and prejudiced man. He stood by his statement, made earlier to the press, that he preferred those who threw baseballs to those who slung mud, and that he would fight tooth and nail to uphold his right and his duty to judge Pete Rose. Occasionally, he confessed, he was a "docile and supine creature," but not now, not with this matter. He was merely waiting until the entire "ecosystem" of the Rose case was presented to him. It was a word he had used some years back, at his beloved Yale, but then, he had added the phrase "like a swamp." The Rose case had become that to him, a swamp and a sewer.

When his interrogation was over, devastated and drained though he was, Giamatti did an extraordinary thing. Rising from his chair, he moved around the table and embraced Stachler.

"You are an honorable man, Mr. Stachler," Giamatti said and launched into a genial reference to the Tafts of Ohio, in whose Cincinnati law firm Stachler practiced. With a man capable of mood swings like this, Stachler thought to himself, you know you're dealing with a very volatile situation.

In the days that followed the deposition, the strategists for major league baseball became profoundly worried, both for their case and for their commissioner's personal welfare. Bart had to get some rest, for he was clearly exhausted. The commissioner had done poorly, and his lawyers knew it. But there was no rest. The Rose case was coming to a climax, to the ninth inning. Who would win and who would lose was a closer call than the public realized. If it came to a trial, it was going to be a bloodbath. The substance of the investigation went against Rose: he had bet on baseball. The process of the investigation went against Giamatti: he had prejudged the case. In all likelihood, both antagonists would be destroyed in a trial. The consequences for baseball itself would be great and unpredictable.

That was no concern of Stachler's. He was preparing for war. So too was baseball, as the legal team of the commissioner acquired an Ohio trial lawyer equal to Stachler in experience and tenacity. They met within a week of Giamatti's deposition.

"Giamatti can not get on that witness stand," baseball's litigator said forcefully. "This case has got to be settled."

Stachler took that under advisement and pushed forward. A few days later, he was in New York to meet with Fay Vincent, who had assumed overall charge of the legal defense of Giamatti's actions on baseball's behalf. Stachler was open to the possibilities of a settlement, just as he put the deputy commissioner on notice that in lieu of a settlement, he planned to present a withering, frontal attack on the despotic institution of major league baseball in the next round of the court case.

"You are not going to want to read it," Stachler said menacingly to Vincent.

To this threat, Vincent collected himself. Leveling a stare at Stachler, and with a tone of controlled passion that spoke more to his deep friendship for Bart Giamatti than to the bluster of opposing attorneys, he said, "Mr. Stachler, you have done more harm to baseball than any single person in seventy years of the game's history."

For the next six weeks, *Rose v. Giamatti* bounced around the legal field of southern Ohio, caroming from Cincinnati to Columbus, from Common Pleas to U.S. Federal Court, to the Sixth Circuit Court of Appeals and back again. The sports pages were filled with terms that fans were happy to ignore: preliminary injunctions versus permanent injunctions, remandings and restraining orders, diversity of citizenship and injunctive relief. If Rose seemed ahead with Judge Nadel's decision proclaiming Giamatti's bias, he was set back again when the decision was discarded as hometown justice and widely criticized as a misguided intrusion of the court system into a private, administrative matter. Rose's legal maneuverings began to be compared with a filibuster. It began to look as if he would finish out the poisonous season as the Reds manager, despite Giamatti's desire to banish him, the Reds desire to fire him, the fans' desire to hang him from the foul pole. As time went on, some owners began to second-guess Giamatti. They complained privately that the commissioner should have suspended Rose first and then held a hearing only if Rose appealed. In Washington, in late July, Giamatti showed his frustration.

"There has been a historic wisdom of the law in this country not to intrude upon private businesses, including baseball," the commissioner said, as a Senate task force was meeting to ponder the expansion of baseball in three years. "This is what happens when the courts intrude. The result is to slow down and make vastly more complex and vastly more frustrating for millions a process which was otherwise very clear, precisely laid out." He did not mention his own role in prolonging the process.

Whoever was winning in the courts, Giamatti was taking control of public opinion. As Rose hid and dodged, dissembled and delayed, Giamatti could say that all he wanted was his rightful hearing on the substance of the charges. That was the only hearing baseball fans cared about as well. Did Rose do these awful things or didn't he? To hell with this talk about rights. Fans wanted a resolution, a definitive finding. They wanted an end, so they could get back to baseball. It was only these clever, scheming, high-priced lawyers of Rose's,

Giamatti could imply, who were preventing him and the baseball public from getting to the final truth.

Expressions of support and encouragement came to Giamatti from many quarters, including from academics who had never quite understood why Bart had not stayed with them. The president of Boston University, John Silber, wrote: "When you resigned the presidency of Yale to become president of the National League . . . I never understood why you thought the job was any more worthwhile than continuing your work at Yale. That is, I failed to understand until the Rose case came along. Now, it is abundantly clear why the position is worthy of your concern! In fact, I feel foolish for not having known it all along. The American people want their baseball players to be worthy mentors to their children: men who are free from drugs, from gambling, from crime, and above reproach. Your determination to uphold the highest standards of the game is deeply appreciated by all Americans who enjoy baseball and especially by all those who love it."

Giamatti replied with appreciation. "You understand precisely what is at issue and why it is important that institutions like this one are as worthy of defense as institutions like the one that nourished me," Giamatti wrote. "People in baseball ask me all the time how the pressure of this latest episode is. I don't really tell them that compared to what you do and face in the course of a year, this is not really pressure at all."

The commissioner was showing off. It was true that academic politics were more complicated and subtle (and petty). It was true that, in his own mind, Rose's was an open and shut case and that Giamatti considered himself to be absolutely on the right side of the issue. It was true that this talk about due process was all for appearance's sake and not mandatory under major league rules. But Rose was a national—indeed, international—figure, and his case was far-flung in its scope. Its proper resolution had profound implications for the sport Giamatti loved. The national press was on the phone to him every day. The pressure was indeed immense.

In fact, the tension was corroding him internally. His emotional engagement made the physical toll greater than it would have been had he been merely another coldhearted businessman. In July, old friends were shocked at his physical deterioration. He had ballooned to being perhaps eighty pounds overweight, the consequence of too many elaborate lunches at the 21 Club. When overeating was combined with his chain-smoking, the premonition of disaster occurred to many. Yale friends were too polite to confront him about this "sweet negligence." Baseball friends were told to mind their own business when they were brash enough to mention it. Moreover, he became delusional about the stature the Rose case would impart to his career as a national figure. To a dear friend, he talked about using the commissionership as a bridge to national politics, about establishing New York residency, running for the U.S. Senate or the New York governorship, and then for the presidency of the United States! He liked the notion of himself as a second Woodrow Wilson, but a Yale rather than a Princeton version, with more wit and humor.

In this final stage of their conflict, Giamatti's self-indulgence contrasted with Rose's mental toughness.

Then Rose had his own lapse. On July 30 and 31, the *Washington Post* printed a long, two-part series on the scandal, the second part of which contained admissions by Rose that he had bet illegally on sports other than baseball with the likes of Gioiosa, Peters, and Janszen. This was nothing new—Rose had confessed as much to Giamatti in the first, February 20 meeting—but now, the tough customers behind Giamatti saw their opening. Vincent seized on these "public confessions" and asserted in private, to the press, and to the court that Rose's admissions alone were enough to banish him from baseball, quite apart from the question of whether he had bet on baseball. The commissioner's side asked to be liberated from the court's overbroad restrictions: give baseball the freedom of action outside the question of baseball betting. To Reuven Katz, Fay Vincent said bluntly that baseball had every intention of tossing Rose out of the game for his association with undesirables. If the Rose legal team persisted in its battle, baseball would bankrupt Rose as well.

This financial hardball was the turning point. For the first time, Rose had an incentive to settle and a disincentive to continue. Behind the scenes, the serious negotiations got under way. On the surface, *Rose v. Giamatti* loitered on in the courts. In late July, Rose's attorneys were still trying to get their case out of federal court and back into the more friendly venue of state court. But on July 31, that request to remand was denied. Rose appealed. Giamatti responded by setting yet another date for his hearing, August 17, the same date that the Sixth Circuit Court of Appeals would decide Rose's appeal of the July 31 ruling. Regardless of what was decided on August 17 in federal court, there would still be yet another round in federal court. If it got that far, Giamatti would have no choice but to testify in open court and be cross-examined. Avoiding that potential disaster gave baseball its incentive to settle.

Vincent's first offer was banishment for ten years. (That is worth remembering about current-commissioner Vincent's initial thinking on when and if Rose might ever be reinstated to baseball.) Katz did not like the word *banish*. Moreover, he would accept no stiff penalty that would be interpreted as an admission of guilt on baseball betting. There could be no finding that Rose bet on baseball: that was nonnegotiable. How about seven years? Vincent wondered. Katz declined for the same reasons. They wrangled and bantered.

In due course, Katz fell back on the language of the rules. Rule 21 (d) governed betting on ball games. To Katz, that was not applicable. But Rule 21 (f) governed other unspecified misconduct that was not in the best interests of baseball. For infractions of that kind, whatever kind they might be, a club employee could be placed on the "ineligible list." If the infraction was serious enough, a man could be declared permanently ineligible. Once on this death row of baseball, the guilty party could apply for reinstatement after one year.

In this hazy area, the negotiators found common ground and came to an agreement.

At the New York Hilton, at precisely 9:00 A.M. on August 23 and exactly six months after Giamatti's investigation of Rose began, the commissioner stepped before the press and banished Pete Rose forever from the game of baseball. As he stood before the huge banner of Major League Baseball, which might as well have been the American flag, Giamatti's words fell with hammer force. They were crisp, direct, eloquent, passionate, final. Rose was more than fired from his game. He was ostracized, expelled, driven away. He was proclaimed an outcast, an exile, a pariah. He was not employed nor was he employable by any phase of organized baseball, not by a team in the major or minor leagues, not by a broadcast organization that was approved by a team. He could not participate in an Old Timers game that was sanctioned by baseball, nor attend dinners that were approved officially, nor could he set foot in a team clubhouse or front office.

There was something biblical—indeed, Old Testament—about the punishment. Adam had been banished from Eden. Cain had been banished from the presence of the Lord. In the Book of Samuel, the "King doth not fetch home again his banished." It had happened to Cicero in ancient Rome, and in that time, so dear to Giamatti, banishment implied the confiscation of property, as it now did for Rose in the present day. Chaucer and Shakespeare had imposed banishment on their villains. Just as the banished were meant to be cast out in the desert or upon vast oceans, so the banisher was necessarily a

King or an Emperor or a God or a Commissar or a colonial Puritan. Parole or pardon was not implied—it would be "a tad premature" to talk about that just then, Giamatti said—even though he laid out the manner whereby the curse might be lifted sometime in the distant future.

The judgment on Rose was "the sad end of a sorry episode." One of baseball's greatest heroes had "stained" the game, and the game had been hurt. It would emerge stronger, however, for the commissioner's office had come through a difficult test with its absolute powers affirmed and the principle established that no man, no matter how exalted, was above the game itself. For Giamatti, the whole episode had been about two things: living by the rules, and taking responsibility for one's actions. Rose had broken the game's most fundamental rule. Now, he had accepted the game's ultimate punishment. No one should be in doubt that in another similar situation this commissioner would use every legal and ethical means "to root out offending behavior." He would be vigilant in protecting baseball against blemish and disgrace.

The country was witnessing a rare sight. The words alone were surprising: *disgrace, banishment, integrity, authenticity, idealism,* and the *purchase* that the national game had on the national soul. Here was a leader who had been through a difficult and painful and debilitating process, who had agonized and had even been badly mistaken along the way, but who, at the end, spoke plainly and directly from the heart with natural eloquence. He quibbled no longer. He did not get technical or legalistic. There were no pauses or mumbles. Without regret or qualification, he took a simple and clear moral position.

After his formal statement, the first question was whether he personally believed that Pete Rose bet on baseball, including on his own team. No doubt, Giamatti expected the question. The technical legal agreement between the parties had specifically avoided the issue. An agreement existed only because it had been avoided. For days, the lawyers had wrangled over the question, and it had been agreed that there would be no formal finding.

A formal finding, Giamatti said now, could only come out of a formal hearing, and Rose had not wanted a formal hearing. Giamatti had been asked for his personal opinion, someone reminded him. Had Giamatti been almost any other leader in America, especially if he had been legally trained, his answer would have deflected the question with a literal response. That was not Giamatti. The country deserved a definite, final, clear resolution to this appalling episode. The agreement did not bar him from expressing his personal outrage.

This was a moment, as he had stated in a lecture on leadership a year before, for moral courage.

"In the absence of a hearing and therefore in the absence of evidence to the contrary," he began looking down, shuffling his papers on the lectern . . . and then up, into the eyes of his questioner, "I am confronted by the factual record of Mr. Dowd. On the basis of that, yes, I have concluded he bet on baseball."

If there was a collective gasp at this categorical denunciation, it was abroad in the land rather than in that room in the Hilton. Giamatti's pronouncement was met by the normal bedlam of a crisis press conference. The shouts for his attention filled the room. To the wider world, this moment of leadership was stunning and uplifting. Leadership, not baseball, had suddenly become the real focus of the event. Giamatti had moved onto the level he loved: the metaphorical level, where baseball was not simply a game but a treasured American institution, and he was more than the baseball commissioner—he was an American leader. He was showing the leaders of other American institutions that absolute, sincere, passionate stands were possible. Not that Giamatti had thought all this out. He was operating on instinct. He was always at his best when he did that.

For an hour he took questions from the press. He tugged on his ear and squinted to hear above the constant whirring and the flashing of cameras. His eyes flashed through the dark bruise-like circles that now extended halfway to his ears. He was a study in olive, in black, in dark blue. His jovial comfort with the press was evident. He fell back effectively on the theatrical gesture when he needed it. As Giamatti strained to hear it, someone asked about counseling for Rose, as if he might be simply a sick man suffering from an addiction.

"Treatment? . . . ah, treatment," Giamatti sighed with familiarity, as if the subject was an eccentric, old friend. The topic had been discussed between Vincent and Katz back in April, as Katz had offered (and Vincent had rejected) treatment as the keystone of Rose's penalty. "With all due respect, my friends, I do not practice psychology or psychiatry by remote control." It would be inappropriate, even patronizing for him to suggest that "Mr. Rose" was ill or in need of treatment. Nevertheless, if an application for a pardon was to be persuasive in a year or in any way supportable, Mr. Rose might want to "reconfigure his life in ways, I assume, that he would prefer."

A few minutes later, a reporter wondered if he found it troubling that only a few hours after Rose had signed the agreement putting him on the permanently ineligible list, Pete was in Minneapolis merrily signing and hawking baseballs on television for forty dollars apiece.

Giamatti expelled a marvelous Falstaffian sigh, the sigh of a jolly, generally tolerant father who was running out of patience with a naughty child. Rose's behavior was for Mr. Rose to change. In the absence of "strappado"—the medieval method of extracting a confession by tying the suspect's hands behind his back, hoisting him upward by his hand straps with a pulley, and then dropping him—he could not compel Rose to say or do anything. Once Rose had signed the agreement, he was cast out of baseball. In Minneapolis, he was a "free citizen on the permanently ineligible list." That was not a category he would advise any in the room to join, Giamatti said with a twinkle, for it was a category of one. He paused. "I will say that confident steps toward rehabilitation ought to [follow] a direction not hitherto taken."

With this brilliant, utterly sincere performance, Giamatti elevated himself to heroic stature in America. By banishing a sports hero, he became a moral hero to the nation. "I will be told that I am an idealist," he had said in his formal statement. "I hope so. I will continue to locate ideals I hold for myself and for my country in the national game, as well as in other of our national institutions."

With that, he touched and moved the nation. The country noticed him as it never had before. A splendid future stretched out before him. A scourge had been cleansed from the hallowed national game. Baseball was safe in Giamatti's hands, and that was good.

Going into the morning, the Rose team felt it had a marvelous settlement. Pete had avoided the formal finding on baseball betting. He stood convicted only of the gambling he had admitted directly to Giamatti and the press, and had a real expectation that he would be back in baseball in a year's time. The day before, only a half hour before Rose signed the suspension agreement, Giamatti spoke directly with Katz on the phone—the only time they had talked in the six months of the investigation. Giamatti had assured Katz that he had an "open mind" about reinstatement. There was no fixed number of years in Giamatti's mind—not ten or five or two years for Rose's exile. It soon became clear that Giamatti was thinking in more epic ways than that.

With rising confidence, Katz suggested that he would be in touch with the commissioner in a few months to discuss the mechanics of a reinstatement application. Then Vincent's flat voice came on the line: Katz should talk with him about any such idea, not with the commissioner. When Katz and Vincent had finalized the legal agreement a few days earlier, Katz had asked for a gag rule on both sides: the agreement should speak for itself. Vincent had declined. The commissioner might want to express his opinion at some juncture about the settlement, Vincent said. He would not want Commissioner Giamatti to feel constrained.

Now, in Katz's living room in Cincinnati, as Rose watched the Giamatti press conference in the company of his advisers, his shock and dismay at the commissioner's damnation was profound. After days of haggling over the precise barrister's language, Giamatti had rendered the agreement virtually irrelevant. In all likelihood, this had been the Giamatti-Vincent plan all along. Get a technical agreement that forced Rose to drop his lawsuit and suspended him indefinitely, to accent Rose's right to apply for reinstatement under the rules in a year's time, and then undermine it all with Giamatti's imperial condemnation. As he listened, Rose was dumbfounded. This was not what he had agreed to at all. If this was an example of Giamatti's "good faith," what could be said about Giamatti's "open mind" about reinstatement?

Grimly, the entourage made its way to Riverfront Stadium for Rose's own press conference. Pete Rose was learning quickly what banishment meant. Only through the sufferance of the Reds was he permitted to hold his press conference in the stadium—the stadium that was every bit as much the House of Rose as Yankee Stadium had been the House of Ruth. All the moments of glory had come down to this moment of disgrace. As Katz stepped forward to remind the press of what had been agreed to, Rose struck an unsympathetic pose against the white, perforated soundboarding. His hair was spiked. His square, fleshy face was haunted. His eyes darted. His mouth turned down unpleasantly in a pout. His blockhouse frame was poured into a dark suit. There was something altogether wrong about the scene; Rose was out of his element. The contradiction of his position was obvious: how could one deny betting on baseball and accept baseball's ultimate penalty as fair? It made no sense.

Contrition was nowhere in his demeanor. Reinstatement was his right, he seemed to be saying. He would be out of baseball "a very short period of time," and he tied his certain reprieve to the first birthday of his infant daughter, happy not so much for that family celebration as for the fact that two days later he could apply for reinstatement. If he had any female supporters left in the country, he no doubt lost the last of them with that statement.

Still, he had his sympathetic moments. In motion, his mouth

lost its pout. At times, he was near tears. How much baseball and the Reds meant to him was clear, just as it was clear how much he had thrown away. What was he going to do in the next year? he was asked.

"Nothing . . ." he mumbled uncertainly, as if he hadn't thought about that until now. "I'll have to do without baseball for the first year since I was seven or eight years old." He bit his lip to control himself.

What did he think about Giamatti's remarks? "I was a little surprised at some of his remarks," Rose replied. Then his old humor flickered, "and some of them I didn't understand, I might add." For a fleeting second, Giamatti's erudition seemed profoundly unfair.

Why had he agreed to this settlement if he was innocent?

"This could have went on for another year," he said with grammar once so enjoyed and now, next to Giamatti's eloquence, so pathetic. "I was tired of it."

"Pete! Do you think you have a gambling problem? And if so, will you seek any sort of rehabilitation?" someone shouted.

"I don't think I have a gambling problem," he replied. "Consequently, I will not seek any help of any kind."

Several hours before the hapless Reds took the field against the last-place Pirates on August 25, 1989, the empty stadium lacked the trappings of celebration or mourning or even relief. Cincinnati was exhausted with controversy. For six months, this garden had become a place of chaos and dishonor. Like Rose, the people were tired of it. The fans had been unable to come to the ballpark and suspend their disbelief. Their angel had become Lucifer. Once his glories had been theirs. They had been happy to have their city defined by him and his values. Now his shame and dishonor were theirs.

By the batting cage the players whispered out of the hearing of the horde of national press, there to ignore their now-meaningless game and devour instead their maudlin and ambivalent emotions. Somewhere in the stadium, engineers and technicians tinkered with the electronics of the huge scoreboard near the massive beer and cigarette signs that appointed the top of the stadium. In times past, Rose had been asked to endorse these products, but he had refused. "I would rather not do a commercial for anything I wouldn't want kids to go out and buy," he had said. In his contract, he had promised never to do anything that would tarnish the image of the game.

In the subdued clubhouse, Hamilton Joe Nuxhall hunched before his locker where his old Reds uniform sentimentally hung. The old pro, now the beloved radio announcer for the Reds, was a figure of grief and despair. He loved the guy. "It hurt me when Pete said, 'I don't need any help.' Try something, get some advice, something," Nux said, as if he was trying to pull back Rose's horrid performance of the day before and make it different. He made a half-hearted reference to Rose's competitive spirit, but he knew no one was listening now. There was no bitterness toward Giamatti. "The prohibition on gambling is right there in the contract," Nuxhall said. "I've had twenty-two of them."

An hour later, the Reds languorously took the field and got plastered 12–3, despite the twenty-eighth homer, a towering blast to right, by the mighty and beautiful Eric Davis. The lowly Bucs produced seventeen hits.

The atmosphere in the Reds locker room afterward was churlish. Soiled uniforms piled up in the center of the gray carpet as the press gathered around the goats of the night and around those who had not played but who were finally ready to spill their guts about Rose. The starting, and the losing, pitcher, Rick Mahler, sat crouched by his locker, like a cornered and wounded animal. Wasn't he distracted out there? Wasn't he thinking about Pete? Hadn't the heart gone out of the team that night? The questions were akin to a fat pitch.

"You guys are trying to read it too deep," Mahler said snappishly. He just made a bad pitch to Gary Redus in the dreadful third with two on, two out, and three runs in already. The score was suddenly, insurmountably, 6–0.

At the other end of the antiseptic cinder-block clubhouse, with its garish glossy red painted to eye level, the journeyman outfielder, Dave Collins, was ready to unburden himself. Collins and Rose went back ten years, back to the glory days of the 1980 Phillies, and so his candor came as a surprise. Of course, the Rose scandal had affected the team. The players had had to deal with it in their own way, in silence and forbearance. You'd come to the ballpark every afternoon, wondering what new revelation was coming out in the papers that day or what lie Rose might be caught in tomorrow.

As for the game that night, Collins had a performer's sense of a sour crowd. The fans had been sedate, unengaged, inattentive. In his postgame dirge, the caretaker manager, Tommy Helms—as much an undertaker as a caretaker at this moment—echoed the sentiment. Even if his thankless job was to play out this dreadful season and get fired, still it had annoyed him that the fans were talking to one another rather than watching the game. They should have stayed at home. The next day, the Reds rebounded, winning by one run behind their ace stopper, John Franco.

Meanwhile, in the days after the banishment, Giamatti tried to relax at his Edgartown cottage on Martha's Vineyard. Little in his life over the past six months had been elevating. He had suffered. The Rose case broke his heart. He retreated from it now with a sense of vindication as well as sadness . . . and a deep certainty that justice had been done. A few strands remained to be knitted up. His phone rang off the hook, until he finally had to turn a deaf ear. Until he could log a few walks on South Beach, the Rose case was closed.

As Giamatti tried to unwind, Rose had given his first interview after his banishment. Stretched out on his couch, he howled betrayal. He had chosen to wear a T-shirt that was then being marketed on Fountain Square. It featured a picture of Rose in uniform in the early days, his right hand grabbing his genitals and his face carved in cockiness: "Bet on this, Bart" the message read.

That brought another round of calls to Martha's Vineyard. In his exhaustion, Giamatti would say only that Rose's comments did not sound like a "positive step toward the future."

Hours later, Giamatti was dead.

It was world news. His old rival for the Yale presidency, Henry Rosovsky, heard the flash in his hotel room in Jakarta and was amazed that the newscasters treated the news as if a major world leader had died. The Mets owner, Fred Wilpon, heard it somewhere in New Jersey and quickly commanded his private pilot to fetch him and fly him to the Vineyard. George Bush was in Kennebunkport. With sadness, the president recalled that he had spent an evening with Giamatti discussing Pete Rose. West of Cincinnati, in Riverside, about a mile from the house where Rose grew up, the mood was different. On the outside of a sports bar, the owners had hung a professional sign: RIVERSIDE—HOME OF PETE ROSE AND PROUD OF IT. When the news of Giamatti's death came over the television, which was propped on a ledge over the bar, the clientele broke out in a song from the *Wizard of Oz:* "Ding, dong, the witch is dead, the wicked, wicked witch is dead. . . ."

At Fenway Park that night, the Red Sox lost 7–2 to the Seattle Mariners and slipped a game back of first place, as the Blue Jays beat the Twins in Toronto.

Epilogue

IN THE YEAR after baseball's final resolution of the Rose case, the wheels of the justice system ground slowly toward a resolution of his legal troubles. A certain inevitability marked the process. It had begun more than a year before the first reports about Rose's betting on baseball had appeared and, as early as 1988, was pointing toward a jail term.

The government had an unassailable case. Rose had hidden $354,968 of income from card sales and memorabilia in the years 1985 and 1987. He had cheated the government out of $162,703 in taxes, and he was also subject to substantial tax evasion charges for the years 1984 and 1986. In a brokered compromise in April 1990, the federal prosecutors agreed to drop the charges for 1984 and 1986 in exchange for a guilty plea for the years 1985 and 1987.

In July 1990, when Rose finally stood before a federal judge in Cincinnati, it was difficult to imagine any modern American figure who had fallen so far, so fast. Since his banishment from baseball, there had been talk about his rehabilitation, his treatment, the "reconfiguration" of his life, to use Giamatti's phrase. But Rose remained bitter and unrepentant. And even as he stood before Judge Arthur Spiegel, he continued to deny the undeniable. He would not or could not admit that he bet on baseball. Fixed in his mind, perhaps, was the notion that if he confessed to baseball's ultimate offense, he could never attain baseball's highest honor: to be inducted into the Hall of Fame.

Before Judge Spiegel, his voice cracked. He spoke of his loss of dignity and self-respect. One could believe him, there in that tense, packed walnut-paneled courtroom, although the words seemed new and the concepts unfamiliar to him. "I am very shameful to be here in front of you," he said, but it remained unclear just how remorseful Rose really was. He was surely sorry that he had been caught, and that he and his family had suffered. He had lost nearly everything, and those who reveled in biblical punishment could rejoice in the fact that he was headed toward bankruptcy.

On August 22, 1990, as prisoner #01832-061, he had been in the penitentiary three weeks when he sat down to write to his counselor, Reuven Katz. He had been thinking about things, and he wrote to his friend from the heart.

> I know that I must have embarrassed you as a friend and as my long-time attorney. I can only say that I'm very sorry and that it won't happen again. I also have a lot of making up to do to my wife and children. I'm looking forward to living my life with them, when I get out. Maybe we can once again reach the top.
>   Being here is the most humiliating experience of my life. For you or Bob [Pitcairn] to see me here would be even more humiliating, so I wish you wouldn't worry about coming to this dump for a visit. It won't be long until I am home.

After his death, the outpouring of affection for Bart Giamatti was extraordinary. Memorial services at Yale and Carnegie Hall blended scholars and athletes, statesmen and literary figures. On the Yale College campus, a stark, black granite bench was dedicated as only the fourth memorial to a Yale figure in the university's history. Its inscription was a quote from Giamatti: "A liberal education is at the heart of a civil society, and at the heart of a liberal education is the act of teaching."

The occasions were touching for their emphasis on Giamatti's unfulfilled promise, for the universal sadness about premature death, and for their simple appreciation of a wonderful human being. At the Yale commemoration in October 1989, the will to reclaim Giamatti to etch his lasting reputation as a teacher rather than as a man of baseball was strong. "He was a great teacher," his friend Peter Brooks told a crowded Woolsey Hall, "and he never ceased to be a teacher." That was as close as Yale wished to get to the collision between Rose and Giamatti at the ethical home plate of baseball. Indeed, there was a visceral distaste at Yale at the way its noble prince would be linked forevermore with this elemental baseball player, Pete Rose.

In pondering Bart in death, Brooks had remembered their work together back in 1970 on a collection of poetry, a collection, Brooks said, which they both hoped—naively—would pay their children's college education. He recalled one poem in particular, which Giamatti loved. Written by Giacomo Leopardi, a nineteenth-century Italian, it was about the frailty of the human voice, about voices of the past, and the silence of the present.

> Dear to me always was this lonely hill,
> and this hedgerow, that cuts the greater part
> of the horizon farthest from my view.
> But gazing out from my seat here
> I shape the endless spaces there beyond,
> and the transcendent silences and deepest
> quiet, in my thought; until, almost,
> the heart is for a moment terrified.
> And as I hear the wind stream through these woods,
> I then begin to match this voice to that
> infinite silence; and I remember the eternal
> and the dead seasons, and that living present
> giving its own sound. And so amidst
> this vast immensity, my thought drowns;
> and sinking in this sea is sweet to me.

Postscript:
Of Fame
and Honor

IT WAS THE UNIQUENESS of the late and much missed Commissioner of Baseball, A. Bartlett Giamatti, that he could speak with eloquence to the wider significance of baseball to American life. In no debate is he more sorely missed than the issue of whether Pete Rose should be inducted into the Baseball Hall of Fame.

As a scholar of Renaissance poetry and Greek mythology, Bart would have seen the issue of Rose's induction not as a question of fame, but of honor. Pete Rose is the most famous baseball player in modern history. He will be remembered a hundred years from now with Ty Cobb and Babe Ruth when the names of Mickey Mantle and Carl Yastrzemski have long since been forgotten. Rose does not need a sterile, brass plaque to certify this fame.

Induction into the Hall of Fame is the highest honor baseball has to give. The induction ceremony is a time for the baseball world to gather in celebration. They gather to honor a player, a uniquely American game, and more than that, as Bart Giamatti understood better than anyone, to honor an American institution.

How could such a ceremony of honor be held for Pete Rose? To honor a disgraced player who disgraced the game? To write the very sentence shows its impossibility. The ceremony alone would tear the game apart. It would be like gathering to dedicate a glossy new presidential library for Richard Nixon, two years after he resigned the presidency in disgrace, or like the U.S. Senate gathering reverentially as Senator Joseph McCarthy lay in state, only a few years after he was officially censured.

During his famous press conference, only a week before he died, Giamatti was asked about whether Rose should be inducted into the Hall of Fame. The matter was for the baseball writers of America, he said, not for a handful of baseball executives. He would not presume to instruct the writers on the relation between "life and art."

It is inconceivable to me that, had he lived, Giamatti would have countenanced the decision of the Hall of Fame managers to deny the baseball writers their right to vote on Rose's induction. Giamatti had too high a regard for sportswriters, partly because he had tried to be one himself. He admired the writers' verve and sense of fun, but saw them as mature professionals, who would approach their solemn duty responsibly. To deny them the right to vote is to deny the writers their one act of history. As a scholar of history and a writer himself, Giamatti would have been offended by this disqualification.

For once, the writers had a difficult and important ethical question to ponder: Would the great museum of baseball be cheapened by Rose's presence in its Hall of Honors? Or would Cooperstown be trivialized by his absence? Giamatti would have trusted the scribes to make the right choice.

You cannot honor Pete Rose, but you cannot ignore him either. You cannot treat him as a pariah, as baseball now does, without serious consequences. Baseball is hounding Rose in his private life, denying him the right to celebrate past glories with his former teammates, blocking him from the broadcast booth, stripping him, in their most trivial and petty act, of the chance to put on a 1927 Detroit Tigers uniform for a bit part in a Hollywood movie.

You cannot do that without creating tremendous sympathy for Rose. You turn him into the victim of a biblical curse that goes way beyond an appropriate punishment that fits his baseball crime. From his mythic heroes in the Renaissance and ancient Greece, Bart would have known better.

There is a solution to this thorny Hall of Fame question. If Cooperstown truly represents the history of baseball, how can it overlook the game's all-time hit leader and the game's all-time tragic figure?

Put Pete in the museum wing at Cooperstown. Have the best of the curators fashion an exhibit about the great moments of this great baseball career, including the famous collision at home plate with Ray Fosse in the best All-Star game ever played two decades ago. And let the exhibit portray the decline and fall of Pete Rose as well.

Museums are supposed to educate as well as entertain. Let the Pete Rose exhibit explain why gambling is baseball's capital crime. Let it teach why Pete Rose's gambling struck at the integrity and the authenticity of the game. Let it show why Bart Giamatti was so passionate, almost operatic, about this form of cheating.

Such an exhibit would be true to the real legacy of Pete Rose, and the final triumph of Giamatti as a teacher.

Acknowledgments
and Sources

IN THE FIRST WEEKS of labor on this book, in the summer of 1989, I soon learned that research for a "sports book" is no less exacting than for a major political biography. Fourteen books had already been written about Pete Rose, including his 1970 and 1975 autobiographies, which I found valuable for his early years and the formation of his public persona. Supplementing this body of work was a drawer full of newspaper and magazine references at the Cincinnati Public Library, equal in size to the entries for John F. Kennedy. Soon the trial records of Rose's associates and the voluminous Dowd Report to Commissioner A. Bartlett Giamatti (and its nine attendant volumes) would be added to the published record. The process began to feel very much like the experience with my previous biography, of John Connally, in researching the Warren commission files and poring through the trials of Watergate figures.

With Rose's banishment from baseball, Bart Giamatti's death, Rose's conviction for tax evasion, and his incarceration, the story had moved from being merely about a great and flawed sports figure to the level of a morality tale, a clash of cultures and values, and, ultimately, an American tragedy. After Giamatti died and the concept for the book was transformed into a dual biography, I found the raw material on Giamatti to be as deep as the Rose material was wide. Apart from Giamatti's books and articles, his papers are deposited in the manuscript division of the Sterling Library of Yale University. There archivists Bill Massa and Judith Schiff guided me with courtesy and professionalism. Other archivists who were of great help for

Giamatti's early life were Mary Kates at the Holyoke Public Library, Patricia Albright at Mount Holyoke College Library, and Ruth Quattlebaum at the Andover Library. For other Giamatti materials at Yale, as well as introductions to Giamatti friends (and adversaries) on the faculty, I thank Rad Daly, the secretary of the University, and Walter Littel of the Public Information Office.

I am especially grateful to Mary Giamatti for her graciousness and good cheer in what had to be the sad and difficult chore of talking about her son, then so recently taken from her, as well as to Bart's brother, Dino Giamatti, who was equally welcoming and forthcoming. In Giamatti's wide circle of friends, I found a heartfelt pleasure in talking about Bart, which went to the depth of affection that lingers for him. Because he was a profoundly private man behind his buoyant exterior, I thank the following people for their insights into Bart's inner persona, as well as their insights into the reasons why the game of baseball so captured the imagination of this Renaissance scholar: Peter Brooks, Dick Cavett, Jaroslav Pelikan, Frank Ryan, William Brainard, Joe Benanto, Lance Liebman, Steve Umin, Eli Jacobs, Bud Selig, Peter O'Malley, Henry Rosovsky, Joe Vining, George Steinbrenner, Maxine Singer, John McSherry, William Bundy, Cyrus Vance, Strobe Talbott, DeWolfe Fulton, Peter Knipe, Donald Dell, Maynard Mack, John Wilhelm, Robert Hollander, Don Kagan, Fred Wilpon, Lou Conti, Charles Feeney, John Hersey, Lawrence Lucchino, John Wilkinson, Robert Brustein, Dan Catlin, and Bob Bose. There were others, of course, and I thank them collectively.

Because most of the book was written during the year between Rose's banishment from baseball and his incarceration in federal prison, there were subtleties and delicacies on the Rose side of the house. A few wise and forthright individuals who must remain nameless will appreciate the depth of my gratitude to them, as will, I hope, the following: Judge Gilbert Bettman and Marianna Bettman, Bud Harrelson, Ray Fosse, Robert Walker, Don Zimmer, Bill Giles, Marty Brennaman, Joe Nuxhall, Dave Bristol, Jim Leyland, Tom Lasorda, Bernie Wrublewski, Larry Bowa, Larry Shenk, Tim Sullivan, Dallas Green, Jim Feist, Bill Holmes, Judge Arthur Spiegel, Dave Parker, Judge Carl Rubin, Pappy Nohr, Ron Darling, Earl Weaver, Ben Kaufman, Joe Webb, Willie DeLuca, Don Burroughs, Eness Jim, Richard Lehr, and Tom Baldrick. Of special help was Robert Harris "Hub" Walker, from whose book, *Cincinnati and the Big Red Machine*, I profited, and who provided me with useful, unpublished background materials.

Other books of value were these:

Alexander, Charles C. *Ty Cobb*. New York: Oxford University Press, 1984.

Anderson, Sparky. *The Main Spark*. Garden City, N.Y.: Doubleday, 1978.

Asinof, Eliot. *Eight Men Out*. New York: Henry Holt & Co., 1963.

Brooks, Peter, and A. Bartlett Giamatti, eds. *Western Literature*. Vol. 3, *The Modern World*. New York: Harcourt Brace Jovanovich, 1971.

Brustein, Robert. *Making Scenes*. New York: Random House, 1981.

Collett, Ritter. *The Cincinnati Reds*. Cincinnati: Jordan Powers Corp., 1976.

Gammons, Peter. *Beyond the Sixth Game*. Boston: Houghton Mifflin, 1985.

Giamatti, A. Bartlett. *Earthly Paradise and the Renaissance Epic*. Princeton: Princeton University Press, 1966.

———. *The University and the Public Interest*. New York: Atheneum, 1981.

———. *Exile and Change in Renaissance Literature*. New Haven: Yale University Press, 1984.

———. *Take Time for Paradise*. New York: Summit, 1989.

Hood, Robert E. *The Gashouse Gang*. New York: Morrow, 1976.

Hunter, Thomas C. *Beginnings*. New York: Thomas Y. Crowell, 1978.

Pallone, Dave. *Behind the Mask*. New York: Viking, 1990.

Robinson, Frank (with Dave Anderson). *Frank*. New York: Holt, Rinehart & Winston, 1976.

Rose, Pete, and Roger Kahn. *Pete Rose: My Story*. New York: Macmillan, 1989.

Spink, J. G. Taylor. *Judge Landis and 25 Years of Baseball*. St. Louis: Sporting News Publishing Co., 1974.

Wheeler, Lonnie, and John Baskin. *The Cincinnati Game*. Wilmington, Ohio: Orange Fraser Press, 1988.

Pamphlets

Dittly, Bernard, Ruth Hess, Mary Johnson, Matthew Kettler, and William Kunkemoeller. "Riverside Pride: A History of the Civil, Welfare Club, Inc." Neighborhood Studies Project of the Cincinnati Historical Society, Cincinnati, 1982.

Newspapers and Magazines

American Scholar, Atlanta Journal, Atlanta Constitution, Andover Bulletin, Boston Globe, Cincinnati Enquirer, Cincinnati Post, Cleveland

Plain Dealer, Eagle-Tribune (Andover, Mass.), *Esquire, Gentlemen's Quarterly, Harper's* magazine, *Holyoke Transcript Telegram, Houston Post, Inside Sports, Life, Lynchburg News and Daily Advance* (Lynchburg, Va.), *Mail Tribune* (Medford, Oreg.), *Mount Holyoke Alumni Quarterly, Ms., New Haven Register, New Journal* (New Haven, Conn.), *New York Daily News, New York Post, New York Times, The New Yorker, Newsweek, Oregonian, Penthouse, People, Philadelphia Inquirer, Philadelphia Post, Playboy, Providence Journal Bulletin, Readers Digest, St. Petersburg Times, Saturday Evening Post, Sport, Sporting News, Sports Illustrated, Tampa Tribune, Time, Trenton Times, U.S. News & World Report, Vineyard Gazette* (Martha's Vineyard, Mass.), *Washington Post, Yale Daily News.*

Legal Papers

Dowd Report. Report to the Commissioner and Volumes 1–8. New York: Office of the Commissioner of Baseball, May 9, 1989.

Rose v. Giamatti. Civil Action A-8905178. Court of Common Pleas, Hamilton County, Ohio.

- Complaint for Injunctive Relief, Declaratory Judgment and Damages, June 19, 1989.
- Affidavit of A. Bartlett Giamatti, June 21, 1989.
- Cross Examination of John Dowd, June 23, 1989.
- Deposition of A. Bartlett Giamatti, June 29, 1989.

Report of investigation, re "Substantiated Failure [by Peter Edward Rose] to file CMIR's for an accumulative amount of $121,197.54 from Japan to the United States." U.S. Customs Service, March 27, 1986. (Obtained by the author through the Freedom of Information Act.)

United States v. Gioiosa, Criminal No. 1-89-038. U.S. District Court, Cincinnati.

United States v. Peters. Criminal No. 1-89-034. U.S. District Court, Cincinnati.

In the preparation of the manuscript, I thank, as always, the careful work of my friend and colleague Alfreda Kaplan; John Milton Leary, baseball's consummate fan, for his research; and for their help with the picture section, Bob Medina and Arthur Sulzberger at the *New York Times* and Mary Sullivan at Yale University.

Index